Diagnostic and Remedial Reading for Classroom and Clinic

SIXTH EDITION

Diagnostic and Remedial Reading for Classroom and Clinic

Robert M. Wilson
UNIVERSITY OF MARYLAND

Craig J. Cleland
MANSFIELD UNIVERSITY

MERRILL PUBLISHING COMPANY
A Bell & Howell Information Company
Columbus   Toronto   London   Melbourne

Cover Photo: Kevin Fitzsimons

Published by Merrill Publishing Company
A Bell & Howell Information Company
Columbus, Ohio 43216

This book was set in Paladium.

Administrative Editor: Jeff Johnston
Production Coordinator: Sharon Rudd
Art Coordinator: Gilda M. Edwards
Cover Designer: Brian Deep
Photo Editor: Gail L. Meese

Photo credits: Jean Greenwald/Merrill, pp. xxiv, 3, 22, 26, 29, 58, 105, 122, 136,
180, 194, 219, 226, 240, 252, 279, 303, 337, 354, 364, 406, 407; Irma
McNelia/Merrill, pp. 14, 164, 185, 277, 297, 358; courtesy of Keystone View Company, p. 78; Jerry Harvey, p. 82; David Williams, pp. 100, 143, 183, 265, 332,
451; Jan Smyth, p. 243; David S. Strickler, p. 312; Bruce Dart, pp. 372, 451;
Charles Quinlan, p. 390; courtesy of National Captioning Institute, p. 347;
courtesy of Med-Tech Photo Service, p. 396.

Library of Congress Catalog Card Number: 88-63290
International Standard Book Number: 0-675-20640-5
Printed in the United States of America
1 2 3 4 5 6 7 8 9—92 91 90 89

To Karen for her patience, love, and encouragement.
C.J.C.

To all my students who have helped me understand the reading process. And, to my wife, Marcia, who lets me try out new ideas in her elementary school.
R.M.W.

Preface

Point of View

In many areas of scientific inquiry, authors take extraordinary care to keep their personal beliefs and biases out of their published works. The field of education, however, requires that teachers blend knowledge, skill, compassion, intuition, and beliefs in making hundreds of informed professional judgments each day. It would be impossible (and undesirable) for teachers to divorce themselves from their personal beliefs. Similarly, our beliefs and biases have played a major part in writing this book, and we wish to state them at the outset in order to help the reader evaluate the ideas that follow.

We believe that good teaching involves assessment and planning guided by careful, daily observations. It requires that teachers evaluate student strengths and needs and adapt instruction accordingly. In both diagnosis and remediation, we recognize the importance of focusing on student strengths in attempting to correct areas of weakness. This is particularly important for students who have experienced prolonged failure in reading, because reading failure breeds low self-concept, feelings of inadequacy, and avoidance behaviors. Throughout this text, we have presented ways of addressing skill deficits without slighting affective concerns.

We are convinced that effective remediation of reading difficulties is inextricably tied to building students' communicative skills in listening, speaking, and writing. Therefore, we have included numerous suggestions for developing these related abilities. We have also found children's literature to be a particularly powerful resource in strengthening students' reading skills. Unfortunately, all too often, poor readers spend most of their time "reading" workbooks, worksheets, and flash cards.

Reading comprehension is emphasized in all chapters because we believe reading *is* comprehension. Because no single approach will be successful with every student, we have considered many different approaches, strategies, and techniques. Finally, we believe that diagnostic and prescriptive teaching properly falls within the domain of the classroom teacher. We are inspired by the many fine teachers with whom we work.

Audience and Purpose

This text has been written for pre-service and in-service teachers who wish to gain a fundamental knowledge of diagnostic and remedial reading. We have assumed that readers have some basic knowledge and experience in teaching developmental reading and a firm grounding in educational psychology. While we have presented ideas in considerable detail, we have avoided become overly technical or theoretical. In the final analysis, we hope the reader will find this book practical.

Organization and Features

Although selected chapters of the text may be read out of sequence, the book follows a logical progression to develop an understanding of the diagnostic and prescriptive process. In chapter 1 the reader is introduced to the difficulties encountered by poor readers and the personal and societal consequences of those difficulties. This opening chapter also discusses two different approaches to diagnosis: on the one hand, attempting to identify causes; on the other, seeking to treat the symptoms of reading difficulties. Chapter 2 overviews the diagnostic sequence and presents several important principles for guiding diagnosis. Chapter 3 examines some of the uses (and misuses) of standardized tests and equips the reader with background knowledge to better understand the diagnostic chapters that follow. Intellectual, physical, and emotional correlates to reading success are discussed in chapter 4. Classroom and clinical diagnosis are examined in chapters 5 and 6, respectively. In each case, diagnosis is presented as a decision-making process that is altered to fit the needs of the individual student. Chapters 7 through 10, examining the various aspects of reading remediation, discuss many valuable approaches, strategies, techniques, and materials for working with students experiencing reading difficulties. The diagnostic and remedial reading needs of handicapped students are discussed in chapter 11. Working with these students often requires a multidisciplinary approach; it is important that both classroom teachers and reading specialists know how to adapt instruction to meet the unique learning needs of the handicapped. In chapter 12, diagnostic and remedial reading applications of emerging microcomputer and closed-caption television technologies are explored. Chapters 13, 14, and 15 discuss ways of organizing the total school reading program in order to deliver needed services to students effectively. Once again, the emphasis is on a cooperative effort—combining teachers, resource people, administrators, and parents to plan the best possible diagnostic and remedial reading program.

To help readers gain a thorough understanding of the material, we have begun each chapter with a "Chapter Emphases" section to introduce the featured topics and distill the major ideas into several succinct statements. Readers are encouraged to use these statements to gain an overview of each chapter prior to reading and to use them after reading in reflecting on the ideas presented.

End-of-chapter summaries bring closure to the chapters; however, these summaries are not intended to take the place of a thoughtful and careful reading of the text. The glossary at the back of the text has been revised and expanded to foster the reader's understanding of unfamiliar and technical vocabulary.

The editorials, which were first introduced in the fourth edition, have been well received. These short essays recount ways in which individual teachers and administrators have adapted the text material in working with their students. We view such a process as being at the heart of this text, and we are pleased to feature quite a few new editorials in this edition. As is evidenced in the experiences of these teachers, effective diagnostic teaching is not a single regimen of instruction; rather, it is a dynamic process that evolves in the hands of skillful and caring teachers who expand on ideas and make them their own.

New in This Edition

A great deal has happened in the field of reading in the four short years since the last (fifth) edition of this book. Many sections have been updated and expanded to keep pace with the rapid change. Two entirely new chapters have been added: one on uses and interpretation of standardized tests and one on microcomputer and closed-caption television technologies. Another chapter, previously entitled "Readiness Activities," has been thoroughly rewritten and expanded to reflect a different focus as well as recent developments in whole language and literacy development. In this chapter, considerable attention is given to language underpinnings of reading abilities and the need for poor readers to be exposed to the power of children's literature. New insights into metalinguistic awareness and its relationship to reading acquisition are also examined. Throughout the rest of the book, new information has been added in such areas as neurological problems, curriculum-based assessment measures, comprehension teaching strategies, reliability and validity, English as a second language, metacognition, reading/writing connections, and signing to improve reading ability. Appendixes listing tests, remedial materials, and computer software programs have been completely revised and updated to include new products on the market and revised editions of old favorites.

Additional Resources

Readers wishing to further study some of the topics in the text are directed to the "Suggested Readings" sections at the end of each chapter. These readings both expand on chapter topics and offer alternative points of view. The appendixes contain updated listings of commercial tests, remedial materials, and microcomputer software.

We trust that this sixth edition will provide a strong foundation in the study of diagnostic and remedial reading. It is our sincere hope that this text will encourage incentive for further study in this important and fascinating field.

Acknowledgments

We are grateful for the opportunities of working with a wonderful group of colleagues, both at our universities and in the local schools. These fine teachers contributed to this book through countless interactions but most especially by the spirit in which they teach their students. We would also like to thank our students, both present and former, who themselves taught us much. We are pleased and grateful that several of our former students consented to write editorials for this edition.

Several other people deserve special thanks for their work on this sixth edition. We thank Gordon Browning, Cynthia Bowen, Bea Liswell, Diane Strohecker, and Anita Demsey for their helpful suggestions and careful work on new and updated appendixes. Robert Wilson thanks the Reading Center Staff at the University of Maryland for their rich interactions. He also thanks Barbara Kapinus of the Maryland State Department of Education, who always manages to point to new directions. Craig Cleland is grateful for the encouragement of his colleagues at Mansfield University, particularly the members of the Education and Special Education departments with whom he works each day. He especially thanks his present and former chairpersons, Bob Putt and Luke Pfluger, for their continued support. Appreciation is also extended to Kallie Richardson, Frances Seaborn, and George Mullen for the support they extended in the manuscript preparation stages.

The work of many others who contributed to past editions of this text remains in this sixth edition. They are Margery Berman, Robert Duffey, William Druckmiller, Ward Ewalt, Donald McFeeley, Louise Waynant, and Marcia Wilson.

Merrill submitted this text's manuscript to many reviewers. Our thanks go to Elinor Ross, Tennessee Technological University; Lawrence L. Smith, State University of New York, College at Buffalo; Barbara J. Walker, Eastern Montana College, Charles E. Matthews, College of Charleston, and Victoria T. Risko, Vanderbilt University.

We also wish to thank Alden Waitt for her careful copy editing and the many fine photographers who contributed to this edition.

Our families have been wonderfully supportive and endlessly patient through the countless hours that went into the preparation of this edition. Craig

Cleland thanks his wife, Karen, daughter, Allison, and parents, Jack and Mary Cleland, for their understanding and encouragement. Robert Wilson thanks his wife, Marcia, and the rest of his family, Rick, Judy, and Rebecca; Jim, Nancy, Jennifer, and Andrea; and Sharon, Russell, Matthew, and Evan for their total support.

R.M.W.

C.J.C.

Contents

CHAPTER 4.   Intellectual, Physical, and Emotional Diagnosis

CHAPTER 5.   Classroom Diagnosis

When Students Encounter Difficulties

CHAPTER OUTLINE

Problems Readers Encounter
Problems Teachers Encounter
Problems Readers Take with Them to School
Ramifications of Low Achievement in Reading
Types of Reading Difficulties
Diagnose for Symptoms or Causes?
School Screening Committees
Special Considerations
Instructing Low-achieving Readers

CHAPTER EMPHASES

Most low-achieving readers face problems that are largely out of their control.

Many teachers face problems that are largely out of their control.

By focusing on readers' strengths, reading skills are most effectively developed and refined.

The effects of low achievement in reading are borne by some students throughout life.

In diagnosis, both symptoms and causes of reading difficulties should be assessed.

Educators often refer to low-achieving readers as *problem readers, dyslexic, learning disabled,* or *language disabled.* Such labels give the impression that something is wrong with the reader. In most cases of low achievement in reading, however, the problem is not *within* the reader; it is *encountered by* the reader. The educator's responsibility is to help the reader overcome the problem. In this chapter, some of these problems will be examined, along with their implications for teaching students with reading difficulties.

Problems Readers Encounter

Prejudice

Some readers encounter discrimination because of race, sex, social status, appearance, or some other perceived difference. Readers of any age, but most certainly beginning readers, can quickly feel that something is wrong with them when they encounter prejudiced treatment. When a reader encounters prejudice and receives discriminatory treatment, the motivation to make the effort needed to learn to read is dampened.

Instruction

When instruction is geared to the achieving readers, those who are achieving slowly or not at all can be quickly left behind. Catching up can be difficult even when the spirit is there and is almost impossible when the reader gets so far behind that the desire to try is gone.

Materials

When the materials used for instruction are too difficult, reading can be frustrating. Readers can quickly develop the attitude that reading is difficult and unrewarding.

Grouping

Readers who are assigned to a group in which all students are experiencing difficulty with reading can easily become discouraged. They all know that their group is proceeding at a slower pace than the others and may start to believe that they are, in fact, slow.

Labels

When another person labels a low-achieving reader, it is difficult for that reader to maintain a positive self-concept. Furthermore, such labels are difficult to remove.

*Labeling can cause
low self-esteem.*

Humiliation

Public displays of the readers' progress are humiliating to the low-achieving readers. No amount of encouragement can motivate those readers who must sit in a classroom and see their names on a chart that indicates that they are not doing well.

Indeed, the list of problems students encounter seems endless. Others include uninterested parents, problems at home, difficulties with peer acceptance, and inappropriate instructional materials. The point is that some readers encounter serious problems that are not of their doing. When this happens, they are likely to get the message that something is wrong with them and become so discouraged that they stop trying. The labels, special groupings, and special instructional materials that result only confirm this message.

Teachers cannot be blamed for all the problems of low-achieving readers. Many teachers do not have the resources that would enable them to provide the type of instruction necessary for all readers to be successful.

**Problems
Teachers
Encounter**

Class Size

For no good reason, classrooms have been constructed to accommodate thirty or more students. To provide efficient instruction to over thirty students at one time is an extremely difficult task.

Pressure

Parents, administrators, supervisors, and many others can apply great amounts of pressure on teachers. One of the worst pressures is to satisfy others that all readers are reading up to grade level. This expectation is unreasonable, but the pressure does exist; consequently, many readers are instructed with materials far too difficult for them to use successfully.

Nonteaching Duties

In some schools, teachers must spend too much time making reports, managing lunch counts, supervising hall behavior, and other such nonteaching duties. While necessary, these duties often interfere with time that should be allotted for instruction.

Materials

Many teachers face teaching their students with inadequate or insufficient materials. Learning suffers in those cases in which the teacher cannot make adjustments to overcome the inadequacy of the materials provided.

Preparation

Some teachers enter their teaching careers with extremely poor preparation. Colleges and universities that do not provide prospective teachers with adequate instruction and experience in reading, language, measurements, and psychology must bear part of the responsibility for poor teaching. A desire to teach well will not make up for poor teacher preparation.

Testing

In some schools, testing has reached an unbelievable level. Tests for intelligence, readiness, phonics, spelling, reading achievement, reading subskills, writing, and arithmetic are often required at the beginning, midpoint, and end of the year. Some students spend most of the first month of the school year in testing situations. Not only does this cut into instructional time, but it can well lead to a series of frustrating experiences, especially for the low-achieving readers who do not test well.

Some students have personal problems that cause them difficulty learning to read. These types of problems cause low achievement far less often than those just discussed. Illness, physical or emotional handicaps, and limited intellectual ability cause some readers great difficulty with the reading process. Public laws have pinpointed the need for placing such students in the most advantageous learning environment to enhance the development of their academic and social skills. Chapter 4 will provide more detailed information about the problems that some readers take with them to school.

Low achievers not only face obstacles that interfere with achievement, but they must also face the task of overcoming the difficulties that low achievement creates. These difficulties occur in school, with peers, and at home with their parents.

In School

In school, where students often are pressured to achieve grade level performance, low achievers are a source of never-ending disappointments. Whether the pressure is subtle or direct, the readers themselves and the teachers sense failure. Teachers may react by giving up on them or by feeling that they are indifferent, lazy, or troublesome. These reactions may be followed by punishment that usually fosters a hostile attitude between the teacher and these students who are ill-equipped to accept hostility. Frustrated by the rejection and the labels, these readers either can not or will not work independently. As more and more frustrating materials are heaped on them, they are likely to busy themselves with noneducational activities and finally decide that learning is just not worth the effort. As they fall behind in their classroom work, they may be faced with the continual threat of repeating a grade. Excessive absenteeism and complete rejection of the school program are inevitable as they proceed through school, being promoted on the basis of age alone. The reading level of high school dropouts tells the rest of the story. Penty says, "More than three times as many poor readers as good readers dropped out of school before graduation."[1]

Not all low achievers become dropouts; however, the strained school-pupil relationship raises dropout probabilities. Furthermore, some students will drop out emotionally although they continue to attend class. Psychological dropouts can be found in every school; they generally create problems for both the teacher and their success-oriented peers. In either case, the situation is critical.

With Peers

Although peers often treat them kindly, it is not uncommon for low achievers to be teased and taunted. They are not with the "in" group and are often found alone at play as well as in the classroom. Other children are not likely to seek their ideas for committee work because they perceive their contributions as limited. Rejection encourages them to seek companionship with others in the "out" group. A further complication occurs with the repetition of a grade, which places them one year behind their peers. They clearly recognize that they do not "belong" either in the group with which they are placed or with their peers. If they continue to meet peer group disapproval, they become highly susceptible to undesirable influences, the consequences of which can be seen in the reports of police authorities who handle juvenile delinquents. Harris and Sipay state that "reports of a high incidence (approximately 60–65%) of reading or learning disability in delinquent children and adolescents are fairly common."[2] Of course, all low achievers do not turn to delinquent behavior, but continued rejection from peers makes these students more susceptible to undesirable influences.

With Parents

Parents become anxious when their children are not succeeding in school. They may try to solve the problem by pressuring their children to make greater efforts. This often means piling on more of the same type of frustrating work that makes them reject school. When such children balk, they are often compared to siblings or playmates. Seemingly ashamed of their children's behavior, parents often will look for someone to blame. Students are not blind to this shame and rejection, and they too will look for someone to blame. Even more important, they are likely to look elsewhere for that acceptance that all children need from their parents.

By observing these readers, it can be concluded that the ramifications of their difficulties are felt not only by them, but also by the school, peers, and family. Their inability to solve their own problem causes the future to look incurably bleak.

Into Adulthood

Further problems emerge as low achievers reach adulthood. Post-high school educational options are usually limited, and job opportunities are restricted to unskilled labor that requires little reading skill. The problem is a huge one. Right to Read reports that "an estimated 1.4 million adults report that they cannot read or write in any language. More than 20 million are functionally illiterate."[3] *Functional literacy* is defined as having sufficient reading skills for surviving in a reading-based society. Right to Read once funded sixty-seven literacy projects in thirty-five states at a cost of $5.2 million.[4] So, the problem is not just the reader's; our society must face it as a serious gap in the development of human potential and correct it where it is first encountered—in the schools.

From one point of view, it appears that the reading and writing skills of adults have improved over the years. Weber points out, on the other hand, that the reading demands of our society have increased more rapidly than have improvements in literacy.[5]

In 1969, Allen reported that 25 percent of the students in school are likely to experience frustration in reading.[6] By adjusting instructional programs so as to minimize problems that readers face, that percentage could be reduced drastically.

Not all of those who experience difficulty in learning to read follow the patterns discussed here. Many are capable of making reasonable adjustments, usually with the help of understanding teachers and parents. The problem facing these teachers and parents becomes determining a way to help students maintain self-esteem while adjustments are made to allow for successful learning.

Students experience difficulty with learning to read for various reasons. For purposes of categorization, these can be classified into three types of difficulties.

First, students may be experiencing difficulty with reading because for some reason they do not read as well as their abilities indicate they should. They should not be judged by their reading skills in relation to their grade levels in school, but, rather, in relation to their potentials. Slow students reading below their grade levels in school may experience learning difficulties, but this does not necessarily imply that they are retarded in the development of their reading skills. On the other hand, more able students, although reading well above their grade levels, may be considered low achievers when their reading levels fall short of their intellectual potentials. Accurate assessment of the reading levels and abilities of students lets the teacher determine whether readers are operating below their potentials. For example, in Table 1–1 Ruth is operating consistently with her ability; Beth is not.

Second, students may have difficulty when, with the exception of a specific skill deficiency, all measures of their reading are up to their levels of potential. They read satisfactorily in most situations, but they have a specific weakness. Although their deficiencies are difficult to locate because most of these students' reading skills appear normal, once located, they are readily corrected through the precise nature of the remediation necessary. For example, since many adults read slowly, they have a specific skill deficiency. They can perform on tests and seem to read very well, but their slow speeds make reading tiresome and reduce their inclinations to read. Students, while appearing to read well, also may have specific skill deficiencies with speed, oral reading fluency, word attack, comprehension, and study skills.

TABLE 1–1. Ability Compared to Reading

Student	Grade Placement	Ability Level	Reading Level
Ruth	4	3	3
Beth	4	6	3

The third type of reading difficulty occurs when, in spite of reading skills consistent with their potential, students lack the desire to read. LeGrand-Brodsky reports that 6 percent of the American population over the age of sixteen do not read anything at all and that 30 percent are nonbook readers.[7] Strang points to this problem when she says, "If the book is interesting they read it eagerly and with enjoyment. . . . Students confronted with drab, uninteresting reading material show the opposite pattern. They read reluctantly, they skip and skim so that they can get it over with more quickly."[8] These factors discourage students from using available skills and tend to dampen the desire to read. Lack of desire to read should be considered an important reading problem because often there is no other apparent difficulty. Clinic reports for such students show that they are frequently subject to ridicule and disciplinary action, since it is often assumed that there is no excuse for their poor reading habits. An understanding of the students' reaction to reading, however, will indicate the need for adjustment of the school situation to help develop a better attitude toward reading.

Diagnose for Symptoms or Causes?

When it becomes apparent that a student has difficulty learning to read, a basic decision must be made. Should the diagnosis be based on a survey of the symptoms, or should it attempt to determine causation? Or should both be considered?

If the cause of the problem can be determined, it would certainly help in diagnosis. However, causation is often difficult (and many times impossible) to determine. For example, if the reader cannot organize information read for speedy recall, then strategies are available to correct that cause of the difficulty. If, however, the cause is some type of minimal brain dysfunction, it may never be diagnosed—not even in the best medical facility. To continue diagnosis and withhold instruction in such a case would be foolish. A look at the following examples may be helpful for understanding assessment of reading difficulties for symptoms and causes.

Example 1: Tony

Tony is not alone. He is one of many students across the country who, day after day, sits in an elementary school classroom in which he encounters reading situations well beyond his ability. Tony, however, may be ranked among the fortunate; his teacher, Mr. Coley, realizes that Tony cannot read well enough to do fifth-grade work. He quickly discovered that Tony could read accurately at the third-grade level and that he could read only with frustration at the fourth-grade level. He noticed that Tony refuses to attack unknown words, and, on the rare occasions when he does, his pronunciation is inaccurate.

He also noticed that Tony's reading is characterized by word pronunciation without fluency, that he is uncomfortable in the reading situation, and that he seems hindered by what the teacher calls "word reading." A quick check of the school records indicates that Tony is average in ability but that each year he seems less responsive to reading instruction.

After carefully considering the information available to him and his own analysis of Tony's reading performance in the classroom, Mr. Coley implemented a two-pronged program to supplement Tony's regular reading. First, he encouraged Tony to read for meaning by providing highly interesting reading material at a low level of difficulty; second, he taught essential phonic skills from the sight words that Tony knew. Realizing that Tony's problem might be deeply rooted, he asked for an evaluation by a reading specialist. This approach to the situation reflects an interested, informed classroom teacher analyzing a student's problem and attempting to correct it, while waiting for the services of the reading specialist.

When the reading specialist, Mrs. Ruark, saw Tony, she knew that a careful diagnosis would be essential. She realized that, among other things, she needed to have complete information concerning Tony's ability, his knowledge of word attack, his comprehension skills, and his emotional stability. Therefore, the specialist began thorough diagnosis to establish the cause of the problem; without such diagnosis she could not properly recommend a corrective program.

This example illustrates two different reactions to Tony's symptoms. The classroom teacher used a pattern of symptoms to implement a program of correction. The specialist realized that the problem could best be understood by a more careful study of the student. Both the classroom teacher and the reading specialist reacted appropriately. The teacher instituted a corrective program as quickly as possible after carefully considering the symptoms, his basic concern being the continuation of Tony's educational program. The specialist initiated a diagnostic program, attempting to determine the cause of Tony's difficulty in order to recommend the most appropriate program of remediation.

To clarify further the difference between symptoms and causes of reading difficulty, we define *symptoms* as those observable characteristics of a case that lead to an educated guess about a reader's difficulties. Teachers must look for reliable patterns of symptoms so that an appropriate program of correction can be initiated with minimal delay to the student's educational progress. Harris and Sipay state that "many of the simpler difficulties in reading can be corrected by direct teaching of the missing skills, without an intensive search for reasons why the skills were not learned before."[9] Average classroom teachers lack the time, training, and materials to conduct thorough diagnoses. Instead, they must observe students to find a reliable pattern of behavior on which to base correctional instruction. The procedure involves these three steps:

1. Examining observable symptoms, combined with available school data.
2. Forming a hypothesis based on the observed pattern.
3. Beginning instruction.

With the possibility of referral in mind, teachers must continue to formulate and conduct the most effective corrective programs possible within the limitations of the classroom. Reference may be made to chapter 2 for patterns of symptoms applicable to the classroom diagnosis of readers.

Causation may be defined as those factors that, as a result of careful diagnosis, might be accurately identified as being responsible for the reading difficulty. Robinson presents data to support the multiple nature of causation in reading difficulties.[10] The reading specialist is acutely aware that, since there is rarely just one cause for a given problem, a careful examination for causation is necessary. Poor home environment, poor physical health, inadequate instruction, lack of instructional materials, personality disorders, and many other factors have been identified as interfering to some degree with the development of reading skills.

The reading specialist realizes that if causes can be determined, programs of prevention are possible; Robinson states, "Preventive measures can be planned intelligently only if causes of difficulty are understood."[11] For example, the cause in Tony's case could have been a lack of auditory discrimination skills for learning phonics or an overemphasis on isolated word drill in earlier grades. The reading specialist, after a diagnosis designed to determine causes, sets the groundwork for a program of correction. For Tony's teachers, this could involve revision of portions of the reading curriculum for all grades or establishment of a more thorough readiness program in the early grades. Thus, a careful diagnosis is the first step toward the implementation of a preventive program.

The reading specialist may also emphasize causation to find the most effective program of correction, especially with the more seriously retarded reader. Strang states, however, that diagnosis is complex and that causes are difficult to uncover.[12] If Tony's classroom teacher's program of correction is not effective, a more thorough diagnosis will be essential. This is the other function of the reading specialist. By her diagnosis she will be able to assist the classroom teacher with recommendations to implement the most effective program.

Just because specialists look for causation and classroom teachers for patterns of symptoms in no way prevents classroom teachers from being aware of possible implications and complications concerning the causes of reading problems; nor does it excuse them from gathering as much diagnostic information as possible. The more informed they become about causation, the more effective they will become in analyzing patterns of symptoms. As Harris and Sipay state, they should be "able to carry out the simpler parts of a diagnostic study."[13] At the same time, teachers must instruct all students in their care, and this obligation generally precludes thorough diagnosis in any one case. It is also possible that after careful diagnosis the reading specialist will not yet be able to identify the causes of the student's reading difficulty. However, if causative factors can be determined, they can serve as an excellent springboard for corrective instruction.

Example 2: Bill

"Bill, how many times have I told you not to hold your book so close to your face?" Despite repeated efforts to have him hold his book at the proper distance, his teacher, Ms. Beath, noticed that Bill insisted on this type of visual adjustment. Recognizing this as a symptom of a visual disorder, she began to observe him more closely. She noticed unusual watering of the eyes and an unusual amount of blinking, especially after long sessions of seat work. In response she adjusted the classroom situation to allow Bill maximum visual comfort (i.e., regulating visual activities to shorter time periods and assuring Bill the most favorable lighting conditions). Realizing that he might have a serious problem, the teacher referred him to a vision specialist.

The teacher's job was to recognize the symptoms and react: first, by adjusting Bill's physical setting to enable him to perform as comfortably as possible; second, to refer him to a specialist for necessary visual correction.

Mr. Nash, the reading specialist, reacted to Bill differently. He saw the symptoms of the difficulty and realized that referral was a possibility. However, in this case, a visual screening test involving near-point vision[14] was administered first to determine whether Bill's problem was a visual disability or a bad habit.

In all physical problems, referral to the proper specialist is the appropriate action for personnel in education; therefore, the reading specialist and the classroom teacher considered referral of Bill for visual analysis. However, their approaches differed. Ms. Beath observed a pattern of symptoms that told her that there was a good possibility that impaired vision was interfering with Bill's educational progress. Since education is her first responsibility, the teacher's proper reaction was to adjust the educational climate so that Bill could operate as effectively as possible. She also was obligated to make a referral for visual analysis. The reading specialist, however, was not immediately confronted with Bill's day-to-day instruction; rather, he was obligated to determine as accurately as possible whether vision was the factor interfering with Bill's education. Thus, he attempted to screen Bill thoroughly before making recommendations for visual referral or for adjustment of the educational climate.

Example 3: Evan

Evan was known as a daydreamer. His present teacher, Ms. Paz, confirmed that his attention seemed to drift off, but she also noticed that he did not participate in discussions and was unable to respond to questions about material he had just read. One day she called Evan to her desk and asked him to read orally for her. Evan did so with ease and fluency. She then asked him a series of questions and found that he disliked reading the stories in the reading book. He became very interested in discussing crabbing, his favorite activity. She found that his father took him crabbing every possible weekend on Chesapeake Bay.

Armed with information that he had the necessary reading skills and was interested in crabbing, Ms. Paz conferred with the media specialist to find some books that might interest Evan. The media specialist had two books about crabbing, *Chesapeake* and *Beautiful Swimmers*. She also had several editions of a high school publication named *Skip Jack*. Evan was delighted with these books. He studied them carefully, without daydreaming. He still seemed bored by the other reading he was expected to do, so Ms. Paz referred him to a reading specialist, Mr. Fowler.

Mr. Fowler was impressed with Ms. Paz's efforts. Evan seemed open and eager to talk about crabbing. Mr. Fowler found that Evan was in command of his reading skills and could read almost anything he wanted. He also confirmed that Evan seemed to be interested only in crabbing. After giving Evan an interest survey, however, he found that Evan was also interested in boating, soccer, photography, and swimming. This information provided numerous opportunities to select materials that would interest him. Ms. Paz arranged with the media specialist for Evan to always have available at least one book on a topic of his interest. Once he found reading personally enjoyable and meaningful, Evan's general interest in learning improved.

Again the teacher and the reading specialist assisted each other to determine how to best help Evan. The reading specialist, with instruments available and time to use them, was able to find Evan's areas of interest. His recommendations to Ms. Paz helped her to get Evan on task. Once involved in interesting material, Evan found school stimulating and informative.

These three examples illustrate the roles of teachers and reading specialists in diagnosis. The relationship between causes and symptoms is a delicate and sometimes confusing one. Educators, however, must deal with both symptoms and causes as they work to provide the best educational climate for their students.

School Screening Committees

Many schools have organized all resource personnel into screening committees to handle teacher referrals. These committees meet regularly with the principal to make decisions based on all diagnostic information available. A committee is likely to include specialists in reading, special education, language disabilities, and speech, as well as the school nurse, psychologist, principal, and guidance counselor. Multiple input helps prevent diagnostic errors. The referring teacher usually attends. When it is determined that the child is handicapped, the parent is present and actively participates in decision making.

When all available information has been considered, an educational plan is developed and responsibilities assigned to the most appropriate persons for instruction. Periodic reports of progress are reviewed by the committee. When the child is handicapped, the parent must approve the program by signing the plan. In these cases the plan is called an Individualized Education Program (IEP) and is mandated by federal legislation, Public Law 94–142.

Several advantages of screening committees have been noted:

1. The principal is informed of the specialists' work.
2. Principals maintain records so that parents can be informed of progress.
3. Specialists, working together, find less conflict of interest among themselves.
4. Overlapping of responsibilities diminishes.
5. The school's complete resources can be used to aid students in becoming successful learners.

In each case described on the preceding pages, screening committee action would have been appropriate and helpful.

Two groups of students need special consideration as teachers plan for their instruction: those who come from cultures different from those of their teachers and those who have been identified as handicapped.

Cultural Differences

Much has been written about students who come from different cultural environments. Some claim these students come to school with a cultural handicap and thus label them *disadvantaged.* Others attribute their difficulty in school to their cultural background, implying not only differences but undesirable influence as well. Labels such as "disadvantaged" and "undesirable" hold no value for diagnosis and create assumptions that hurt students. Numerous children from poor families or minority groups *do* have difficulty in school. Students from restricted urban environments and isolated rural environments may be far below their peers in reading skills.

However, the environment alone cannot be blamed for the reading difficulty. Indeed, evidence also points to a lack of equal educational opportunity.[15] Yet culturally different children usually come to school with fully developed language and with wide backgrounds of experiences. Teachers must recognize culturally different students as having distinct and valuable cultures. They can be taught if their strengths are evaluated and their programs adjusted to those strengths. For example, since they can talk, they can be taught through the language-experience approach. Therefore, variations in technique are recommended on the basis of diagnosis. Cohen claims, "Learning disability patterns as measured on clinic tests of disadvantaged retarded readers do not differ markedly from the learning disability patterns of middle-class children who are retarded readers."[16]

In research with low-income black students in inner-city schools, it has been found that almost all students produced larger portions of standard English than divergent English.[17] One or two divergent usages may attract teacher attention even when the student uses as many as twenty standard usages. Concentration on these uses may cause students to feel inadequate. Very low correlations exist between divergent usage and ability to listen to standard English. Apparently the user of divergent English has ample opportunities to listen to and comprehend standard English.

When working with these students, teachers should remember that *different* does not mean *deficient.* If we can accept a different dialect as a natural and effective means of communication, the students can develop positive self-concepts. Teaching with the dialect is not advocated; but teachers should accept dialect when communicating with students.

13

Teachers should remember that different does not mean deficient.

Teachers should be mindful of how the values of a divergent culture differ from their own. McDermott cites numerous instances of low achievement when "a group in power educates the children of a minority group." He cites such factors as communication interferences, lack of understanding about motivation stimuli, and failure to understand cultural values.[18] If teacher-student relations are strained by a lack of understanding, then learning to read can become very difficult. Smith refers to it as *risk taking.*[19] If the readers do not believe that a given reading situation is worth the risk of embarrassment or humiliation, they will not try. One obvious solution is to make risk taking worthwhile: that is, no penalty or punishment for the risk taker who fails. Another solution is to study the different culture to enhance the possibilities of effective teacher-student relationships.

The third problem with teaching students from different cultures occurs when English is not the student's native language. The difficulty may involve a student completely unfamiliar with English and a teacher completely unfamiliar with the student's language, or a student skilled in, but not completely comfortable with, English. Unfortunately, the students in both situations respond to English slowly and create the false impression that they lack intelligence. Teachers in these situations need help, and volunteers or other teachers who know the child's native language must be used to bridge the gap until the student learns to communicate comfortably in English.

Students' strengths should always serve as the focus for instruction. Teachers must adopt strategies that involve acceptance of the student and that encourage risk taking.

Handicaps
                                                    15

When
Students
Encounter
Difficulties

Public Law 94–142 has mandated specific educational processes for handicapped students. The mentally retarded, hearing impaired, deaf, speech impaired, visually impaired, seriously emotionally disturbed, deaf-blind, learning disabled, and multiple handicapped are all included in this provision.

As teachers diagnose and instruct the handicapped, they should give attention to the interpretation of the laws as they appear in the *Federal Register.*[20] Basically, they call for full educational opportunities for all handicapped children. Individualized education programs must be written for each handicapped child. These programs are to be implemented in as normal a schooling situation as possible and should be evaluated periodically.

Low achievers in reading may or may not be classified as handicapped. Reading is included under the term *specific reading disability*, when it can be determined that the low achievement in reading is due to some type of disorder in the psychological processes.

Teachers and reading specialists need to be familiar with all school policies that concern the handicapped—who makes the decisions, where everyone's responsibilities lie, and the established procedures for developing IEPs.

Instructing Low-Achieving Readers

Reading is a skill. Like all skills, it is developed and refined through practice. Practice activities must be planned so that the readers can complete them with speed, fluency, and accuracy. If they are designed to fit the readers' strengths, then the readers can refine their reading skills. If they are designed to fit their weaknesses, then it is likely that they will be practicing slow, nonfluent, inaccurate reading and will be learning to read in that manner. Specifically, teachers should:

1. Select reading material so that the readers encounter little difficulty understanding the material and are highly accurate. (See chapter 5 for details on acceptable word pronunciation criteria.)
2. Plan skill activities so that the student can achieve success with them. Low achievers have often had plenty of failures and need no more.
3. Plan alternative strategies for all activities. When the readers stall on an activity, help should be provided immediately or other activities initiated. Continued frustration with too difficult an activity leads to negative self-concept.
4. Encourage student decision making whenever possible. Students are likely to pick those activities that are of most interest to them and those that they can complete successfully.

Suggestions for activities designed to focus upon strengths will be provided in the various chapters that deal with instructional strategies.

The following selected authorities provide additional insight into the necessity of focusing on readers' strengths:

- Waetjen stresses that "if a person is accepted and valued and esteemed, he becomes an inquiring person and he actualizes himself."[21]
- Raths claims that "if our meanings gained from our experiences are frowned upon, are devalued—it constitutes a rejection of our life, and that is intolerable to everyone of us so treated. . . ."[22]
- Bowers and Soar say that "the more supportive the climate, the more the student is willing to share, the more learning will take place. . . ."[23]
- Cohen asserts, "tolerance for failure is best taught through providing a background of success that compensates for experienced failure. . . ."[24]
- Prescott stresses, "the unloved child who fails is in double jeopardy. . . to his insecurity is added the feeling of inadequacy, and he becomes more and more reluctant to try again with each failure."[25]
- Smith notes that "attention is likely to be focused on what each child finds incomprehensible in order to 'challenge' them [sic] to further learning. Anything a child knows already is likely to be set aside as 'too easy.' Paradoxically, many reading materials are made intentionally meaningless. Obviously, in such cases there is no way in which children will be able to develop their ability to seek and identify meaning in text."[26]
- High success rates have a positive impact on student learning while low success rates have a negative impact.[27]

While planning work for students experiencing reading difficulty, some time should be spent developing techniques that will help them develop a desire to learn. For example, the Institute for Research on Teaching reports that low achievers' major strategy for working independently at their seats is to get finished as quickly as possible.[28] They see that their teachers are pleased when they get finished with their work within a specified time period. These students often do not monitor their efforts to determine if the activities make sense. They need techniques for self-monitoring their activities. For example, the teachers might ask these low achievers questions such as, "What did you learn from that activity?" "How will this type of work help you with your reading?" "Do you know why you were asked to do this work?" This procedure not only focuses on making sense of the work, but it also forces the teachers to make sure seat work activities are meaningful.

If activities focus on strengths, school can be a happy, fun-filled environment for all learners. As Margaret Mead put it, "If learning to read were seen as a path to individual triumphant success. . . each child's mastery of reading could, in its own way, be celebrated."[29]

Summary

When students encounter difficulty learning to read, the reactions of teachers and parents are crucial. Attempts to apply more pressure, to label, and to focus on weaknesses can complicate the difficulty. Careful diagnosis followed by instruction that focuses on strengths can enable many low achievers to succeed and develop an "I can do it" self-concept.

Notes

1. Ruth C. Penty, "Reading Ability and High School Dropouts," *Journal of the National Association of Women Deans and Counselors* (October 1959), 14.
2. Albert J. Harris and Edward R. Sipay, *How to Increase Reading Ability*, 8th ed. (New York: Longman, 1985), 316.
3. Albert J. Harris, "Adult Illiteracy: Changing the Statistics," *Reporting On Reading* 5, no. 3 (1979): 6.
4. Ibid.
5. R. Weber, "Adult Illiteracy in the United States," in *Toward a Literate Society: A Report from the National Academy of Education,* ed. John B. Carroll and Jeanne Chall (New York: McGraw-Hill Book Co., 1975).
6. James Allen, "The Right to Read—Target for the Seventies" (Address given to the National Association of State Boards of Education, 23 Sept. 1969).
7. Katherine LeGrand-Brodsky, "Hope for Reading in America: Practically Everyone Reads," *The Reading Teacher* 32, no. 8 (May 1979): 947.
8. Ruth Strang, *Diagnostic Teaching of Reading* (New York: McGraw-Hill Book Co., 1969), 106.
9. Harris and Sipay, *How to Increase Reading Ability*, 201.
10. Helen M. Robinson, *Why Pupils Fail in Reading* (Chicago: University of Chicago Press, 1946), 219.
11. Robinson, *Why Pupils Fail in Reading*, 219.
12. Strang, *Diagnostic Teaching of Reading*, 26.
13. Harris and Sipay, *How to Increase Reading Ability*, 201.
14. Distance of eyes from print—twelve to fifteen inches.
15. James S. Coleman et al., *Equality of Educational Opportunity* (Washington, D.C.: U.S. Department of Health, Education, and Welfare, 1966).
16. S. Alan Cohen, "Cause vs. Treatment in Reading Achievement," *Journal of Learning Disabilities* (March 1970), 43.
17. Walter N. Gantt, Robert M. Wilson, and C. Mitchell Dayton, "An Initial Investigation of the Relationship Between Syntactical Divergency and the Listening Comprehension of Black Children," *Reading Research Quarterly* 10, no. 2 (1974–75): 193–208.
18. Ray P. McDermott, "The Ethnography of Speaking and Reading," in *Linguistic Theory,* ed. Roger Shuy (Newark, Del.: International Reading Association, 1977), 153–85.
19. Frank Smith, *Understanding Reading*, 2d ed. (New York: Holt, Rinehart & Winston, 1978), 20.
20. *Federal Register* 42, no. 163 (Tuesday, 23 Aug. 1977).
21. Walter B. Waetjen, "Facts about Learning," in *Readings in Curriculum,* ed. Glen Hass and Kimball Wiles (Boston: Allyn and Bacon, 1965), 243.
22. Louis E. Raths, "How Children Build Meaning," *Childhood Education* 31 (1954): 159–60.
23. Norman D. Bowers and Robert S. Soar, "Studies in Human Relations in the Teaching-Learning Process," *Evaluation of Laboratory Human Relations Training for Classroom Teachers* (Chapel Hill, N.C.: University of North Carolina Press, 1961), 111.
24. S. Alan Cohen, *Teach Them All to Read* (New York: Random House, 1969), 231.
25. Daniel A. Prescott, *The Child in the Educative Process* (New York: McGraw-Hill Book Co., 1957), 359.
26. Frank Smith, *Understanding Reading*, 166.

27. James H. Block, "Success Rates," in *Time to Learn*, ed. Carolyn Denham and Ann Lieberman (Washington D.C.: U.S. Department of Education, 1980), 95–96.

28. Linda M. Anderson, "Student Responses to Seatwork," *Research Series* no. 102, Institute for Research on Teaching, Michigan State University, July 1981.

29. Margaret Mead, Editorial inside front cover, *The Reading Teacher* 28 (October 1974).

Suggested Readings

Bond, Guy L., Miles A. Tinker, Barbara B. Wasson, and John B. Wasson. *Reading Difficulties: Their Diagnosis and Correction*, 5th ed. Englewood Cliffs: Prentice-Hall, 1984. For another viewpoint of the disabled reader's characteristics, see chapter 3 of this text.

Denham, Carolyn and Ann Lieberman, eds. *Time to Learn*. U.S. Dept. of Education, National Institute of Education, 1980. Reports the findings of a National Institute of Education-funded study which examined the learning behaviors of students in the areas of reading and mathematics. Time spent on successful academic learning tasks resulted in superior student achievement, while time spent on unsuccessful activities interfered with student achievement.

Smith, Frank. *Understanding Reading*, 2d ed. New York: Holt, Rinehart & Winston, 1978. Essential text for those interested in understanding the processes in reading. Smith brings theory from a psycholinguistic base and applies it to various activities involved in learning to read.

Waetjen, Walter R., and Robert R. Leeper, eds. *Learning and Mental Health in the School*. Washington, D.C.: Association for Supervision and Curriculum Development, 1966. Several chapters by different authors illustrate the necessity for consideration of a theory behind instructional strategies. The writings of Syngg are especially valuable regarding the necessity to focus on student strengths.

Joseph G. Czarnecki

is a reading supervisor for the Anne Arundel County Public Schools, Maryland.

Mrs. Howell, a fourth-grade teacher, entered the principal's office for the first School Screening Committee meeting of the year. She brought up John, an alert but shy boy from a school outside the county. No records from the previous school had arrived, but already Mrs. Howell was worried.

John functioned best in a basal with a stated readability of 2.5; his math and other subject work were on grade level; he was having considerable difficulty with both manuscript and cursive handwriting; he couldn't work independently and had a poor self-concept. John was being tutored at home three times a week in reading and handwriting. Mrs. Howell was pleased with John's progress in the basal but would like to be able to pinpoint specific strengths and weaknesses in his reading and improve his weak self-concept.

After discussion, the group made these recommendations: (1) Expedite the transfer of records from John's previous school; (2) Obtain results from speech screening; (3) Proceed with an in-school assessment (Slosson Intelligence Test and Metropolitan Reading Achievement Test); (4) Ascertain the objectives of the after-school tutoring program; (5) Continue to gather information on strengths and weaknesses through the teacher's daily interactions with the student; and (6) Try to have all information available at the next committee meeting.

The next meeting included the principal, the special education teacher, the school psychologist, the pupil personnel worker, and the nurse. They heard the following assessment results: Slosson Intelligence Test = 115, Metropolitan Achievement Test = 2.2. They then hypothesized that John had above average ability, was functioning at least two years below grade level in reading only, and demonstrated a low interest level and success in school tasks.

The group made the following recommendations: (1) Obtain permission to administer the WISC–R; (2) Administer an informal inventory to provide a more specific listing of reading strengths and weaknesses; (3) Invite parents in to obtain more information about John's perceptions of himself and school, his home situation, and his tutoring program; and (4) Be prepared to review all data and make final recommendations to the school team and parents at the next meeting.

At the next meeting, both of John's parents were present. The school gave them all the access ment data: (1) WISC–R results indicated slightly above-average intelligence with a wide scatter in verbal and performance sections. Strengths were visual discrimination, visual sequencing, and commonsense reasoning. Weaknesses were in auditory and visual memory and spatial visualization; (2) The informal reading inventory detected strengths in using syntax clues and decoding both long vowels and vowel digraphs. Weaknesses were detected in using semantic clues, decoding blends and short vowels, and reading intact units of meaning (phrases, short sentences).

His parents said John's learning and attitude problems began when a younger brother was born. His mother said she had been working with John one hour per night (in addition to tutorial help) in reading and handwriting. She said these sessions were frustrating and often ended with John in tears.

The group concluded: (1) John's assessment information indicated a disability in one or more basic psychological processes. According to county and federal guidelines, this would qualify him for reading assistance from the special education teacher; (2) Since John felt incompetent and frustrated in reading tasks and because he would now be receiving specialized help in school, the home tutoring program should be terminated. Further, the parent should replace mutually frustrating nightly work sessions with opportunities to go to a library or bookstore to select high-interest, low-readability material, followed by brief positive (10 to 15 minute) sessions to share what had been read or to have silent reading sessions. The parents were also involved in a discussion of factors and practices that contributed to feelings of self-worth, including opportunities to point out successes and strengths to John in both academic and non-academic situations; (3) The Individual Education Plan should include diagnostic lessons to supplement the existing information on strengths and weaknesses in both comprehension and word attack skills; assignment of tasks that reduced the amount of writing and provided high probability of success; close coordination with classroom teacher and parent; and scheduled review of program and progress in sixty days.

In the ensuing months, the teacher and parents detected gradual improvements in John's self-esteem, reading skills, and task completion. His parents reported a more positive home environment and growing interest in school.

Joseph G. Czarnecki

Introduction to Diagnosis

CHAPTER OUTLINE

Some Myths about Diagnosis
Types of Diagnosis
Steps in Diagnosis
Diagnostic Procedures
Sources of Data
Guidelines for Diagnosis
Diagnosis for Strengths

CHAPTER EMPHASES

*Three types of diagnosis are
recommended for reading
assessment.*
*Assessment of the educational
environment is as important as the
assessment of the reader's
behavior.*
*Diagnosis for readers' strengths has
many positive features.*

If one views diagnosis from the medical viewpoint, an inaccurate perception of educational diagnosis will result. Medical diagnosis is the examination of the nature and circumstances of a diseased condition. However, the notion that a diseased condition causes educational achievement problems is misleading since such conditions are seldom the cause of low achievement. Educational diagnosis involves external factors such as the assessment of the home and school environments, the personal health and attitude of the learner, the learner's skills, and the self-report of the learner.

In the classroom, when first signs of difficulty appear, the readers' educational environment should first be examined. Is that environment a favorable one for the readers? Can easy-to-make changes remedy the situation so that learning efforts can become successful? If so, it is not necessary to involve the readers in testing activities; rather, teachers should make the changes and continue with instruction. For example, several readers may have had difficulty responding to instruction in a comprehension lesson. By evaluating the instructional procedures in the lesson, the teacher may find that several new terms were used in the text and that they were the key to understanding the material. While planning the lesson, the teacher may have missed the importance of these key terms and made no plans to introduce them. By going back and introducing the new terms, the teacher may note that the difficulty originally noticed has disappeared.

Teachers need to develop the habit of keeping careful notes about adjustments that prove effective. These notes can lead to a pattern of observed student behavior. When such patterns are observed again and again, a reliable assessment of student behavior becomes possible. Occasional observations of a particular type of behavior create unreliable impressions.

| Some Myths about Diagnosis | All teachers use diagnostic strategies as they teach. Teacher-made tests, observations of student behavior, and notations in student records are used by all teachers to assist in effectively understanding students. Some myths persist, however, that keep teachers from being as effective as they might be. |

Myth 1 Diagnosis requires the use of specially designed tests. To the contrary, effective diagnosis is usually best achieved by using teacher observation and informal evaluations. The testing situation creates unnatural behavior with some students, and the results are often misleading.

Myth 2 Group standardized tests provide useful information regarding individual students. Not true. Group standardized test results provide very little useful information on individual students. (See discussion in chapter 3.)

Myth 3 Diagnosis requires highly trained personnel. As in all other areas of education, there are levels of competence in diagnosis.

All teachers use diagnostic procedures every day. Those with more preparation are probably more efficient, but teaching requires continual assessment.

Myth 4 Diagnosis calls for a case-study report. Notes from diagnostic observations should be maintained but in a very simple format. Case-study approaches are generally used when the reading difficulty is severe and a reading specialist has been asked to assist.

The preceding clarification of the myths often associated with diagnosis will aid in discussing the types of diagnostic procedures. Three types of diagnosis prove useful at various times.

Informal On-the-Spot Diagnosis

Teachers constantly assess student performances during instruction. Student responses to questions, writing activities, and general class participation provide teachers with informal input about student progress. When difficulties arise, adjustments are made on-the-spot to help students achieve success.

Classroom Diagnosis

If, after informal adjustments have been made, students continue to have difficulty, more structured diagnostic efforts may be initiated. Here the teacher sets some time aside to work individually with a student to determine what is causing the difficulty. Testing might be involved in an attempt to determine the degree of skill development in a given area. Those findings are checked against data in school records. Classroom instruction is adjusted to see if the student can then respond successfully.

Clinical Diagnosis

When instructional adjustments prove unsuccessful and reading difficulty increases, a reading specialist may be called in. Generally, clinical diagnosis will take place outside the classroom and involve specific skills testing and diagnostic lessons with the student. Recommendations for instructional adjustments will be made and the teacher and reading specialist can evaluate the success of those adjustments together. Clinical diagnosis may also involve specialists in speech therapy or special education, or involve the referral of the student to an outside diagnostic agency such as a college reading clinic.

Teachers should constantly assess student performance during instruction.

Steps in Diagnosis	The following steps will provide a better understanding of the relationships among the types of diagnosis.

The classroom teacher first makes an informal on-the-spot diagnosis and adjusts instruction accordingly. If this fails, the teacher conducts a classroom diagnosis and individualizes instruction. Should this step prove unsuccessful, the teacher can refer the student to a reading specialist for a more thorough analysis via clinical diagnosis. Instruction is then adjusted according to the recommendations of the specialist. If this entire sequence cannot produce the desired results, the necessity for other referrals is likely. A single failure will not likely cause the teacher to move immediately to the next type of diagnosis; rather, the teacher will use each diagnostic step thoroughly and repeatedly, if necessary, before moving to the next. Further, teachers should keep in mind that referral is possible at each step in diagnosis (see Figure 2–1).

Since all effective learning relies on informal on-the-spot diagnosis and its subsequent follow-up, one might assume that this type of diagnosis will occur in good teaching. Further, the types of diagnosis are not clearly separated; classroom teachers may use the reading specialists' clinical diagnostic tools when appropriate. All types of diagnosis include observation of the student to determine the effectiveness of the adjusted instruction.

Diagnostic Procedures	Specific procedures will vary with the diagnosis of the difficulty and type of treatment initiated. The following treatment procedures for each type of diagnosis should be considered flexible.

The procedures used with informal on-the-spot diagnosis are related to the instructional procedures used. When the teacher notices that students are experiencing difficulty, an immediate instructional adjustment is made in order to facilitate learning. Some examples may be helpful.

- Margi was not responding well to her teacher's questions on the material she had just read. When the teacher changed the type of question from literal to interpretive, Margi responded very well. Her teacher noted that Margi could deal better with the literal questions after she was successful with the interpretive ones.
- Roy read orally in a slow, choppy manner, only mispronouncing about one word out of fifteen. Roy was encouraged to practice reading orally to himself, and he soon became fluent and accurate.
- Catherine was the lowest achiever in her reading group. She knew it and so did the other students. Her self-concept as a

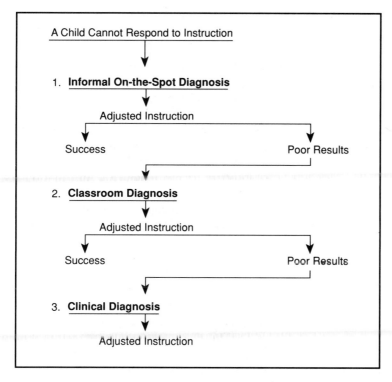

FIGURE 2–1. Steps in Diagnosis

reader was poor. Her teacher made arrangements for Catherine to tutor a young child in a lower grade for fifteen minutes each morning. This tutoring caused an instant change in Catherine's attitude because she felt worthwhile helping someone else.

- Joe was reading well in reading class, but he seemed to encounter great difficulty doing assignments in his science text. His teacher noticed that the science text introduced a large number of new words at the beginning of each chapter. By using those new words in contexts that Joe could understand, his teacher could help him with those words before he encountered them on his own. His science assignments improved immediately.

Of course, informal on-the-spot diagnosis and its subsequent follow-up do not always work this nicely. At times, attempted adjustments miss their purpose, and the difficulty continues. If repeated informal on-the-spot adjustments do not have the desired effect, then a classroom diagnosis, allowing for a more careful look into the factors causing the difficulty, becomes necessary.

Classroom Diagnosis

Classroom diagnosis entails a more formal assessment than does informal on-the-spot diagnosis. When students are in a failure pattern and informal adjustments do not help, carefully planned classroom observation and testing become necessary.

Procedures for classroom diagnosis include the following:

IDENTIFICATION. The classroom teacher is in the best position to notice potential problem areas. In this way, classroom diagnosis is actually under way by the time the student's problems have been identified; informal on-the-spot diagnosis has previously established certain diagnostic information that the teacher will use in classroom diagnosis.

The tendency for educators to wait until a problem is well developed before acting on it can be avoided by increased attention to classroom diagnosis at all age levels, including first grade. Through immediate attention to the first symptoms of reading difficulty the number of low-achieving readers can be reduced.

ASSESSMENT OF THE EDUCATIONAL ENVIRONMENT. The classroom teacher should make notes on such factors as the instructional strategies, grouping and seating arrangements, and materials used in the classroom. These factors should then be carefully examined to determine if modifying any of them would create a more successful learning environment.

GATHERING AVAILABLE DATA. The classroom teacher next searches for information about the student and organizes it for consideration during the diagnosis.

The classroom teacher is in the best position to notice potential problem areas.

School records, interviews with past teachers, health reports, and other sources provide considerable data concerning the student's past development, successes, and failures. Notes made during informal on-the-spot diagnosis can prove extremely useful, particularly if the teacher making the classroom diagnosis did not conduct the previous one. Other sources of data include:

- *Limited testing.* When necessary, classroom teachers may administer and interpret tests designed to provide information in the difficulty area. Testing, of course, is limited by the time that teachers have for individual testing as well as their skill in using the instruments.
- *Direct observations.* Using the information available at this stage of classroom diagnosis, teachers should observe students in various reading situations with particular attention to verifying other diagnostic information. When observations and other data complement previous findings, the next step can be taken. When they do not support each other, there is a need for reevaluation, more observation, possible testing, and new conclusions.

FORMULATION OF HYPOTHESES. From the patterns observed, the teacher will form hypotheses about adjusting instruction for the group or individual and about the possibility of referral. By looking for patterns, one reduces the chances of error often caused by relying on one observation or test score.

ADJUSTING INSTRUCTION. Once instructional hypotheses have been formed, teachers adjust instruction and test each hypothesis. For example, if the diagnostic hypothesis is "Jack will read more fluently if I reduce the level of

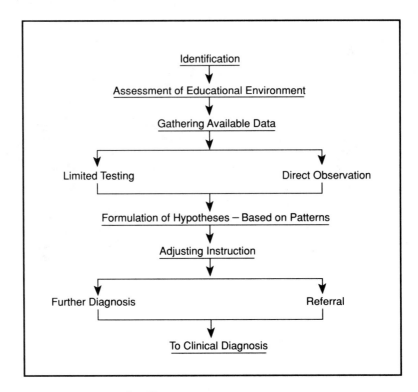

FIGURE 2-2. Procedures for Classroom Diagnosis

difficulty by one grade level," then the teacher finds materials at the level indicated and places Jack in a learning situation. If, in fact, Jack can read fluently in these new materials, then the hypothesis is accepted. If he cannot, then it is back to the diagnostic procedures to develop another hypothesis.

Classroom diagnosis *is* time consuming. However, teachers can minimize the amount of time needed if they use existing records, conduct the diagnosis during times other students are occupied, and collect diagnostic data daily over a period of time. As teachers gain proficiency with diagnostic procedures, they will find them less time consuming. Figure 2-2 summarizes the procedures in classroom diagnosis.

Clinical Diagnosis

Clinical procedures may be implemented through individual study of the student outside of the classroom. These procedures are listed here and described in Figure 2-3.

REFERRAL. The reading specialist has the advantage of starting to work with a student who has been referred. The classroom teacher has either attempted classroom diagnosis or determined that the student needs clinical diagnosis. All available information about the student should be forwarded to the reading specialist at the time of referral. Many times the referral comes from parents. The specialist should consult with the classroom teacher to obtain as much information as possible in these cases.

ADMINISTRATION OF A BATTERY OF TESTS. Using a tentative evaluation of a student and that student's needs, the reading specialist proceeds with the administration and analysis of a battery of tests to gather objective data on the student's reading skills.

OBSERVATION OF PATTERNS. The reading specialist carefully observes behavior patterns during the testing. Combined with test scores and the specialist's analysis of the reading responses on tests administered, these observations will be useful in grouping relevant data into meaningful patterns.

FORMULATION OF HYPOTHESES. From the observable patterns, the reading specialist then forms tentative hypotheses concerning the causes of the problem.

CONSIDERATION OF RELATED DATA. Once the hypotheses have been formed, the specialist weighs related data from parent and teacher conferences, school

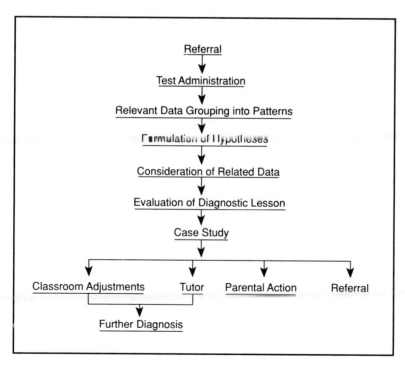

FIGURE 2–3. Procedures for Clinical Diagnosis

records, and previous diagnostic results. When the specialist finds that the related data support the hypotheses, the diagnosis gains validity; at other times conflicting information forces reconsideration of the original hypotheses. In many cases, further testing or reexamination of test results is needed for clearer insights into the difficulty.

EVALUATION THROUGH DIAGNOSTIC LESSONS. The lessons conducted during a clinical diagnosis are brief and specifically related to the diagnostic hypotheses. Parts of the lessons should be directed to the student's strengths and parts to the student's weaknesses. Short-term diagnostic sessions provide further validation of the diagnosis.

FORMULATION OF RECOMMENDATIONS AND REFERRALS. After consideration of all relevant data, the reading specialist develops a case study that includes recommendations for adjustments of school programs, remedial treatment, parental action, further testing, or necessary referral.

The time needed for effective clinical diagnosis will vary with the age of the student, the effectiveness of classroom diagnosis, and practical matters such as clinician load. Normally, a clinical diagnosis should take one to two hours. In some cases, however, much more time is needed due to the involved nature of the case.

While clinical diagnosis has the advantage of highly individualized study and the use of precise instruments for evaluation by a carefully trained person, it has the following limitations:

- The clinic situation involves one-to-one interaction, while the classroom situation necessitates working with others. Thus, the behaviors of students in the two situations will probably differ.
- Since the teacher and the reading specialist are two different people, students will naturally react to each in a different way.
- After the reading specialist checks diagnosis with the diagnostic teaching lessons, the teacher may be unable to make necessary instructional adjustments.

For these reasons, the specialist should discuss the results of the diagnosis with the teacher, in addition to providing a written report. To illustrate the techniques recommended in the report, the reading specialist should offer to work with the student in the classroom for one or two lessons.

Clinical diagnosis often establishes a need for further action for the reading specialist, such as the following:

- Reporting the results of the clinical diagnosis and their interpretation to a screening committee.
- Reporting and interpreting the results of the diagnosis to parents.
- Preparing teachers to use special instructional techniques through in-service sessions.

- Consulting with medical or psychological personnel when referrals are made.
- Instructing the student for a period of time when individual or small-group attention is needed.

While conducting any type of diagnosis, teachers should be aware of the available sources of data. At times one can become so involved with testing that other sources of data are overlooked. Some of the other sources, however, are much more useful than test results.

Informal on-the-spot diagnosis relies heavily on observed student behavior, school records, and reports from others. Since most of this diagnosis takes place during instructional time, the only test results available are from teacher-made tests, which are normally used to assess the effectiveness of the instruction.

Classroom diagnosis relies on school records, observations of teachers, reports from past teachers, interviews with students and parents, records from home visits, and test results. In classroom diagnosis, the teacher also obtains important data from the assessment of the educational environment.

Data for clinical diagnosis include reports from psychologists, medical personnel, or speech therapists. Other useful data come from interviews and questionnaires, diagnostic lessons, and tests. In clinical diagnosis, heavy reliance is placed on a variety of testing instruments. Physical screening tests, intelligence tests, attitude surveys, and a host of reading tests are available for use in clinical diagnosis.

In each type of diagnosis, information from the student can be very useful, though it is often overlooked. How does the reader see the difficulty? What are the reader's perceived strengths? What is his or her perception of the learning environment? These types of data from readers are useful for planning instructional programs.

Several guidelines should be kept in mind when entering into diagnostic activities. While they may not be applicable in every instance, failure to use them when indicated can drastically interfere with student performance.

Establish Rapport

Students will perform best in a relaxed environment where a good rapport with the supervisor present encourages a cooperative attitude. The classroom teacher, through daily contact with students, has a better opportunity for establishing this kind of situation than a reading specialist, who meets with students outside of the normal classroom setting. Both, however, should strive to make students comfortable so that inhibitions do not affect performance, thus resulting in inaccurate assessment.

Provide Individual Study

Since many group testing situations produce unreliable results, individual study is essential. Individual sessions with students reduce those competitive activities that are frustrating to low-achieving readers.

Provide Group Study

Evaluation of students as they interact can offer useful diagnostic insights. Diagnostic results that come from data collected during individual study only are often difficult to apply. Students' reactions in groups may be quite different from their performances during individual study. Both types of data are needed for a thorough diagnosis.

Resist Temptations to Coach

When students are experiencing difficulties, teachers' first reactions are often to try to help them by trying to coax or by coaching a correct answer. In most teaching situations, that response is the appropriate one. In diagnosis, however, the teacher must remember that the ultimate goal is to get the most accurate picture possible of a student's capabilities. Supportive encouragement is important; coaching answers from students may give a false picture of their abilities.

Maintain Efficiency

An efficient diagnosis includes only tests and observations likely to help the examiner determine the difficulty. There is a tendency to rely on a systematic diagnostic procedure regardless of the needs of the student, creating pointless testing situations which are often frustrating experiences. An efficient diagnosis, then, includes those measures needed by the educator to arrive at a solution; it eliminates those of questionable value to the objectives of the diagnosis.

Search for Patterns of Performance

Single observations of a reader's performance can lead to unreliable conclusions. A consistent pattern of performance over time, or over different testing situations, increases the probability that the results are a true indication of the reader's skills. For example, it would be best to check the student's reading comprehension skills with several passages at the same level. If a student scores well on one and poorly on another, it is difficult to determine whether the difficulty lies in the passage or the reader's comprehension. By checking on a few more passages, the teacher could confirm or reject that suspicion with more confidence.

Effective diagnosis is a continuous process of observing students, posing hypotheses to guide instruction, and reevaluating approaches and strategies as instruction proceeds. Teachers should remember that diagnosis is ongoing and does not end with testing. In fact, some of the very best diagnosis is informally conducted by teachers in the course of their day-to-day instruction.

Diagnosis for Strengths

Diagnostic reports of students experiencing reading difficulties usually focus on areas of weakness, with no mention of strengths. However, because instructional adjustments must start with areas of strengths, deliberate effort should be given to uncovering them in diagnosis. What students know is important. What they do not know can be implied from what they do know. By shifting the focus of a diagnosis to discovering a student's strengths, all those involved with the student begin to adopt a new outlook. The referring teacher views the student differently. Because many other past interactions with educational agencies have tended to stress the negative aspects of their child's academic performance, parents also appreciate learning positive things about their child. Perhaps the most positive result, however, is the opportunity to discuss diagnostic results with students in terms of their strengths. Such conferences leave students feeling worthwhile.

When diagnosing for strengths, teachers must look for student performances that demonstrate comfort, fluency, accuracy, and speed. These can be observed during instruction or testing. Satisfactory test scores evaluated without these characteristics of performance may be misleading in attempts to identify strengths. The following are examples of diagnostic activities for strengths:

- Instead of listing skill weaknesses on a phonics test, list those skills that were noted as accurate and well developed.
- Determine comprehension levels at which students can respond with comfort and accuracy. Report those levels as suggested starting levels for instruction.
- Note skills demonstrated in oral reading and report them as skills that should be practiced and reinforced.
- Ask the student to indicate his or her perceived reading strengths. Then set up a diagnostic situation in which those strengths can be demonstrated.

Diagnosis for strengths does not preclude noting areas in need of attention, however, it does add a pleasant and positive dimension to diagnosis.

Summary

The three types of diagnosis discussed in this chapter have an important place in reading diagnosis. Each uses data that are available and procedures that are effective in that type of diagnosis. Guidelines for diagnosis are provided to help teachers avoid some of the activities that interfere with effective diagnosis. Diagnosing for strengths is recommended.

Suggested Readings

Askov, Eunice, and Wayne Otto. *Meeting the Challenge.* Columbus, Ohio: Merrill, 1985. The authors present corrective elementary reading instruction from a perspective that weds diagnosis and instruction in a continual and dynamic fashion.

Barr, Rebecca, and Marilyn Sadow. *Reading Diagnosis for Teachers.* New York: Longman, 1985. Using a sample case format, this text presents a diagnostic model that describes reading behaviors in terms of print translation strategies, word meaning knowledge, and comprehension abilities.

Collins-Cheek, Martha, and Earl H. Cheek. *Diagnostic-Prescriptive Reading Instruction.* 2d ed. Dubuque, Iowa: Wm. C. Brown, 1984. Chapter 2 discusses the teacher's role in diagnosis and remediation. In chapter 15, the authors describe how the various parts of diagnostic-prescriptive teaching fit together.

Jaggar, Angela, and M. Trika Smith-Burke, eds. *Observing the Language Learner.* Newark, Del.: International Reading Association, 1985. The authors of this volume present varied ideas for gaining knowledge about students through watching them work and read. The naturalistic observations correspond directly with instruction.

Marzano, Robert J., Patricia J. Hagerty, Sheila W. Valencia, and Philip P. DiStefano. *Reading Diagnosis and Instruction: Theory Into Practice.* Englewood Cliffs, N.J.: Prentice-Hall, 1987. In chapter 7, the authors present an ethnographic model for guiding the selection of diagnostic devices and interpreting diagnostic findings.

Rupley, William H., and Timothy R. Blair. *Reading Diagnosis and Remediation: Classroom and Clinic.* 2d ed. Boston: Houghton Mifflin Company, 1983. The authors make a strong case in chapter 6 for a study of the educational environment. They include a teacher effort scale to aid in evaluations of instructional programs.

EDITORIAL

Judith O. Smith

is a doctoral student at Penn State University, University Park, Pennsylvania.

I can still see them: John, a forty-eight-year-old man who could not spell even the simplest words; Ivan, young father of two and a math whiz, but with no high school diploma and no job; Yvonne, a struggling single mother; Rose, a grandmother who never got beyond elementary school. All were unemployed and desperate enough to swallow their pride to attend summer classes in their former elementary school. These remarkable adults taught me, their teacher, some valuable lessons about the diagnosis of reading problems in children.

My students were keenly aware of their past failures and were reluctant to participate in any situation in which they felt they would not succeed. They had a real aversion to taking tests, the very first task they were asked to do. How then could I begin to pinpoint their strengths and weaknesses so that I could tailor instruction to them individually?

My strategies were the following:

1. Because the class was held in an elementary school, which I perceived as threatening to my students, I tried to create the most relaxed atmosphere possible. I brought coffee and allowed them to take breaks whenever needed, except during formal testing procedures. Extra reading materials in the classroom included magazines in which they had expressed interest.

2. I never based my diagnosis on a single standardized test which yielded "grade levels" for these adults. I emphasized students' strengths and reminded them that they had many skills and experiences that had enabled them to survive to this point. Thus, they saw that I viewed them as intelligent human beings in spite of their limitations, and I believe that they eventually viewed themselves this way too.

3. I took responsibility for my students' learning. If they weren't succeeding, my first step was to look at my teaching and the learning environment. I told my students that if they weren't learning, it might be because I hadn't figured out how to teach in a way that was appropriate to them

Students became very open about what did and didn't work for them. They were less likely to see themselves as failures, and I was better able to tailor my teaching to their needs.

The summer went by very quickly. Some students progressed rapidly; others seemed to move at a slower rate. I found that I had to continue to emphasize the students' strengths. Whenever they were frustrated, it showed immediately. Honest praise was given when any progress was made.

More advanced students were preparing to take the General Educational Development (GED) test to earn a high school equivalency diploma. Reading comprehension was extremely important in three of the five subtests which typically presented selections of text followed by multiple-choice questions. Diagnosis had to be an ongoing process. We worked in small groups of two or three and through discussion were able to pinpoint areas of difficulty and discuss test-taking tips.

I learned to use materials that were relevant to the students. John did not want to learn spell-ing by traditional memorization techniques. We worked successfully in the format of the GED test he hoped eventually to take. One reluctant reader was enticed by the prospect of passing his driver's test. So we worked from the *Pennsylvania Manual for Drivers* and appropriate grade-level books about hunting, another of his interests. Ivan, the math whiz, would work on his reading skills as long as he was allowed some time for math afterwards.

John never did become a good speller, but he eventually passed the GED test and got a job. Yvonne and Ivan also earned their diplomas and both are now attending college. Rose continues to study and is so pleased with her own progress that she has recruited her daughter to attend class with her. I left the class in the hands of another teacher so that I could pursue my own studies. The summer was an extremely rewarding experience. I'm not sure who learned the most—the students or the teacher.

Judith O. Smith

Standardized Test Interpretation

CHAPTER OUTLINE

Diagnosis As Decision Making
Selecting Standardized Measures
Interpreting Standardized Tests
Responsible Uses of Standardized
    Testing
New Directions in Standardized
    Testing

CHAPTER EMPHASES

*Standardized tests can be one useful
    source of information to aid
    teacher decision making.*

*Norm-referenced and criterion-
    referenced standardized tests assess
    student abilities by comparing
    performance to two different
    standards.*

*Reliability, validity, and usability are
    three important considerations in
    evaluating the measurement
    capabilities of a standardized test.*

*A knowledge of common testing
    terminology and scores is
    necessary to properly interpret
    standardized test results.*

*To avoid improper use of standardized
    tests, teachers should be familiar
    with some of the major limitations
    associated with them.*

S tandardized testing is a widespread, almost universal, practice in education, and a huge industry has sprung up to support it. Every year, millions of dollars are spent (and all too often misspent) on standardized tests by school districts all over the country.

Good reasons exist for questioning the effectiveness of standardized testing. Teachers report that, although they must allot valuable classroom time for their students to take the tests, when the results arrive they are of little practical value. Principals complain of test results that do not seem to be accurate reflections of their students' abilities. Curriculum coordinators search the results for suggestions to guide their instructional programs but sometimes find little relationship between what their reading programs teach and what the standardized tests assess. And, at all levels, standardized tests are misinterpreted and their results misused. According to the 1985 Report of the Commission on Reading, "the proper attitude toward standardized tests is one of balance. Tests yield information that is of some value, but its significance should not be exaggerated out of proportion."[1]

Proper use of standardized tests requires test users to understand what these diagnostic devices can and can not do. It is also important to be able to correctly interpret test results. Most importantly, test users should understand the rightful place of standardized tests in the diagnostic process.

Diagnosis As Decision Making

When diagnosis is mentioned, many people immediately think of tests and testing. Diagnosis, however, is far more than that. In its simplest sense, diagnosis is decision making. Each day, teachers make literally hundreds of professional decisions in the course of their everyday work. Some of those decisions are fairly trivial and require very little thought; others are momentous and affect students' lives in profound ways.

Example 1: Mrs. Winston

Billy was a mystery to third-grade teacher Mrs. Winston. Some days in the lowest reading group Billy would appear to be the most able reader in the group, yet on other days, he seemed to be hopelessly over his head. Was attitude, ability, or some other factor responsible for Billy's reading group difficulties? What steps could Mrs. Winston take to help Billy be successful?

Example 2: Mr. Sheenan

Mr. Sheenan, the reading specialist, was troubled by Beth. She had been referred to him for evaluation by her seventh-grade science teacher with a report that she was generally interested in science and attentive in class but was having a great deal of difficulty with homework assignments in the textbook. Were her difficulties related to reading ability, study habits, or something else? Was she having similar difficulties with other content area subjects? What could be done to help Beth?

Example 3: Mrs. Gilbert

As she reviewed the standardized test results for her building, Mrs. Gilbert, principal of Mill Creek Elementary, became more and more concerned. According to reports forwarded to her by the testing company, her school was below national averages for reading. If only she could pinpoint the problem! Mrs. Gilbert turned back to the printout to see if she could identify what was wrong.

All these educators are faced with decisions; however, the paths they follow to their decisions may be quite different. In order to make informed professional decisions, each will attempt to gather as much relevant information as possible on which to base the decision. The first place each may be tempted to turn may be a standardized test; however, standardized testing is only one source of information and, in many cases, a faulty source of information at that.

Teachers should remember that diagnosis is most accurate when it is systematic, naturalistic, and considers multiple indicators of student abilities. Systematic diagnosis requires the teacher to assess students' abilities over time rather than in a single testing session. Student abilities are variable and may be affected by mood, fatigue, carelessness, or inattention. When students are observed over a period of time, the resulting decisions are more likely to be accurate.

Naturalistic diagnosis requires that measures used to assess student abilities resemble "real" reading tasks to the degree possible. Most reading takes place in fairly long segments of text arranged in paragraph form, and reading is thought to be successful when the reader is able to understand the central message intended by the author. Unfortunately, the type of reading required by many assessment instruments is so limited and artificial that it might be argued that only in testing situations does this type of reading exist. Some "reading comprehension" tests, for example, only require students to read one to three sentences and then fill in a missing word. Isn't reading comprehension far more than that?

Diagnostic decisions that are based on a single measure of student ability may be misleading for a variety of reasons. First, reading is a complicated human behavior with many overlapping and interacting components. It would be difficult for a single assessment device to pinpoint individual strengths and weaknesses and also reveal how they interact in the reading process. Second, all tests are flawed. When too much dependence is placed upon any single measure, the teacher increases the possibility that the resulting decisions will be off the mark.[2] Observations of students in learning situations, self-reports of students, teacher-made tests, and standardized measures can all have a role in making good diagnostic decisions. Conversely, a diagnosis that ignores any of these sources of potential information may be incomplete and misleading.

If taken as one source of diagnostic information, standardized tests can provide useful information for assisting diagnostic decisions. Regrettably, too often standardized tests have been relied upon as sole determinants of student abilities, and scores from standardized tests have been misused. In order to use standardized test information in a responsible manner, it is first necessary to understand something of test construction, interpretation, and limitations. Historically, standardized tests have been among the most used and most misinterpreted diagnostic measures of all.

Selecting Standardized Measures

Characteristics of Standardized Tests

With the many tests now available, it is often difficult for teachers to know which would give the most assistance in making a particular diagnostic decision. A knowledge of how standardized tests are constructed and the nature of validity, reliability, and usability can aid teachers in making good choices.

There are two major types of standardized tests that account for most testing measures currently on the market—norm-referenced and criterion-referenced. The term "referenced" in each name reminds the test user that information derived from using the test gains its meaning by comparing it to the reference system used to construct the test. In the case of a norm-referenced test, the reference system is the group of individuals the test authors used to determine average performances on the test. A criterion-referenced test, on the other hand, uses the test itself as the reference system. The test is designed to represent mastery or competence of a particular skill or skills. The test itself serves as a yardstick against which to measure student performance.

Norm-referenced tests usually are constructed using a six-step process. First, educational objectives are written that identify the goals of the test. Second, questions are written that seek to assess the test objectives. In the third step, the questions are assembled into a pretest. The pretest is given to a small sample group of individuals who are similar to those for whom the test is being designed. Based on the performance of the sample group, the test authors refine the questions to eliminate misleading, biased, or otherwise poorly written items. Fourth, a final copy of the test is assembled. Fifth, the test is given to a large, representative, national group called the norming population. Their average performances on the test determine the scoring standards. Finally, results from the test are statistically analyzed to determine the test's reliability and validity (more on these terms later). At times, poorly constructed standardized tests have resulted when test authors have bypassed one or more of the steps described above.

Most standardized criterion-referenced tests are also constructed using a six-step process. First, a general description is prepared of the overall test goals. Second, a large number of individual skill objectives are written that specify in great detail each of the skills being assessed. Third, questions are written that correspond to each of the individual skill objectives, usually with several items corresponding to each objective. Fourth, the questions are pretested to eliminate misleading and biased items. Fifth, a final copy of the test is written, and cutoff scores are derived to represent mastery levels on the test. Sixth, reliability and validity trials are run.

Norm-referenced and criterion-referenced tests are constructed in these different ways to serve different purposes. Decisions concerning which type of test is most appropriate will depend upon whether the teacher is interested in assessing student performance by comparing it to a national norming group (norm-referenced) or by assessing student mastery of a specified set of objectives (criterion-referenced). In either case, teachers should carefully examine a test's goals and objectives to determine their relationship to the instructional program.

Validity, Reliability, and Usability

VALIDITY. How well does a test accomplish the purpose for which it is used? In order to adequately consider validity of a particular test, teachers must consider their reasons for using it. Most test authors attempt to establish the validity of their test by comparing the results of their test with another test, usually one of established reputation. This is called concurrent validity. A measure may also be valid if the content of the test represents an adequate sampling of the knowledge and skills it is designed to measure. This is called content validity. A test is said to have predictive validity if that test score can be used to predict some future achievement with accuracy.

Concurrent validity is reported by means of a validity coefficient. These figures usually appear as decimals (such as 0.70). For purposes of interpretation, the decimal must be squared (0.49) to find the percent (49 percent) of the variance measured, in common, by each test. Bartz presents a "rule of thumb" for interpretation of validity coefficients when he states that "validity coefficients may range anywhere from .20 and up, with the .60 to .70 range considered quite high."[3] Although this is the most widely used approach to validity, Johnston notes that it is the least desirable. "This approach can naturally result in a rather circular argument, since two tests can intend to measure the same trait, be highly correlated, and still fail to measure what they were intended to measure."[4]

From a validity standpoint, it is more important to consider the degree to which the test items are capable of measuring the ability in question and the degree of match between the test objectives and those of the school curriculum. Published tests, particularly norm-referenced group tests, are at a considerable disadvantage in satisfying either of these crucial validity concerns.[5] Criterion-referenced measures may bear a greater relationship to the classroom curriculum than many norm-referenced tests. A criterion-referenced test should also be examined to determine which skills have been identified, how clearly skill objectives have been stated, and how well the test items assess those skills.

RELIABILITY. Has the test measured consistently? Has the test measured by chance? If students were to retake the test, would they obtain the same scores? All tests are subject to error; therefore, most test authors provide information about a test's error factor in the user's guide. Two types of error factors commonly reported are reliability coefficent and standard error of measurement. Reliability coefficients are usually reported in decimals (such as 0.93). Reliability coefficients below the 0.90 level cause concern about test reliability. Test reliability is usually determined by one or more of the following four methods:[6]

1. Test-retest, where students take the same test more than once and results are compared.
2. Parallel forms, where student performance on alternate test forms is compared (i.e., Form A and Form B).
3. Split-test, where total test reliability is estimated from student performance on test halves. (Reliability coefficients obtained by the split-test method are generally higher than those found by the other methods.)[7]
4. Item data, where the internal consistency of the test items is examined by determining the degree to which individual items are interrelated in the abilities they assess. In other words, how homogeneous is the test?

The standard error of measurement is related to test reliability. Although the reliability coefficient represents the testing instrument's freedom from error, the standard error of measurement denotes the extent to which error does exist in a test score. It tells the amount a student's obtained score might be expected to vary from that student's hypothetical true score. Suppose Bill obtained a score of 9.5 units on a test that had a standard error of measurement of 0.4 units. It could be estimated with about 68 percent certainty that his true score is within the range 9.1 to 9.9 units. The certainty concerning Bill's true score increases to approximately 95 percent if the range is expanded to 8.7 to 10.3 units. The standard error of measurement denotes the *average* error of measurement for a given test. Errors of measurement are greater for students who score very high or very low than for those scoring in the middle or average ranges of the test.

When one is using a criterion-referenced test, part of determining the reliability involves determining that an adequate number of items have been used to assess each given skill. If too few items have been used, an erroneous estimate of student skill may result, because guessing or carelessness may significantly affect a student's performance. If too many items are related to a given skill objective, student fatigue may hamper performance. Therefore, criterion-referenced tests should have a sufficiently limited overall focus to enable an adequate number of items to assess each individual educational objective.[8] That is, it would be better to measure fifteen objectives well than to attempt to measure thirty objectives and end up with a test that measures poorly.

USABILITY. Although validity and reliability are important concerns, test selection must also consider how practical the test is to use. Is the test affordable? Is it easily scored? How are results reported? How long does the test take to administer and score? How much special training is required to administer the test? Are alternate forms available for pretesting and posttesting? Will results offer clear directions for subsequent remediation? All these questions are important; however, teachers must guard against selecting tests on the basis of usability alone. Some easily administered and scored tests lack reliability and validity.

Putting It All Together

Reliability, validity, and usability are crucial factors in selecting a test that will suit a teacher's purpose. When a test has low reliability, interpretation of the test is impossible because the measurement may be error laden. A fairly reliable test that has low validity proves useless because of uncertainty of what abilities are being measured. For example, a readiness test might be limited to alphabet knowledge and be very reliable. However, to make decisions about student readiness on the basis of such a test would not be valid, because there are many variables associated with readiness other than alphabet knowledge.

A test can be reliable but not valid; however, the reverse is not possible. In order for a test to have high validity, it must measure consistently. And, the most reliable and valid test is of little use if a school district is unable to afford it or if the teacher has difficulty scoring it.

Ideally, tests should be rated high in all three areas—reliability, validity, and usability. Unfortunately, all tests are flawed and teachers must make selection decisions accordingly. Evaluation of a test should start with validity. If the test does not accurately assess the ability that the teacher wants to measure, questions of reliability and usability are irrelevant. Ultimately, the ability of a test to accurately measure what the teacher sets out to measure should remain the primary concern. If the test's validity is acceptable, the reliability of the measure and the usability of the test should be considered.

The Normal Curve

The normal curve is a bell-shaped mathematical model that describes how a very large population would be expected to perform on a well-constructed measure of ability (see Figure 3–1). It is a means of illustrating the natural spread that occurs whenever human attributes or abilities are measured. The vast majority of people are found to be grouped somewhere around the average with relatively few people being found to be very high or very low. If twenty-six-year-old men were tested for jumping ability, for example, a few professional athletes might be expected to jump extraordinarily high, most men would tend

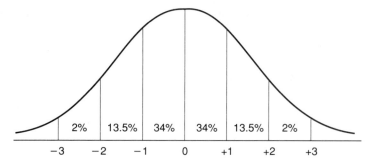

FIGURE 3-1. The Normal Curve with Standard Deviations and Approximate Percentages

to group around a similar average height, and a few men would barely be able to get off the ground. There are very few Michael Jordans in this world.

The normal curve is useful in interpreting performance on norm-referenced tests, because if the standardization population was carefully chosen to represent the general population, their scores on a well-constructed test will approximate a normal curve. Their scores are then used to calibrate the test. A fourth-grade designation is given to the raw score obtained by average fourth graders from the standardization population. A second- or third-grade designation might be assigned to the raw score obtained by low-achieving fourth graders from the standardization group.

Measures of Central Tendency

Mean, median, and mode are three terms used to describe the tendency of scores to be grouped around the average. A mean is an arithmetic average. It would be the midpoint of a normal curve that bisects the curve into two mirror parts. In a group of scores, the median is the score that represents the middle of the distribution when the scores are arranged in ascending or descending order. The mode is the most often occurring score in a group of scores. If the group is very large and their performance approximates a normal curve, the mode would be expected to fall in the mid-range; however, on some tests that may not be the case. Of the three measures of central tendency, the mean is the one most often reported from standardized tests.
Two examples:

"A" Scores: 2, 3, 1, 4, 4, 1, 3, 5, 4
Mean = 3   Median = 3   Mode = 4

"B" Scores: 5, 15, 25, 10, 25, 40
Mean = 20   Median = 20   Mode = 25

Range and standard deviation are two useful ways ot describing the degree of spread in a group of scores. The range is determined by subtracting the lowest score from the highest score. The range of the "A" Scores in the above example is 4. The range of the "B" Scores is 35.

Standard deviations represent performance in relationship to the mean of a normal curve. On a well-constructed test, approximately 68 percent of those taking the test would be expected to score within one standard deviation on either side of the mean. Approximately 95 percent of test takers would be expected to score within two standard deviations on either side of the mean. If the mean for a given test was 50 and the standard deviation was 5, approximately two-thirds of all those taking the test would be expected to score between 45 and 55; approximately 95 percent would be expected to score between 40 and 60. A teacher, who received a printout reporting that Billy had scored a 62 on the test, would realize that Billy had done extremely well indeed as compared to all those having taken the test.

Types of Scores

There are several different types of scores that are commonly reported from standardized testing. In each case, proper interpretation of the score requires the test taker to understand how the score was derived and what the score represents.

GRADE EQUIVALENTS. "Matt scored a 6.2 reading score on this group, norm-referenced achievement test, and he's only in third grade! He must be able to read sixth-grade level materials." Is this judgment warranted? Absolutely not! However, grade equivalents are often misinterpreted in this manner because parents, teachers, and administrators fail to consider how grade equivalents are assigned.

Grade equivalents are the most often reported score on norm-referenced standardized tests.[9] The test user should bear in mind, however, that norm-referenced tests are comparisons between the performance of the test taker and the standardization group on which the test was normed. In the preceding example, if Matt scored a 6.2, it only indicates that he scored well above average in comparison to the standardization group. It is entirely possible that the third-grade test that he took did not even contain any sixth-grade-level reading material on it.

The widespread misinterpretation of grade equivalents led the International Reading Association in 1981 to adopt a resolution recommending against their use.

WHEREAS, the misuse of grade equivalents promotes misunderstanding of a student's reading ability and leads to underreliance on other norm-referenced scores which are much less susceptible to misinterpretation and misunderstanding, be it RESOLVED, that the International Reading Association strongly advocates that those who administer standardized reading tests abandon the practice of using grade equivalents to report performance of either individuals or groups of test-takers. . . .[10]

PERCENTILES. When percentiles are used, the comparisons between test takers are more evident. Percentiles denote the position of the obtained score in an overall group of 100 scores. For example, if a student scored at the 40th percentile on a norm-referenced test, it would mean that the student earned a score that equaled or surpassed the score obtained by 39 percent of the persons in the comparison group and that approximately 60 percent of persons in the comparison group earned a higher score.

The interpretation of a percentile score requires the test user to consider the group against which the students' performances are being compared. Does the percentile reflect the student's performance in relation to the standardization population? Or does the percentile compare the student's performance against other students in that school or district?

Because the performances of individuals tend to group around the average, percentiles have a tendency to "bunch up" in the middle ranges (see Figure 3–2). This means that a difference of 5 percentiles between two students' scores in the upper ranges is likely to reflect a greater difference in their abilities than a 5-percentile difference in the middle ranges.[11]

STANINES. A stanine is another type of comparison score. It divides the normal curve into nine segments. Therefore, a stanine of 5 denotes average per-

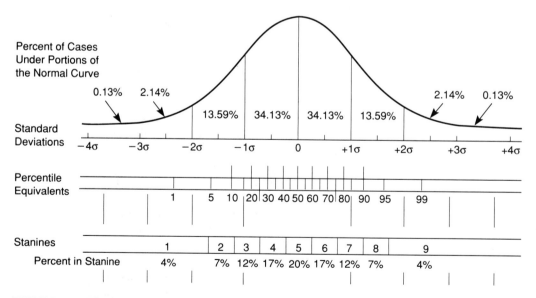

FIGURE 3–2. The Normal Curve with Standard Deviations, Percentiles, and Stanines

formance, a stanine of 1 represents very low performance, and a stanine of 9 represents very high performance.

Because they are based on the normal curve, more scores will fall in the fifth stanine than in any other (see Figure 3–2). Over one-half of all scores would be recorded in stanines 4, 5, and 6. One of the weaknesses of stanines is that because they are such gross measures, they can distort differences between students.

An example:

Student	Raw Score	Stanine
Jan	45	5
Tim	56	5
Sue	57	6

In the above example, if stanines were the only scores considered, Jan and Tim would appear to have earned the same score, and yet, a quick perusal of their raw scores indicates that Tim did much better on the test than Jan. On the other hand, Sue would appear to have scored higher than Tim if stanines were the only score considered. She did score higher but only by one item, and the error factor in any standardized test would make the differences in their performances negligible. Nevertheless, if a teacher only looked at stanines, he or she might conclude that Jan and Tim had earned the same score and that Sue had scored much higher than Tim.

STANDARD SCORES. Standard scores are also related to the normal curve. When standard scores are reported, it is usually necessary to know the mean and standard deviation in order to interpret them. An example of a standard score is an intelligence quotient (IQ). Intelligence quotients are based on a mean of 100 and a standard deviation of approximately 16. Therefore, if a student obtained an intelligence quotient of 128, it could be assumed that the score represented well above average performance.

Out-of-Level Testing

Out-of-level testing may be a useful means of increasing the reliability of a standardized test. It is based on the notion that when students take a test that is too difficult for them, the result may reflect frustration, guesswork, and inaccuracies. Out-of-level testing in reading matches the level of the test to the reading level of the student.

Out-of-level testing should only be done if the standardized test is technically equipped to yield out-of-level scores. Because scores on standardized tests are based on comparisons to the standardization group, teachers cannot merely allow a fifth grader to take a third-grade test and then interpret the score using the third-grade norming tables. Fortunately, many major test authors now make out-of-level testing relatively easy. Sometimes out-of-level norms are provided in the user's manual; other times, raw scores obtained from out-of-level testing can be converted to scaled scores and then to on-level scores. Some tests even come with short locator tests that recommend an appropriate level of the test for each student.

Studies that have examined out-of-level testing suggest that it enhances the reliability and suitability of assessment for low-achieving students but that it does not necessarily raise their obtained scores. Upper-grade students may actually score lower when given out-of-level tests,[12] and out-of-level testing may raise the scores of primary students.[13] Regardless, if out-of-level norms are available for a norm-referenced test, such testing should be considered a more fair and accurate testing alternative for poor readers.

Responsible Uses of Standardized Testing

Deceptively Precise

Standardized tests are popular because they are easy to administer and because they give an illusion of precision. The printouts that are returned from the testing companies list all sorts of scores for each student—grade equivalents in decimal form, national and local stanines and percentiles, diagnostic profiles of strengths and weaknesses. It looks so scientific and precise that it's easy to lose sight of exactly what the information represents. Many teachers would be surprised to learn that, for diagnostic purposes, teacher-made tests often have more value than standardized measures.[14]

Other Limitations

Standardized tests, although widely used, have serious limitations. Some of those limitations include:

1. Many are group measures with all the attendant limitations related to misunderstanding of directions, lack of motivation, inattention, or loss of place on the test or answer sheet.
2. They are often timed tests. Therefore, speed becomes a factor, and slower-reading students may be at a decided disadvantage.
3. Multiple choice is the most commonly used testing format. This only requires a student to recognize the correct answer from among several alternatives. Often this is easier than coming up with an answer without assistance. Multiple choice also encourages and rewards guessing.
4. There may be little correspondence between the test items and the school curriculum, raising serious validity concerns.
5. The standardization population may have been sufficiently different from the user group to make interpretation of norms meaningless.
6. The reading abilities that are measured on the test may be artificially fragmented into single skills and fail to adequately assess the interrelated nature of real reading skills.

7. Especially on criterion-referenced tests, skills may be measured by a relatively small number of items.
8. Oftentimes, as has been noted, student standardized test performances have been misinterpreted.

Proper Uses

Faced with this list of limitations, what are the proper uses for standardized tests? Group tests contribute most to the diagnostic process when they are used to evaluate the performances of large student groups rather than individuals. For example, they may provide principals with some objective evidence to evaluate how well their schools compare with a national average. Group tests might also be used to assist in curricular reform, helping to identify those items or skills that an entire class or an entire school finds difficult.

Reading specialists might use individually administered standardized tests as one more piece of information to aid in diagnostic decision making. Standardized tests also may be used to assist in making tentative grouping decisions or to suggest the need for further assessment. Teachers should always attempt to use multiple measures in making assessment decisions.

Room for Improvement

In the last twenty years, knowledge in the field of reading has expanded by leaps and bounds. Research has indicated new theoretical conceptions of reading and helped to improve the ways in which reading is taught. Materials for teaching reading have been transformed so that they bear little resemblance to their predecessors. So why haven't standardized tests changed to keep pace?

Farr and Carey note that standardized tests of reading have changed little in the last fifty years. Their formats have remained relatively unchanged, and their underlying assumptions have been remarkably resistant to the evolution of modern reading theory.[15] A quick look at a few of the issues that might be addressed in updating standardized testing follows in the next section.

Some Current Questions

PRIOR KNOWLEDGE/TOPIC INTEREST. Increasingly, definitions of reading have come to recognize the central importance of what a reader knows in determining what a reader understands. Reading comprehension involves an interaction between the information presented by an author and the reader's own prior information related to that topic. Readers' prior knowledge enables them to construct meanings by making inferences, filling in gaps, and making connections between various textual ideas.

Ironically, test authors have sought to assure that readers' prior knowledge would have little influence on assessment. They carefully eliminate questions that are answerable through general knowledge and not through reading the selections.[16] This is a tricky issue. Clearly, reading tests should measure a student's reading ability, but how can prior knowledge be factored into that assessment to reveal its influence on comprehension?

Although it appears clear that prior knowledge aids reading comprehension, what is the effect of topic interest on standardized test performance? Obviously, readers may possess more background knowledge of, and pay greater attention to, those reading selections that interest them. However, schools require students to read from all sorts of materials, some of which they will find interesting, and some of which they will not. What role should topic interest play in standardized assessment?[17]

FOCUS OF ASSESSMENT. Most authorities acknowledge that reading is a complex behavior in which many factors interrelate to create a whole greater than the sum of its parts. Standardized assessment, however, often encourages test users to think of reading as a collection of subskills. These tests often attempt to assess skills in isolation from other skills and to report "profiles" of student abilities broken down into subskill areas. However, reading in real-life situations belies such neat categorization schemes. It is a much more holistic process. Perhaps, in the years to come, assessment instruments will be developed that better incorporate the integrated nature of reading.

It is also generally accepted that the processes and strategies readers employ vary with individuals and are an important key to understanding readers' strengths and needs. Most standardized assessments, however, are more concerned with the products of reading than with the in-process deliberations of the reader. Typically, students are asked multiple-choice questions to assess how well they have "read" a selection or have mastered a particular skill. These tests appear to assume that everyone reads in the same manner and that all readers ascribe the same importance and meanings to what they read. What is the influence of processes and strategies on reading ability, and what sort of tests can best assess in-process deliberations of the reader? It is hoped that standardized reading tests of the future more adequately consider these important questions.

Summary

Diagnosis of student abilities requires teachers to make many informed, professional decisions. Diagnosis is most accurate when it is systematic, naturalistic, and considers multiple indicators of ability. When properly selected, administered, and interpreted, standardized tests provide useful information to aid reading diagnosis.

There are two major forms of standardized tests, norm-referenced and criterion-referenced. Norm-referenced tests compare student performance to the group of students on whom the test was standardized. Criterion-referenced tests compare student performance to mastery of certain skills that the test seeks to assess.

Reliability, validity, and usability are major considerations in selecting appropriate tests for educational uses. Reliability refers to the ability of the test to yield consistent results. Validity refers to the test's ability to accurately assess what it purports to assess. The test's ease of administration, scoring, and interpretation is referred to as usability.

To professionally interpret standardized test results, teachers need a basic knowledge of characteristics of the normal curve, measures of central tendency, measures of variability, and types of scores. Teachers also should be aware of the major limitations associated with standardized tests. In the future, it is hoped that refinements to standardized tests will make them even more useful in reading diagnosis.

Notes

1. Richard C. Anderson et al. *Becoming a Nation of Readers: The Report of the Commission on Reading* (Washington D.C.: National Institute of Education, 1985), 101.
2. W. James Popham, *Educational Evaluation* (Englewood Cliffs, N.J.: Prentice-Hall, 1988), 82.
3. Albert E. Bartz, *Basic Statistical Concepts in Education and the Behavioral Sciences* (Minneapolis: Burgess Publishing, 1976), 343–44.
4. Peter H. Johnston, "Assessment in Reading," in *Handbook of Reading Research*, ed. P. D. Pearson et al. (New York: Longman, 1984), 162.
5. Roger Farr and Robert F. Carey, *Reading: What Can Be Measured?* 2d ed. (Newark, Del.: International Reading Association, 1986,) 148–52.
6. David A. Payne, *The Specification and Measurement of Learning Outcomes* (Lexington, Mass.: Xerox College Publishing Co., 1968), 129–40.
7. Bartz, *Basic Statistical Concepts*, 343–44.
8. W. James Popham, *Criterion-Referenced Measurement* (Englewood Cliffs, N.J.: Prentice-Hall, 1978), 182.
9. Tom Kubiszyn and Gary Borich, *Educational Testing and Measurement: Classroom Application and Practice*, 2d ed. (Glenview, Ill.: Scott Foresman, 1987), 331.
10. International Reading Association, "Misuse of Grade Equivalents," *The Reading Teacher* 35, no. 4 (January 1982): 464.
11. James F. Baumann and Jennifer A. Stevenson, "Understanding Standardized Reading Achievement Test Scores," *The Reading Teacher* 35, no. 6 (March 1982): 648–54.
12. Lawrence L. Smith et al. "Using Grade Level vs. Out-of-Level Reading Tests with Remedial Students," *The Reading Teacher* 36, no. 6 (February 1983): 550–53.
13. Thomas G. Gunning, "Wrong Level Test: Wrong Information," *The Reading Teacher* 35, no. 8 (May 1982): 902–5.
14. Dennis Searle and Margaret Stevenson, "An Alternative Assessment Program in Language Arts," *Language Arts* 64, no. 3 (March 1987): 278–84.
15. Farr, *Reading: What Can Be Measured?* 204–6
16. Anne M. Bussis and Edward A. Chittenden, "Research Currents: What Reading Tests Neglect," *Language Arts*, March 1987, 302–8.
17. R. Scott Baldwin, Ziva Peleg-Bruckner, and Ann H. McClintock, "Effects of Topic Interest and Prior Knowledge on Reading Comprehension," *Reading Research Quarterly* 20, no. 4 (Summer 1985): 497–504.

Suggested Readings

Boehm, Ann E., and Mary Alice White. *The Parent's Handbook on School Testing.* New York: Teacher's College Press, 1982. In nontechnical language, the authors attempt to demystify standardized testing. They discuss test score interpretations and suggest questions that parents might ask to better understand their children's school progress.

Farr, Roger, and Robert F. Carey. *Reading: What Can Be Measured?* 2d. ed. Newark, Del.: International Reading Association, 1986. The authors discuss varied issues related to reading assessment. Chapter 5 examines reading tests and reliability and validity concerns.

Gearheart, Bill R., and Ernest P. Willenberg. *Application of Pupil Assessment Information.* 3d ed. Denver: Love Publishing Co., 1980. In chapter 2 the authors overview terms and concepts important in standardized test interpretation. Chapter 3 discusses the usefulness of different types of tests to answer educational questions.

Mehrens, William A., and Irvin J. Lehman. *Using Standardized Tests in Education.* 4th ed. New York: Longman, 1987. This book offers a thorough (and somewhat technical) discussion of the important aspects of standardized test use.

David W. Sikorski

is a school psychologist for Intermediate Unit No. 17 in Tioga County, Pennsylvania.

SETTING: Faculty Conference Room, Hometown Elementary School, 7:30 A.M.

Principal: As you all know we are here to discuss John B's progress and possible promotion into seventh grade for next year. As you are aware, the school psychologist's report indicates that John demonstrates a well above average range of intellectual functioning. Standardized testing over the years has failed to explain his less-than-satisfactory classroom performance.

Classroom teacher: John has made progress this year, according to the year-end Comprehensive Achievement Battery. His percentile rankings on all subtests place him at or above fifty, according to the test's grade norms.

Reading teacher: My evaluative test data reveal that John scored a 6.3 grade-level equivalent, a gain of almost two grade levels since September.

Educational diagnostician: According to my Diagnostic Reading Survey, John scored in the fourth and fifth stanines for word decoding, reading comprehension, and vocabulary skills. He really has made nice gains this year.

Principal: So, we all agree that John has acquired grade-appropriate skills for entrance into seventh grade. I just knew he could do it! His parents will be so proud.

Oh, there's John arriving at school now. For goodness sakes! I don't know how many times I've told John *he is not allowed to park his car* in the school superintendent's parking spot!

Although the above illustration is exaggerated, it identifies a score comparison dilemma that can lead to the masking of more serious problems requiring educational intervention. This issue of norms usage is important. Are test norms based on normative samples of age or grade? In John's case, one set of norms for intelligence was based upon age, and other sets of norms for achievement were based upon grade level. Because John B. was so much older than other students in the sixth grade, grade-level norms gave a distorted view of his achievement, and a serious mistake appears to have occurred. Is it possible that a true learning disability has been overlooked?

Standardized test scores do give educators a point of comparison that can help them to better understand each student. The goal of such testing should be to identify students' needs and talents in order to develop the best educational programs possible. Educators must be careful with norm-referenced tests and use them in a manner consistent with the published normative samples. Comparisons based on totally different normative samples invalidate testing results, recommendations, and program development.

David W. Sikorski

Intellectual, Physical, and Emotional Diagnosis

CHAPTER OUTLINE

Intellectual Diagnosis
Physical Diagnosis
Emotional Diagnosis

CHAPTER EMPHASES

An understanding of the role of intelligence and the limitations of intelligence testing is critical in reading diagnosis.

Realistic goals can be set when students are measured in terms of their expectancy rather than their grade-level placement.

Physical factors influence reading growth.

Symptoms of emotional disturbances can both cause and be the effect of reading difficulties.

Students benefit when teachers make informed referrals.

Reading is not an isolated behavior. It encompasses intellectual, physical, and emotional aspects within the reader. In making an accurate reading diagnosis, student functioning in these areas should be assessed. Diagnosis of intellectual, physical, and emotional problems may require the assistance of professionals with specialized training outside the reading field. However, classroom teachers and reading specialists should be knowledgeable concerning these kinds of diagnoses because teachers are ultimately responsible for their students' daily instruction.

Intellectual Diagnosis

Estimates of intellectual ability are useful in diagnosing reading difficulties. An estimate of the student's ability can assist the teacher in setting realistic instructional goals. Such goals should be flexible, however, because even the best measures of intelligence are subject to error. Therefore, recognition of the advantages and limitations of measures of intelligence is essential for interpretation of such data in a reading diagnosis.

Low intelligence should not be considered the cause of reading difficulties. In fact, intelligence is related to reading difficulties only in relation to the ability of the school to adjust the educational program to the abilities of various types of students. Intelligence—or lack of it—does not prohibit students from reading up to their potential; rather, school programs, which are often geared to the majority of average students, do not give ample consideration to those at the extremes (intellectually able and less able students), and so difficulty results. The inability of a given situation to provide the necessary adjustments often causes these students to become low achievers. Ross suggests:

> If a child fails to learn, look for a different way of teaching. Don't look for something that is wrong inside the child. Chances are that your teaching method and the child's way of learning are out of phase. Neither the child nor you are to blame for that, but you *can* be blamed if you don't try something else.[1]

Although accurate measures of intellectual performance are essential to the diagnosis of reading difficulties, the intelligence of a given student per se seldom causes the student's failure to learn.

Complications of Intellectual Testing

The educator's tendency to misuse test scores by grasping at high or low scores as the basis for division between low achieving, average, and above-average readers complicates the use of intelligence tests. How many students have been mislabeled by these tests can only be estimated. A brief review of some of the limitations of intelligence tests will indicate the difficulties encountered when such data are used in diagnosis.

DEFINITIONS OF INTELLIGENCE. Measurement of intellectual ability is complicated by the lack of agreement among authorities as to what constitutes intelligence. To some theorists, intelligence is the ability to think abstractly, while others define it as an individual's learning rate. Still others view intelligence as an individual's ability to adapt to novel situations.[2] With such a lack of agreement about the definition of intelligence, it is not surprising that intelligence tests differ widely in the abilities that they assess. Pragmatically, intelligence can be defined as performance on a given intelligence test.

RELIABILITY AND VALIDITY. Because intelligence is such an elusive notion, it is difficult to measure consistently and accurately. Of the many dimensions that intelligence must surely have, most intelligence tests measure only a few; some measure only one. Presumably, the most prominent aspects of intelligence have been included in the best constructed tests. Some tests, however, purport to measure more than can reasonably be expected. Listening comprehension, for example, is sometimes considered a significant aspect of intelligence. If a test of listening comprehension reports a student's score in mental age, however, such a score would be misleading, because mental age constitutes more than the ability to listen and understand. Another complication arises when a given test requires specifically learned skills, such as reading. The test's validity is weakened because the test score also measures the reading achievement of the test taker.

Many intelligence tests contain items that depend on cultural experiences. Students from cultures other than those on which the test was normed may score significantly lower than students from cultures similar to the ones on which the test was normed. In such cases, the test cannot be considered a valid measure of intelligence.

Chance and error may also influence a student's intelligence test performance. Teachers are reminded to check each test's standard error of measurement and to consider test score performance in light of that information. It is better to think of intelligence test scores as representing low, average, or high performance than to be unduly impressed by a "precise" score.

TEST ADMINISTRATION AND INTERPRETATION. Even the best constructed intelligence tests are difficult to administer and interpret. Despite the efforts of the American Psychological Association to prevent it, persons other than qualified psychologists often administer intelligence tests. Many of these people have no training and work without directed supervision. Thus, they often make serious errors in test administration, scoring, and interpretation. Tests administered by untrained personnel should not be considered useful information in a reading diagnosis.

Group Intelligence Tests

Group tests of intelligence are inappropriate for students suspected of having reading difficulties. Many group tests require that students read in order to take the test. Obviously, if they cannot read well, their scores will reflect poor reading as well as low intelligence, and the two will be hopelessly confused. Further, rapport is difficult to establish in group testing. For students who have been subjected to considerable failure, any group test may threaten them further and result in a poor performance. Also, many of the group tests on the market have very poor reliability, making score interpretation nearly impossible. Helms and Turner comment on the disadvantages of group intelligence tests in stating:

> The tests are further limited in that they are highly reliant on verbal abilities, not only for just one dimension of intelligence, but also because the child must *read* all of the directions and questions. Being a poor reader, or simply making an error in reading a statement, may result in a wrong answer. Another, more subtle, disadvantage is the inability of the examiner to know the physical and emotional state of the child.[3]

Awareness of the limitations inherent in measures of intellectual performance will lessen the possibility that intelligence test scores will be used or interpreted improperly. To best assess intellectual performance, at least one of the measures of intelligence must be individual and nonreading in nature. Major discrepancies between test scores constitute justifiable reasons for referral for psychological examination.

Considering the limitations of intelligence testing (particularly group testing) it seems inconceivable that school reading personnel would use such scores to control admission to a program to aid those having reading difficulty. However, many schools limit admission to reading programs to those with group intelligence test scores above a certain score. Such a practice seems indefensible and should be changed, since a student who needs help might well be overlooked. Furthermore, that same student might score much higher on an individual measure. Discrimination of this type is based on a lack of knowledge of the instruments being used. Instead of relying on such scores, other options are available, such as the following tests.

Potential Reading Ability Measures Suitable for Clinical Diagnosis

REVISED STANFORD–BINET INTELLIGENCE SCALE. The Stanford–Binet test may only be administered and scored by personnel with formal course work and laboratory experience. The test will yield a mental age and intelligence quotient in a range from preschool to adult. The test measures several aspects of intelligence and is heavily verbal. It takes about one hour to administer, is individual in nature, and requires precise administration and interpretation for reliable results.

WECHSLER INTELLIGENCE SCALE FOR CHILDREN-REVISED (WISC-R). Another popular and accurate test of intellectual performance, the WISC-R (see Figure 4–1) requires individual administration and should be given by personnel who have had formal course work and laboratory experience. Measuring several aspects

WISC-R RECORD FORM

Wechsler Intelligence Scale
for Children—Revised

NAME _____ AGE _____ SEX _____

ADDRESS _____

PARENT'S NAME _____

SCHOOL _____ GRADE _____

PLACE OF TESTING _____ TESTED BY _____

REFERRED BY _____

WISC-R PROFILE

Clinicians who wish to draw a profile should first transfer the child's *scaled scores* to the row of boxes below. Then mark an X on the dot corresponding to the scaled score for each test, and draw a line connecting the X's.*

	Year	Month	Day
Date Tested	____	____	____
Date of Birth	____	____	____
Age	____	____	____

VERBAL TESTS   PERFORMANCE TESTS

Information · Similarities · Arithmetic · Vocabulary · Comprehension · Digit Span

Picture Completion · Picture Arrangement · Block Design · Object Assembly · Coding · Mazes

Scaled Score □ □ □ □ □ □   Scaled Score □ □ □ □ □ □   Scaled Score

Scaled Score		Scaled Score		Scaled Score
19	· · · · · ·	19	· · · · · ·	19
18	· · · · · ·	18	· · · · · ·	18
17	· · · · · ·	17	· · · · · ·	17
16	· · · · · ·	16	· · · · · ·	16
15	· · · · · ·	15	· · · · · ·	15
14	· · · · · ·	14	· · · · · ·	14
13	· · · · · ·	13	· · · · · ·	13
12	· · · · · ·	12	· · · · · ·	12
11	· · · · · ·	11	· · · · · ·	11
10	· · · · · ·	10	· · · · · ·	10
9	· · · · · ·	9	· · · · · ·	9
8	· · · · · ·	8	· · · · · ·	8
7	· · · · · ·	7	· · · · · ·	7
6	· · · · · ·	6	· · · · · ·	6
5	· · · · · ·	5	· · · · · ·	5
4	· · · · · ·	4	· · · · · ·	4
3	· · · · · ·	3	· · · · · ·	3
2	· · · · · ·	2	· · · · · ·	2
1	· · · · · ·	1	· · · · · ·	1

*See Chapter 4 in the manual for a discussion of the significance of differences between scores on the tests.

NOTES

	Raw Score	Scaled Score
VERBAL TESTS		
Information	____	____
Similarities	____	____
Arithmetic	____	____
Vocabulary	____	____
Comprehension	____	____
(Digit Span)	(____)	(____)
Verbal Score		____
PERFORMANCE TESTS		
Picture Completion	____	____
Picture Arrangement	____	____
Block Design	____	____
Object Assembly	____	____
Coding	____	____
(Mazes)	(____)	(____)
Performance Score		____

	Scaled Score	IQ
Verbal Score	____	* ____
Performance Score	____	* ____
Full Scale Score		____

*Prorated from 4 tests, if necessary.

FIGURE 4–1. Record Form of the Wechsler Intelligence Scale for Children–Revised. (Copyright © 1974, 1971 by The Psychological Corporation. Reproduced by permission; all rights reserved.)

of intelligence, the WISC–R yields performance and verbal scores, with the verbal score normally considered the more valid predictor of performance in reading. With poor readers, however, the performance score probably provides the better measure of reading potential. The students' verbal scores may be limited by the same factors that limit their performance in reading. Vance summarized the results of twenty-five studies which attempted to identify a WISC–R profile that was characteristic of poor readers. Although Vance reported the presence of several general patterns of strengths and weaknesses among poor readers, he cautioned against the application of those patterns to individual students because the findings were based on group results.[4]

Moore and Wielan compared the WISC–R performances of students who had been referred for reading diagnosis with those of students from the general population and found that both groups evidenced similar amounts of test-score scatter.[5] Although the WISC–R may provide some useful insights into the intellectual abilities of students, teachers should use caution in using WISC–R results to prescribe reading remediation. This test is not intended to be a diagnostic measure of reading ability. The Wechsler Adult Intelligence Scale (WAIS) may be used with older children and adults. Both the WISC–R and the WAIS take approximately one hour to administer.

KAUFMAN ASSESSMENT BATTERY FOR CHILDREN (K–ABC). Since its publication in 1983, the K–ABC (see Figure 4–2) has been generating a great deal of interest. The K–ABC represents an attempt to measure mental processing independently from achievement. An individual intelligence test designed for children of ages 2.5 to 12.5 years, the K–ABC consists of sixteen subtests and yields four different scores: Sequential Processing; Simultaneous Processing; Mental Processing Composite, a combination of the sequential and simultaneous measures; and Achievement. Because the intelligence batteries and the achievement battery were standardized on the same populations, a student's problem-solving abilities may be compared to that student's general knowledge and grasp of school-related learning. These comparisons may have a special application in the identification of learning disabled children.

The K–ABC can be administered in 30 to 50 minutes to preschoolers and in 50 to 80 minutes to older children. As with the Stanford–Binet and the WISC–R, the K–ABC requires a specially trained examiner for administration and interpretation of the test. The testing battery includes a Nonverbal Scale for use with hearing-impaired students, language-impaired students, or students for whom English is a second language. The items on the Nonverbal Scale are administered in pantomime and the students are directed to respond through gestures. A Spanish version of the K–ABC is available, as are separate sociocultural percentile rank norms for use with other minority students. One unusual departure from other intelligence tests is the K–ABC authors' decision to describe intelligence without the use of the term *intelligence quotient*.

QUICK ASSESSMENTS OF INTELLIGENCE. The Slosson Intelligence Test, Revised; The Detroit Tests of Learning Aptitude-2 (DTLA-2); and the Peabody Picture

K·ABC Kaufman Assessment Battery for Children

by Alan S. Kaufman and Nadeen L. Kaufman

INDIVIDUAL TEST RECORD

Name: Mary B. Sex: F

Parents' names: Rita and James

Home address: 807 S. Lincoln

Home phone: 782-4602

Grade: 4 School: Central Elementary

Examiner: Norma Ehrhardt

SOCIOCULTURAL INFORMATION (if pertinent)

Race: black

Socioeconomic background: mother finished 3rd. grade, housewife, father finished 6th. grade construction worker.

	YEAR	MONTH	DAY
Test date	82	17	15
Birth date	72	8	11
Chronological age	10	9	4

Achievement Subtests $\bar{X} = 100$; $SD = 15$	Standard score ± band of error ___ % confidence	Nat'l. %ile rank Table 4	Socio-cultural %ile rank Table 5	S or W Table 11	Other data
11. Expressive Vocabulary	±				
12. Faces & Places	87 ± 8	19	35		8-9
13. Arithmetic	92 ± 8	30	70		9-6
14. Riddles	99 ± 9	47	90	S	10-6
15. Reading/ Decoding	73 ± 8	4	10	W	7-6
16. Reading/ Understanding	67 ± 8	1	5	W	7-3

Sum of subtest scores: 418 — Transfer sum to Global Scales, *Sum of subtest scores* column.

Mental Processing Subtests $\bar{X} = 10$; $SD = 3$	Scaled Score: Sequential	Scaled Score: Simultaneous	Scaled Score: Nonverbal	Nat'l. %ile rank Table 4	S or W Table 11	Other data
1. Magic Window						
2. Face Recognition						
3. Hand Movements	10			50		11-9
4. Gestalt Closure		14		91	S	above 12-6
5. Number Recall	11			63		above 12-6
6. Triangles		8		25		8-0
7. Word Order	6			9	W	6-6
8. Matrix Analogies		9		37		9-9
9. Spatial Memory		7		16		8-3
10. Photo Series		9		37		9-9
Sum of subtest scores	27	47				

Transfer sums to Global Scales, *Sum of subtest scores* column.

Global Scales $\bar{X} = 100$; $SD = 15$	Sum of subtest scores	Standard score ± band of error ___ % confidence Table 2	Nat'l. %ile rank Table 4	Socio-cultural %ile rank Table 5	Other data
Sequential Processing	27	93 ± 8	32	50	10-3
Simultaneous Processing	47	95 ± 6	37	80	9-8
Mental Processing Composite	74	93 ± 6	32	70	9-10
Achievement	418	81 ± 4	10	30	8-8
Nonverbal		±			

Global Scale Comparisons

	Indicate >, <, or ≈		Circle the significance level
Sequential	≈	Simultaneous (Table 10)	(NS) .05 .01
Sequential	≈	Achievement (Table 10)	(NS) .05 .01
Simultaneous	>	Achievement (Table 10)	NS .05 (.01)
MPC	>	Achievement (Table 10)	NS .05 (.01)

AGS®

FIGURE 4-2. The Individual Test Record from the Kaufman Assessment Battery for Children. *(Copyright © 1983 by American Guidance Service Inc. Reproduced by permission; all rights reserved.)*

Vocabulary Test–Revised (PPVT–R) are examples of easy-to-administer, quick assessments of some of the behavior that indicates intelligence. Although, strictly speaking, the Peabody Picture Vocabulary Test–Revised is a test of receptive vocabulary for standard American English and not general intelligence, the Peabody is included here as a quick assessment of intelligence because it is used as such by many. Although the PPVT–R does tap hearing vocabulary and experience, two important abilities related to reading potential, it does not accurately assess innate ability.[6]

Each of these quick tests may be given by a teacher who is familiar with the instrument and has had practice in administering it. These abbreviated measures should be treated cautiously, since their brevity can lower their reliability. If scores obtained on these tests are exceedingly high or low, a more careful assessment of intelligence should be conducted. Because the test can be administered quickly, the constructors had to eliminate many of the aspects of intelligence and rely, in some cases, on only one. This raises the question of validity. The predominantly verbal composition of the Slosson, Revised; PPVT–R; and several of the subtests of the DTLA–2 may cause many poor readers to score low. For all these reasons, such tests should be used only as initial indicators of student potential.

LISTENING COMPREHENSION. Listening comprehension, or *auding*, is another quick and easily assessable indicator of reading potential. It usually requires that the student listen to read-aloud passages of increasing difficulty and then answer comprehension questions about their content. Listening comprehension is considered an indicator of reading potential because it reveals, in part, the level at which concepts can be understood and language interpreted independent of word recognition abilities. It is most appropriate for use with younger students because many secondary readers will have silent comprehension levels that exceed their listening comprehension levels. Other difficulties, such as poor attention and general comprehension deficits, may also adversely affect an auding score.

ARITHMETIC COMPUTATION. For students who have attended school for two or more years, a test of arithmetic computation, not involving verbal problems, may be useful in estimating reading potential. Arithmetic computation requires three abilities related to reading achievement: abstract reasoning, manipulation of a symbol system, and visual perception. However, it cannot be used routinely for estimating reading potential. Many students who experience difficulties with reading also have difficulties with arithmetic. Further, when students react with emotional rejection toward the school environment, their achievement is likely to suffer in both reading and arithmetic. Arithmetic computation should be viewed only as a possible indicator of reading potential when students score significantly higher in tests of arithmetic computation than in reading tests. Even then, arithmetic computation should not serve as the only indicator of reading potential because it is essentially an achievement measure.

Other measures of intellectual performance are available for clinical diagnosis; however, most of them require special preparation and laboratory experience, as do the Stanford–Binet, the WISC–R, and the K–ABC.

Potential Reading Ability Measures Suitable for Classroom Diagnosis

THE STANFORD-BINET, WISC-R, AND K-ABC. These tests are not normally administered by the classroom teacher, but their scores are often found in the school records of students experiencing reading difficulties. The other tests mentioned under clinical diagnosis can be administered by a classroom teacher as part of normal school procedure or as a part of classroom diagnosis.

GROUP INTELLIGENCE TESTS. Although group intelligence tests are inherently unsatisfactory in reading diagnosis, several of them do separate reading and nonreading factors. The California Test of Mental Maturity, for example, provides a mental age (M.A.) and intelligence quotient (IQ) for both language and nonlanguage performance. The teacher who uses this type of test and finds a major discrepancy between the two scores (such as nonlanguage IQ = 125, language IQ = 100) should be looking for other signs of intellectual performance because the student may be capable but hindered in the language section by lack of reading ability. Other measures of reading potential, such as those mentioned under clinical diagnosis, should then be checked, or the student should be referred for an individual intelligence examination. However, unless group intelligence tests have nonlanguage features, they are not useful in estimating the reading potential of students who read poorly. Even then, their usefulness is highly questionable.

TEACHER OBSERVATION. The experienced teacher often can estimate reading potential through direct observation of the student's response to various school activities. Students demonstrate their intellectual abilities thousands of times each day in school tasks and problem-solving situations. Specifically, observable examples of intellectual abilities include:

- Ability to listen and speak effectively in class discussions
- Ability to achieve more successfully in arithmetic than in subjects that require reading
- Ability to interact effectively in peer group activities
- Ability to demonstrate alert attitudes toward the world
- Ability to perform satisfactorily on spelling tests
- Ability to think in abstract terms and mentally perform complex functions
- Ability to understand scientific concepts

Such observations obviously cannot be considered reliable indicators of reading potential. Teacher observation always includes the possibility of teacher bias; teachers often see just what they are looking for. As an example, a teacher's observation may be influenced by previous test scores and prior impressions of the student. However, lack of ability in these observable areas often provides the first indication of a difficulty. By such observations, students who have been intellectually misjudged may be referred for more accurate evaluations.

Grade-Level Expectancy

How often have you read an editorial in the newspaper which decries the fact that many students graduate from high school unable to read at a twelfth-grade level? This reflects a common expectation held by most parents and many teachers that all students should be reading at or above grade level. If a pupil is reading below grade level, many individuals would target that student for remedial attention. Grade-level expectancy, while well intentioned, is misguided and stems from a lack of knowledge of how standardized, norm-referenced tests are constructed and lack of awareness of the other alternatives that exist for helping to set reasonable goals for students. The following example may help illustrate some of the problems involved when students' achievement is compared merely to their grade level in school.

Example: Lisa, Kelly, and Janet

Lisa, Kelly, and Janet are all in the same fourth-grade class. Their teacher, Mr. Walker, gave them a reading test at the beginning of the year and found the following reading grade levels: Lisa, 3.3; Kelly, 4.4; and Janet, 4.9. From this evidence Mr. Johnson concluded that Lisa was reading poorly, Kelly was reading well, and Janet was reading very well. He resolved to see that Lisa received as much help as possible.

Suppose, however, that Mr. Walker also knew the information about the girls provided in Table 4–1. Would it change his assessment of their achievement and his expectations for their progress?

Comparing Reading Achievement to Reading Expectancy

An alternative to comparing students' reading achievement to their grade level is to compare students' achievement to the best indication of their reading potential or expectancy. Reading potential can be estimated in many different ways, but in each case the underlying idea is similar. Instead of comparing a student's reading achievement to the student's grade level, the student's achievement is compared to facts known about the student's true ability. This can help teachers set realistic goals for the student and identify candidates for remedial attention.

TABLE 4–1. A Comparison of Three Fourth-Grade Students 69

Name	Grade Level	Reading Level	Chronological Age	IQ	Grades Repeated
Lisa	4.0	3.3	9.4	82	0
Kelly	4.0	4.4	10.2	101	1
Janet	4.0	4.9	9.3	140	0

A comparison of the best estimates of reading potential with the best estimates of reading achievement will result in an arithmetical difference. When potential exceeds achievement, the concern is that the student is not working up to capacity. The larger the difference, the more serious the degree of reading difficulty.

MENTAL AGE FORMULA. Perhaps the most common technique of estimating the seriousness of the reading difficulty is a simple comparison of mental age with reading age. Mental age can be computed as follows:

$$\text{M.A.} = \frac{\text{C.A.} \times \text{IQ}}{100}$$

M.A. = mental age
C.A. = chronological age
IQ = intelligence quotient

Reading achievement scores are most often reported as grade equivalents. In order to convert a grade equivalent to a reading age (R.A.), it is necessary to add 5.2 to the grade equivalent. When a student's reading age is subtracted from the student's mental age, the resulting difference is interpreted as the student's degree of reading difficulty.

HARRIS FORMULAS. Harris has proposed two formulas for estimating reading expectancy which give priority to the student's mental age but which also consider the student's chronological age.[7] The first formula contends:

$$\text{Reading Expectancy Age} = \frac{2(\text{M.A.}) + \text{C.A.}}{3}$$

The resulting reading expectancy age (R Exp A) can be converted to a grade equivalent by subtracting 5.2. This reading expectancy grade equivalent can then be compared to the student's reading achievement scores to give an estimate of the student's degree of reading difficulty.

Harris also suggests that a reading expectancy quotient (R Exp Q) be computed. In this second formula, a reading age (R.A.) is found by adding 5.2 to the student's reading achievement grade equivalent score. Then, that reading age is divided by the R Exp A found using the previous Harris formula.

$$\text{Reading Expectancy Quotient} = \frac{\text{R.A.} \times 100}{\text{R Exp A}}$$

Harris provides general guidelines for interpreting the reading expectancy quotient. In general, the lower the R Exp Q, the greater the degree of reading difficulty indicated. Quotients below 85 are interpreted as representing a *severe disability*, quotients in the range 85 to 89 represent a *probable disability*, and quotients of 90 to 110 represent *normal limits*.[8]

BOND AND TINKER FORMULA. Bond and Tinker use the number of years that the child has received formal reading instruction as a factor in estimating reading expectancy (R.E.).[9] Their formula yields a reading expectancy grade equivalent which can be compared to a student's reading achievement scores to give an indication of the student's degree of reading difficulty.

$$\text{R.E.} = (\text{IQ}/100 \times \text{yrs. of reading instruction}) + 1.0$$

The Bond and Tinker formula assumes that most children, regardless of their intellectual ability, will begin first grade with an expectancy of 1.0 and that thereafter their reading expectancy will climb as a function of their general intelligence and the amount of reading instruction that they receive. A student of average intelligence would be expected to achieve one year's growth in reading for each year of reading instruction. A more able student would be expected to make accelerated progress, while a less able student would be expected to achieve at a slower than average rate.[10]

In using the Bond and Tinker formula, teachers should consider three factors. First, they must understand that the phrase *years in school* does not mean the student's grade placement, but rather, the actual number of school years completed. Therefore, for a student who has a grade placement of 4.8 and who has not accelerated or repeated a grade, the appropriate entry would be 3.8 for years in school. (For this formula, kindergarten does not count as a year in school.) Second, teachers must have accurate data concerning the grades repeated or accelerated. Third, they should be aware that the addition of 1.0 years in the formula is to compensate for the manner in which grade norms are assigned to tests, 1.0 being the zero month of first grade.

Advantages and Limitations of Expectancy Formulas

Each of these expectancy formulas has its own unique advantages and limitations. The mental age formula, while easy to use, relies on mental age as a single factor in estimating reading expectancy. As a result, expectancies tend to be unrealistically high for young students of superior ability. In effect, this formula expects that bright students will be reading when they enter school. For example, a student who is 6.0 years old on the first day of first grade and who has an IQ of 140 would have a mental age of 8.4 and a reading expectancy grade equivalent of 3.2.

The Harris formulas seek to mitigate the effect of mental age somewhat by including the student's chronological age in the expectancy computation. Once again, however, schooling or lack of it is not directly considered. In the case of the student described here who is just entering first grade, the Harris formula would yield a reading expectancy grade equivalent of 2.4.

The Bond and Tinker formula includes years of reading instruction as a variable and so gives a more realistic estimate of expectancy for very young students. The beginning first grader in our example would have zero years of reading instruction and so would be assigned a reading expectancy grade equivalent of 1.0 by the Bond and Tinker formula. However, this formula tends to overestimate the reading expectancy of very low-functioning students and underestimate the reading expectancy of older highly able students.

Degree of Difference Between Achievement and Expectancy

When selecting candidates for remedial attention by comparing students' achievement and expectancy, teachers should consider the grade placement of the students. Many students may fall slightly short of their reading expectancy yet would not be viewed as having serious reading difficulties. Older students can bear a larger variance between potential and achievement without the severe ramifications that occur with younger students.

The scale in Table 4–2 may be useful in selecting a cutoff point between a tolerable difference and one that is sufficient to interfere with the child's progress in reading and other subjects. Tolerable differences are presented in this table by individual grade groupings. Although this scale should not be adhered to rigidly, it does provide reasonably useful limits. However, since diagnosis includes considerably more analysis than the estimation of potential and achievement, the educator should not evaluate progress in reading by this technique alone.

When selecting the method for computing the degree of reading difficulty, the following factors should be considered:

- The number and type of students selected as candidates for remedial attention in reading will vary with the method employed.
- Each method is only as good as the instruments used to obtain the scores for its computation.
- A student with a specific skill deficiency may not be discovered by these types of formulas.

TABLE 4–2. Degree of Tolerable Difference Between Potential and Achievement

End of Grade	Tolerable Difference (in Years)
1, 2, and 3	0.5
4, 5, and 6	1
7, 8, and 9	1.5
10, 11, and 12	2

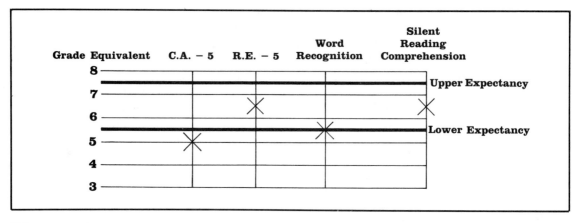

FIGURE 4-3. Comparing Expectancy Range with Other Reading Variables

In Figure 4-3, a student's scores have been plotted. This ten-year-old boy has a 5.5-word recognition level and a 6.0 silent reading comprehension score. His reading expectancy level is 6.5 and the two heavy lines reflect the standard error plus and minus the actual potential score.

Although neither reading performance score is as high as the reading expectancy, both fall within the standard error of the reading expectancy score. This treatment of expectancy scores expresses to all who receive the report that the score should not be taken as a precise measure.

Example Revisited

Returning to the example of the three fourth-grade students (see Table 4-1), Mr. Walker decided to compute reading expectancies to see if his initial impressions about the girls were justified. This is what he found.

Lisa's mental age was computed to be 7.7. When Mr. Walker placed this mental age in the Harris formula, he found that she had a reading expectancy age of 8.3 and a reading expectancy grade equivalent of 3.1. These expectancies compared favorably with Lisa's reading age of 8.5 and her reading achievement level of 3.3. Mr. Walker found Lisa's reading expectancy quotient of 102 to be well within normal limits. Using the Bond and Tinker formula, it was found that Lisa's reading expectancy level was 3.5. Mr. Walker concluded that, although Lisa was reading below grade level, she was reading pretty well in terms of her potential or expectancy.

Kelly's mental age of 10.3 led Mr. Walker to a Harris reading expectancy age of 10.3 and a reading expectancy grade equivalent of 5.1 (due primarily to the fact that she was older than the average fourth grader). He found, however, that Kelly's reading expectancy quotient of 93.2 still fell within normal limits. Mr. Walker further noted that Kelly's Bond and Tinker reading expectancy level was 5.0 as a consequence of her repeating a grade. Nevertheless,

Kelly's reading achievement level of 4.4 was within a tolerable difference of her potential.

In Janet's case, Mr. Walker found mixed results. Her Harris reading expectancy age was 11.8. When Mr. Walker compared this to Janet's reading age of 10.1, he found that Janet's reading expectancy quotient of 85.6 placed her in the range of probable disability. Surprised, Mr. Walker computed a Bond and Tinker reading expectancy for Janet and found it was 5.2. This figure compared much more favorably with Janet's reading achievement level of 4.9. Mr. Walker resolved to talk with the reading specialist about Janet.

Thus, reading expectancy formulas can provide a better standard for judging reading achievement than grade-level expectancy alone. However, expectancy formulas are not without their problems. Although they helped to explain Lisa's below-grade-level achievement, two different formulas painted two different pictures in Janet's case. Once again, the teacher is encouraged to consider reading expectancy as a measure against which to compare reading achievement but not to put undue emphasis on any single test score or reading expectancy computation.

Some Additional Cautions

Many students could fail to receive the help they need if potential formulas are used as the only indicators of need. Students with specific skill deficiencies or attitudinal problems might well be missed. Students with low potential scores might need a language development program prior to or in conjunction with the start of a reading program.[11] On any one given day, a student might score differently on the reading tests. These and many other problems call for examiners to evaluate the total reader, not just the test scores. Attention to the reader's responses during testing may be more important than the resulting score. How the use of potential fits into classroom and clinical diagnosis is discussed in chapters 5 and 6.

When a physical limitation interferes with a student's potential or performance, it can be considered a cause of a reading difficulty. Whose job is it to assess the severity of a physical disability? Although physical limitations are recognized first in a classroom or clinical diagnosis, medical personnel or other specialists are responsible for specific identification of the problem, prescription of corrective measures, and recommendations to teachers for adjusting instruction. Both the reading specialist and the classroom teacher can refer students either on the basis of reliable patterns of symptoms or as a result of certain screening devices available to educators.

Specifically, the areas of physical diagnosis of reading difficulties include general, visual, auditory, and neurological health. Limitations in these areas that are serious enough to interfere with performance in reading will most likely also interfere with general educational performance. However, a general

Physical Diagnosis

educational deficiency does not necessarily indicate a physical disability, nor does a physical disability always cause a learning deficiency.

General Health

Large numbers of students are not healthy enough to profit efficiently from the instruction provided, even under the best conditions. Educators should know these aspects of general health that should be evaluated in the diagnosis of reading difficulties.

MALNUTRITION. Malnutrition causes the student to lose weight or lag behind in physical and mental vitality. Malnutrition does not necessarily show itself in loss of weight, however. Many suffering from nutritional imbalance are quite chubby due to an overconsumption of starches. The sluggish behavior that results may interfere with school performance.

GLANDULAR DEFECTS. The endocrine system regulates many important bodily functions. Endocrine disturbances, particularly those involving the thyroid, may adversely affect reading performance. Hypothyroidism, a thyroid deficiency, often causes obesity and a lack of mental alertness. Hyperthyroidism, a thyroid excess, may cause extreme weight loss, irritability, and an inability to concentrate on school tasks.

MENTAL OR PHYSICAL FATIGUE. Caused by lack of sleep, poor sleeping habits, lack of exercise, or overexertion, mental or physical fatigue can cause students to be inattentive and easily distracted in a learning situation. Unfortunately, in recent years we have seen an upswing in the number of students who come to school both mentally and physically fatigued due to late night television viewing.

POOR GENERAL AND PHYSICAL CONDITION. Often characterized by frequent illness, poor general physical condition causes a lack of stamina with resulting gaps in the educational program. Factors such as overweight, underweight, dental problems, or hay fever can result in difficulty with school tasks. Alertness to signs of poor health is essential in a reading diagnosis. Many such cases are first identified by individual attention to a student's performance during diagnosis.

The classroom teacher also uses information from school records, reports from the school nurse and the family doctor, information from the parents, and observable symptoms that are characteristic of students with general physical deficiencies to identify physical problems. Sluggishness, inattentiveness, failure to complete assignments, apparent lack of interest, sleeping in school, and general lack of vitality often are symptoms that cause a student to be labeled *lazy* or *indifferent*. Classroom teachers should observe these symptoms, contact the home to report the problem, and make medical referrals when appropriate. At the same time, they should adjust the instruction to make the learning environment as comfortable as possible for the student. This adjustment may take the form of relaxing the tension caused by the student's apparent indifference, allowing the fatigued student a program of varied activities and necessary rest periods, and, when necessary, following the recommendations of medical personnel.

It does not take a medical report to make us aware that all students, not just those with reading difficulties, need good health for optimal school performance. Necessities such as adequate rest, a balanced diet (particularly a good breakfast), annual physical checkups, and large doses of play activity after school are vital requirements for good school performance.

One of the reading specialist's responsibilities in diagnosis is to evaluate reports received from medical personnel in terms of the total case picture of the student involved and to recommend the appropriate classroom adjustment or remedial program.

Visual Diagnosis

Deficiencies in visual ability and ocular comfort may impede a student's reading growth. Recent reports state that from 15 to 40 percent of students need professional visual attention. The relationship of vision to low achievement in reading is complicated, since many students with visual problems are not low achievers. Carefully conducted research shows a relationship between certain types of visual deficiencies and failure in reading and also that certain visual disabilities and ocular discomfort greatly interfere with students reaching their reading potentials.[12] In general, functional problems such as awkward eye movements and poor fusion cause reading difficulties more often than organic difficulties such as nearsightedness, farsightedness, or astigmatism. A review of some of the aspects of vision and ocular comfort will clarify the relationship.

ACUITY. Acuity, the clearness of vision, is normally measured at far-point targets (a Snellen Chart twenty feet away from the student). Such screening tests of acuity provide information concerning the student's acuity at the far point (such as the ability to see the chalkboard). The results of this type of visual screening are expressed in terms of what the average person can see at twenty feet. The term *20/20* means that a person can see at twenty feet the same target that a person with normal vision can see at twenty feet. However, this test, when used alone, cannot detect all visual deficiencies. People do not normally read targets that are twenty feet from the eyes; neither do they read with one eye at a time. The eyes must efficiently move from one target to another, rather than merely fixing on and identifying a target. Kelley claims, "The misconception that the Snellen Chart will do an efficient job of screening out students who need visual care is a major block in the road of those trying to establish good school visual screening programs."[13]

Screening devices to measure near-point acuity should be used in diagnosing a low achiever, although they generally require more time and training to administer properly. One who successfully reads the Snellen Chart may still have a visual deficiency that is causing problems in reading. The farsighted reader, seeing far-point targets better than near-point targets, may pass the Snellen Chart yet not see efficiently enough to read with comfort at the near point. The nearsighted reader, who sees near-point targets better than far-point targets, is likely to fail at reading the Snellen Chart; but, while obviously limited by a visual defect, he or she may still read effectively in most cases. Therefore, effective visual screening must measure both far- and near-point acuity. This need has been partially met by the development of a type of chart for use at a fourteen-inch distance. The following additional techniques are generally desirable for accurate near-point screening.

BINOCULAR FUSION. Binocular fusion involves the ability of the brain to blend or fuse the image from each eye into a single adequate image. If the eyes do not work in perfect harmony, a double image or blurring may result. In an effort to ease the discomfort of seeing a double image, the brain will often suppress the vision of one eye. Such a condition is called *amblyopia* or *lazy eye*. Undetected, amblyopia may cause a loss of acuity in the suppressed eye. *Strabismus* involves poor coordination of the eye muscles necessary to focus effectively and often results in double vision or blurring of the image. Students experiencing binocular fusion difficulties should be referred to a vision specialist. Left untreated, students may confuse letters and words, frequently lose their place when reading, and experience visual discomfort or fatigue.

OCULAR MOTILITY. Effective reading requires the efficient operation of the eye in motion. In particular, ocular motility refers to fixations, pursuit, saccadic movement, accommodation, and convergence. Although these important abilities are seldom evaluated in a school screening, classroom teachers and reading specialists should be aware of these and refer students suspected of having difficulties with ocular motility for a thorough vision examination.

- *Fixations.* Fixations are the moments that the eyes stop and focus on a graphic display. In the reading act, the eyes must fix on a word group, move to the right, fix on another word group, then sweep back and take hold of the next line. This process is not innate but learned. Students who are grossly inefficient at this task of left-to-right eye movement or accurate fixation will likely experience reading difficulty.
- *Pursuit.* Eyes should be able to follow a moving target smoothly, not stopping and starting, but following with an effortless, fluid movement. This ability would be required in reading a moving sign or in shifting the eyes efficiently from desk work to the blackboard.

- *Saccadic movement.* Accurate change of fixations from one word to another or from the end of a line of print to the beginning of the next line is an important ocular-motor skill related to reading. When deficient in this skill, students lose their places, skip words, and read more slowly than necessary.
- *Accommodation.* When students look at targets that are at varying distances, the eyes must instantaneously adjust the focus. Many classroom reading tasks require good accommodation abilities.
- *Convergence.* Focusing on an object that is close to the eyes requires each eye to turn inward. If a student has difficulty converging, reading performance will be severely impaired.

A number of screening devices and procedures are available that a teacher might be trained to use. In screening visual abilities related to most school reading tasks, these procedures represent a marked improvement over the traditionally used Snellen Chart.

A test using a telebinocular provides near- and far-point screening of visual acuity, binocular fusion, color perception, and stereopsis (the ability to judge the relative distance between two objects). The proper administration and analysis of this test requires supervised experience to assure reliable results. The telebinocular screens the visual skills related to the ability of the eyes to fix only on a stationary target (see photo and Figure 4–4).

The reading specialist must also be concerned about the eyes as they operate in reading situations. The Spache–Binocular Reading Tests provide an analysis of binocular vision during the reading act. In these tests, the student looks at a card that has been placed in the telebinocular and reads a story containing some words that only the right eye can see and some that only the left eye can see. By marking the student's responses, the examiner can determine the degree that each eye operates in the reading act. Referral is based on certain characteristics that are identified in the accompanying manual.

A pocket flashlight is used to screen pursuit, saccadic eye movements, accommodation, and convergence. Holding the light upright in front of the eyes, the examiner asks the student to look at the light. The examiner then moves the light in an area eighteen inches from the eye in straight vertical, horizontal, and diagonal lines twelve to eighteen inches in length, and then in a circle with a radius of about twelve inches clockwise and counterclockwise. Referral should be considered if (1) students cannot follow the light without moving their heads, even after being told to hold still; (2) the reflection of the light cannot be seen in both of a student's pupils at all times; or (3) the eye movements are saccadic (that is, they follow the light jerkily instead of smoothly). To test converging power, the light is again held eighteen inches from the eye, moved slowly to a position one inch directly between the eyes, and held for one second. Since some students do not understand what they are to do the first time, referral should be recommended only if this fixation cannot be held after three attempts.

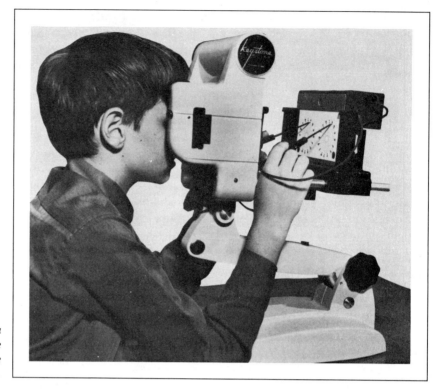

*An example of a
student using the
Keystone
Telebinocular.*

(Caution should be observed in screening vision through use of a pocket flashlight since some individuals may not be able to tolerate the direct light.)

Not having any of this screening equipment available, classroom teachers must rely on a pattern of symptoms observable in the reading act or in other school situations. When teachers observe a combination of symptoms (listed in Table 4–3), the possibility of a visual impairment exists. The first level of vision referral will ordinarily be to the school nurse; however, if screening equipment is limited to the Snellen Chart, the classroom teacher should report the observed behavior to the parents with the recommendation of a complete visual examination by a vision specialist. Until the student receives treatment, the teacher should make every effort to provide a comfortable and efficient visual environment. This may be accomplished by placing the student in a position of optimal lighting, eliminating glare, adjusting seating to ease board work, or reducing the reading load.

VISION REFERRAL PROBLEMS. Because most educators have little or no formal background in vision assessment, referral decisions are fraught with uncertainty. Does this student *really* have a vision problem? Are the student's difficulties severe enough to warrant referral? What if I refer this student and then find

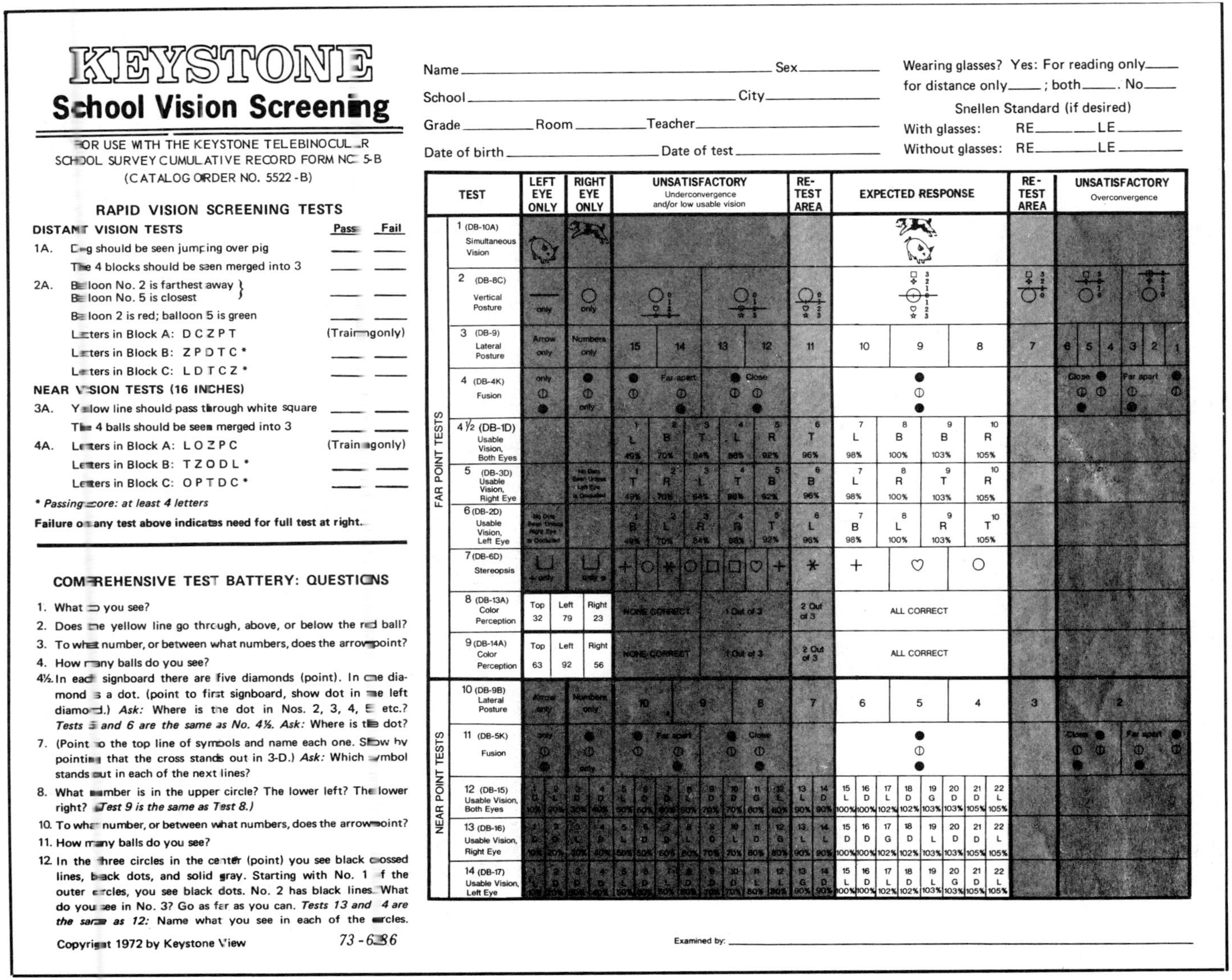

KEYSTONE
School Vision Screening

FOR USE WITH THE KEYSTONE TELEBINOCULAR
SCHOOL SURVEY CUMULATIVE RECORD FORM NO. 5-B
(CATALOG ORDER NO. 5522-B)

RAPID VISION SCREENING TESTS

DISTANT VISION TESTS — Pass / Fail

1A. Dog should be seen jumping over pig ____ ____
The 4 blocks should be seen merged into 3 ____ ____

2A. Balloon No. 2 is farthest away; Balloon No. 5 is closest ____ ____
Balloon 2 is red; balloon 5 is green ____ ____
Letters in Block A: D C Z P T (Training only)
Letters in Block B: Z P D T C * ____ ____
Letters in Block C: L D T C Z * ____ ____

NEAR VISION TESTS (16 INCHES)

3A. Yellow line should pass through white square ____ ____
The 4 balls should be seen merged into 3 ____ ____

4A. Letters in Block A: L O Z P C (Training only)
Letters in Block B: T Z O D L * ____ ____
Letters in Block C: O P T D C * ____ ____

** Passing score: at least 4 letters*

Failure on any test above indicates need for full test at right.

COMPREHENSIVE TEST BATTERY: QUESTIONS

1. What do you see?
2. Does the yellow line go through, above, or below the red ball?
3. To what number, or between what numbers, does the arrow point?
4. How many balls do you see?

4½. In each signboard there are five diamonds (point). In one diamond is a dot. (point to first signboard, show dot in the left diamond.) *Ask:* Where is the dot in Nos. 2, 3, 4, 5 etc.? *Tests 5 and 6 are the same as No. 4½. Ask:* Where is the dot?

7. (Point to the top line of symbols and name each one. Show by pointing that the cross stands out in 3-D.) *Ask:* Which symbol stands out in each of the next lines?
8. What number is in the upper circle? The lower left? The lower right? *Test 9 is the same as Test 8.)*
10. To what number, or between what numbers, does the arrow point?
11. How many balls do you see?
12. In the three circles in the center (point) you see black crossed lines, black dots, and solid gray. Starting with No. 1 of the outer circles, you see black dots. No. 2 has black lines. What do you see in No. 3? Go as far as you can. *Tests 13 and 14 are the same as 12:* Name what you see in each of the circles.

Copyright 1972 by Keystone View — 73-6386

Name ____ Sex ____
School ____ City ____
Grade ____ Room ____ Teacher ____
Date of birth ____ Date of test ____

Wearing glasses? Yes: For reading only ____ for distance only ____; both ____. No ____
Snellen Standard (if desired)
With glasses: RE ____ LE ____
Without glasses: RE ____ LE ____

	TEST	LEFT EYE ONLY	RIGHT EYE ONLY	UNSATISFACTORY Underconvergence and/or low usable vision	RE-TEST AREA	EXPECTED RESPONSE	RE-TEST AREA	UNSATISFACTORY Overconvergence
FAR POINT TESTS	1 (DB-10A) Simultaneous Vision							
	2 (DB-8C) Vertical Posture	only	only					
	3 (DB-9) Lateral Posture	Arrow only	Numbers only	15 14 13 12	11	10 9 8	7	6 5 4 3 2 1
	4 (DB-4K) Fusion	only	only	Far apart Close				Close Far apart
	4½ (DB-1D) Usable Vision, Both Eyes			1 L 49%, 2 B 70%, 3 T 84%, 4 L 88%, 5 R 92%	6 T 96%	7 L 98%, 8 B 100%, 9 B 103%, 10 R 105%		
	5 (DB-3D) Usable Vision, Right Eye		No Dots Seen Unless Left Eye is Occluded	1 T 49%, 2 R 70%, 3 L 84%, 4 T 88%, 5 B 92%	6 B 96%	7 L 98%, 8 R 100%, 9 T 103%, 10 R 105%		
	6 (DB-2D) Usable Vision, Left Eye	No Dots Seen Unless Right Eye is Occluded		1 B 49%, 2 L 70%, 3 R 84%, 4 R 88%, 5 T 92%	6 L 96%	7 B 98%, 8 L 100%, 9 R 103%, 10 T 105%		
	7 (DB-6D) Stereopsis	+ only	only					
	8 (DB-13A) Color Perception	Top 32, Left 79	Right 23	NONE CORRECT / 1 Out of 3	2 Out of 3	ALL CORRECT		
	9 (DB-14A) Color Perception	Top 63, Left 92	Right 56	NONE CORRECT / 1 Out of 3	2 Out of 3	ALL CORRECT		
NEAR POINT TESTS	10 (DB-9B) Lateral Posture	Arrow only	Numbers only	10 9 8	7	6 5 4	3	2
	11 (DB-5K) Fusion	only	only	Far apart Close				Close Far apart
	12 (DB-15) Usable Vision, Both Eyes	1 D 10%, 2 L 20%	3 D 30%, 4 D 40%	5 L 50%, 6 G 50%, 7 D 60%, 8 L 60%, 9 D 70%, 10 D 70%, 11 G 80%, 12 L 80%	13 L 90%, 14 D 90%	15 L 100%, 16 D 100%, 17 L 102%, 18 D 102%, 19 G 103%, 20 D 103%, 21 D 105%, 22 L 105%		
	13 (DB-16) Usable Vision, Right Eye	1 D 10%, 2 G 20%	3 L 30%, 4 D 40%	5 L 50%, 6 D 50%, 7 D 60%, 8 L 60%, 9 D 70%, 10 L 70%, 11 D 80%, 12 G 80%	13 L 90%, 14 L 90%	15 D 100%, 16 D 100%, 17 G 102%, 18 D 102%, 19 L 103%, 20 D 103%, 21 D 105%, 22 L 105%		
	14 (DB-17) Usable Vision, Left Eye	1 L 10%, 2 D 20%	3 D 30%, 4 D 40%	5 L 50%, 6 D 50%, 7 L 60%, 8 D 60%, 9 D 70%, 10 D 70%, 11 L 80%, 12 L 80%	13 G 90%, 14 D 90%	15 L 100%, 16 D 100%, 17 L 102%, 18 D 102%, 19 L 103%, 20 G 103%, 21 D 105%, 22 L 105%		

Examined by: ____

FIGURE 4-4. Record Form of the Keystone School Vision Screening Form. *(Copyright © 1972 by the Keystone View Company. Reproduced by permission; all rights reserved.)*

TABLE 4–3. Signs of Possible Eye Trouble in Children

Behavior	Appearance	Complaints
Rubs eyes excessively	Crossed eyes	Eyes itch, burn or feel scratchy
Shuts or covers one eye, tilts head or thrusts head forward	Red-rimmed, encrusted or swollen eyelids	Cannot see well
Has difficulty with reading or other close-up work	Inflamed or watery eyes	Dizziness, headaches, or nausea following close-up work
Blinks more than usual or is irritable when doing close-up work	Recurring styes	Blurred or double vision
Is unable to see distant things clearly		
Squints eyelids or frowns		

Signs of Possible Eye Trouble in Children was reproduced with permission from the National Society to Prevent Blindness, 500 East Remington Road, Schaumburg, Illinois 60173, a not-for-profit organization that provides sight-saving programs and services through its twenty-seven affiliates/divisions.

that there was no visual difficulty? Abrams places the referral process in perspective:

> The responsibility of the teacher or educator is to *detect* the visual problem, not to *diagnose* visual difficulties. . . . The diagnosis and treatment of a visual problem rightly belongs in the realm of the vision specialist who is trained to handle such problems.[14]

Kelley comments on the reluctance of educators to overrefer:

> The cardinal purpose of school visual screening procedures is to refer children who may need visual care. It generally is considered more serious for a screening program to *fail to refer* a child in real need of care than for it to *refer* a child not actually in need of care.[15]

The schools, through their reluctance to refer, have permitted many students to operate daily with eye strain that leads to more complicated, permanent problems. All students should have periodic visual examinations by a specialist. Since most schools do not assume this responsibility, it remains a parental obligation. The teacher, then, should not hesitate to refer any student who demonstrates symptoms of visual difficulties.

Changes in the eyes will occur even following visual adjustment, complicating the referral decision even more. The nature of school, requiring hours of near-point visual activities, may make it necessary for lenses to be changed periodically. Therefore, the teacher should not hesitate to refer students who have symptoms of visual discomfort even if they are wearing glasses.

Another complication of referral occurs when the strongly motivated student, despite experiencing visual strain and discomfort, completes schoolwork and shows no sign of academic deficiency. Again, this student, showing symptoms listed in Table 4–3, should be referred without hesitation before possible damage occurs.

Finally, the choice of to whom the referral should be made is often confusing. The term *vision specialist* has been used to avoid confusion. A vision specialist may be an optometrist, an ophthalmologist, or an oculist. A competent specialist in any of these fields should be considered satisfactory for referral. Ophthalmologists and oculists are medical doctors who have specialized in vision problems. The optometrist has a doctor's degree in optometry. Each is qualified to prescribe corrective lenses and visual training. In the case of eye disease, an optometrist will refer the patient to the ophthalmologist or oculist. Regardless of the type of degree held by the vision specialist, educators should make an effort to seek out those who have a special interest in the visual development of students and in the problems of functional vision that relate to reading achievement.

A form such as the one illustrated in Figure 4–5 will aid the vision specialist in understanding the reasons for referral and provide him or her with basic educational information that can aid in a complete diagnosis.

The educator's tone when making a referral is especially important. If the educator's tone is dictatorial, conflict with both vision specialists and parents may occur. The referral should be stated in a manner such as "Since Jason appears to be having serious difficulties reading and since he has not had his eyes checked recently, we would like you to take him to a specialist for an examination. As we start to work with Jason, it will be best to correct any visual disorder first. If he has none, then we will not need to be concerned about visual disability."

In summary, both the reading specialist and the classroom teacher should be alert to the possible presence of visual problems in students who are experiencing reading difficulties. Teachers should observe students' classroom behaviors and use screening devices to guide referral of possible problem cases. Under no circumstances should the classroom teacher or the reading specialist

Walter was screened visually and did not perform satisfactorily in the following area(s):
near-point acuity near-point fusion
His/her present reading level is begining third grade,
but his/her reading potential is about upper 6th grade.
Will you please inform us if, after your examination, a visual deficiency may have been causing this student some difficulties in reading?

Ms. Carlotte Vasquez
(Signed)

FIGURE 4–5. A Visual Referral Form

consider a battery of screening devices, no matter how highly refined, as a substitution for a thorough eye examination and visual analysis. Screening tests, at best, are limited to their designed function—the identification of those in need of visual attention.

Auditory Diagnosis

Obviously, students who cannot hear adequately face problems in school. Many students with auditory limitations are placed in special schools or special classes for the deaf and hearing impaired so that they can receive specialized education. Many others with hearing losses, however, remain in regular school situations. School nurses have usually been able to identify these students early and to refer them to specialists.

Auditory problems affect reading in several ways. Students with a significant hearing loss are likely to find phonic instruction beyond their grasp because of a distortion of sounds or the inability to hear sounds at all. Most auditory deficiencies concern high-frequency sounds; therefore, because of the high frequency of many of the consonant sounds, the most common limitation that a hearing deficiency places upon a reader is in consonant recognition and usage. Hearing losses in lower frequency ranges may result in vowel difficulties. Students with hearing difficulties are also hindered by inability to follow directions since they may not hear them clearly. They are likely to lose their places in oral reading activities when listening to others, fail to complete homework assignments, and appear inattentive and careless.

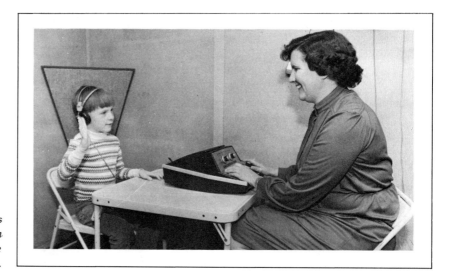

When the child thinks he hears a sound from the audiometer, he raises his hand.

Teachers should understand the difference between the student who is unable to hear a word and the one who is unable to discriminate between sounds. In the first case, the student has a hearing loss that is a physical problem, and, in the latter, the student has an auditory discrimination problem that has educational implications. (Auditory discrimination will be discussed in chapter 5.)

Ideally, auditory screening should include a test of pitch (frequency) ranging from low to high and one to measure varying loudness (decibels). This screening can be adequately conducted using an audiometer (see photo and Figure 4–6), an instrument adaptable for either group or individual auditory testing. Although opinions vary concerning a satisfactory audiometer score, a screening score that reports a loss of twenty-five decibels at 500, 1,000, 2,000, and 6,000 frequencies, and thirty decibels at 4,000, adequately indicates possible interference with reading instruction and that such a student should be referred.[16]

It is unlikely that the classroom teacher has the time, experience, or equipment to conduct the screening mentioned here. Classroom teachers have been

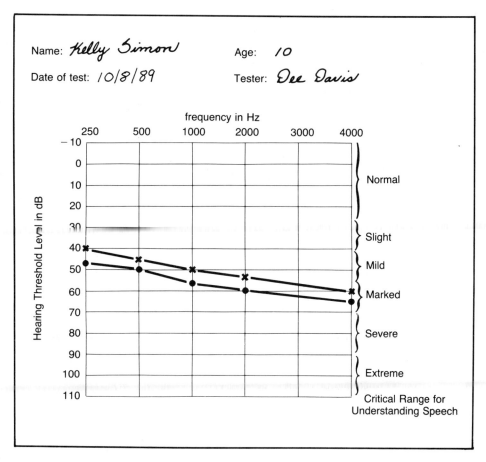

FIGURE 4–6. An Audiogram Charted for a Student with a Mild Hearing Loss (x = left ear, • = right ear)

advised that a watch-tick test or a whisper test is possible in the classroom. However, classroom teachers are reluctant to use these tests, perhaps because they have not had enough supervised experiences with them and the possibilities of overreferral are too great. Therefore, the classroom teacher should rely on a pattern of the symptoms listed in Table 4–4 that, when observed in a student who has failed in reading, is justifiable cause for referral.

Normally, the student is referred to the school nurse for audiometric screening. Then, in an effort to encourage as much success as possible in the classroom, the teacher should move the student's seat so that it is in the center of a discussion area, close to the teacher, and away from outside distractions such as radiators, fans, air conditioners, and traffic noises. A teacher must also be willing to repeat assignments for this student to assure that they have been properly understood.

Referral outside the school normally would be made to a general practitioner, an audiologist, or to an otologist. An audiologist is a professional who has particular expertise in hearing assessment and rehabilitation. An otologist is a medical doctor who specializes in physical examinations of the ear. Often an audiologist and an otologist will function as a team. Referrals to one of these specialists should be made in terms of the observed symptoms of auditory difficulty which prompted the referral, with a request for results of the audiometric examination and suggestions concerning appropriate classroom adjustments if an educationally significant hearing loss is found.

Although the reading specialist may not plan to conduct an audiometric examination with every student, such an examination should be made when the student exhibits difficulties in speech or phonics instruction which may be related to a hearing problem. The specialist should take into consideration the observed onset of hearing related difficulties since this will have an important impact on educational planning for the student. For example, if a hearing loss occurs sometime after the primary grades, the student will have had the benefit of receiving basic instruction in sound-symbol correspondences while having unimpaired hearing. The remedial program for such a student would differ from that recommended for a student who began school with an educationally significant hearing loss.

TABLE 4–4. Symptoms Justifying Auditory Referral

Physical Symptoms	Behavioral Symptoms
Speech difficulties (particularly with consonant sounds)	Inability to profit from phonic instruction
Tilting the head to listen	Inability to follow directions
Cupping of the ear with the hand in order to follow instructions	General inattentiveness
Strained posture in listening situations	Excessive volume needed for comfortable radio listening
Persistent complaints of earaches	
Inflammation or drainage of the ear	
Reports of persistent buzzing or ringing in the head	

Neurological disorders remain the most confusing of the physical factors which may impede reading growth. Authorities differ markedly regarding the incidence, identification, referral, and treatment of students who are neurologically impaired. Often these differences can be traced to varying perspectives on the problem: medical, educational, or psychiatric. However, even among professionals of similar background, there are often differences due to the imprecise nature of diagnostic knowledge and procedures.

Neurological disorders may be divided into two groups: cases of established, known brain damage and cases in which brain damage is suspected but not verified. Little evidence can be found to support the idea that neurological disorders resulting from known brain damage are a major cause of low achievement in reading. Bond, Tinker, Wasson, and Wasson state, "Among children who have not yet acquired the ability to read, there are a very few who have sustained known brain damage before, during, or after birth."[17] In the case of suspected brain damage there is considerably less agreement. Some would attribute virtually all reading disabilities to presumed brain damage. Others would place the incidence of suspected brain damage among poor readers at a much more modest level. Robinson named neurological disorders as one of the causal factors in 18 percent of the cases in her classic study.[18] (In working with poor readers who have been referred to a university reading clinic, it is found that much less than 18 percent show symptoms of abnormal neurological patterns.)

Teachers, faced with the prevailing confusion in the field, may be uncertain about their role in the identification of neurologically impaired students. As with other factors that may contribute to a reading difficulty, the teacher's primary responsibility is to carefully observe and decide which students may warrant referral for a neurological evaluation. Referral of a student should always be based on an observed pattern of symptoms and should only be made when a student fails to respond after the best available diagnosis and remedial instruction or when identification of the student will enable the student to receive needed special services. In the absence of these two cases, a referral may cause the student more harm than good. In recent years, a proliferation of classification labels that have been associated with neurological disorders has emerged. Dunn reports twenty-three different terms that are used to describe brain-damaged children ranging from "clumsy child" to "psychoneurologically disordered child."[19] Unless identification results in either better educational planning or better services for the student, the negative label, an unfortunate by-product of identification, may hinder more than help the student.

Symptoms of neurological problems fall into two categories—physical and educational. Physical symptoms include:

- *Physical incoordination.* Grossly awkward walking, running, writing, etc., in relation to overall physical development.

- *Hyperactivity.* Inability to concentrate that causes the child to rarely complete assignments, annoy others, and appear disinterested.
- *Headaches.* A history of persistent headaches.
- *Speech impediments.* Persistent blockage of speech or articulation difficulties that are peculiar for the child's age.
- *Visual incoordination.* Poor saccadic eye movements, inability of the eyes to focus or to hold to a line of print.

Educational symptoms of neurological problems include:

- *Average or better than average intelligence.* General educational development deficient in terms of valid measures of intelligence.
- *Phonic blending deficiency.* Knowledge of sounds but inability to blend them into words.
- *Poor contextual reader.* Knowledge of a sight vocabulary but difficulties when those words are encountered in sentences.
- *Slow reading speed.* Poor reading rate, even with easy or familiar material.
- *Poor auditory discrimination.* Inability to discriminate between sounds of letters, without evidence of an auditory acuity deficiency.
- *Distractibility.* Inattentiveness to designated tasks.
- *Abnormal behavior.* Overreaction to stimuli (e.g., laughing after others have stopped).
- *Poor ability to remember sequences.* Although apparently normally intelligent, difficulty in remembering verbal and nonverbal sequences.
- *Difficulties with visual perception.* Difficulty with spatial orientation often manifested in reversals of letters or words.

Obviously, these symptoms in isolation do not necessarily indicate a neurological disorder. A *pattern* of these symptoms that includes four or more of these indicates that a neurological disorder might exist. Students with this quantity of symptoms, whether identified in classroom or clinical diagnosis, should be considered legitimate referrals for neurological examinations.

Clements summarizes the ten most frequently cited characteristics of minimal brain dysfunction from over 100 publications in the following list:[20]

1. Hyperactivity
2. Perceptual-motor impairments
3. Emotional lability
4. General coordination defects
5. Disorders of attention
6. Impulsivity
7. Disorders of memory and thinking

8. Specific learning disabilities in reading, arithmetic, writing, or spelling
9. Disorders of speech and hearing
10. Equivocal neurological signs and electroencephalographic irregularities

An initial referral should be made to a pediatrician who has a background in diagnosing neurological disorders and is sympathetic to the educational realities of the classroom. During the first office visit, the pediatrician will conduct a neurological examination and obtain a detailed case history. If he or she detects evidence of a neurological disorder or notes a history of such factors as birth difficulties, head injury, or severe diseases accompanied by prolonged periods of high fever, further specialized testing may be recommended. (Hartlage and Hartlage discuss diagnostic evaluation in more detail.)[21]

The reading specialist, upon receipt of the neurological report, relates the findings to other information gathered for the case study. The relationship of neurological problems to the entire case history must be considered in the recommendations for educational adjustment.

The classroom teacher, while waiting for the neurological report, should relieve the student from unnecessary frustration by relaxing tension and providing reading experiences in the area of the student's strengths. If the report indicates that the student does not have a neurological problem, the teacher will continue with the classroom diagnosis in an effort to find the area where correction should start. However, if the report does reveal a neurological problem, the classroom teacher should refer the student to a reading specialist, who will conduct a careful case evaluation, noting all educational aspects and precise recommendations concerning remedial techniques.

In attempting to meet the needs of the neurologically impaired student, cooperation and communication among professionals is essential. Medical personnel need to remember that a label alone does nothing to help a student. Neurologically impaired students represent a heterogeneous group for whom no single treatment routine may be expected to be successful. Medical specialists should attempt to be as descriptive as possible of the student's specific neurological strengths and weaknesses. This will enable the reading teacher to make informed educational decisions concerning remedial approaches to pursue for that particular student.

Similarly, educators can perform an excellent service to medical specialists in providing feedback concerning the observed effect of medical treatment. Classroom teachers can be invaluable in monitoring the effects of drug therapy treatment. Students who evidence attention deficit disorders are most often prescribed one of two central nervous system stimulants, methylphenidate (Ritalin) or dextroamphetamine (Dexedrine).[22] Teachers are in ideal position to notice changes in a student's attention to school-related tasks as well as the student's general ability to function in the classroom. These observations can aid the physician in evaluating the treatment's benefit or detriment to the student, and in adjusting subsequent prescriptions.[23]

Based on an examination of current literature, Gentile, Lamb, and Rivers suggest that students experiencing reading difficulties because of neurological problems often have difficulties with symbol-language relationships, depression, and classroom behavior. They suggest that teachers can help these students by directing remedial instruction to the students' strengths rather than their weaknesses and by offering strong emotional support. Techniques and approaches that have been successfully used with some neurologically impaired students include the language experience approach, the neurological impress method, repeated readings, comprehension-monitoring, and audiovisual approaches with nonprint media that bypass the students' neurological difficulties with print (see chapters 8, 9, and 10).[24]

Finally, Abrams reminds us that neurologically impaired students may be frustrated by events and conditions beyond their control. These students deserve an extra measure of our compassion and understanding.

> We must recognize that children who have experienced severe reading disabilities have packed a lifetime of pain into a few years. Much of this pain has been associated with the struggle to maintain their dignity in spite of an organism that refuses to be efficient. . . . The best thought out strategies and programs established by the most learned people can have little lifelong value or durable impact if the interpersonal relationship patterns are impersonal, insincere, or patronizing. We strongly believe that it is the manner in which contact with the child is maintained that determines the success or failure of anything else.[25]

Emotional Diagnosis

Emotional difficulties, when considered in terms of reading difficulties, create cause-and-effect confusion. Sometimes emotional disturbances cause reading difficulties; however, many emotional problems are not the cause, but the result, of reading failure. Unfortunately, often no clear line of distinction exists. When emotional disturbances cause reading difficulties, performance in all learning areas suffers. Often, it is in the diagnosis of a reader that this area of difficulty is first uncovered; however, assessing the severity of the difficulty is properly the task of psychological personnel. Conversely, although emotional reactions may complicate a reading diagnosis, they are often not the cause but rather an effect of the reading failure itself. Most students who encounter difficulty in learning to read exhibit some symptoms of emotional conflict, and these symptoms often diminish or disappear with effective instruction after the diagnosis. In summarizing the research, Bond, Tinker, Wasson, and Wasson conclude, "Examination of all the evidence does make it fairly clear that emotional maladjustment is much more frequently the effect than the cause of reading disability."[26] An effective diagnosis may result in relieving the student of some home and school pressures by exposing the fact that the student's difficulty is not due to a poor attitude or a low level of intellectual potential but rather to a skill deficiency, which, when corrected, will permit the student to perform as expected.

The classroom teacher and the reading specialist must be aware that most students with reading difficulties react emotionally to their failure through such behavior patterns as refusing to read, not enjoying school, disliking their teachers, or causing problems at home. Assessment of emotional adjustment is complicated for several reasons. First, an individual's behavior is often inconsistent and unpredictable. For example, when frustrated, an emotionally disturbed student may lash out in defiance on one occasion and another time, with similar provocation, may react by being withdrawn and quiet. Second, an individual's personality traits change over time. Therefore, an assessment of personality must be considered as an indication of a student's personal adjustment at a given point in time. Third, an individual's personality is complex and is made up of the interactions of many factors. Nunnally states, "One of the impediments to discussing the measurement of personality is that there are so many different kinds of attributes that are included under the name."[27] The more thorough an understanding the teacher has of the intrafamilial, peer, and school relationships, the better the likelihood of an effective diagnosis. The teacher should observe the student in reading situations, note pertinent emotional reactions, include those reactions in the diagnosis, and consider them in the recommendations. However, these reactions should be labeled cautiously as causative of a reading difficulty because their presence does not necessarily make the student a candidate for referral.

Realistically recognizing their limitations as detectors of emotional difficulties and at the same time recognizing the emotional entanglement of these types of students, teachers and reading specialists follow similar diagnostic procedures. Through the cooperation of all the educators in contact with the student, information may be assembled concerning the student, the home, the school situation, and the student's behaviors in peer group encounters.

Information Concerning the Student

Due to their daily contact with the student, classroom teachers are in a unique position to obtain valuable information about the student's reactions to many situations. Often the reading specialist must rely on information supplied by the teacher, by the parents, or from a personal interview with the student. Useful information would include the following:

- The student's attitude toward family, school, teacher, and friends
- The student's awareness of behavior and learning problems and the student's suggestions for their improvement
- The student's attitude toward reading and the student's self-assessment of his or her own reading skill
- The student's development of worthwhile personal goals and the student's level of commitment toward reaching those goals

Gathered informally by the classroom teacher or formally by the reading teacher, all information in doubtful areas must be checked for reliability. One can do this easily by comparing reliable sources. A student may have claimed to be earning B's and C's in school. The educator will rely more readily on the student's other statements about school if, when checking the school records, one finds that the student does indeed make B's and C's.

Formal personality testing can also prove useful in determining emotional difficulties. The California Test of Personality, one of the more popular instruments for classroom use, provides standardized evaluations of the student's reactions to questions concerning personal and social adjustment. This test may be administered individually or in classroom-sized groups. Since adequate performance requires that the student possess reading skills close to the grade level of the test, the very poor reader will be unable to read the questions. In evaluating the California Test of Personality, one should not place undue emphasis on any low set of scores; however, such scores may be considered indicative of areas of potential personality problems. (Scores indicating the necessity for referral are described in the test manual.) Final verification will not come from this type of testing but rather from careful teacher observation and referral to psychological personnel.

Personality testing using incomplete sentences provides an informal way of obtaining valuable information. The student is expected to respond to several incomplete sentences, such as "I like books, but . . . ," "My home is . . . ," "I like my brother and. . . ." The most reliable use of this type of information is noting patterns of responses and verifying them by direct observation of the student in situations where these responses may be reflected in behavior. Again, the examiner should be cautioned against excessive analysis of any slightly deviate responses and urged to leave to psychological personnel the final assessment of the emotional stability of the individual being tested.

Paper-and-pencil personality tests are considered inherently weak, because students often anticipate what they consider acceptable responses. Ebel notes:

> Much of personality has to do with typical behavior in actual situations. But the behavior exhibited on a paper-and-pencil test is a limited, artificial kind. Even if a student knows with reasonable accuracy how he would behave in the situation described (and often he does not know) he may find it advantageous to report something else. It is possible for an examinee to "fake good" on most personality tests if he chooses to do so.[28]

Furthermore, these tests tend to record "of-the-moment" responses. Those who have had bad days may score poorly on such tests; however, twenty-four hours later, they may score many points higher. When this occurs, the scores obtained obviously have severely limited use in the diagnosis of emotional problems.

To note personality characteristics in a more natural situation, students should be observed at play. An investigation of play behavior may be based on the following types of questions: Do they play with others their own age? Does it appear that they are accepted by their peers? Do they play fairly? Do they play enthusiastically? Answers to such questions provide further analysis of the total behavior pattern without the limitations of paper-and-pencil tests. Caplan and Caplan believe that the analysis of free play has definite advantages in emotional diagnosis:

> Since it is impossible to determine exactly what goes on in a child's mind or to get children to talk like adults, specialists who work with distressed children have found that much can be learned about them from watching them at play during which most children are able to reveal both their imaginary and real life.[29]

Silvern summarizes the current research:

> All of the studies reviewed take the position that the child's social ability/social interaction is reflected in the child's play. By observing a child's play we can make assumptions about the child's social interactions. Play, then, is the vehicle for *examining* socialization.[30]

Both of these authorities suggest that play analysis has particular value with younger children.

A Study of the Home

Although home visits are uncommon as a result of a reading diagnosis, under certain circumstances such visits are profitable. When it appears that situations at home are impeding the student's language or emotional development, the educator who hopes to improve these conditions must make a home visit. In cases where a home visit would be of little value, one may gather information concerning home conditions through parental interviews or questionnaires. These are constructed to obtain information on the socioeconomic status of the home, availability of books, intrafamilial relations, parental efforts to assist the child, general family activities, and overall acceptance of the child in the home.

Abnormal home conditions should be brought to the attention of appropriate personnel (school officials, home-school visitors, social workers, and psychologists). Neither the classroom teacher nor the reading specialist can justifiably offer unsolicited advice to parents about home conditions unrelated to the student's educational progress. At times, parents will turn to an educator and ask for consultation. Although it depends upon the individual situation, an educator is normally acting outside the proper professional role in offering advice in such cases. Offering advice concerning domestic affairs implies that one has training or information about effective solutions.

Tragically, many students today live under the specter of child abuse and neglect. An estimated 3 percent of school-age children are at risk of serious physical injury from their parents each year. Add to that number the many other children who suffer each year from physical neglect and emotional mistreatment, and the number of children affected is staggering. Teachers are in a unique position to help these students by being in daily contact with them. Although other professionals may see children only infrequently, teachers see children every day and should be alert to physical and behavioral signals that may indicate the need for referral. Symptoms of child abuse and neglect include the following:

- Evidence of repeated injuries that are unexplained and apparently nonaccidental in origin.
- Frequent complaints of abdominal pain.
- Recurrent bruises, welts, wounds, fractures, or burns.
- Consistent hunger, underweight, or failure to thrive.
- Poor hygiene, inappropriate dress, or unattended physical problems.
- Evidence or report of sexual abuse.

In addition to the physical signs of abuse, teachers should be alert to behavioral indicators of child abuse. Students who display severe changes in mood, unusual apprehension of adults, or irrational fear of punishment may be victims of abuse.[31]

When child abuse is suspected, the teacher's professional duty is to report those suspicions to the proper authorities. In some areas this will be the building principal or other school administrator; in other areas abuse cases should be reported directly to local child service agencies. Because the physical safety of the child may be at stake, the teacher should not hesitate to refer any suspected case. If abuse is suspected, the teacher should neither interview the parents concerning the matter nor conduct a home visit. The teacher or school need not *prove* abuse—that is up to the appropriate child protective agency. The teacher's sole responsibility is to initiate timely referral.

Social workers may also be helpful in less severe instances if the teacher has reason to attribute a student's poor classroom performance to difficulties at home. These professionals are skilled in working with parents and investigating home situations. Some large school systems have found it worthwhile to have professional social workers on their staffs.

A Study of the School

The classroom teacher gathers relevant data for a classroom diagnosis and submits it to the reading specialist for case analysis. Information relating to attendance, ability to work and play with others, and reactions to various types of frustration should be obtained from the school. Teachers should note the student's behavior patterns in a wide variety of group settings. In this day of increased parental access to student records, subjective comments and anecdotal records are seldom included in a student's school records. When such notations are available, they should be considered in the diagnosis. When behavior patterns are not described in a student's records, they should be sought out through interviews or questionnaire responses from the teacher. Diagnosis that attempts to suggest instructional directions, without considering student behaviors, is incomplete and probably faulty.

If the educator is to be effective in obtaining such information, students and parents must be assured that it will be handled confidentially. A confidential approach on the part of both parents and educators is necessary for reliable data collection.

A number of characteristics exhibited in the school setting may serve to identify a student as a candidate for psychological referral. According to the definition of *seriously emotionally disturbed* included in Public Law 94–142, this student is one who exhibits one or more of the following characteristics over a long period of time and to a marked degree, which adversely affects educational performance:

1. An inability to learn which cannot be explained by intellectual, sensory, or health factors
2. An inability to build or maintain satisfactory interpersonal relationships with peers and teachers
3. Inappropriate types of behavior or feelings under normal circumstances
4. A general pervasive mood of unhappiness or depression
5. A tendency to develop physical symptoms or fears associated with personal or school problems[32]

Each of these characteristics obviously can be expected to interfere with a student's ability to benefit from reading instruction. Once again, the proper response of the classroom teacher is to refer the student for examination and to make appropriate classroom adjustments pending the outcome of the evaluation.

Classroom adjustments for the student suspected to be emotionally disturbed or for the student who consistently displays antisocial behavior should be designed around clear limits and planned successes. Students should be clearly told what is expected of them in the classroom and should be made aware of the consequences of their actions. Sometimes teachers are reluctant to be firm with the emotionally disturbed student, and yet, the resulting ambiguous standards for classroom behavior may be confusing to the student. At the same time, teachers should be both fair and consistent. Vacc recommends "straight talk" in working with these students.

> Some children, however, will change their behavior for the better almost immediately if it is clearly stated by the teacher how they should behave. The teacher should tell the child that they are going to work together to change the behavior that is causing problems in school and with friends and that the child is going to participate in changing his or her own behavior with the instruction of the teacher.[33]

Another key to working with emotionally disturbed students is to plan for success. Failure situations that produce frustration should be minimized so that students come to expect success. This, in turn, will help to build trust and rapport between the students and the teacher. Students learn that the teacher will not ask them to do something they are incapable of doing. This newfound confidence often will inspire a student to greater achievement. If the frustrating situations are removed that caused either avoidance or hostility in the past, the undesirable behaviors may also diminish. Glass, Christiansen, and Christiansen give some insights into how these suggestions may be translated into classroom practice.

> Since it is understood that many students have a fear of failure in addition to anxiety over learning, traditional testing is minimized and academic lessons are made as informal and relaxing as possible. Emphasis is placed on pointing out correct responses rather than incorrect responses. As the students' academic skills and self-confidence increase, more challenging academic tasks are provided.[34]

The classroom teacher must be willing to give such students special considerations; negative reactions can only drive the student to further reject the learning process and environment. At the same time, the teacher has an obligation to the other students in the classroom to provide an environment conducive to learning. If disruption occurs, alternative strategies for dealing with the emotionally disturbed student must be found.

Classroom teachers should also work to prevent complex emotional disorders. Their reactions, for example, to a student's initial signs of frustration and failure in a situation may cause the student's acceptance or rejection of a temporary solution. Although students must be challenged in school, not all will meet these challenges with the same degree of success. Teachers may relax tensions and feelings of failure by their attitudes toward the efforts of the less successful. All students must succeed in school. Teachers should emphasize the successes of all but particularly the less successful. However, they should beware of false praise—students resent it. Instead of false praise, they should structure situations in which, with a little effort, a student can legitimately succeed and be praised. More of these types of techniques are discussed in later chapters.

All information and notations concerning the student's emotional behavior should be included and evaluated in the case analysis. The reading teacher should apply the recommendations for the necessary educational adjustment. If the classroom teacher, after instituting these recommendations, finds further complications, the student should be referred to the reading specialist.

Referral decisions are never easily made. The teacher must carefully weigh the potential benefits to the student against the anxiety that referral often creates on the part of students and parents. Teachers are reminded to base referral decisions on a pattern of behaviors and not on test performance alone. Test scores may be a first indicator of student need; however, abnormal scores should always be confirmed by systematic teacher observation of the student's performance. Clearly, in the final analysis, students are better served when a referral is made and no difficulty is found than when no referral is initiated and a problem is allowed to persist.

Summary

Reading is a complex act made up of the interaction of many factors. Intellectual, physical, sensory, emotional, social, and neurological factors all contribute to reading success or failure. The teacher must possess an awareness of the manner in which each of these areas influences the development of reading skill. Knowledge of diagnostic procedures and of referral avenues will enable the teacher to make the most complete assessment of a student's reading difficulties.

Often the types of assessment discussed in this chapter must be undertaken by a specialist from outside the education field. However, teachers should understand the relationship of these areas to reading achievement and be familiar with some of the technical terminology associated with diagnosis in these varied areas. Just as reading itself is a complex act composed of a variety of aspects, a complete reading diagnosis must sometimes encompass the expertise of specialists from many fields.

Notes

1. Alan O. Ross, *Psychological Aspects of Learning Disabilities and Reading Disorders* (New York: McGraw-Hill Book Company, 1976), 168.
2. Arnold J. Lien, *Measurement and Evaluation of Learning* (Dubuque, Iowa: Wm. C. Brown Company, 1976), 142.
3. Donald B. Helms and Jeffrey S. Turner, *Exploring Child Behavior* (Philadelphia: W. B. Saunders Company, 1976), 492.
4. Booney Vance, "Intellectual Characteristics of Reading Disabled Children," *Journal of Research and Development in Education* 14 (Summer 1981): 11–21.
5. David W. Moore and O. Paul Wielan, "WISC-R Scatter Indexes of Children Referred for Reading Diagnosis," *Journal of Learning Disabilities* 14 (November 1981): 511–14.
6. Eugene A. Jongsma, "Test Review: Peabody Picture Vocabulary Test-Revised," *Journal of Reading* 25 (January 1982): 360–64.
7. Albert J. Harris and Edward R. Sipay, *How to Increase Reading Ability*, 8th ed. (New York: Longman, 1985), 152–54.
8. Ibid., 154–57.
9. Guy L. Bond, Miles A. Tinker, Barbara B. Wasson, and John B. Wasson, *Reading Difficulties: Their Diagnosis and Correction*, 5th ed. (Englewood Cliffs, N.J.: Prentice-Hall, 1984), 42–45.
10. Ibid., 42–43.
11. John J. Pikulski, "Assessing Information about Intelligence and Reading," *The Reading Teacher* 29 (November 1975): 162.
12. Charles R. Kelley, *Visual Screening and Child Development* (Raleigh: North Carolina State College, 1957), 11.
13. Kelley, *Visual Screening and Child Development*, 11.
14. Jules C. Abrams, "The Psychologist-Educator Views the Relationship of Vision to Reading and Related Learning Disabilities," *Journal of Learning Disabilities* 14 (December 1981): 566, 567.

15. Kelley, *Visual Screening and Child Development*, 11.
16. John Salvia and James E. Ysseldyke, *Assessment in Special and Remedial Education* (Boston: Houghton Mifflin, 1978), 336.
17. Bond, Tinker, Wasson, and Wasson, *Reading Difficulties*, 61.
18. Helen M. Robinson, *Why Pupils Fail in Reading* (Chicago: University of Chicago Press, 1946), 218.
19. Lloyd M. Dunn, "Minimal Brain Dysfunction: A Dilemma for Educators," in *Brain Damage in School Age Children*, ed. H. Carl Haywood (Washington, D.C.: Council for Exceptional Children, 1968), 163.
20. Sam D. Clements, *Minimal Brain Dysfunction in Children*, (Washington, D.C.: GPO, 1966), 13.
21. Lawrence C. Hartlage and Patricia L. Hartlage, "Application of Neuropsychological Principles in the Diagnosis of Learning Disabilities," in *Brain Function and Reading Disabilities*, ed. Lester Tarnopol and Muriel Tarnopol (Baltimore: University Park Press, 1977), 111–46.
22. Laurie L. Humphries, "Medication and Reading Disability," *Journal of Research and Development in Education* 14 (Summer 1981): 54–57.
23. Barbara Bateman, "Educational Implications of Minimal Brain Dysfunction," *The Reading Teacher* 27 (April 1974): 662–68.
24. Lance M. Gentile, Patrice Lamb, and Cynda O. Rivers, "A Neurologist's Views of Reading Difficulty: Implications for Remedial Instruction," *The Reading Teacher* 39, no. 2 (November 1985): 174–82.
25. Jules C. Abrams, "Minimal Brain Dysfunction and Dyslexia," *Reading World* 14 (March 1975): 227.
26. Bond, Tinker, Wasson, and Wasson, *Reading Difficulties*, 83.
27. Jum C. Nunnally, *Educational Measurement and Evaluation*, 2d ed. (New York: McGraw-Hill, 1972), 469.
28. Robert L. Ebel, *Essentials of Educational Measurement* (Englewood Cliffs, N.J.: Prentice-Hall, 1972), 520.
29. Frank Caplan and Theresa Caplan, *The Power of Play* (Garden City, N.Y.: Anchor Press/Doubleday, 1973), 54.
30. Steven B. Silvern, "Play As an Avenue for Social Growth," *Journal of Research and Development in Education* 14 (Spring 1981): 110.
31. Donald F. Kline, *Child Abuse and Neglect: A Primer for School Personnel* (Reston, Va.: Council for Exceptional Children, 1977), 17–25.
32. Department of Health, Education, and Welfare, "Education of Handicapped Children," *Federal Register* 42 (23 Aug. 1977): 42478.
33. Nicholas A. Vacc, "Coping with the Behaviorally Disturbed Child in the Classroom," *Viewpoints in Teaching and Learning* 55 (Summer 1979): 32.
34. Raymond M. Glass, Jeanne Christiansen, and James L. Christiansen, *Teaching Exceptional Students in the Regular Classroom* (Boston: Little, Brown and Company, 1982), 88.

Suggested Readings

Geoffrion, Leo D., and Karen E. Schuster. *Auditory Handicaps and Reading*. Newark, Del.: International Reading Association, 1980. This annotated bibliography provides an excellent starting point for anyone researching information on this important subject.

Hammill, Donald D., ed., *Assessing the Abilities and Instructional Needs of Students*, Austin: Pro-Ed, 1987. The sections on assessing reading and assessing socioemotional development provide many valuable insights and techniques.

Harris, Albert J., and Edward R. Sipay. *How to Increase Reading Ability*. 8th ed. New York: Longman, 1985. Harris and Sipay discuss several techniques for the use of mental age in determining reading expectancy scores. Included in chapter 6 are useful charts for determining reading expectancy ages and quotients.

Hartlage, Lawrence C., and Patricia L. Hartlage. "Application of Neuropsychological Principles in the Diagnosis of Learning Disabilities." In *Brain Function and Reading Disabilities*, ed. by Lester Tarnopol and Muriel Tarnopol. Baltimore: University Park Press, 1977. Pp. 111–46. The authors discuss neuropsychological assessment instruments, their interpretation, and subsequent prescription. A comprehensive neurological assessment battery is listed, and several illustrative cases are presented.

Salvia, John, and James E. Ysseldyke. *Assessment in Special and Remedial Education*, Boston: Houghton Mifflin Company, 1978. Although a number of the topics contained in this chapter receive excellent treatment in this text, the reader is particularly urged to review chapter 16 which discusses visual and auditory assessment.

U.S. Department of Health, Education, and Welfare. *Child Abuse and Neglect*, Washington, D.C.: HEW, 1977. This self-instructional text developed for Head Start personnel presents useful information regarding the characteristics, reporting, treatment, and prevention of abuse and neglect.

Weintraub, Sam, and Robert J. Cowan. *Vision/Visual Perception.* Newark, Del.: International Reading Association, 1982. This annotated bibliography contains useful research references related to vision and visual perception.

EDITORIAL

Nancy M. Jaquish

*is a first-grade teacher in the Wellsboro
School District, Wellsboro, Pennsylvania.*

It was already the last week of August. For me,
this last week of summer vacation also meant the
first week of preparation for the coming school
year. Driving to my school, I felt that same sense
of excitement and anticipation that comes with each
new school year.

Upon my arrival, I noticed that the class lists
were posted on the door. Anxiously, I perused the
list to see if I could recognize any of the names—
and did I ever! I had been assigned the one child
everyone had hoped not to get. Although only six
years old, Larry had a reputation for his disruptive
behavior both in the classroom and on the
playground. Thinking back on remarks I had heard
last year about Larry, I feared that this school year
was going to be quite a challenge.

The first weeks of school were a testing time
for both Larry and me. He wanted to see just how
long I would tolerate his disruptive behavior, and
I wanted to see exactly what he could do
academically. When testing Larry for placement in
a reading group, I found him to be working below
his expectancy level, even though he had an
average intelligence and no physical problems. My
next step was to investigate his home environment.

The conference that I had with Larry's legal
guardians was very enlightening. Because he had
been physically abused for the first two and a half
years of his life, Larry was placed in a foster home,
where he had been for the last four years. Although
Larry was very young when he was abused, the
trauma still remained with him, and he was just
now beginning to show some signs of improvement
in his behavior at home.

After this conference, I had to rethink my
strategy for working with Larry. I now knew that
Larry's emotional problems were probably causing
his reading difficulties, which, in turn, were causing
more emotional problems. I realized that before
Larry could succeed academically, he needed to
develop his self-esteem. Encouraging Larry to do
his best and praising him daily helped to foster a
positive image of himself. Also, Larry's reading
program focused on his strengths which assured
him some success and helped to increase his
confidence.

Larry's progress was slow, but I was
eventually able to see some improvement, both in
his reading and in his behavior. I was especially
proud of him when one of his kindergarten teachers
remarked to me how much better Larry seemed to
be doing this year. He had come a long way, but
he still had a long way to go.

Being aware of Larry's social and emotional
background helped me to be more compassionate,
understanding, and patient with him. Although
Larry will probably never overcome all the effects
of his traumatic early years, I am hopeful that his
accomplishments in first grade will be a positive
influence on him during his remaining school years.

Nancy M. Jaquish

Classroom Diagnosis

CHAPTER OUTLINE

The Learning Climate
Implementing Classroom Diagnosis
Questions to Pinpoint Diagnostic
    Findings
Interests, Habits, and Attitudes
Record Keeping
Four Final Questions
Early Identification

CHAPTER EMPHASES

*The first task in classroom diagnosis
    should be assessing the learning
    climate.*
*Classroom diagnosis involves the
    observation of student behavior,
    limited testing, and assessment of
    interests and attitudes.*
*Student strengths and needs should
    receive equal attention.*
*Records of classroom assessment are
    essential.*

The classroom teacher, who has a relatively long acquaintance with a student, relies heavily on informal observation, systematic observation, informal testing, and student self-assessment for educational diagnosis of difficulties in reading. The classroom teacher considers the learning climate, the various causes of reading difficulties, the possible instructional adjustments that can be made, and the continuous assessment of student progress.

The Learning Climate

When teachers notice that certain students are experiencing difficulties in reading, their first step should logically be to conduct a quick assessment of the learning climate. Although it would be impossible to note all aspects of the learning climate in each teacher's classroom, a brief look at some important factors may prove helpful.

1. Is the climate one in which students are comfortable? Are such aspects as ventilation, lighting, and room cleanliness appropriate for learning? Because reading requires vigorous attention to the tasks at hand, physical discomfort can easily cause difficulties. Most of the physical aspects of discomfort can be adjusted easily once noticed.
2. Is the climate one that fosters communication? Are there any signs that students are experiencing difficulty communicating with the teacher or with other students? The threat of ridicule or failure can discourage some students from even attempting to communicate. Students are well aware of the risks involved in attempting to communicate. When risk taking is not worthwhile, communication becomes difficult and it may appear as though the students are not able to respond. Risk taking and communication can be improved by:
   - Starting comprehension discussions with personal questions that all students can answer without the fear of being wrong. For example, if the starter question is, "What did you like most about this story?" all students can respond without the fear of being wrong.
   - Focusing on a discussion about what has been read, as opposed to a teacher-questioning session. For example, after using a personal starter question, the teacher and students can discuss agreements and disagreements about the responses of others. By staying away from a questioning session in which the students are penalized for being wrong, the spirit of communication can be developed.
   - Staying at the eye level of the students instead of standing in front of them.

- Encouraging student-to-student communication and teaching students to regard the thoughts of others as important even when they disagree.

These and other aspects of facilitating risk taking and communication will be discussed in detail in chapter 10.

3. Are the materials for instruction appropriate? Are the materials suited to the reading levels of the students who are experiencing difficulty in reading? If not, then there may be no need for further assessment. The materials should be adjusted and the students observed to see if the difficulties disappear.

4. Are there opportunities for individualizing portions of instruction? Do all students have to complete the same assignments in the same amount of time or are there alternatives? If alternatives do not exist, can they be developed? Many readers appear to be having difficulty when they are attempting activities that are not appropriate for them, either because the activities are not geared to the students' strengths, or the time allotted for completion is not sufficient.

Numerous aspects of the learning climate may be assessed to determine if reading difficulties can be attributed to the climate instead of the student. The four mentioned here are common causes of difficulties that incorrectly appear to be within the student. Other common aspects that may be examined include inappropriate class size, inappropriate instructional strategies, discriminatory treatment of students, and the effect of labels that are attached to certain students.

Observing Student Behavior

If the learning climate seems appropriate and if a student is not able to respond when the climate is adjusted, then the classroom teacher needs to observe and assess that student's behavior to determine where the difficulties might lie. Some examples of the types of behaviors to look for follow.

1. Do the students have difficulty with reading comprehension activities? If students are not effectively gaining meaning from their reading, then they are reading nonsense. When reading without gaining meaning, the student makes many errors that may appear to be vocabulary problems or problems with word attack skills. In this chapter several approaches to assessing comprehension skills will be presented.

2. Are the difficulties most apparent when the students are reading in the content areas? Many students do satisfactory work in teacher-directed reading lessons but seem to have considerable

difficulty with independent reading in content-area books. The particular books, the assigned activities, and the nature of the difficulties need to be assessed. For example, the answers to the following questions would be helpful:

- Are students having difficulty with all content books or just certain ones? If certain ones, why?
- What features of the books creating the difficulty can be identified? Are readability levels too high?
- Can the assigned activities be changed to make the reading of content books an easier task? Are new concepts introduced prior to independent reading? Are new vocabulary words discussed?
- Are study guides available for student use? If not, are the students certain of the specific tasks in the assignment?

3. Do oral reading activities seem to be difficult for these students? Many students can read silently and answer questions but cannot read that same material orally with fluency. Assessment of the nature of the difficulty should be made before further oral reading activities are planned.

4. Do these students read accurately with good comprehension, but so slowly that they never finish their reading when others do? A slow reader causes real problems for the teacher. These readers hold up the entire group while others wait until they finish their reading.

Implementing Classroom Diagnosis

Classroom diagnosis can take place before, during, or after instruction. Each technique has distinct advantages and limitations and most teachers use each of them at times.

Diagnosis before Instruction

Prior to planning instruction, the level of skill development of students should be known. This information can be collected from sources such as past school records, student self-assessments, and tests.

School records contain a variety of information ranging from very useful to completely useless in nature. When using this information, teachers should first try to assess the reliability of the data found in school records. Teacher comments, test scores, health information, and past scholastic performance are usually found in school records. Unfortunately, much of this information is in the form of global information and is of little use. For example, test scores usually indicate total test scores and give little indication of how these scores were obtained. A low score on an IQ test may appear in the records as an intelligence quotient; however, if the test itself were available it might show that the student did satisfactorily on all but one section, and that that section lowered

Appropriate classroom climate is important for effective independent reading.

the total score. In many instances, however, useful data are found in school records, so they should be examined prior to initiating testing. If, for example, a teacher is curious about a student's intellectual ability, the school records may contain several indicators of that ability, making additional testing unnecessary. When those indicators provide consistent data and have been collected at different times in the student's schooling, they can be used with some degree of confidence. If, however, these indicators are not consistent or have been collected over a short period of time, one should use them cautiously.

Student self-assessment provides surprisingly useful information. Numerous professionals use self-report as one of the first steps in diagnosis: the doctor wants to know how you are feeling, the dentist wants to know which tooth hurts, and the lawyer wants to know a client's opinion of the problem. Many students have very accurate perceptions of their difficulty and are willing to discuss those perceptions. The following questions are useful in getting the students thinking about how reading is working for them:

1. Do you think you read better, worse, or about the same as other students in your class?
2. What do you do best when reading?
3. What causes you the most difficulty when reading?
4. Are you reading a book for fun? (If the answer is yes, ask for the name of the book.)
5. If you were to describe reading to a kindergarten child, what would you say?
6. Why do you read books? For fun, information, because you have to, or for another reason?
7. What could your teacher do to make reading easier for you?

After assessing the reading skills of the students who have already provided teachers with a self-report, teachers can better help them understand themselves as readers. Students make accurate self-reports more than 50 percent of the time. Accuracy is determined by comparing student self-reports with data collected during diagnosis. Many teachers attempt to determine the strengths and weaknesses of their students by testing them before instruction. They use these test results as they plan future instruction and as they plan for grouping students. Five basic types of testing instruments are available for classroom diagnosis: prepared informal inventories, teacher-made informal inventories, cloze tests, maze tests, and criterion-referenced tests.

The type of information needed for diagnosis should determine which testing instrument is selected. Some instruments are designed to measure the progress of groups of students, while others are designed to provide information on individual students. Some help teachers obtain information concerning the reading levels of students, while others provide information on skill development. By first determining what type of information they need, teachers can make intelligent choices. The following descriptions provide an overview of the various types of instruments available for classroom diagnosis.

PREPARED INFORMAL INVENTORIES. Several publishing companies and many school districts have prepared informal testing instruments that are useful for classroom diagnosis. Informal inventories are usually developed by teachers from the actual materials the students will be expected to use during instruction. Inventories already prepared for teachers generally use a sampling technique, where words are selected from a sampling of commonly used reading materials. Other inventories include paragraphs for oral and silent reading. Teachers using these instruments can obtain measures of the students' oral reading accuracy and silent reading comprehension as well as skill development. The paragraphs are usually evaluated through the use of readability formulas or taken from materials that have been graded previously.

One commercially prepared informal instrument is the Botel Reading Inventory (Revised). This inventory contains four major sections. The Word Recognition Test requires students to read graded lists of words orally. The Word Opposites Test requires the student to identify antonyms in graded word lists. It can also be used for reading expectancy when the teacher reads the words to the student (see Figure 5–1). The Decoding Test contains four sections: letter naming, beginning consonant sound/letter awareness, rhyme sound/letter pattern awareness, and decoding syllable/spelling patterns. The Spelling Placement Test consists of frequently used spelling words. Parts of this inventory are group tests, while other parts must be administered individually. Testing can be conducted quickly and provide teachers with a survey of their students' strengths.

Results, such as those in Table 5–1, can be useful in placing students in suitable books and in making initial decisions about areas of needed instruction.

A third-grade teacher with this type of diagnostic data early in the school year can make grouping decisions and book placements with considerable confidence. Betty and Simone's scores look very much alike on the first two subtests

BOTEL READING INVENTORY **B**

Word Opposites Test (Reading)

Directions: Pick a word in each line which
means the opposite or nearly the opposite of
the numbered word. Draw a line under it.
Example:
1. work   find   <u>play</u>   stop

Name _____

Date _____

Teacher _____

(First)

	A	**a**	**b**	**c**
1.	father	birthday	<u>mother</u>	children
2.	boy	shoe	train	<u>girl</u>
3.	in	eat	one	<u>out</u>
4.	big	away	<u>little</u>	around
5.	here	live	find	<u>there</u>
6.	morning	please	<u>night</u>	horse
7.	up	there	from	<u>down</u>
8.	him	bag	ask	<u>her</u>
9.	go	<u>stop</u>	boat	kitten
10.	yes	saw	<u>no</u>	fish

Score _____%

FIGURE 5–1. Botel Reading Inventory, Word Opposites Test, by Morton Botel.
(Copyright © 1978 by Follett Publishing Company. Used by permission.)

but not so much alike in spelling. The same can be said for Linda and Maria.

Another prepared informal inventory, the Individual Evaluation Procedures in Reading,[1] features passages taken from the content areas of literature, science, and history. It measures ability levels from primer level to tenth grade and has two forms. The examiner starts by administering a word recognition test to determine probable starting levels for the graded passages. Since some readers do well when reading basal-type stories, but have difficulty in content materials, this inventory proves particularly useful.

TABLE 5–1. Botel Reading Inventory Sample Results

Student	Word Recognition*	Word Opposites*	Spelling % Correct**			
			Grade 1	Grade 2	Grade 3	Grade 4
Betty	2–1	2–2	100	85	70	
Simone	2–1	2–2	85	70	—	—
Janet	2–1	2–2	100	90	70	—
Les	2–2	2–2	100	80	60	—
Mae	3–1	3–2	90	90	80	60
Linda	3–1	3–1	100	100	90	60
Maria	3–1	3–1	100	80	60	—
Jane	3–2	4	100	100	90	70
Joan	3–2	5	100	100	100	90
Jose	4	5	100	100	90	70

*Grade level equivalents.

**Testing stops when a student scores below 80 percent.

TEACHER-MADE INFORMAL READING INVENTORIES (IRIs). Teachers can develop informal tests having the same features as those prepared commercially. Using the material from which they intended to teach the students, teachers can assess a reader's abilities to recognize words, read orally, and read silently for comprehension. Many school systems develop IRIs for use by their teachers. Constructing such instruments can be time consuming and requires considerable knowledge of both the reading process and test construction. Interpretation can be even more difficult. Powell raises serious questions concerning traditional norms used on informal inventories.[2] Others also have found the subject of norms for informal inventories rather perplexing.[3] Betts is acknowledged as creator of the IRI as a functional measurement instrument.[4] Since then, Powell has conducted numerous studies attempting to establish criteria that teachers can use when interpreting informal inventories.[5]

Powell's latest study of criteria for interpretation of informal reading inventory results can be applied by a study of comprehension, word recognition, and other systematic behavior. Powell states, however, "The comprehension dimension is the most important of the three in determining final placement. When comprehension drops below the criterion for a given level, then it matters not what happens on the other two dimensions."[6]

Powell contends that the comprehension and word recognition criteria will vary with the difficulty of the material. His criteria can be seen in Table 5–2.[7]

These criteria are based on oral reading at first sight. The criteria were determined by comparing IRI scores with scores on cloze tests. Word recognition errors in oral reading include insertions, omissions, mispronunciations, substitutions, unknown words, and transpositions. Other errors such as repetitions, disregarding punctuation, nonfluent reading, etc., should be noted and evaluated diagnostically but should not be used for determining word recognition scores for IRIs.[8]

TABLE 5–2. Informal Reading Inventory Scoring Criteria by Performance Grade Level

Performance Level	Word Recognition	Comprehension
Independent		
1–2	1/17	80 +
3–5	1/27 +	85 +
6 +	1/35 +	90 +
Instructional		
1–2	1/8–1/16	55–80
3–5	1/13–1/26	60–85
6 +	1/18–1/35	65–90
Frustration		
1–2	1/7–	55–
3–5	1/12–	60–
6 +	1/17–	65–

A student reading a second-grade book would be considered to be reading independently when making only one word recognition error per seventeen running words. A student reading from a fourth-grade book would be considered to be reading at the frustration level when making one or more word recognition errors for every twelve running words. Powell checked this criterion against a dependent criterion, on a test of comprehension at each level cited. Test results can be used in much the same manner as that suggested for commercially prepared informal inventories. A major advantage of teacher-made inventories centers around the ability to make the test cover a wider range of reading materials than do many commercially prepared tests. The larger sampling tends to produce more reliable results. However, two serious problems occur with their construction. The teacher may have difficulty selecting materials and asking questions that are accurate measures of the student's development and grading the materials accurately.

However, with some training, teachers can select materials and ask questions that are accurate measures of the student's development. Also, they are more capable of interpreting the results when they have developed the instrument themselves. However, without training and without a thorough knowledge of the skills of reading, many sloppy, inaccurate, relatively useless instruments have been developed. Also, publishers tend to pay little attention to the readability level of materials even if they place grade-level numbers on the books.[9] Even then the readability level is generally an average of the readability levels of the individual pages. Through readability checks on several basals, teachers become aware that a "fifth-grade" basal can range in readability level from second to eighth grade.[10] If the teacher uses these materials for an informal inventory and happens to select pages that are at the extremes of the ranges (second- and eighth-grade levels in the examples), the assessment of a student's reading ability will be inaccurate. For example, the *Autobiography of Malcolm X* was rated at readability levels of fifth, eighth, and tenth grade when the examiner used three different readability formulas.[11] Today, many teachers use microcomputer software packages to aid them in selecting graded passages for informal inventories (see chapter 12).

A problem exists with matching performance prior to instruction with any given material. In fact, mismatching probably occurs all too frequently. A student tendency to change reading ability with the material's content contributes to the mismatching. Books tend to be inaccurately matched with their grade level, particularly in the content areas. Informal inventories provide more useful information than standardized tests, even considering their limitations. With teacher-made inventories, mismatching is reduced since the student is tested from samples of the same material in which instruction will take place.

CLOZE TESTS. Closure testing may help circumvent the problem of mismatching and labeling. Cloze tests constructed from the same materials students are expected to use can provide useful information concerning the students' abilities to work with various types of printed materials. The procedure for closure testing is to select several passages of at least 150 words from the various books to be used and retype the selections, deleting every fifth word. All proper nouns as well as the entire first sentence should be left intact, as in the following example.

> Mary had a little lamb. Its fleece was white ＿＿ snow.
> Everywhere that Mary ＿＿ the lamb was sure ＿＿ go.

Then the student reads the selection, supplying the omitted words. Older students can write the words in; younger students can read the passage to you orally. A score is determined by counting the number of words actually used by the author as *correct* responses.

A score of 40 percent or higher indicates that the book should not be above the reader's level.[12] A score below 40 percent indicates that the book is probably too difficult. The student will need more help reading it or should be permitted to use easier material. The use of closure eliminates the necessity of matching a grade-level score with a book because the test derives from the same types of material that the student will be expected to read. Closure tests are easily constructed, scored, and interpreted. While they are not flawless, they may be the most useful type of testing instrument available to the classroom teacher for use prior to instruction.

A word of caution is necessary. Considerable research is being conducted with closure testing materials. Adjusted norms have been reported indicating possible differences from the 40-percent criterion mentioned. As one works with students of different ages and with materials from different content areas, adjusted norms can be expected. The teacher should watch for reports of such changes for the most useful application of closure in reading diagnosis.

Two problems arise when using cloze tests for reading diagnosis. First, the tests are usually very frustrating to students who are operating in reading material above their instructional level. If, after five or six deletions, the student has made serious mistakes concerning the meaning of the passage, then the reader is working with nonsense. Many give up—refusing to try any more items because they know that what they are doing does not make sense.

The second problem concerns grading a cloze test. The exact word of the author must be presented in order to be considered correct. Synonyms do not count, nor do creative entries. This scoring procedure is annoying to many teachers who must mark an entry as an error when they know that the student has obtained the meaning of the author. The following example illustrates this.

> Test item: The owner of the ＿＿ dog was Mike.
> Correct response: The owner of the *huge* dog was Mike.
> Incorrect student response: The owner of the *big* dog was Mike.

The student is not helped at all if, in the next sentence, the clue is "Mike's big dog likes ＿＿ ." Now the response "big" looks accurate. Nevertheless, the teacher must mark *big* incorrect if the 40-percent criteria is to be used.

MAZE TESTS. An adjustment to cloze tests called *maze tests*[13] has been made to overcome some of the objections raised to cloze testing. As in cloze tests, every fifth word is deleted. However, three alternatives are given. So, given the sentence, "The men were working at the oil well," a maze test would look like

at
"The men were working in the oil well."
big

Two of the three words are the same part of speech so that they would both be syntactically correct. The other is not acceptable syntactically and makes nonsense out of the sentence.

Maze tests require the students to obtain scores of 70 percent or better for the material to be appropriate for their instruction. Scores from 65 to 75 are an indication that teacher direction is necessary for successful comprehension of the material.

Some school faculties develop maze tests for all their basic texts. Assembled by a faculty, these tests can be constructed easily and placed in the school office for future use. New students can be given a few of these and placed with a high degree of accuracy. When other students are experiencing difficulty with working in a given book, a quick use of a maze test can provide data concerning the difficulty of that material for those students.

When a maze test seems to indicate that the material is above a student's instructional level, a new sample of material can be selected for the maze test.

CRITERION-REFERENCED TESTS (CRTs). Unlike standardized norm-referenced tests that compare students with one another, CRTs are designed to reveal any one student's ability to demonstrate a specific skill. However, the CRT's effectiveness in reading diagnosis is limited to whether the objective of the test is important and whether the test can measure the objective.

For each objective judged important, several test items are developed. The student's ability to respond to the test items in relation to that specific objective will become one indicator of the degree to which the student has learned the objective. It is easier to develop items for some objectives than others. For example, one can easily construct a test item to determine if a student can substitute the initial consonant *t* to make new words from *mop*, *sip*, and *sin*, but it is much more difficult to construct a test item to determine if a student can obtain the main idea from a complicated paragraph.

Numerous CRTs are finding their ways into classrooms. Table 5–3 shows Stallard's[14] report on some of the variables that need to be considered when choosing a CRT for classroom use. The wide range of objectives and items for sampling each objective and the variance in what is considered mastery make test selection and interpretation difficult. The tests are often justified as a management system for teachers; however, unless interpreted cautiously, they can lead to mismanagement, calling for the teaching of unimportant subskills and locking all students into the identical path to reading. The teacher should use only

TABLE 5–3. Characteristics of Fifteen Objective-Based Reading Programs. *(From Cathy Stallard, "Comparing Objective-Based Reading Programs. Journal of Reading, October 1977. Reprinted with permission of the International Reading Association.)*

	1	2 A/B	3	4
Rationale presented in book or booklet form			X	X
Grade levels included in program	K–Adult	K–6 / K–6	1–6	1–6
Categories of skills included in program				
Bilingual reading skills				
Comprehension skills	X	–/X	X	X
Creative reading skills		–/X		
Interpretive or critical reading skills		–/X		X
Oral reading skills				
Readiness skills	X	X/–	X	X
Secondary or content area skills	X	–/X	X	
Self-directed or independent reading skills				
Study skills		–/X	X	X
Vocabulary skills	X		X	X
Word attack skills	X	X/–	X	X
Total number of objectives in program	450	32/31	428	343
Percent of test items correct to demonstrate skill mastery	95%	100/ 84%	75– 100%	50– 80%
Average number of test items per skill	2–3	17/12	3	5
Average number of specific activities for teaching each skill		10+ / 20+		
Consultant services available		X/X	X	X
In-service training of teachers available	X	X[f]/X[f]	X	X[e]
Procedures for including teacher-made objectives in tests	X	[e]		
Purchaser selects desired objectives from catalog				

1. Criterion Reading	6. PRI	11. Wisconsin Design
2A. Croft Word Attack	7. Read-On	12. ORBIT
2B. Croft Comprehension	8. SCORE	13. PLAN
3. Fountain Valley	9. SOBAR	14. High Intensity
4. IPMS	10. ICRT	15. SARI
5. Performance Objectives		

TABLE 5-3 (continued)

5	6	7	8	9	10	11	12	13	14	15
X	X		X			X	X	X	X	
K–6	K–6.5	1–4	1–8	1–6	1–8	K–6	K–12	K–12	1–Adult	K–8
				X						
X	X	X	X	X	X	X	X	X	X	X
						X				
	X		X	X	X	X	X	X	X	
								X	X	X
	X	X	X					X	X	
X			X		X	(X)[b]	X	X	X	
						X		X	X	
			X	X	X	X	X	X	X	
X		X	X	X	X	X		X		X
X	X	X	X	X	X	X	X	X	X	X
312	172	60	800+	463	329	309	335	1100	475	95
	80%	90%	66.7 75,100%[d]	d	d	80%	75%	66–80%[d]	80%	90–100%
	3–4	15–20	3+	3	4	12–25	4	3–4	10	20
	8					14+		5+		2+
X	X[e]		X			Y	Y		)([e]	)(
X	X		X		X	X[f]	(X)[b]	X	X	X
			X						X	
X			X	X			X		X	

[a]Each number designates a particular program. [b]Being developed. [c]75% is "proficiency" level, 100% is "mastery" level; individual user chooses criterion level desired for the class. [d]Mastery level is established by individual user of program. [e]Available on request. [f]In-service programs are also designed to be training sessions for district personnel who intend to conduct in-service training for others in their district.

113

those parts of such tests that relate to what they think is important. This applies particularly to phonics subskills.

Teacher-constructed CRTs give the teacher the opportunity to develop large numbers of items to sample the students' behavior. Large sampling tends to increase the reliability of tests. When few items are included to measure a given type of behavior, CRTs have the same reliability problems as standardized tests (see chapter 3).

Diagnosis during and after Instruction

In classroom diagnosis, observation of the student's ability to respond to instruction is of prime importance. Through the direct observation of the student's responses, the teacher can avoid some of the time-consuming, costly, and sometimes questionable testing commonly linked to diagnosis. Also of prime importance is the continued assessment of the learning climate. That climate can change rapidly and without notice unless continuous assessment is made. Student self-assessment should also occur continuously. As students' attitudes and self-concepts as readers change, teachers should note the changes and adjust instruction according to those changes. Instead of the formal questionnaire, as was suggested in diagnosis before instruction, self-assessment can be informal and occur during and after instruction. A simple, "How well do you think you did on this activity?" can provide important information for the teacher. If the students think they did very well and the teacher assesses their performances poorly, then conferences should be held. During conferences it can be determined whether the students understood the assignment, the expectations, and the form of the final product.

Skills assessment during and after instruction depends heavily on the teacher's ability to observe various types of student behavior. Equal weight should be given to the student's performance on individual seat work and on teacher-made tests. Attention to task, enthusiasm, cooperative spirit, and efficient study habits can also be observed during instruction. At times, teachers are too busy to make accurate observations during instruction and must rely on the cooperation of others. Other teachers, the principal, the reading specialist, an aide, or a parent volunteer can be asked to help. If three or four students are experiencing difficulty, these students can be observed using a checklist for several minutes apiece. If an observation is made every fifteen seconds for five minutes, the teacher will have twenty pieces of data. Information from observations can be noted on a form such as in Figure 5–2.

Using this form, an entry for each activity is used to indicate whether the student is working with the teacher in a group, with the teacher individually, or independent from the teacher. Only two check marks are needed for each observation: (1) was the student on-task, off-task, or was it not possible to determine and (2) with what type of materials was the student supposed to be working? If the pattern in Figure 5–2 were to continue, it would tell the teacher that

Student's Name *Rebecca*　　　Date　5/14/89

a *independent*　b _____　c _____

	On task?			Working with		
Observation	Yes	No	?	Letters	Words	Sentences
1	✓					✓
2	✓					✓
3		✓		✓		
4		✓		✓		
5	✓				✓	
6	✓				✓	

FIGURE 5–2. Example of Systematic Observation Record Keeping

Rebecca goes off task when working independently with letter-type activities but is on task when working with sentences.

The teacher can now examine those letter exercises and see if they can be made more appealing; talk with Rebecca about her on-task and off-task behavior to see if she has any ideas about how to improve her concentration; or change to more sentence exercises so that Rebecca can benefit as much as possible from her school activities. Obviously, any behavior could be substituted for those shown; however, it is important to observe as few as possible at one time. Trying to observe too many types of behavior at one time can be confusing and produces unreliable results.

To assess reading behavior during and after instruction, the teacher will want to identify the context in which that behavior occurs. Is behavior during teacher-directed instruction the same as behavior while working independently or with an aide? Does a given student work better alone or with another student? When working alone, does the type of activity seem to generate different kinds of behavior? For example, some students may work quite well with the teacher, be completely inadequate when working at assigned work independently, and then work quite well again when working with a classmate. If the only sample of behavior were taken when working at assigned seat work, a distorted perception of the student's reading behavior would be obtained.

For the purpose of diagnosis, student behavior should be assessed in four reading situations.

1. Behavior while working with word recognition and word meaning activities
2. Behavior while reading orally
3. Behavior while reading silently
4. Behavior while responding to silent reading to demonstrate understanding of what has been read

The order of these activities does not indicate their importance. Usually the last one will be the most important source of data. Given a specific objective, however, any one of the four may be the most important in a given situation. For each activity, the teacher will try to obtain answers to the following questions:

- *What is the instructional level?* Teachers must determine at which level each student can respond most effectively to instruction; normally, it is a point at which the student makes errors but does not fail completely. Teachers have numerous opportunities to observe students reading different types of materials. They realize that students do not have one instructional level, but several. In social studies materials, a given student may read at levels considerably above materials read in other areas. As a student encounters materials that are obviously too hard, teachers must adjust instruction by either increasing assistance through word introduction and concept development prior to reading or by reducing the difficulty of the material by selecting different books.
- *Specifically, what types of skills do the readers possess? What are their reading strengths?* Diagnostically, the teacher looks for those skills that the students have apparently mastered. For example, if a student always attacks the initial portion of the word accurately, initial consonants may be listed as mastered. The teacher also notes observed patterns of errors. Thus, both strengths and needs are noted.
- *What classroom adjustment can be used to teach to the students' strengths? What adjustments can be made to assist students in areas of need?* By starting with adjustments that permit students to demonstrate strengths, success experiences can be developed. Awareness of adjustments that will help students in the areas of need will help teachers plan for continued student development.
- *Which activities seem to generate the most enthusiasm on the part of the student?* Teachers should note the expression of interest or enthusiasm for learning since all teachers need to know which types of activities motivate their students and which types seem to bore or frustrate them.

To answer each of these questions, teachers directly observe students in three reading situations: word recognition and word meaning exercises, oral reading, and silent reading. Reading situations differ from skill areas in that each situation requires the use of one or more of the skills for acceptable performance. Improvement in the skill areas usually results in improvement in reading situations when the diagnosis has been effective in establishing the instructional strengths and needs of students. Word recognition exercises provide teachers with information concerning the ability of a student to handle words in isolation. Since almost all reading activities require dealing with words in context, word recognition diagnosis is of little value. However, it does give the teacher some insight to the student's word knowledge. Word meaning exercises focus on the various meanings of words. Again, in isolation most word meanings are vague. What does *bank, ball, run, happy,* or *awkward* mean without a sentence of support? And service words such as *if, and, on,* and *when* carry meaning only as they relate to other words. Observation of students in oral reading provides teachers with the best insight into their overt reading behavior. It provides teachers with their only observation of the overt reading behavior of students when reading in context. Obviously, oral and silent reading require somewhat different behaviors. Oral and silent reading probably are more similar for beginning readers and become less similar as readers gain maturity. Silent reading provides teachers with the best situation to determine the comprehension performance of students. Observations in each situation provide important information for teachers to complete the picture of a student's reading performance. Teachers add these observations to any testing information that they may have and formulate diagnostic hypotheses that they will attempt to interpret into instructional adjustments.

WORD RECOGNITION AND WORD MEANING. Scores from word recognition and word meaning assessment activities can be used as a basis for selecting passages for initial oral and silent reading diagnosis. Some analysis of performance with words in isolation can be conducted. Teachers need to observe patterns of performance in the various reading situations in order to develop sound diagnostic hypotheses. Each observed behavior pattern should be followed by a statement of diagnosis that considers both strengths and weaknesses. Strengths generally indicate areas in which a student is making a positive effort; therefore, attitudes as well as skills are reflected. The following are examples of observed student behavior and possible assessment implications.

1. The student refuses to pronounce words even after a delay of up to five seconds.

   strengths: none known

   weaknesses: may not know the word; may lack word attack skills

2. The student hesitates but finally pronounces a word after a delay of two to five seconds.

   strength: may be using word attack skills or delayed recall of word form at sight

   weakness: may not be in sight vocabulary

3. The student partially pronounces the word but fails to pronounce entire word accurately (e g , *ta* for *table*).

   strength: uses graphic cues for the portion of word pronounced (in this case, initial consonant and vowel sound)

   weaknesses: may not be in sight vocabulary; may have difficulty in word attack with unpronounced portion of word (in this case, word ending)

4. The student substitutes one word for another while maintaining the basic word meaning (e.g., *kitten* for *cat*).

  strength: may have clue to word meaning through association

  weakness: may be disregarding graphic cues

5. The student can pronounce a word accurately but does not know its meaning.

  strength: uses graphic cues

  weaknesses: may need concept development; may have worked so hard to pronounce the word that attention to meaning was not possible

6. The student reverses letter order (e.g., *was* for *saw*, *expect* for *except*).

  strength: may be observing graphic cues

  weaknesses: may have directional confusion (orientation); may not be in sight vocabulary

Observations noted during word recognition activities should be verified in oral and silent reading activities.

ORAL READING. Teachers should observe oral reading to determine how students use graphic and semantic contextual cues in reading. Some signs of thoughtful oral reading are:

1. The student repeats words or phrases. Four types of repetitions should be considered.
   - Student successfully changes first response to match text.

     strengths: may be using context (semantic) clues; may be using graphic cues

     weaknesses: none known
   - Student attempts to correct but is unsuccessful.

     strength: may be aware of semantic cues

     weakness: may be unable to utilize graphic cues in semantic setting
   - Student simply repeats portion that was initially correct.

     strength: may be attempting to improve intonation

     weakness: may be biding for time to attack forthcoming segment of the passage
   - Student changes an initially correct response.

     strength: may be changing passage into a more familiar speech pattern

     weakness: may be biding for time to attack forthcoming segment of the passage or searching for meaning.

2. The student omits words. Two types of omissions should be considered.

- The omission distorts meaning.
  - *strengths:* none known
  - *weaknesses:* may not be reading for meaning; may not be in sight vocabulary
- Omission does not distort meaning.
  - *strength:* may be reading for meaning
  - *weaknesses:* may have too large an eye–voice span; may not be in sight vocabulary

Omissions occur infrequently and account for less than 7 percent of oral reading errors; 93 percent of the time they do not distort the meaning of the sentence.[15]

3. The student inserts words. Two types of insertions should be considered.

- The insertion distorts meaning.
  - *strengths:* none known
  - *weakness:* may not be using semantic cues
- The insertion does not distort meaning.
  - *strength:* may be embellishing the author's meaning
  - *weakness:* may have too large an eye–voice span

Insertions also occur infrequently and account for less than 6 percent of oral reading errors; 94 percent of the time they do not distort the meaning of the sentence.[16]

4. The student substitutes a word or nonword for the word in the passage. Substitutions account for more than 87 percent of oral reading errors.[17] When such a substitution occurs, it can be analyzed according to graphic, syntactic, and semantic information.[18] Such an analysis considers qualitative as well as quantitative considerations. The qualitative aspects rest heavily with the student's reaction to the passage in a meaningful context.

Example: Student reads: "the big title was"
Text was: "the big table was"
Graphic: initial—accurate
medial—error
final—accurate
Syntactic: accurate, a noun for a noun
Semantic: error, major change in meaning

Example: Student reads: "boy hurried down"
Text was: "boy hustled down"
Graphic: initial—accurate
medial—variance
final—accurate
Syntactic: accurate, a verb for a verb
Semantic: not accurate but acceptable

These three types of oral reading behavior need to be considered in terms of how they relate to one another. Individually the strengths and weaknesses include the following:

- Student fails to use graphic cues.

    strengths: uses graphic cues for portions of words accurately pronounced; may be using syntactic and semantic cues

    weaknesses: may fail to use all graphic cues available; may not be in sight vocabulary

- Student fails to use syntactic cues.

    strength: may be using graphic cues

    weaknesses: may fail to use syntactic cues in the language; may not be in sight vocabulary

- Student fails to use semantic cues.

    strength: may be using graphic and syntactic cues

    weaknesses: may not be in sight vocabulary; may be concentrating on pronunciation instead of meaning; may not be familiar with concepts

5. The student fails to observe punctuation.

    strengths: none known

    weaknesses: decoding may be so difficult that punctuation is ignored; may be unaware of the function of punctuation

6. The student observes all punctuation via pauses and inflection.

    strengths: using semantic cues; knows cues implied by punctuation

    weaknesses: none known

7. The student loses place during oral reading.

    strengths: none known

    weaknesses: may have directional confusion; may be reading meaninglessly; may have visual problem; may be overconcentrating on decoding

8. The student reads word-by-word (all words pronounced accurately, but slowly, with pauses between them and without much expression).

    strength: may be using graphic cues

    weaknesses: may not be using semantic cues; may have insufficient sight vocabulary

9. The student exhibits difficulty when asked questions, although he or she accurately pronounces all words.

    strength: may be using graphic cues

    weaknesses: decoding may be so consuming that comprehension does not occur; may have inadequate conceptual development; may have poor verbal memory

Reading assessment does not normally include oral reading comprehension as an important skill, especially when the reader is reading orally without reading silently first. Teachers should ask questions after oral reading to help the readers know that all reading should be purposeful. Comprehension errors of passages read orally should always be confirmed in silent-reading situations.

Symptoms observed during oral reading should be based on materials that the student can read at 90 to 95 percent accuracy. All symptoms observed during attempts to read frustrating material are invalid because the difficulty of the material creates unnatural error patterns.

SILENT READING. Assessment of silent-reading tasks can be made during the silent reading itself and in comprehension activities that follow silent reading. Comprehension assessment is difficult but very important. If all other reading skills are functioning well but the readers are not obtaining meaning, then they are not reading. On the other hand, if other reading skills are incomplete but the readers are obtaining meaning, then they are functioning as readers. During silent reading, teachers can observe several instances of overt behavior that may aid in the total diagnosis:

1. The student moves lips and makes subvocalized sound during silent reading.
   - *strength:* appears to be working on graphic cues
   - *weaknesses:* may be overworking decoding; may be trying to remember what is read; may be a habit carried over from excessive oral reading
2. The student points to words with fingers.
   - *strength:* may be using touch to keep place or to emphasize words
   - *weaknesses:* orientation skills may need touch support; may be having decoding difficulties
3. The student shows physical signs of reading discomfort (e.g., rubbing of eyes, extreme restlessness, constant adjustment of book).
   - *strength:* may be persevering with task
   - *weaknesses:* possible difficulty of material; possible physical deficiencies (vision, nutrition, etc.); possible emotional reaction to frustration

The important diagnostic aspect of silent reading is, of course, the ability of the student to demonstrate an understanding of the author's message. Five important considerations must be noted.

1. What types of questions are to be asked: literal questions that call for facts and details; interpretive questions that call for paraphrasing and drawing inferences; or problem-solving questions that call for critical and creative responses and evaluative thinking?

The student's ability to demonstrate an understanding of the author's message is important in diagnosis of silent reading problems.

2. What situation is the student facing when answering questions? A recall situation calls for the reading material to be unavailable during questioning. A locate situation encourages the student to find the answer in the reading material. Locating opportunities appear to have a great effect on a student's ability to respond to questions at all levels.
3. Was the student aware of the purposes for silent reading?
4. How much exposure has the student had to the reading material? Are the responses expected after a single reading or after study and reexamination of the material? Different performances may obviously be expected depending on the amount of exposure to the material.
5. How much time has elapsed between the reading of the material and the student's response to it?

The following procedure is suggested for silent-reading comprehension diagnosis.

1. Have the students read the story for a set purpose. At times the purpose is set by the teacher and at other times it is set by the students.
2. After the students have finished reading, give them a few minutes to think about what they have read and then ask them to retell as much of the story as they can. From this the teacher can assess the personal meaning that various students were able to derive from the story.
3. Start questioning in a recall situation and with interpretive questions. Davey found that students answer literal questions more

accurately when questioning starts with interpretive questions than they do when questions start with literal questions.[19] Then ask literal and problem-solving questions.

4. Permit students to return to the passage and locate the answers to questions missed in a recall situation.

Steps 3 and 4 give teachers six comprehension scores from questioning. Using the number or percent of accurate responses, these scores can be charted, as in Figure 5–3.

The following behaviors may be observed during the question-reaction period of a silent-reading lesson.

1. The student can decode the material but cannot respond to literal questions in a recall situation.

    strength: may be using graphic, semantic, and syntactic cues

    weaknesses: may have poor (visual) memory; may need concept development related to material read; may be overconcentrating on graphic cues

2. The student can decode the material and can respond to literal questions in a locate situation.

    strengths: may be using graphic, semantic, and syntactic cues; may be able to locate literally stated ideas

    weaknesses: none known

3. The student can respond to literal understanding questions but cannot interpret those ideas into own words.

    strengths: may be using graphic, semantic, and syntactic cues; uses literal understanding

    weaknesses: possible overconcentration on graphic cues; possible load difficulty; possible failure to reflect on the author's ideas

Student: *Sarah*	Grade: *7*	
	Reading situation	
Type of response	**Recall**	**Locate**
Interpretive	*60%*	*80%*
Literal	*50%*	*100%*
Problem solving	*70%*	*80%*

FIGURE 5–3. Example of Comprehension Record Keeping Form for Diagnostic Use

4. The student can respond literally and can interpret the author's ideas but cannot apply ideas to problem-solving situations.

    strengths: may be using graphic, syntactic, and semantic cues; uses literal understanding; uses interpretation

    weaknesses: may lack problem-solving skills; possible misunderstanding of the problem

5. The student can retell the story accurately but cannot answer teacher-made questions related to it.

    strengths: shows literal understanding; uses sequence skills

    weakness: may have inability to anticipate teacher questions

6. The student can answer teacher-made questions when allowed to study and reexamine passage but not after a single reading.

    strength: gains meaning when allotted sufficient time

    weakness: may need repeated exposure for comprehension

7. The student can answer teacher-made questions immediately after reading but is unable to do so a day or so later.

    strength: may have short-term memory

    weakness: may not have adequate long-term memory

8. The student can answer questions covering short passages but is unable to do so on longer passages.

    strength: may have short-term memory

    weaknesses: may have inadequate long-term memory; may lack organizational skills

Teachers should collect observational data relating to comprehension over a period of time. A given comprehension failure might be as attributable to story content, reader interest, or reader motivation on a given day as it is to reading ability. Once a consistent pattern is observed, teachers can make diagnostic hypotheses and start to make needed instructional adjustments in the reading program.

Three Cautions

Teachers must be cautioned of three aspects in observing reading behavior. First, observation of reading behavior is a learned skill. Teachers must consistently practice, habitually keep careful records, and double- and triple-check findings. Obviously one repetition in an oral reading situation cannot determine a diagnostic hypothesis. Also, classroom observations may lead to a dangerously fractionalized view of the reader. Every reader is more than the sum of skills listed on the preceding pages. The classroom teacher needs to pull back periodically during diagnosis and observe the whole reader. Such observations may reveal that the reader is always on-task, enjoying the reading activities, helping others, and happy. Perhaps such observations are more important than a listing of skill strengths and weaknesses. At least they should be recorded as equally important information.

Second, many readers do very poorly during the initial efforts to respond in a diagnostic setting. They are attempting to determine what is expected of them and may be quite nervous since they do not know what is going to happen next. For this reason, students should be allowed to respond to a practice passage of relatively easy material. In this case, student performance on the first passage read orally would not be counted in the assessment. Similarly, the student response to the first silent-reading passage would not be counted. Our interest is in determining how well these students can read, so we want to provide the best assessment situation possible.

Third, in comprehension assessment the reader's prior knowledge of the content of the passages being read is going to have an effect on how well that story is comprehended. It is possible to be fooled completely about a reader's comprehension skills or lack of them. For example, most adults have considerable knowledge about the events surrounding the assassination of President John F. Kennedy and would feel very comfortable reading a passage or two about the day of his assassination in Dallas. If, however, the passages to be read were about the Battle of Hastings, most of these adults would be a bit uncomfortable because they cannot bring much prior knowledge to that event in history. If comprehension were to be assessed using one of these two events in history, undoubtedly most would choose the passages about President Kennedy's assassination. Therefore, in classroom assessment of reading comprehension it will prove helpful to assess comprehension over a period of time using a variety of passages.

From word recognition, oral reading, and silent-reading data, teachers should seek answers to questions in the following skill areas:

Questions to Pinpoint Diagnostic Findings

PREREADING-READINESS SKILLS. If answers to questions in this area are *yes*, remedial suggestions can be found in chapter 8.

1. Do language skills appear to be underdeveloped?
2. Do speech skills appear to be underdeveloped?
3. Does dialect usage appear to cause difficulty?
4. Do visual or auditory problems appear to be causing discomfort?
5. Do visual discrimination skills appear to be underdeveloped?
6. Do auditory discrimination skills appear to be underdeveloped?
7. Do reversals occur frequently enough to cause confusion?
8. Does student frequently lose place during reading?

SIGHT VOCABULARY. If answers to questions in this area are *yes*, remedial suggestions can be found in chapter 9.

1. Does student misread small, similar words?
2. Do words missed represent abstract concepts?
3. Do word meanings appear to be confused?
4. Does student know words in context but not in isolation?
5. Does student appear to know words at end of a lesson, but not the next day?

WORD ATTACK. If answers to questions in this area are *yes*, remedial suggestions can be found in chapter 9.

Phonics

1. Does student use graphic cues? Which graphic cues are used?
2. Does student attack small words accurately but not larger ones?
3. Does student seem to know sound-symbol relationships but seem unable to use them during reading?

Structural

1. Do words missed contain prefixes or suffixes?
2. Are words missed compound words?

Contextual

1. Does student appear to ignore syntactic cues?
2. Does student appear to ignore semantic cues?
3. Does student appear to ignore punctuation cues?

COMPREHENSION. If answers to questions in this area are *yes*, remedial suggestions can be found in chapter 10.

1. Do large units of material seem to interfere with comprehension?
2. Do comprehension difficulties occur with some types of comprehension and not others? (Literal comprehension is weak but interpretive is strong.)
3. Does student respond when given opportunities to retell stories from a personal point of view?
4. Does student have difficulty using locating skills?
5. Does student have difficulty understanding material read in content areas?
6. Does student reorganize what has been read so that it makes sense from a personal point of view?
7. Does student fail to comprehend most of what has been read?

Teacher observations and teacher-made tests are curriculum based. Deno refers to them as curriculum-based measures (CBM).[20] They are, without a doubt, the most relied-upon assessment techniques used by classroom teachers, and they might well be the most valid. They let teachers determine whether the students can comprehend the science book they are using. If they can, it doesn't really matter what the test data indicate. Teachers use CBM every day to evaluate student progress during and after instruction. CBM can also be used prior to instruction to determine what students already know about the content to be studied. By using CBM prior to instruction, teachers can determine how to focus on strengths or needs. The repeated use of CBM adds to its attractiveness because there can be multiple data collection points, which adds respectability to the assessment data collected. For example, if a student scored between 90 and 100 percent on teacher-made tests over a period of three months, the teacher can safely assume high performance. Nave found teacher judgments about student performance in materials used for instruction to be at least as valid as test scores.[21]

By using CBM, teachers can avoid the problem of matching a test score with a given text. For example, if a student earned a grade equivalent of 4.3 on a standardized test, can the teacher assume that the same student can read a fourth-grade textbook in social studies? But that would be an inaccurate assumption (see chapter 3).

One problem with CBM is reliability. Have the CBM tests been carefully developed? Do the teachers know how to interpret the CBM test results or the CBM observations? The use of CBM over many data collection points tends to reduce this limitation. And the matter of validity reappears. Even though these CBM assessments are developed from the materials used for instruction, do they really measure comprehension of the important concepts in the material, or do they evaluate the understanding of details, important or not? Again, it becomes a matter of using several measures to assure accurate diagnosis in the classroom.

An evaluation of student interests, habits, and attitudes is an important part of classroom diagnosis. Teachers, through regular observation of student performances, are in the ideal setting to note changes in interests, habits, and attitudes. Effort should be made to note effective and ineffective habits that seem to vary considerably from those of the average student. The reading specialist will likely ask the classroom teacher for information concerning interest, habits, and attitudes; therefore, observations should be noted carefully. Specifically, classroom teachers should obtain answers to the following questions:

**Interests,
Habits, and
Attitudes**

1. What uses do students make of free reading opportunities? Do they appear eager to use free time for reading, or is reading only the result of constant prodding?
2. Do students appear anxious or reluctant to read orally? Silently? Does there appear to be a difference in attitude between oral and silent-reading situations?

3. Are signs of reluctance noticeable in reading situations only or in all learning situations? If difficulty occurs only in reading then it may be the act of reading that is causing the reluctance. If reluctance is observed in all learning situations, then an analysis of the learning environment is needed.

4. In what reading situations are students most or least effective? Do students tend to enjoy providing answers orally as opposed to writing them? Do questions that call for summaries get better results than specific questions? Students often develop habits as a result of what has been expected by other teachers.

5. Do students have to be prodded to finish reading assignments? If they cannot work without supervision even when specific assignments have been made, unsupervised reading situations should be avoided in initial remedial instruction.

6. What types of book selections do the students make in the library? Considerable information can be obtained about interests by noticing the types of books chosen from the library. Remedial efforts should start with the type of material in which students have indicated an interest.

Answers to these questions will become important guides to the initial remedial sessions. Teachers will find it useful to record these findings so that they will have a record of accurate data. Although these questions will be answered mostly by informal observation, teachers should give them special attention and become active agents in collecting information.

At times, it is not possible to obtain precise *yes* or *no* answers to such questions. In these cases, teachers should continue to observe the readers until they can substantiate accurate error patterns. Specifically, teachers may provide students with individualized exercises to do independently, go over their responses, and have a short conference about their responses. As a part of informal, on-the-spot diagnosis, this technique can be useful in verifying classroom diagnosis. Suppose, for example, that one has diagnosed irregular patterns of difficulty with final consonant sounds. Several carefully prepared exercises with final consonant sounds can be developed, administered, and analyzed for the purpose of verification. Further verification can come from information available in school records, parental interviews, past observations, classroom diagnostic tests, and subsequent instruction.

Pencil-and-paper interest surveys can be used to obtain information about areas that motivate students. However, interests change rapidly, making the results of a survey inappropriate several weeks from the time it was administered. Sample questions for an interest survey might include:

1. What things do you like to do when you get home from school?
2. If you could wish for three things for your future, what would they be?
3. Name three of your favorite television shows.

4. Do you enjoy participating in sports? If so, which sports?
5. Do you have any hobbies? If so, what are they?

Such questions tend to provide the teacher with natural areas of interests. Books and articles about these areas can now be read in the classroom by these students. Lessons can be planned to feature activities related to the interests of the students.

Classroom diagnosis effectiveness will rest to a large extent upon the records teachers keep. The type of records will vary with the purpose of the diagnostic activities. Figure 5–4 shows an example of group record keeping. An entire class can be monitored by this type of record using no more than two sheets of $8\frac{1}{2}$ " $\times$ 11 " paper. Another type of group record can be used to monitor student progress over time. The teacher can determine what data are available and periodically assess student behavior in those areas.

Students in this record were placed according to the Botel Word Opposites (Reading) Test. The teacher periodically asks individual students to read orally a 100-word passage. Their oral reading accuracy is sampled in this manner. Note that in Figure 5–4 Ron appears to be having considerable difficulty with his accuracy in the 3^1 reader. Then, over time, the teacher jots down impressions received about each student's responses during comprehension lessons. Ron again seems to be doing poorly. Having obtained this type of information, the teacher may consider placing Ron in material that he can handle with better comprehension and better oral reading accuracy. Using this type of record and updating the data several times during the year will assist in keeping students in appropriate materials for instruction.

Another type of record keeping involves a detailed account of the reading skill development of individual students. Such records are time consuming to develop and probably would be maintained only on the students about whom a teacher is most concerned. These records would include test scores and data from teacher observations and would be collected periodically. Figure 5–5 can be adapted for individual record keeping.

Records can also be kept on an informal basis. Using a 5" $\times$ 8" index card for each student, the teacher can jot down important behavior noted dur-

Name	Botel WO	Oral Reading Accuracy	Comprehension	Placement Reader Level
Pat	3^2	97%	Good	3^2
JoEllen	4	99%	Fair	3^1
Ron	3^1	95%	Poor	3^1
Maria	3^1	90%	Good	4^1

FIGURE 5–4. Example of Group Record Keeping

Name _Klyde Martin_ Age _12_ Teacher _D. Keller_
Grade _6_ Date record initiated _October 1988_

	Date _Oct. '88_ Scored	Date _May '89_ Scored
Scores:		
Word Recognition	3.5	4.5
Oral Reading Accuracy	4.0	5.5
Silent Reading		
Recall Comp.	4.5	6.0
Locate Comp.	6.0	7.0
Strengths:		
Word Recognition		
Oral Reading Behavior		_greatly improved_
Silent Reading Comprehension	_comprehension using location skills_	
Weaknesses:		
Word Recognition	_pronounced words in isolation_	_improved_
Oral Reading Behavior		
Silent Reading Comprehension		_improved_
Interests and Attitudes		_He is interested in music, art, and the outdoors. He plays center for the school basketball team._
Comments:		_He is sensitive about his inability to read well and is embarrassed when talking about it. Interest in art could be springboard to reading activity._

FIGURE 5–5. Example of Individual Record Keeping Form

9/12	Administered Botel Word Opposites Test—Jim scored at 3^2 level.
9/15	Jim comprehended well in the 3^2 material.
10/3	Jim appears to have trouble completing assignments in his social studies book. I'll try to introduce new concepts.
10/7	After introduction of new concepts, Jim comprehended material in his social studies book well.

FIGURE 5-6. Example of Informal Record Keeping

ing any lesson. Dates and behavior observed serve as a suitable record of student progress. Figure 5–6 shows the types of entries that may be recorded.

As the teacher makes decisions about record keeping formats, care should be taken to assure that the records do not create unreasonable demands. Careful records should be maintained on a few important types of behavior instead of inaccurate records on many types.

Teachers should reflect on the answers to the following four questions to complete an effective classroom diagnosis and to assist them in establishing more clearly the validity of their findings.

1. Did the students make the same error in both easy and difficult material, or did the observed errors indicate frustration with the material? Teachers are most interested in the errors made at the instructional level, the level at which they hope to make improvement. All readers make errors when reading at their frustration level; these errors, however, normally do not lead to diagnostic conclusions, for these are not the errors upon which remediation is based.

2. Were the errors first interpreted as slowness actually an effort on the part of the reader to be especially careful and precise and to be reflective? Beware of diagnostic conclusions drawn from the students' responses to questions, especially when timed standardized tests are used or when testing situations make the reader aware of being evaluated. Many students have been taught to be impulsive with their responses when, in fact, reflective behavior may be considerably more desirable.

3. Can students be helped as a result of classroom diagnosis, or is further diagnosis necessary? Further testing with any of the instruments mentioned under clinical diagnosis is appropriate when the teacher has the knowledge of their proper use and interpretation and has the time to use them. At this point, however, the services of a reading specialist may be required.

4. Did the students appear to concentrate while being directly observed, or did they seem easily distracted? Children who appear to be distracted during observation may have produced unreliable symptoms.

The diagnostic task consists of observing individuals through analysis of symptoms and associating the symptoms to appropriate skill areas. Then, the significance of the errors must be determined and that information organized in terms of practical classroom adjustments. Under only a few circumstances will diagnosis be concluded at this point. An ongoing process, diagnosis will normally continue during the remedial sessions, always attempting to obtain more precise information concerning the readers. Morris believes that this is the important advantage for the classroom teacher. He states, "To the teacher . . . the challenge is to get to grips more directly with the problem and by working with the individual pupil try to understand what is leading him astray."[22] We would add that an additional challenge would be to determine more precisely the skills, strengths, and deficiencies of the student.

Early Identification

Teachers are capable of making early identifications of children who are likely to experience difficulty in school. In Maryland, a multidisciplinary task force worked two years to develop assessment instruments to identify children with potential learning handicaps.[23] They found the best device for such identification to be systematic teacher observations. At the University of Maryland reading clinic, we found a similar result when asking teachers to identify potential reading problems. They identified them more accurately than did the tests that we administered. In some schools, early identification occurs in kindergarten. When accompanied by specific symptoms, such identification assists teachers in modifying educational programs to increase the possibilities of success. Some children might best start with a phonics-based program; others might profit from one that stresses sight learning. Some succeed best when the initial program uses the language-experience approach, and others need multisensory techniques. Such programs have the potential to assist students' successful start in school and avoid several years of failure.

Several problems are related to early identification programs. First, if they stop with identification, thus only labeling a student, they may do more harm than good. Second, when tests are relied upon heavily, many students become erroneously identified and others are not identified when they should be. Third, providing teachers with checklists of behavior that may cause learning problems may result in self-fulfilling prophecies. For example, if a teacher is told that children in first grade who make reversals may have serious reading problems, teachers might react to children so identified in such ways that create nonlearning. Finally, parents can be aroused to such a state of anxiety as to alarm the child.

If early identification programs are implemented, several safeguards should be applied to avoid these problems. Early identification should never be made using a single testing instrument. Children who have been initially identified should be reevaluated periodically. Early identification programs should be accompanied by instructional adjustments. Parents should be informed of the program and the advantages it offers their children. All early identification programs should be carefully monitored and periodically evaluated to be certain they are effective.

Summary

Classroom diagnostic assessment involves the observation and testing of student behavior. It also involves the assessment of the learning climate. Classroom diagnostic assessment can take place before, during, or after instruction. Teachers are encouraged to diagnose for strengths as well as for needs. Evaluation of student self-appraisal is a recommended tactic for classroom diagnosis.

Teachers should develop some type of record keeping to reflect classroom diagnosis. These records are used to assess skill development, to aid in communication with other teachers and parents, and to evaluate the success of instructional adjustments.

Notes

1. Thomas A. Rakes, Joyce S. Choate, and Gayle Lane Waller, *Individual Evaluation Procedures in Reading* (Englewood Cliffs, N.J.: Prentice-Hall, 1983).
2. William R. Powell, "The Validity of the Instructional Reading Level," *Diagnostic Viewpoints in Reading* (1971): 121–33.
3. William K. Durr, ed., *Reading Difficulties* (Newark, Del.: IRA, 1970), 67–132.
4. Emmett A. Betts, *Foundations of Reading Instruction* (New York: American Book Co., 1946).
5. William R. Powell, "Revised Criteria for the Informal Reading Inventory" (Speech presented at International Reading Association, New Orleans, La., 3 May 1974).
6. Ibid., 11.
7. William R. Powell, "Measuring Reading Informally" (Paper presented at International Reading Association, Houston, Tex., 1978), 9.
8. Ibid., 9.
9. Robert E. Mills and Jean R. Richardson, "What Do Publishers Mean by Grade Level?" *The Reading Teacher* 16, no. 5 (March 1963): 359–62.
10. Lowell D. Eberwein, "The Variability of Basal Reader Textbooks and How Much Teachers Know About It," *Reading World* 18, no. 3 (1979): 259–72.
11. Mae C. Johnson, "Comparison of Readability Formulas" (Ph.D. diss., University of Maryland Reading Center, College Park, Md., 1971).
12. Earl F. Rankin and Joseph W. Culhane, "Comparable Cloze and Multiple Choice Comprehension Test Scores," *Journal of Reading* 13 (December 1969): 194.
13. John T. Guthrie et al., "The Maze Technique to Assess, Monitor Reading Comprehension," *The Reading Teacher* 28, no. 2 (November 1974): 161–68.
14. Cathy Stallard, "Comparing Objective-Based Reading Programs," *Journal of Reading* 21, no. 5 (October 1977): 36–44.
15. Karen D'Angelo and Robert M. Wilson, "How Helpful Is Insertion and Omission Analysis?" *The Reading Teacher* 32, no. 5 (February 1979): 519–20.
16. Ibid.
17. Ibid.
18. Kenneth S. Goodman, "Analysis of Oral Reading Miscues: Applied Psycholinguistics," *Reading Research Quarterly* 5 (Fall 1969): 9–30.

19. H. Beth Davey, "The Effect of Question Order on Comprehension Test Performance at the Literal and Interpretive Levels" (Faculty research paper, University of Maryland, Reading Center, College Park, Md., 1975).

20. Stanley L. Deno, "Curriculum-Based Measurement: The Emerging Alternative," *Exceptional Children* 52, no. 3 (1985): 219–32.

21. Dorothy Nave, *Teacher Judgement As a Primary Measure of Reading Performance* (Ph.D. diss., University of Maryland, College Park, Md., 1982).

22. Ronald Morris, *Success and Failure in Learning to Read* (London: Oldbourne, 1963), 159.

23. *Reading in Maryland* (Baltimore: Division of Instruction, Maryland State Department of Education, 1974–75).

Suggested Readings

Cunningham, Patricia Marr, Sharon V. Arthur, and James W. Cunningham. *Classroom Reading Instruction*. Lexington, Mass., D. C. Heath, 1977. This text provides numerous examples of classroom diagnosis through the use of teacher observation of student behavior during instruction.

Deboer, Dorothy L., ed. *Reading Diagnosis and Evaluation*. Newark, Del.: International Reading Association, 1970. This IRA collection features early identification, use of testing, and formal approaches, emphasizing the diagnostic aspects of reading.

Durr, William K., ed. *Reading Difficulties*. Newark, Del.: International Reading Association, 1970. The second section, "The Informal Inventories," includes six articles by different authors on the various aspects of informal inventories. Readers who are unfamiliar with informal techniques will want to study this section.

Farr, Roger, and Robert F. Carey. *Reading: What Can Be Measured?* 2d ed. Newark, Del.: International Reading Association, 1986. This is an excellent paperback that looks at the value and limitations of the various measuring instruments used in reading. A valuable resource for teachers.

Geyer, James R., and Jane Matanzo. *Programmed Reading Diagnosis for Teachers: With Prescriptive References*. Columbus, Ohio: Merrill, 1977. For those who want practice coding and analyzing reading behavior, this book may be interesting. Aside from specific practice exercises, case studies are included for prescription writing. Suggested answers are provided throughout.

Goodman, Kenneth S. "Analysis of Oral Reading Miscues: Applied Psycholinguistics." *Reading Research Quarterly* 5 (Fall 1969). Pp. 9–30. Goodman states his case for oral reading analysis in this article. This view of the reader as a processor of language cues is important for those who wish to become skilled diagnostic teachers.

Johns, Jerry L. et al., *Assessing Reading Behavior*. Newark, Del.: International Reading Association, 1977. This monograph is an annotated bibliography on the topic of informal reading inventories and will provide the reader with a useful reference to many of the issues involved in the use and interpretation of them.

Stallard, Cathy. "Comparing Objective-Based Reading Programs." *Journal of Reading* 21, no. 1 (October 1977). Pp. 36–44. Stallard discusses criterion-referenced testing programs and instructional programs. The coverage is useful for those considering a commercial program for their students.

EDITORIAL

Marian E. Baker

is a multigrade teacher in the Chesapeake Conference of Seventh-day Adventists, Baltimore, Maryland.

The second grading period was just beginning. All sixteen students in my one-room multigrade school were progressing successfully on their individualized study programs. I had taught most of the children before and was looking forward to a good school year. As I was preparing to leave the school, the office telephone rang. The mother introduced herself and asked if I remembered her; I did. She began to cry and asked if her son could be accepted into our school program. I remembered the chubby, freckle-faced child. His sister had been in my classroom six years before. Stanley was now ten and in the fourth grade, but he could not read, the mother reported. His sister, I recalled, had also had reading difficulty. The following day Stanley and his parents arrived for an interview. On the next Monday he walked shyly through the classroom door and proudly told me he had come to learn to read.

Stanley was a rugged, athletic ten-year-old. He was curious about virtually everything and socially well adjusted. His math skills were average for his grade level, as was his general knowledge and problem-solving ability. His participation in class discussion and activities was commendable. Still, he could not read.

During the initial interview with Stanley and his parents, I had learned that Stanley had previously attended three different schools and had repeated second grade. Halfway through third grade he had been placed in a remedial classroom. His mother felt that his needs had not been met, and that he had not been challenged. Stanley's previous school records were requested but would not arrive until April.

To facilitate Stanley's academic progress, he was teamed with other students for the reading of content area subjects. I soon observed that Stanley drew pictures and diagrams of nearly everything he studied. He handled and touched manipulative aides and teaching materials much more than the other students. I also noticed that when Stanley was unable to do these things, he did not retain concepts and information well.

Informal reading surveys revealed that Stanley could identify at sight all upper- and lower-case letters. He could write the alphabet from memory and write any letter he was asked to write. He could identify only a few initial consonant sounds, only occasionally identify consonant sounds in medial or final positions, and could identify no vowel sounds. Stanley was able to identify familiar names and common survival words.

Using the information that had been gathered from interviews with the parents and the student, from observations made in the classroom and on the playground, and from the informal reading surveys, an instructional plan was created that would emphasize Stanley's strengths and interests.

Stanley began to make steady progress in his efforts to learn to read. As he recognized his own success, his progress became even more rapid. Together, he and I periodically reassessed the reading plan. By the time his records arrived in April, Stanley was reading well into second-grade level.

My experience with Stanley made me wonder how many other students sit in our classrooms never realizing their desire to learn to read because care is not taken to discover their strengths and learning styles. The use of careful diagnosis and observation made it possible to develop an appropriate reading program for Stanley—a program that enabled him to be a successful reader.

Marian E. Baker

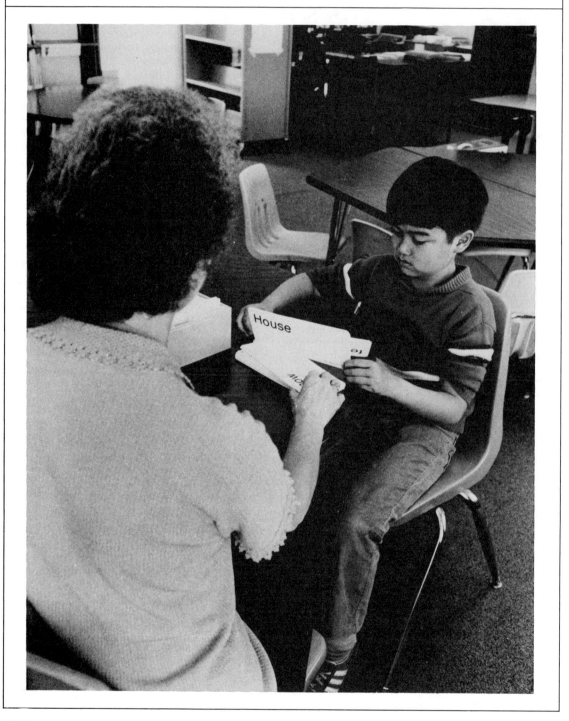

Clinical Diagnosis

CHAPTER OUTLINE

Referral
Initial Screening
The Interview
Extended Diagnosis
Case Reporting

CHAPTER EMPHASES

Clinical diagnosis is individual.
Clinical diagnosis is systematic.
Clinical diagnosis is not problem free.
*Clinical diagnosis involves varying
    levels of assessment.*
*Clinical diagnosis relies on behavior
    patterns.*
*Clinical diagnosis relies on diagnostic
    lessons.*
*Clinical diagnosis relies on data
    interpretation.*
*Clinical diagnosis relies on record
    keeping.*

Clinical diagnosis is conducted by a reading specialist using a variety of assessment techniques to collect the data needed to plan instruction or make recommendations for instruction. In clinical diagnosis, the student is usually evaluated outside the classroom. This involves taking the student to a testing area in the building or to a testing facility out of the building.

Clinical diagnosis features an individual evaluation of the reader and the reading situation and is required when the best efforts at the classroom level have not resulted in helping the student become a successful reader. Its purposes are the same as those of classroom diagnosis, as are the questions that are asked. When all or portions of the classroom diagnosis are not effective, the classroom teacher makes a referral request. However, sometimes parents, resource people, or teachers may make the referral. Occasionally a student will make a self-referral, asking for specific help in some aspect of reading.

The major advantages of clinical diagnosis are:

1. It is individual in nature.
2. It is conducted by specially trained professionals.
3. It uses the best assessment instruments available.
4. It releases the classroom teacher to perform other responsibilities.
5. It uses a variety of professional resources.
6. It uses data from a variety of sources.

These advantages may make clinical diagnosis sound superior to and more desirable than classroom diagnosis, and sometimes it is. But clinical diagnosis is complicated with severe limitations, such as:

1. Evaluating a reader in an individual setting does not necessarily provide information about that reader's behavior in a group setting.
2. Matching clinical data with instructional procedures and materials is an error-ridden procedure.
3. Conflicting clinical data can lead to confusion instead of enlightenment.
4. Clinical diagnosis tends to focus on the deficiencies of the reader while overlooking deficiencies in the learning climate.

This chapter will offer suggestions of ways to overcome, or at least minimize, these limitations. Clinical cases lead to the belief that clinical diagnosis should be continuous. That is, once the initial assessment recommendations are made, the reader's progress should be continuously monitored to assure a successful outcome. Most readers who receive adjusted instruction recommended by a clinical assessment make spectacular progress; however some do not. And some of these do not respond even after continued instruction adjustments and continued assessment. In other words, all of the questions as to why students fail in learning to read have not yet been answered. Some of the difficulties seem to be caused by subtle, untestable problems in the learning climate or within the reader.

Development of an "I-can't" attitude is one of the most severe problems within the reader experiencing difficulties. The likelihood that remediation will prove ineffective due to a reader's low self-esteem increases when he or she has a severe failure syndrome; has seldom or never experienced success in reading; and has been in this situation for three or more years. The reading specialist should approach clinical assessment with these thoughts in mind. The following suggestions for clinical diagnosis can be adapted to each unique situation.

Referral

Various systems are used to refer students to reading specialists. These systems not only refer the readers, but also serve as starting points for collecting data to be used in clinical diagnosis.

In the school setting, a screening committee might be the referral agency. That committee gathers all available information concerning the referred readers and forwards that data with the referral. When referrals are made outside the school (to a college reading clinic, for example) the receiving agency usually asks for data from the referring agency. The referral form shown in Figure 6–1 is used when parents refer their children to the University of Maryland reading clinic. It provides important preassessment data and often prevents serious mistakes in assessment activities. For example, by using the information on the form in Figure 6–1, the specialist knew in advance that this child had been retained in second grade. That information could prevent reading expectancy level computing errors.

Besides obtaining information from referring parents, outside agencies should examine existing school records. They contain information regarding test scores, classroom diagnosis, health, and school progress that can help in a clinical diagnosis.

Initial Screening

Because most reading specialists lack the time to adequately service all the students referred to them, they should establish a screening procedure. The purpose of screening is to obtain a rough estimate of the student's reading skills. The screening results can then be evaluated by the referring committee who will decide what sort of help the student needs. Screenings in out-of-school clinical agencies save hours of diagnostic time. It is estimated that about one-third of the students referred for clinical diagnosis have no reading difficulties. These referrals are usually based on a decline in school grades, concern raised by an article in the press, or interest in the reader's development without concern that difficulties exist. Obviously, a full-blown clinical diagnosis in such cases is unnecessary.

When screening decisions are made, the reading specialist should remember the diagnostic guideline, "Maintain Efficiency." Screenings should be designed to obtain a maximum of useful information in the minimum time required for accurate results. Screenings should include some indication of student interests,

University of Maryland   College of Education   Reading Center

Date *September 9, 1989*

Child's Name *Daniel C. Wagner*   Birthdate *02-08-77* Grade *6*
Mother's Name *Frances E. Wagner* Occupation *store manager*
Business Phone *1-203-445-8394*
Father's Name *James C. Wagner* Occupation *Cabinet Maker*
Business Phone *1-203-445-8394*
Home Address *222 Poquonnock Rd.* Child's School _____
College Park, Ct.   06340   Address _____
                         Zip Code

Home Phone *445-4216*   Principal *Mrs. Mildred Brown*

Reason for referral to University of Maryland Reading Clinic
Classroom teacher suggested it. They have met with no success at his school.

Please be sure to fill out the attached questionnaire and return all of this to the University of Maryland, College of Education, Reading Center, College Park, Maryland 20742.

Place an X on the line following each question and add comments when appropriate.

	Not at all	Perhaps	Certainly
	1	2	3

1. Do you believe health problems have affected your child's reading?   X
If 2 or 3, please comment_____

_____

	Not at all	Perhaps	Certainly
	1	2	3

2. Do you believe attitude problems have affected your child's reading?   X
If 2 or 3, please comment_____

FIGURE 6-1. A Referral Form for Clinical Diagnosis

140

	Not at all 1	Perhaps 2	Certainly 3

3. Do you believe teaching procedures have affected your child's reading?

If 2 or 3, please comment _They use the same set of readers for all children even when a given set does not work well._

	Not at all 1	Perhaps 2	Certainly 3

4. Do you believe teacher attitude has affected your child's reading?

If 2 or 3, please comment _____

	Not at all 1	Perhaps 2	Certainly 3

5. Do you believe problems at home have affected your child's reading?

If 2 or 3, please comment _I never learned to read well. Maybe it is my fault._

	No 1	They tried, but 2	Very well 3

6. Do you believe the school authorities have responded to your child's problem?

Please comment _The teachers seem to care but the school does not even provide special help for those having trouble with their reading._

	No	Yes

7. Is this your first referral of your child for help with reading problems?

If no, please explain _____

8. How many schools has your child attended? (1) 2 3 4 5
9. If your child was retained a grade, what grade? _2nd_

FIGURE 6-1 (continued)

10. Do you believe your child believes that reading is valued in the home?

	Not at all	Some	A lot

(marked X between Some and A lot)

11. How frequently did you read to your child when he/she was:

	Not at all	Occasion-ally	Almost daily
2–4 years old?		X	
5–6 years old?		X	
7–8 years old?	X		
9+ years old?	X		

12. Is your child now reading a book that is not a school requirement?

No	Yes

(marked X at No)

If yes, what book _____

a. Is the mother?

No	Yes

(marked X at No)

If yes, what book _____

b. Is the father?

No	Yes

(marked X at Yes)

If yes, what book *Beautiful Swimmers.*

13. Have there been other reading problems in the family?

No	Yes

(marked X at Yes)

If yes, please comment *As I mentioned, I never learned to read well.*

14. Do you help your child with his/her reading at home?

Not at all	Some	A lot

(marked X at Not at all)

If "some" or "a lot," what do you do? _____

Use back side to tell us anything not included on this side.

FIGURE 6-1 *(continued)*

mental ability, oral reading behavior, comprehension after silent reading, listening comprehension, word attack or study skills, and a diagnostic lesson. Screenings can usually be conducted within two hours.

The following sections explain the steps involved in clinical diagnosis. To make the process more understandable, a fictional student named Walt will be used to illustrate each step and how it helps in accumulating information for a successful diagnosis.

Establishing Rapport

Purpose

1. Relax the reader and develop a communicative atmosphere
2. Obtain information related to reader interests and strengths

Procedures

Because students come to the testing situation in differing degrees of anxiety, clinicians will wish to establish rapport and relax students in a variety of ways. Some clinicians like to use the referral form to guide them in an informal discussion of the student's strengths. Others like to establish rapport and, at the same time, obtain some useful diagnostic information by administering an interest

Establishing rapport helps relax the student and develops a communicative atmosphere.

inventory. Most students enjoy telling about what interests them. Although published inventories exist, some of the best interest inventories are teacher-made. Often interest inventories must be adapted to individual situations and age levels.

Student self-assessments can also be used in establishing rapport. Students can be remarkably insightful concerning their reading strengths and weaknesses; and, by asking them about what they do well and what causes them difficulty, the reading specialist conveys a sense of respect for their opinions. Some clinicians also like to use this opportunity to ask students about their reading strategies and processes.[1]

Students should be invited to ask questions about the purposes of any screening tests that they take. This helps to reassure them that the assessment is a cooperative venture and not an attempt to "trap" or "trick" them into a poor performance. It is always good to keep in mind that many students who have been referred for assessment are mistrustful of testing situations because of unpleasant experiences in the past.

Examples of Instruments

    Interest inventories
    Self-assessment interviews
    Process interviews

Time Needed

Generally about five minutes are necessary. At times, a very shy or very anxious student may require more time to relax and feel comfortable.

Walt example
    Age 12   Grade 7
    Likes school, football, mathematics, cooking, and skateboards.
    Does not care for water sports or history.
    Says he has few friends.

Indication of Mental Ability

In a screening situation, a reading specialist seeks to obtain only an *indication* of mental ability. The careful testing of mental ability would take more time than the entire screening. Therefore, the indication must be evaluated liberally. Using the standard error for a range score is advisable.

Purposes

    1. Determine a reading expectancy level or range
    2. Determine the need for further testing of intellectual ability, i.e., excessively high or low scores or scores that do not fit other available data (teacher observation, listening comprehension,

other scores on tests of mental ability). In these cases, further testing is recommended.

Procedures
In a screening, conduct a quick test of mental ability, which will be supplemented with the reading specialist's observation during the screening. For example, if a reader scores poorly on a test of mental ability, but has a good speaking vocabulary and scores well in reading comprehension, then the ability score's accuracy may be doubted.

Examples of Tests

> Peabody Picture Vocabulary Test–Revised
> Slosson Intelligence Test, Revised
> Receptive One-Word Picture Vocabulary Test
> Word Opposites of the Detroit Tests of Learning Aptitudes–2

Time Needed
Five to fifteen minutes are usually needed.

Walt example
Age 12   Grade 7
Likes school, football, mathematics, cooking, and skateboards.
Does not care for water sports or history.
Says he has few friends.
Ability range: Age 10–12

Oral Reading Testing

This testing can be divided into two subsections, oral reading of isolated words and oral reading in context.

ORAL READING OF ISOLATED WORDS (Word recognition)

Purposes

1. To obtain a quick estimate of reading level to determine the starting point for further testing
2. Informally obtain some quick insights into reader sight vocabulary knowledge and word attack abilities

Procedures
The major purpose for administering a word recognition test is to determine a starting point for silent-reading assessment. Some authorities suggest using rather sophisticated procedures for testing word recognition which employ both timed and untimed responses. Others suggest an in-depth analysis of word recognition errors. In a screening situation, such procedures are too time con-

suming. Examiners will wish to informally note the speed and confidence with which students identify words, but the major purpose is simply for placement in subsequent testing.

Examples of Tests

> New Sucher–Allred Reading Placement Inventory
> Botel Reading Inventory
> Prescriptive Reading Performance Test
> Wide Range Achievement Test-Revised
> Diagnostic Reading Scales-Revised
> Woodcock Reading Mastery Tests-Revised
> Slosson Oral Reading Test
> Informal reading inventory

Time Needed
Five to ten minutes are usually necessary.

Walt Example
Age 12   Grade 7
Likes school, football, mathematics, cooking, and skateboards.
Does not care for water sports or history.
Says he has few friends.
Ability range: Age 10–12
Word recognition: Grade 4

ORAL READING IN CONTEXT

Purposes

1. Determine oral reading level.
2. Determine oral reading comprehension.
3. Evaluate oral reading behavior to gain insight into the reader's oral reading strategies.

The procedures for purpose 3 are different from those for purposes 1 and 2. Since a given screening may involve all three purposes, the procedures for each are presented.

Procedures for Purposes 1 and 2
Many test instruments are available for these two purposes.

Examples of Tests

> Gray Oral Reading Tests-Revised
> Formal Reading Inventory
> Durrell Analysis of Reading Difficulty
> New Macmillian Reading Analysis
> Gilmore Oral Reading Test

Although the directions for administering these tests vary, they all have the following basic ingredients:

- The student reads aloud from graded selections, ranging from simple to difficult.
- The examiner records the reader's responses as outlined by the manual.
- Scores are usually based on a frequency count rather than a qualitative analysis.
- Several comprehension questions are asked that normally provide a measure of the reader's ability to recall specifically stated facts from the story.

The value of oral reading comprehension scores is questionable. During oral reading, most readers are concentrating on pronunciation and fluency. The valuable insights gained from an analysis of oral reading relate to those processes that the reader demonstrates. Comprehension skills are best measured after silent reading. Questions asked after oral reading can be used to show students that reading is a purposeful activity if the teacher begins a lesson with purpose-setting questions and follows oral reading with those same questions.

As with word recognition, many reading specialists prefer to construct informal oral reading tests. Passages are selected from graded materials that the student may be expected to read. Accuracy is recorded as it is on standardized tests of oral reading. Using informal oral reading tests during diagnosis offers the advantage of evaluating students from longer selections and a variety of content. An inherent disadvantage of informal oral reading tests lies in the possibly false assumption that the graded materials used for the tests are, in fact, accurately graded. For example, if a given selection taken from a fifth-grade book is actually at the sixth-grade level, diagnostic conclusions that come from it are faulty. Another limitation relates to how such tests are interpreted. Pikulski states that an informal inventory's usefulness in diagnosis is related to how well the testing material matches the material to be used for instruction.[2] Obviously, if they are mismatched, interpreting results is difficult.

Using oral reading tests as diagnostic tools has several limitations. Disagreement abounds about what constitutes an oral reading error. Certainly, one would recognize such errors as mispronounced words, hesitancy on unknown words, or disregard of punctuation marks as obvious limitations to effective oral reading. But is it an error when a reader repeats words to correct oral reading mistakes? Is it an error when a student stops to use word attack skills on words not known at sight? Or are these examples of the type of behavior teachers want readers to display? Are all errors of equal importance, or do some interfere with reading efficiency more seriously than others? If weights could be developed for various types of errors, would the same weight hold at various grade levels? (For example, would a vowel error made by a first grader be as serious an error as a vowel error made by a fifth grader?)

Tests constructors, in an effort to standardize oral reading tests, have had to establish some easily recognizable arbitrary standards for accurate oral reading. Although these arbitrary systems vary, most of them include markings similar to those listed in the Gilmore Oral Reading Test. Substitutions and mispronunciations are written above the word on which the error was made; omissions are circled; repetitions are underlined; words inserted are put in the appropriate place; punctuation that is disregarded is marked by an *X*; hesitations of two seconds or more are marked by a check mark above the word, and at five seconds these words are pronounced for the reader and two check marks are made. The following paragraph has been marked according to this system.

A spaceman has stepped onto the surface of Mars. He is very careful as he

steps from his capsule. Live television brings the moment to the entire population

of the earth. It is an exciting moment.

This system gives an exact representation of the student's reading. This student made the following errors: hesitated on the word *has* and failed to pronounce the word *stepped* in five seconds; mispronounced *surface* and disregarded the period after *Mars*; repeated *He is very*; substituted *telephone* for *television* and *a* for *an*; omitted *entire*, and added *planet*.

This paragraph illustrates not only the marking system but also the fact that all errors are not equally important. (For example, hesitation on the word *has* is a less serious error than the failure to pronounce *stepped*.)

One can also observe reader strengths from this test. For example, although the first sentence is somewhat distorted, this student seemed to get the passage's basic meaning. The second sentence was read perfectly. The omission of the word *entire* and the addition of the word *planet* did not distort meaning.

Beside the disagreement about what really constitutes an oral reading error, another limitation of oral reading tests concerns their dependence on the ability of the examiner to hear and record accurately the errors that the reader makes. Clinicians need supervised practice to gain proficiency in oral reading test administration. If the examiner is not able to hear or record the responses accurately, the results of testing will be invalid. Through practice, competency can be developed to assure satisfactory administration and interpretation of oral reading tests. However, unsupervised testing without adequate practice can lead to extremely unreliable results.

Time needed for testing oral reading level and determining oral reading comprehension depends, of course, on how many passages need to be read to get to the instructional level. Oral reading diagnosis can usually be conducted in five to fifteen minutes.

Walt example
Age 12   Grade 7
Likes school, football, mathematics, cooking, and skateboards.
Does not care for water sports or history.
Says he has few friends.
Ability range: Age 10–12
Word recognition: Grade 4
Oral accuracy: Grade 5
Oral comprehension: Grade 5

Procedures for Purpose 3

Testing for evaluation of the student's oral reading behavior should be conducted on longer passages than those used for purposes 1 and 2. Goodman and Burke[3] have developed passages for this purpose. Teachers can select passages from materials that students would normally be expected to read in school.

Kenneth Goodman's work (referred to briefly in chapter 5) has influenced the way many are using oral reading in clinical diagnosis.[4] He discourages using oral reading to obtain reading level information and emphasizes using it for linguistic processing information (miscues). Student responses during oral reading are classified qualitatively in terms of the appropriate use of cues. The Gilmore coding system mentioned earlier is also changed to reflect the qualitative classifications.

Many reading specialists have made adaptations of Goodman's ideas for clinical use. Staff members at the University of Maryland reading clinic, for example, have adapted his ideas as a way of looking at oral reading behavior (ORB). Those ideas that most directly affect the ability to make useful recommendations to teachers were modified and used. Basically, with this approach, every response that is in variance to the text is recorded, leaving one word of text on each side of the variant word, for example:

Text: in *the* street
Student response: in *a* street

Then a judgment is made to classify the student variance as a regression, insertion, omission, or substitution. Regressions are further analyzed using the following questions:

1. Did the student change the first response to make a correction?
2. Did the student appear to attempt a correction but fail?
3. Did the student simply repeat a portion that was initially correct?
4. Did the student change a response that was initially correct?

In each of these cases the student might be self-monitoring his or her own comprehension; the reader might have thought that the oral reading did not sound correct or make sense. With such an analysis, one can see that a regression may be classified as good oral reading behavior as well as poor.

Omissions and insertions are judged in terms of whether they changed the meaning of the context. If they do not change the meaning, we can assume that the reader is using semantic cues.

Substitutions, the most important student response in studying oral reading behavior, are evaluated as follows:

1. When making the substitution, did the reader use graphic cues? In what way did the reader display knowledge of phonics or structural analysis?
2. Did the reader use semantic cues? In what ways did the reader demonstrate use of the context?
3. Did the reader use syntactic cues? In what ways did the reader show knowledge of grammar? If the reader uses semantic cues, one assumes the use of syntactic cues. However, if the reader does not use semantic cues but does use syntactic cues, valuable information is obtained about the student's awareness of language.

Obviously, each of these analyses involves some subjective judgment. But with them the reader can be given credit for oral reading strengths even when responses are different from the text. Each of these responses is recorded and all responses in a category are totaled. Then the specialist can say how much of the time a student demonstrates a specific type of oral reading behavior; for example, when the reader makes substitutions, semantic cues are used effectively 75 percent of the time.

The use of this type of oral reading behavior analysis calls for considerable practice. Examiners are urged to use tape recorders, at least during initial efforts, to record variances for this type of analysis.

Goodman and Burke's work may be referred to for a detailed explanation of oral reading miscue analysis.[5] Oral reading diagnosis is of most value for students reading between second- and seventh-grade reading levels. Beginning readers' responses may be related to the method used for instruction. If language experience has been used, the reader may rely heavily on semantic cues; if a phonics method has been used, the reader may indicate heavy reliance on graphic cues. Once the reader is beyond the initial stages of learning to read, one can better determine which cues the reader relies on. Older readers probably use very different behavior in oral reading than in silent reading. Perhaps oral reading analysis becomes less useful as an insight into silent reading behavior as the reader matures. Diagnostic information from oral reading should be interpreted with this caution in mind.

Time Needed for Purpose 3
Usually oral reading behavior analysis is conducted on one passage and takes little testing time (five to ten minutes); however, if the passage is one on which

the reader either makes no errors or makes so many that he or she is reading nonsense, another passage should be selected and more time allotted.

Obviously, a screening can be conducted using all three purposes. If so, time will be added to the screening. Most reading specialists will want to decide which oral reading purpose best suits their needs and evaluate oral reading accordingly.

Walt example
Age 12   Grade 7
Likes school, football, mathematics, cooking, and skateboards.
Does not care for water sports or history.
Says he has few friends.
Ability range: Age 10–12
Word recognition: Grade 4
Oral accuracy: Grade 5
Oral comprehension: Grade 5
Oral reading behavior: High use of semantic cues at fifth-grade level.
  Low use of graphic cues at fifth-grade level.

Comprehension after Silent Reading

Silent-reading comprehension is difficult to accurately assess in an initial screening for several reasons. First, the nature of reading comprehension itself makes assessment problematic. Reading comprehension is a complex, personal process that is dependent on the reader's interest, prior knowledge about the topic, knowledge of text organization, and strategic processes. These factors vary from reader to reader; they also vary from reading selection to reading selection. Therefore, it is not unusual to find a reader who easily comprehends one fifth-grade passage but not another. Second, determination of reading comprehension levels also depends on the measures used to assess comprehension. Comprehension levels can vary several grade levels when different instruments are used.

Purposes

1. Determine the reader's skills in several different aspects of silent-reading comprehension ability.
2. Determine the reader's skills in understanding passages at various degrees of difficulty.
3. Determine the reader's skills in responding to various types of questions.

As in oral reading, the procedures needed to achieve these purposes are different; however, the procedures can be combined so that each purpose is met in a screening situation. Although there are a number of commercially prepared, standardized tests of reading comprehension available, reading specialists gain greater diagnostic flexibility by using an informal reading inventory. These instruments can be more easily adapted to address the three assessment purposes stated above.

Procedures for Purpose 1

Because the procedure used for assessing comprehension affects reader response, teachers and reading specialists can adapt administration of informal reading inventories to gain insights into several aspects of reading comprehension abilities.

1. Prior to reading the selection, read the student the title and a short description of the contents. Ask the student how much he or she already knows about the topic and ask the student to make some predictions concerning what might happen in the selection.
2. Have the reader read for the purpose of retelling the story in the passage. The retelling can be evaluated for completeness, organization, and sequence.[6]
3. Have the reader respond to questions about the story from recall, without the printed material available for referral.
4. Have the reader respond to questions that could not be answered in recall by locating the answers in the material.

Some diagnosticians like to ask older readers to follow these procedures by producing a written summary of the passage. Later examination of those summaries can produce valuable insights into the reader's written organizational abilities.[7]

Procedures for Purposes 2 and 3

The reading specialist will need to decide what type of instrument will be used to assess comprehension. These instruments include prepared tests, informal inventories, cloze or maze tests, and criterion-referenced tests. These same tests are used in classroom diagnosis; however, when used for clinical assessment, they are used on an individual basis, allowing time for different tests and more careful evaluation of reader behavior.

PREPARED TESTS. Several examples of commercially prepared tests that are available for clinical diagnosis of silent-reading comprehension are the following:

Diagnostic Reading Scales–Revised
Formal Reading Inventory
Durrell Analysis of Reading Difficulty
Gates–McKillop–Horowitz Reading Diagnostic Tests
Standardized Reading Inventory
Woodcock Reading Mastery Tests–Revised
Gates–MacGinitie Reading Tests
The Test of Reading Comprehension

Each of these tests differ concerning the amount of time required to administer them, the age group they were designed to assess, and the nature of the reading task. They are capable of providing information about the reader's ability to understand material at different levels. They can also provide information about the reader's ability to respond to various types of questions. The reading specialist will want to be certain that different types of questions are provided, because some tests provide questions that ask for literal responses only.

When selecting a test, the reading specialist should make certain that it is valid and reliable. Information concerning validity and reliability can be found in the technical manual that accompanies each test. Tests with low reliability are measuring too much chance score and are not dependable. Tests that lack validity do not reflect the variables the test was constructed to measure. Another important validity concern is the nature of the comprehension task. To what degree do the testing passages and procedures represent natural reading comprehension? Some reading comprehension measures lack validity because they assess comprehension using extremely short reading selections, whereas most "real" reading takes place in longer selections. (The reader may refer to chapter 3 for a further discussion of the role of reliability and validity in test selection.)

INFORMAL INVENTORIES. Informal inventories, whether prepared commercially or by teachers, provide clinical diagnosis with flexible instruments to assess reading comprehension. The flexibility is feasible because the tests are not standardized, allowing for the three types of assessment suggested under purpose 1. The manipulation of standardized tests interferes with their norms so that the results are meaningless.

Some commercially prepared informal reading inventories include the following:

The Classroom Reading Inventory (Silvaroli)
Informal Reading Inventory (Burns and Roe)
Analytical Reading Inventory (Woods and Moe)
The Ekwall Reading Inventory (Ekwall)

Reading specialists will want to examine each of these and make selections most suited to their school situations. Considerations should include:

1. *Are alternate forms available?* Alternate forms provide flexibility needed for pretesting and posttesting, use of alternate passages for starter examples, and use when assessment about the performance on a given passage can be doubted.
2. *Do the questions reflect varying types of comprehension?* As discussed previously, various types of questions are needed to assess purpose 3.
3. *Do the passages reflect the type of reading material being used in the reader's school?* For example, if the reader has been referred

because of problems reading a content area textbook, are there sufficient content area passages to provide accurate insights into the reader's difficulties?

4. *Have the readability levels of the passages been checked? If so, how?* Passages with unchecked readability levels should be held suspect. It is not enough that the passages have been taken from graded books.

5. *Has the inventory been field-tested? If so, how and where?* Sometimes inventories are published without much field-testing to refine the instrument and set realistic cutoff scores.

Teacher-developed informal inventories have long been used to assess reading comprehension. Generally these inventories are developed using the materials that the students will be reading in school, eliminating the problem of matching test materials with instructional materials. For best results a group of reading specialists should work together to develop the informal inventory. By checking and double checking the passages and the questions, easily made errors can be avoided. Passages should be field-tested and replaced when they do not yield accurate results. Inventory developers should apply the same questions to their tests that apply to commercially developed informal inventories.

The following steps are suggested for developing an informal inventory for clinical diagnosis:

1. *Select passages from instructional material.* Passages should be varied in topic, complete in thought, and of general interest to the grade level of students. Passages should be between 125 and 175 words to assure sufficient length for adequate assessment.

2. *Test the readability of the passages.* If passages are close to the desired readability, sometimes limited rewriting can adjust the difficulty of the passage closer to the needed readability. In general, by reducing the length of sentences and by simplifying the words, the readability is lowered.

3. *Write a title and short introductory lead-in for each passage.* By reading these aloud to the student, the teacher can help to activate the student's prior knowledge.

4. *Develop questions for each passage.* About ten questions should be written to assess comprehension. Questions should elicit literal, interpretive, and problem-solving responses. The number and type of question will vary with the passage content. Each question should be carefully scrutinized to assure that it is clearly stated. Although prior knowledge is an important contributor to reading comprehension, inventory questions should be "passage dependent"; that is, they should require the student to read and understand the passage in order to answer the question.

5. *Field-test each passage on students known to be reading satisfactorily at the passage's grade level.* When reading silently, most

students should be able to answer 70 percent of the questions. If they fall below that, the questions should be reworked. If students answer all the questions, the questions may be too easy or the difficulty of the passage may not be as high as the readability measure would indicate. Preferably, inventories should be used to measure silent, rather than oral, reading comprehension; however, if an oral reading comprehension score is desired, the criteria of success should be lowered to somewhere in the range of 55 to 65 percent.

6. *After making necessary adjustments, use the inventory and keep notes on its effectiveness.* If difficulties occur, continue to adjust the inventory accordingly.

One of the particular advantages offered by informal reading inventories is the opportunity for the reading specialist to carefully observe students reading materials of paragraph length and longer. Systematic observations of the reading act can reveal many valuable insights into students' strengths and needs.

CLOZE AND MAZE TESTS. Cloze tests are constructed directly from the material used in instruction. Every fifth word is deleted, and the student is to supply the missing word. Accuracy scores of 40 percent reflect the 70-percent mark (or instructional level) on the tests previously mentioned. Using a passage with fifty deletions is suggested.

Cloze tests can be used informally to determine how well students use syntactic and semantic cues when reading. In these cases, certain words are deleted (for example, all verbs) to see if the students can supply appropriate words.

Maze testing is a modification of cloze procedures. In maze tests, instead of deleting every fifth word, a three-word choice is provided. For example:

street
The boys walked down the house.
run

The student is to select the most appropriate word. In this type of testing, students are expected to score 70-percent accuracy to determine instructional levels.

Cloze and maze tests can be used to supplement information obtained from informal inventories.

CRITERION-REFERENCED TESTS. Criterion-Referenced Tests (CRTs) can be used in clinical diagnosis, although they are usually more useful for classroom diagnosis since they are group instruments. Reading specialists often develop short CRTs for use in screenings to measure one or more specific objectives. For example, if a screening indicates that the student is having difficulty grasping the author's major ideas, the reading specialist may select several paragraphs and have the student read the paragraphs to obtain the author's main idea. By adding these data to that which was already available, the reading specialist would be adding reliability to the findings of the screening. (See discussion on CRTs in chapter 5.)

From these possibilities for comprehension diagnosis, the reading specialist will need to make a decision concerning what would be most useful. No one decision is appropriate for every case; however, the following suggestions have proven useful in most.

1. Select a good informal reading inventory.
2. Administer it for the retelling purpose.
3. Ask specific questions in a recall situation for important items missed in retelling.
4. Ask specific questions in a locating situation for important items missed in recall questioning.

Time Needed

About twenty minutes are usually necessary. The time needed depends on the number of passages that need to be read to obtain an instructional level.

Walt example

Age 12   Grade 7

Likes school, football, mathematics, cooking, and skateboards.

Does not care for water sports or history.

Says he has few friends.

Ability range: Age 10–12

Word recognition: Grade 4

Oral accuracy: Grade 5

Oral comprehension: Grade 5

Oral reading behavior: High use of semantic cues at fifth-grade level.
  Low use of graphic cues at fifth-grade level.

Comprehension using Informal Reading Inventory:
  4th-grade passage retelling good, recall 90% + locate 10% = 100%
  5th-grade passage retelling fair, recall 70% + locate 30% = 100%
  6th-grade passage retelling poor, recall 50% + locate 20% = 70%
  7th-grade passage retelling poor, recall 20% + locate 30% = 50%

By adding the recall and the locate percentages, the percent of questions answered accurately can be obtained. These data show that Walt's retelling dropped off immediately after the fourth-grade passage and recall dropped off after the fifth-grade passage. Therefore, his retelling comprehension level is fourth grade, his recall level is fifth grade, and his locate level is sixth grade.

Many poor readers have strengths in listening comprehension that exceed their silent-reading comprehension levels. Sticht and James note that, in many cases, listening comprehension levels are higher than reading comprehension levels through the sixth grade. From seventh grade onward, students seem to be about equally likely to be superior in reading or listening.[8] Among poor readers, the percentages favoring listening comprehension are even higher. Not only can listening comprehension measures be used to estimate a student's reading expectancy, but they can also give insights into the student's learning strengths.

Purposes

1. Confirm the data previously recorded to determine a reading expectancy level or range.
2. Gain insights into preferred modes of instruction.

Procedures

Continue to test the student using the inventory selected for silent-reading comprehension assessment. Testing should begin at the student's silent-reading instructional level. The teacher should read aloud each selection slowly and distinctly and test for listening comprehension abilities by using the procedures suggested for silent-reading comprehension.

Time Needed

Five to fifteen minutes are usually necessary.

Walt example
   Age 12   Grade 7
   Likes school, football, mathematics, cooking, and skateboards.
   Does not care for water sports or history.
   Says he has few friends.
   Ability range: Age 10–12
   Word recognition: Grade 4
   Oral accuracy: Grade 5
   Oral comprehension: Grade 5
   Oral reading behavior: High use of semantic cues at fifth-grade level.
      Low use of graphic cues at fifth-grade level.
   Comprehension using Informal Reading Inventory:
      4th-grade passage retelling good, recall 90% + locate 10% = 100%
      5th-grade passage retelling fair, recall 70% + locate 30% = 100%
      6th-grade passage retelling poor, recall 50% + locate 20% = 70%
      7th-grade passage retelling poor, recall 20% + locate 30% = 50%
   Listening comprehension: Grade 6

At this time in the screening, a decision must be made. Is further testing desirable? If so, in what direction should it go? Since Walt scored into the fourth-, fifth-, and sixth-grade levels on all tests, a decision was made to extend the screening to include an assessment of Walt's study skills. If he had scored at the first-, second-, or third-grade level, continued assessment of his word attack skills would have been the next step.

Study Skill Assessment

Purposes

1. Determine if the reader can use reading skills in content materials.
2. Determine if the reader uses effective study techniques.
3. Determine which content area textbooks cause the reader the least difficulties and which cause the greatest difficulties. Try to determine the reasons for the differences.

Procedures

Information about study skills can be gained either through commercially prepared tests or through informal methods. If the student has been specifically referred for evaluation because of reported difficulties with study techniques, the examiner may wish to have a study skills test ready to administer. In most cases, however, informal assessment will be more appropriate in an initial screening; in-depth assessment is more possible during extended diagnosis or during continuing instruction.

Informal assessment of study techniques involves collecting interview data from the student's content teachers and directly from the student. Teachers should be asked questions such as the following:

1. Is the student able to complete independent assignments for class?
2. In what areas does the student show learning and reading strengths?
3. What is your assessment of the student's weaknesses?
4. What instructional adjustments have you been able to make for the student's lack of reading skills?
5. Does the student have any particular difficulties or strengths using graphic aids like maps, tables, graphs, and charts?
6. What is the student's level of ability with reference tools like dictionaries, indexes, and encyclopedias?

The student might be asked questions such as the following:

1. What class or textbook causes you the least amount of reading difficulty? Why?

2. Which class or textbook causes you the greatest amount of reading difficulty? Why?
3. Which tests do you find most difficult to prepare for? How do you go about studying for them?
4. What things that teachers do seem to help you to learn best?
5. How much homework do you get each evening? How long do you work on it and where do you work?

Students might also be asked to read a selection from one of their content area textbooks. The reading specialist can teach a directed lesson and note the student's ability to respond.

Examples of Tests

> Learning and Study Strategies Inventory
> Sequential Tests of Educational Progress
> Diagnostic Achievement Test for Adolescents
> Survey of Reading Study Efficiency

Time Needed
Five to ten minutes are usually necessary.

Walt example
Study skill assessment:
Good in completing mathematics assignments.
Weak in completing social studies and science assignments.
Weak in spelling.

Word Attack Assessment

Purposes

1. Determine if important word attack subskills may be causing reading comprehension difficulties.
2. Identify those important word attack subskills that are the reader's strengths.

Procedures
The usual procedure is to administer a test of identified important word attack skills. (The word *important* is used here because many word attack tests include the assessment of skills that are not useful to the reader.) The reading specialist will need to determine which word attack skills need assessment and then select an instrument or a portion of an instrument that assesses those skills. The amount of time needed to administer tests varies greatly. At this point in

a screening, time becomes crucial because the reader is likely to be weary of testing. Perhaps the selection of a short survey-type test would be most appropriate, saving the more time-consuming tests for extended diagnosis.

Examples of Tests

> Botel Reading Inventory
> Diagnostic Reading Scales–Revised
> Gates–McKillop–Horowitz Reading Diagnostic Tests
> Individualized Criterion Referenced Test–Reading
> Woodcock Reading Mastery Tests–Revised
> Doren Diagnostic Test of Word Recognition Skills
> Criterion Test of Basic Skills

Time Needed

Ten to thirty minutes, depending on the test selected, are usually necessary.

Walt example
We had already decided that Walt did not need a word attack assessment. But, if he had, perhaps the results would show:
    Knowledge of initial consonants: Excellent
    Knowledge of final consonants: Excellent
    Knowledge of short vowels: Very Good
    Knowledge of long vowels: Excellent
    Knowledge of vowel combinations: Good
    Syllabication skills: Weak

Diagnostic Lesson

The final step in the screening is to test out the hypotheses developed from the available data through a diagnostic lesson. In Walt's case, the data available look like this:

Walt example
Age 12   Grade 7
Likes school, football, mathematics, cooking, and skateboards.
Does not care for water sports or history.
Says he has few friends.
Ability range: Age 10–12
Word recognition: Grade 4
Oral accuracy: Grade 5
Oral comprehension: Grade 5
Oral reading behavior: High use of semantic cues at fifth-grade level.
    Low use of graphic cues at fifth-grade level.

Comprehension using Informal Reading Inventory:
   4th-grade passage retelling good, recall 90% + locate 10% = 100%
   5th-grade passage retelling fair, recall 70% + locate 30% =100%
   6th-grade passage retelling poor, recall 50% + locate 20% = 70%
   7th-grade passage retelling poor, recall 20% + locate 30% = 50%
Listening comprehension: Grade 6
Study skill assessment:
   Good in completing mathematics assignments.
   Weak in completing social studies and science assignments.
   Weak in spelling.

From these data several hypotheses may be developed:

- Although Walt is having some difficulty with reading, he has a good attitude toward school and likes mathematics, so opportunities should be developed for him to demonstrate his math skills.
- Walt comprehends best when using both recall and locate situations. He should be encouraged in the use of both recall and locate situations for comprehension in all school subjects.
- Walt's use of semantic cues in oral reading indicates little need for concern. However, it is useful to determine which graphic cues are used and which are ignored. This analysis may help explain some of his difficulty with spelling.

What diagnostic lesson could be useful to deal with these hypotheses? Two possibilities are:

1. A directed lesson with content material, using locating skills at sixth-grade level.
2. A lesson directed toward Walt's locating comprehension skills, using different passages at fifth- and sixth-grade levels.

Of these two, the first is clearly preferable since Walt is in seventh grade, and independent work in content areas is needed. In other cases, the diagnostic lesson could be used to:

1. Determine if the student can respond to the language-experience approach. This lesson might be selected for younger students, culturally different students, or those appearing weak in word attack or sight vocabulary.
2. Determine if the student can read materials in a teacher-directed lesson that the student was unable to read independently. This lesson might be selected for students who appear to have com-

prehension difficulties and who are reading below their grade-level placements.

3. Determine if the student can learn to use a comprehension-oriented study strategy such as SQ3R or personal outlining. This lesson might be selected for older students who are experiencing difficulties remembering what they read in their content textbooks.
4. Determine if the student can respond to different types of questioning procedures. This lesson might be selected for students who displayed difficulties with retelling or recall questions but not with locating questions, or vice versa.
5. Determine if the student would benefit from teacher-directed semantic webbing or mapping. This lesson might be selected for students who appeared to have difficulties with meaning vocabulary, main ideas, or organizational abilities.

Each of these approaches or techniques will be discussed in the chapters on remediation that follow. The goals of a diagnostic lesson are to verify the working hypotheses generated from the data of the screening, obtain some insights into the student's responsiveness to a possible remedial recommendation, and end the diagnostic session with a successful (and, it is hoped, pleasurable) experience. If the diagnostic lesson verifies the screening data, then recommendations can be made with assurance. If it does not confirm the data, then extended diagnosis is recommended, or, if the diagnostic lesson justifies it, the hypotheses can be adjusted to reflect it.

Caution on Initial Screenings

The data collected in this brief manner lead to the formation of working hypotheses that must be tested through extended diagnosis and instruction. The results are *not* conclusive. Although every effort is made to be thorough, there is simply too much involved in the reading process for it to be thoroughly evaluated through a screening. The interview session with the parents and possibly with the student should be approached with caution. No pronouncements of cause and effect and no absolute conclusions are yielded in initial screening; rather, it is the first careful look into the situation.

The Interview

The interview allows the reading specialist and the parents to obtain more information about the student's reading difficulties. Parents come to the interview with a lot of information about their perceptions of their child's reading difficulties and may have difficulty listening until they have the opportunity to share these perceptions. Therefore, the interview should start with a solicitation of information from the parents. Some starter questions might be:

1. Why do you think your child is having difficulty with reading?

163

Clinical Diagnosis

1. Why do you think your child is having difficulty with reading?
2. What have the school personnel told you about your child's difficulty?
3. Why did you refer your child for this screening?

Most parents will respond to these types of questions willingly and unload their concerns. The person conducting the interview should listen carefully, showing interest, but not showing approval or disapproval. When the parents pick up signals that they are on unacceptable ground, they tend to become guarded and less communicative.

Most parents are very perceptive about the difficulties their children are experiencing. Often their comments reinforce or clarify the findings of the screening. In these cases, the interview is a confirming activity. In some cases, the parents tend to concentrate on one aspect of reading, one teacher, or one instructional activity (usually phonics). This type of concentration keeps them from gaining a broad perspective about their children's reading. In these cases, the interview becomes an enlightening activity.

After the parents have expressed their concerns, the reading specialist can then discuss the results of the screening. The following procedures can be followed:

1. Explain each test, give an example of an item from it, and discuss the student's performance on that test. The test score and its interpretation should be given.
2. Summarize all observed behavior.
3. Present implications in the form of working hypotheses. Suggesting conclusions as a result of a screening should be avoided. Rather, state that adjustments will be the first things to try and then reevaluation will be conducted.
4. Ask for questions from the parents.

Some guidelines to follow for conducting interviews that follow initial screenings include:

1. Do not take notes during the interview. Wait until the parents have gone and then write down a record of what transpired. Note taking during an interview tends to make parents uneasy.
2. Do not tape record an interview. Tapes make parents uncomfortable. If you must tape the interview, be certain that all involved know that it is being taped.
3. Do not take sides with the parents against a teacher or a school program. Taking sides in these matters is unethical because both sides of the story are not known.
4. If the screening is to be shared with other school personnel, be certain that the parents know this and approve. An out-of-school

The interview between the parent and the specialist should start with information from the parent.

agency should have written permission from the parents to share any testing report.

5. Attempt to offer plausible recommendations. When possible, make recommendations in such a way that parents are presented with choices to make or alternatives to explore. For example, it may be that the student's needs could be met either through additional school services or through the assistance of an outside clinic or tutor.

A written report of the screening data with implications and suggestions for instruction or extended diagnosis is usually prepared. Such reports, when developed by school personnel, are useful for reference during school staffing meetings. When prepared by out-of-school agencies, they are usually mailed to the school principal.

This text has presented clinical screening procedures in detail. Reading specialists in the schools report that this screening procedure is their most common request for diagnosis; seldom is more detailed diagnosis requested. In a recent survey of a Maryland school district, reading specialists averaged eighty-five individual assessments each year. If this figure is typical for other reading specialists, then time-efficient diagnostic procedures such as those suggested here must be used for thorough assessment.

Extended Diagnosis

After measuring the reader's strengths and weaknesses in sight vocabulary, oral reading, and silent reading, tentative hypotheses are made. From these hypotheses, the reading specialist obtains clues to the reader's strengths and weaknesses in the skill areas and plans further diagnosis. The procedures here are identical to those used by the teacher in classroom diagnosis. Although the questions asked in relation to each skill area are those asked in classroom diagnosis, the resulting conclusions may culminate in further diagnosis, since the reading specialist has more diagnostic tools available and is more qualified to interpret the results. Using these tentative hypotheses, the reading specialist may need to extend the diagnosis to those skill areas that have been identified as needing further analysis.

One basic consideration in clinical diagnosis concerns the possibility that a student may have strength in a certain mode of learning. For example, a reader who may learn effectively when tactile experiences are combined with visual stimuli may not learn through visual stimuli alone. These strengths and weaknesses should serve as guides for instruction.

Intellectual Abilities

Diagnosis may also be extended into intellectual abilities. As discussed in chapter 4, the WISC-R, the K-ABC, and the Stanford–Binet are most commonly used for these purposes. Once again it should be noted that each of these instruments requires a trained examiner to administer and interpret properly. In cases where an in-depth intellectual examination is required, most reading specialists should initiate a referral. Extended intellectual testing is recommended if the student's reading difficulties appear to be mostly attributable to very low intellectual functioning or if a learning disability is suspected. Reading specialists may wish to delay a referral until after appropriate instructional remediation is tried.

Learning Modalities and Strengths

Students differ in their abilities to benefit from various forms of instruction. Modality identification, however, is illusive using commercially prepared tests. Many tests in this area lack validity and reliability. Reading specialists may wish to informally assess learning modalities by carefully observing students in varied learning situations. Which modes of instruction seem to work best with a given student? What strategies does the student appear to use when confronted with an unknown word? How does the student approach reading books, content textbooks, and worksheets? What types of question formats appear to cause the student the most difficulty? Questions such as these may form the basis for teacher observation or be compiled into interview forms, although one difficulty with interviews is students' tendency to give the answer they think the teacher expects. However, many insights into student learning strengths can be gained from careful observation over time.

Concepts about Print

Some students experience reading difficulties because they lack familiarity with the conventions and jargon of written language (see chapter 8). These students may appear confused when confronted with reading tasks, or they may have difficulty distinguishing between "sentences" and "paragraphs." Unfortunately, many teachers take these abilities for granted. Concepts about written language can be assessed through tests such as the Concepts about Print Test and the Test of Early Reading Ability. Students' knowledge of basic instructional terms, such as "between," "widest," "row," and "equal," can be assessed with the Boehm Test of Basic Concepts–Revised.

Visual Discrimination

If visual discrimination skills appear to be deficient, the reading specialist has several diagnostic measures available. Most published reading readiness tests contain measures of visual discrimination. Visual discrimination abilities can also be assessed through informal measures.

The clinician should be certain that diagnostic data will aid in the development of an educational prescription. Generally, informal measures are of most value. Informal testing, using a simple passage or experience story, can be conducted by asking the reader to circle all words that begin with a specific letter after identifying the letter; by asking the reader to underline all words that have a certain ending; or by finding specific letters in a paragraph. The advantage of such informal testing is that the testing medium consists of the actual reading passage.

Auditory Discrimination

If auditory discrimination appears to be causing a problem, further testing using published reading readiness tests or prepared tests such as the Auditory Discrimination Test and the Gates–McKillop–Horowitz Reading Diagnostic Tests may be used. The Goldman–Fristoe–Woodcock Test of Auditory Discrimination assesses discrimination abilities using taped presentations, both "quiet" and "noisy." This provides an assessment of the student's discrimination abilities in varied instructional settings. As with visual discrimination abilities, auditory discrimination can also be readily assessed using teacher-made measures.

Orientation

If the tentative hypothesis identifies orientation as a reading problem, diagnosis often is extended to include an evaluation of eye motion during both oral and silent reading. The student's eyes are monitored closely to determine if they move with an acceptable number of fixations across a printed line, and if they move backwards excessively in regressions. Since everyone makes a certain number of regressions while reading, diagnosis in this area can prove difficult.

Reading specialists should observe groups of good, fair, and poor readers so that they can learn what is expected in the observation of eye movements. Other observations that can lead to suspicions about lack of orientation are behaviors such as peculiar reading posture, placing the book at unusual angles, and losing one's place.

Sight Vocabulary

If the tentative hypothesis identifies sight vocabulary as the problem, a more careful analysis of tests previously administered may determine patterns of sight vocabulary errors (see chapter 5). Durrell suggests that when time is not a factor the word not known at sight should be used to determine if the reader can analyze the word using word attack skills.[9] In such cases, the word recognition answer sheet will have two columns, one for instant pronunciation and one for delayed pronunciaton. If the reader does not know the word at sight but does know it when permitted to examine it, that reader obviously has skills to attack the word properly but has not mastered the word for his or her sight vocabulary. In extended diagnosis, it may also be desirable to assess the student's recognition of functional and survival words such as "exit," "emergency," "stop," and "poison."

Word Attack

If the tentative hypothesis finds a student's word attack skills in need of further diagnosis, the reading specialist should analyze the errors made in word recognition and oral reading, as was done in classroom diagnosis (see chapter 3). A wide range of commercially prepared tests are also available for clinical diagnosis that measure specific word attack skills. Some examples follow:

Diagnostic Reading Scales–Revised
Gates–McKillop–Horowitz Reading Diagnostic Tests
Individualized Criterion Referenced Test–Reading
Botel Reading Inventory
Woodcock Reading Mastery Tests–Revised
Doren Diagnostic Test of Word Recognition Skills

Tests measuring word attack skills vary widely in their time requirements and in the instructional usefulness of their results. Teacher-made, criterion-referenced tests of the various word attack skills often provide the best insight into skill strengths and needs in this area. For example, if analysis of word recognition and oral reading responses indicates that the student has difficulty with word endings, then a test can be constructed that measures only skills dealing with word endings. A standardized word attack test would waste valuable time in such a case.

Reading specialists generally want to see how well a student with specific word attack problems performs on a spelling test. This test should be given at the student's instructional level. Through an analysis of spelling errors, the reading specialist can extend the diagnosis and verify previous findings. Examples of commercially prepared tests which assess spelling include the following:

Botel Reading Inventory
Classroom Reading Inventory (Silvaroli)
Kaufman Test of Educational Achievement
Diagnostic Achievement Test for Adolescents
Peabody Individual Achievement Test–Revised
Test of Written Language

The reading specialist should be aware that many readers have learned to attack words adequately in isolated drill-type exercises but are not capable of performing the same task when they see these words in context. It would be erroneous, therefore, to conclude that students do not have word attack deficiencies simply because they perform successfully on diagnostic tests of word attack skills. Evaluation must be made in an oral reading situation where the student is faced, not with the single unknown word, but with the unknown word in a group of familiar words.

Comprehension

If the tentative hypothesis identifies the need for further diagnosis in comprehension, attention must again be directed to those questions asked in classroom diagnosis (see chapter 5). Clinical diagnosis will be extended to review the history of approaches used in the student's reading instruction. From this type of analysis, the reading specialist can often understand gaps in instruction areas and suggest remedial programs to fill these gaps. In the area of comprehension, the specialist should establish the answers to four questions before proceeding to remediation:

- *Is the reader's poor performance on a comprehension test due basically to weak comprehension skills, or is it more closely related to inadequate vocabulary?* One technique for determining the answer to this question is to make a careful comparison between word-meaning and paragraph-meaning scores. Poorer performance in word meaning usually indicates that a student's vocabulary skills are prohibiting maximum performance in comprehension.

- *Is there a need for further comprehension testing to verify conflicting test scores?* It may be necessary to administer a test that has more items, one that has a better variety of items, or one that measures a certain type of comprehension skill not measured in the previously administered silent-reading test. When students have serious comprehension difficulties, the reading specialist seldom finds one silent reading test satisfactory. If another test is administered, the results of that test should undergo the same diagnostic scrutiny as the previous test. Scores of such tests should not be averaged, however. When more than one test of silent reading is used to diagnose skill strengths and weaknesses, analysis of the responses to types of questions rather than a composite score is critical to clinical diagnosis.

- *Is the reader's poor performance on a comprehension test due basically to slow reading or lack of reading fluency?* In classroom diagnosis, the ability to complete reading assignments in a specific time period is considered; in clinical diagnosis, equal consideration must be given to the reader who fails to complete reading tests in the allotted time or is very slow on untimed tests. This information is not revealed from examining comprehension scores. Rather, the reading specialist should make special note of students who perform adequately on comprehension tasks but who take a long time to do so. Reading fluency is also often related to comprehension abilities. Reading specialists should determine whether comprehension difficulties are related to any lack of fluency observed in oral reading assessments.

- *Is the reader's poor comprehension on specific text exercises caused by the lack of experiences in the content area of the material being read?* A city student unfamiliar with farm life may score poorly on a test story about farming yet be quite capable of comprehending a similar story about city life. Diagnosis, however, is not so easy. While broad areas of experience may be identified, a reader's background of experiences is quite personal and involved and can be difficult to ascertain.

Reading Habits and Attitudes

If the tentative hypothesis identifies reading habits and attitudes as a problem, the reading specialist has found that the student has the basic skills to read adequately but does not care to read. This diagnosis involves a careful consideration of the information from the areas of emotional and physical diagnosis. The student may indicate a poor attitude toward school-type tasks and books or physical discomfort. The study skills tests cited earlier in the chapter may provide useful information for extended diagnosis.

Further evaluation is needed of past efforts made by the school to encourage the sudent to read, assess the availability of books in the school and at home, and evaluate the general atmosphere that may encourage or discourage reading in these situations. A student who can read but normally doesn't is not considered in need of a specialist's attention. The reading specialist is obligated only to make specific recommendations to the classroom teacher. However, fully aware that interests are always changing, the reading specialist will attempt to assess the student's interests either formally through an established interest inventory or informally through interest inventories or a personal interview with the student, the parents, and teacher. Many students, although they are reading as well as possible, are placed in frustrating reading situations daily in school. It does not take a specialist to realize that reading is painful for these students and that they may easily develop a negative attitude toward reading. Information gleaned in such a manner should be included in the diagnostic report.

Diagnostic Batteries

Diagnostic batteries assess a wide range of reading skills and usually report scores in a student profile. Batteries may be found in either group or individual forms, although as a rule, batteries designed for individual administrations are preferred in clinical diagnosis. Some examples of diagnostic batteries include the following:

> Curriculum Referenced Tests of Mastery
> Diagnostic Reading Scales–Revised
> Woodcock Reading Mastery Tests–Revised
> Durrell Analysis of Reading Difficulty
> Gates–McKillop–Horowitz Reading Diagnostic Tests
> Woodcock–Johnson Psycho-Educational Battery
> Kaufman Test of Educational Achievement
> Diagnostic Achievement Battery
> Individualized Criterion Referenced Test–Reading

A careful examination of any diagnostic battery is essential to select one that matches important objectives of the school program. The main advantage of using a diagnostic battery is that the scores of the subtests are comparable because they are standardized on the same population. Another advantage is that there is only one manual and one test to learn to administer and interpret; one does not have the overwhelming job that occurs with some other types of testing combinations. The resulting information will provide an individual analysis of how a student is reading and how the student's skill development is related to total reading scores.

These diagnostic batteries are not without limitations, however. Some are too brief and some are standardized on very small populations, thereby causing reliability problems. Most importantly, reading specialists will find that the tests do not measure the types and degrees of skill that they wish to measure, thus causing validity concerns. Therefore, in clinical diagnosis, it is unlikely that any *single* diagnostic battery will be adequate for a complete diagnosis. Reading specialists may wish to select subtests from individual tests that best correspond to areas they wish to assess.

In a 1983 survey of 100 college and university reading clinics by Rogers et al.,[10] the data in Table 6–1 were reported concerning the frequency of use of various diagnostic instruments.

Diagnostic Teaching

Formulating diagnostic hypotheses from data based on testing situations can lead to a distorted view of the reader. The reader's behavior during instruction must also be considered. An instructional session provides additional data for extended clinical diagnosis.

TABLE 6–1. Test Instruments and Techniques Used in Diagnosis

Instrument/Technique	Rank	Incidence
Informal Reading Inventory	1	57
Visual Screening	2	53
Background Information Form	3	29
Audiometric Hearing Tests	4	26
Phonic Inventories	5	22
Spache Diagnostic Reading Scales	5	22
Informal Interest Inventory	7	21
Slosson Intelligence Tests	8	20
Test of Auditory Discrimination	9	18
Durrell Analysis of Reading Difficulty	10	16
Full Scale IQ (i.e., Wechsler, Stanford–Binet)	10	16
Peabody Picture Vocabulary Test	12	15
Gates–MacGinitie Reading Tests	13	14
School Achievement Records/Grades	13	14
Woodcock Reading Mastery Test	15	12
Reading Miscue Analysis Inventory	15	12
Basic Sight Word Lists (i.e., Dolch)	16	11
Stanford Diagnostic Reading Test	17	10
Gates–McKillop–Horowitz Reading Test	17	10
Wide Range Achievement Test	19	10
Slosson Oral Reading Test	19	8
Gray Oral Reading Test	21	7
Detroit Test of Language Aptitude	21	7
Gilmore Oral Reading Test	22	6
California Reading Test	23	5
Ekwall Reading Inventory	24	4
Botel Reading Inventory	24	4

From "A Research View of Clinic Practicum in Reading Education," by Sue F. Rogers et al. *Reading World* 23, no. 2 (December 1983): 134–46. Used by permission.

Specifically, reading specialists should provide lessons that check their findings concerning reading level, major skill strengths, and major skill needs. For example, if the diagnosis supported an instructional level at 3^1, skill strengths in beginning consonants and directly stated recall, and skill weaknesses in vowels and problem solving, a lesson should be designed to see how the reader operates in each of these areas. Several books—one at the 2^2 level, one at the 3^1 level, and perhaps one at the 3^2 level—can be selected with silent reading followed by questioning in the area of strengths and needs. A short phonics lesson can be developed to see how well the reader handles consonants and vowels.

If the hypotheses are confirmed, the diagnosis becomes more reliable. However, if the student can perform during instruction, new hypotheses should be formulated and tested. Rarely are all hypotheses confirmed. Clinicians who skip the step of diagnostic teaching place themselves in the position of drawing faulty conclusions. Preparing a report on a student that contains faulty conclusions has serious consequences. If specialists expect teachers to use their reports to adjust instruction, they should test their findings in instructional situations. In the reading center at the University of Maryland, diagnostic lessons that follow testing have been found to be of the utmost value.

Occasionally, a full case study seems necessary to complete a diagnostic evaluation. To develop a full case study, in-depth testing is required in the areas of intelligence, verbal performance, auditory skills, visual skills, word recognition, oral reading behavior, silent-reading comprehension, and word attack skills. To these are added medical reports and a developmental history, as well as detailed information from the school and home.

The decision to proceed with a full case study will stem from lack of information on the student and failure of the initial screening to satisfactorily identify the student's strengths and weaknesses. An evaluation of every aspect of the student's educational development, as well as his or her intellectual, emotional, and physical development, is needed. Because of the time, money, and coordination of efforts required, case studies are reserved for those students with the greatest apparent difficulties.

Case Reporting

As in classroom diagnosis, the information accumulated in a clinical diagnosis is useless unless it can be organized for easy understanding. A case report is the typical approach to preparing diagnostic information for clinical use. Although the precise form may vary, the following format should be used so that persons unfamiliar with the student can make optimum use of case information:

1. The first page should contain a concise summary of the essential data included in the report: name, age, address, school, reading ability levels, and a summary statement of diagnostic findings divided into areas of reader strengths and reader needs.
2. The first page should be followed by as many pages of explanation as necessary. The explanation should include all test scores,

the dates the tests were administered, and the name of the test administrator, as well as diagnostic interpretations of the test performance and evaluations of the student's responses. It also should include data from screening tests and referral reports. It is here that the relative importance of each piece of data is evaluated and interrelated and that causative factors may be identified.

3. The third section should consist of a page or two of complete description of the success of the diagnostic lesson.

4. The last pages of the case report should include specific recommendations and referrals. Recommendations are made to the clinic, classroom teacher, and parents, specifying preventive as well as remedial procedures.

The report can best be explained to the teacher in a face-to-face interview. Teachers nearly always have questions about the report that can be answered during the interview. The report will be better understood by the teacher if it has been discussed.

Not long ago, parents were denied specific information concerning test results. Today that has changed; parents have become aware of the need for such information and often demand it. Indeed, they have the right to know this information. It is essential to give parents copies of anything sent to teachers. If reports are misfiled or lost, parents must have copies to replace those lost. Furthermore, parents can often implement adjustments at home to assist with the correction of difficulties.

Since reports often contain technical language, parents will find it helpful to receive the report during a conference. Technical language can then be explained and questions answered.

Pitfalls of Diagnosis

Both clinical and classroom diagnosis may be plagued by certain pitfalls. They include the following:

OVERGENERALIZATION. The tendency to use total test scores without examination of the pattern of test scores; the tendency to draw conclusions before all facts are in; the tendency to rely on the first significant symptom; and the tendency to hazard guesses outside the professional field are all examples of overgeneralizing in diagnosis. Overgeneralizing can be controlled, in part, by making couched statements when all data are not available. For example, instead of saying that a student has a poor home life, one can say that from the data available the home conditions bear watching as a possible cause of the student's lack of educational development. More than merely playing with words, couched statements protect the educational diagnostician and lead to more accurate reporting of diagnostic results.

OVEREXTENSION OF DIAGNOSIS. Extending diagnosis beyond areas which will help arrive at an accurate picture of the student may cause the student to become overly concerned about a reading problem and is therefore a waste of time. In commenting on the disadvantages of extended diagnostic periods, Strang concludes, "He may feel more strongly than ever that something may be wrong with him."[11] Overextension of diagnosis occurs more commonly in the clinic than in the classroom because the clinic provides the most careful study of the reader and a variety of tests. Some clinics suggest that each student receive a complete diagnostic analysis regardless of need. This can only be justified in the interest of gathering research data; however, the expense to the student must always be considered, for not all students can accept large quantities of diagnosis. Nevertheless, every effort must be made to arrive at a true picture of the difficulty. Through the use of initial screenings, selective studies, and indepth case studies, diagnosticians have choices available and can avoid overextension of diagnosis.

ABBREVIATED DIAGNOSIS. A hurried diagnosis often does not investigate a given reading difficulty properly. Insufficient diagnosis is most common in the classroom, where lack of time and materials exert constant pressure on the teacher's efforts. Regardless of the limitations of the classroom situation, the teacher must use all available data to assure that the information obtained is reliable and valid. Abbreviated diagnosis commonly leads to wrong conclusions and, in effect, to waste of time that would have been saved through a more thorough diagnosis. If diagnosticians include the diagnostic teaching lesson as part of their diagnosis, the chance of an abbreviated diagnosis is lessened because unknown factors usually come to light in a diagnostic lesson.

OVERSTEPPING PROFESSIONAL BOUNDARIES. Educators sometimes make statements that are beyond their professional boundaries. The diagnostician must refrain from playing psychiatrist or medical doctor and, instead, refer willingly when necessary. As with overgeneralizing, couching terms in a diagnostic report that goes beyond the field of education will help avoid overstepping professional boundaries. For example, if a telebinocular examination indicates the need for referral, the clinician may write that "poor performance on test four of the telebinocular indicates the need for a professional visual examination." That type of statement is more appropriate than one stating that the poor score on the telebinocular indicates visual problems that need professional attention.

UNFOUNDED STATEMENTS OF FACT. Positive, factual statements made by educators based on evidence that does not justify so strong a statement should be avoided. Couching terms to indicate suspicious areas where more testing may be needed or areas where referral is necessary will be beneficial to all those who are attempting to arrive at a student's difficulty area. An examiner must be certain that positive statements concerning a student's observed difficulties are backed by highly reliable data.

ISOLATION OF FACTORS. Isolated pieces of diagnostic data, test scores, and the like must not be examined without consideration for their relationship to the entire diagnosis. The significance of particular data are often lessened when they are placed in the total picture of a student's reading difficulty. A single group of data or a single test score used in isolation is likely to lead to a distorted picture of the difficulty. Even in the classroom, where time and materials are at a premium, this pitfall should be avoided.

PREVIOUS BIAS. The examiner must be alert to the possible interference of data that are tainted by bias. Bias is often found in the remarks of parents or teachers and can have a definite effect on the direction the diagnosis may take. To circumvent this effect, the examiner may intentionally avoid evaluating data from the parents and teachers until tentative hypotheses are reached.

Difficult Diagnostic Problems

THE SO-CALLED NONREADER. Unfortunately, not all diagnosis falls into neat packages of specific skill deficiencies. Some students appear unable to profit from even the best instruction in any of the skill areas. They cannot learn to read by conventional methods. Abrams estimates this population to be less than 1 percent of the total population of disabled readers.[12] While diagnosis of these students may be the basic responsibility of the reading specialist, the entire resources of the school should be consulted.

Commonly referred to as *dyslexic, neurologically deficient, minimally brain damaged, learning disabled,* or as having a *specific reading disability,* nonreaders have disabilities complicated by multiple factors. They are almost always emotionally involved in their gross failure. They are likely to be physically deficient and may appear slow. Trying to please the teacher often no longer interests them. Diagnosis has failed to identify a consistent behavior pattern. Educators have attempted to teach them by all known methods, each of these methods has failed.

Effective diagnosis calls for an interdisciplinary approach to these students. Every effort should be made to seek out sources of difficulties. Some school districts are establishing special facilities for such students. Carefully trained teachers work in coordination with personnel from other disciplines to establish meaningful educational programs for these troubled learners. It is often necessary for these students to be diagnosed in clinics that have been established to work efficiently with them. But prior to making a referral to an outside clinic, the reading specialist should visit the clinic to evaluate the clinic's philosophy, assessment procedures, remedial programs, and success rates.

In some cases, despite all efforts, these students continue to fail. Multidisciplinary efforts are continuously explored in hopes of establishing new areas of diagnosis and remediation for them. Screening committees assure that the most appropriate resource personnel work to diagnose and remediate these students. Early identification programs followed by early intervention hold some promise. Multisensory techniques are often employed effectively. However, the search continues for diagnostic and instructional techniques that will make school life more pleasant and successful for these students.

While educators working in these areas may be well qualified and well intentioned, some caution is advised. First, labeling students as dyslexic is little help and can cause serious damage to a learner's self-concept. Rather, clinicians should present information about the students' strengths and needs as specifically as possible and avoid the use of general terms which have no diagnostic use. Second, the formulation of special schools and special classes is a procedure that might cause more harm than good to the student. Chapter 11 presents some of these difficulties. Finally, the attempt of some educational groups to specialize in one or more of these labeled groups of students can run the risk of creating a feeling among other educators that these students are not their concern. The notion that someone else should deal with difficult students is faulty and should be challenged.

THE CULTURALLY DIFFERENT. Another group that appears to be experiencing severe difficulty in traditional programs consists of students with cultural backgrounds that differ from the general population. Their language and their experiences are not likely to correspond to the instructional materials that they are expected to use. Mismatching students from low-income homes with books designed for middle- and upper-class children has been common.

Diagnostic instruments that use stories based on middle-class concepts (Dick and Jane going on a vacation in the suburbs) put poor students at a disadvantage in the testing situation. Interpretation of low reading and intelligence scores must be in terms of the students' different cultural backgrounds.

Aside from considerations such as these, culturally different students should be diagnosed using the questions suggested in this chapter. Strengths should be noted and used. Deficiencies should be worked with through the students' demonstrated strengths. Focusing on strengths is extremely important for establishing good diagnostic and remedial relationships with these students.

In all likelihood these students will be urged to try harder and make more effort while being compared with successful students from the cultural majority. McDermott, discussing the high rate of failure among some groups, states, "Almost invariably, such problems arise when a group in power educates the children of a minority group."[13] He attributes the problem to lack of communication and failure to understand what motivates those who are different from ourselves.

McDermott's position is confirmed by Williams and his associates who developed the BITCH tests (Black Intelligence Test of Cultural Homogeneity).[14] They found that inner-city black students could perform well on this test but suburban whites found passing it impossible. The test is used to help develop an awareness of the cultural bias that exists in many of the commonly used tests.

If some students come to school and hear a strange language and experience strange customs, it is likely that they will not enter into a situation conducive to communication. The error clinicians and teachers can make is to assume that their silence indicates lack of ability. Once that error is made, the entire diagnostic effort becomes invalid.

Due to the immigration of large numbers of Asians, Hispanics, and Africans into American society, many students attending school do not use English as their first language; indeed, many do not use English at all. These students and their teachers are usually assisted by English-As-a-Second-Language (ESL) trained educators. However, the day-to-day education of these students is the responsibility of the entire school staff. Efforts must be made to help them learn English while at the same time respecting their first languages and the cultural customs that go with them.

Summary

Clinical diagnosis is normally conducted on individual students. It relies heavily on observations of student behavior and the results of testing. Clinical diagnosis has obvious advantages and several severe limitations.

Understanding the purposes and procedures involved in an initial screening is crucial to clinical diagnosis. Initial screenings involve interviews, questionnaires, testing, and diagnostic lessons. Initial screenings are followed by instruction with continuous evaluation or extended diagnosis. Extended diagnosis relies heavily on testing.

The reading specialist must avoid the seven pitfalls that can lead to erroneous diagnostic conclusions and invalid diagnosis. The reading specialist must also be aware of the difficulties in diagnosing nonreaders and readers from different cultural backgrounds.

If clinical diagnosis is seen as a part of an ongoing diagnostic and instructional program and not as an end in itself, then successful learning can be provided for many readers who do not now experience it.

Notes

1 For an example of a process interview, see Karen Wixson, Anita B. Bosky, M. Nina Yochum, and Donna E. Alvermann, "An Interview for Assessing Students' Perceptions of Classroom Reading Tasks," *The Reading Teacher* 37, no. 4 (January 1984): 346–52.

2. John Pikulski, "A Critical Review: Informal Reading Inventories," *The Reading Teacher* 28, no. 2 (November 1974): 143.

3. Yetta M. Goodman and Carolyn L. Burke, *Reading Miscue Inventory—Manual* (New York: Macmillan Publishing Co., 1971).

4. Kenneth S. Goodman, "Analysis of Oral Reading Miscues: Applied Psycholinguistics," *Reading Research Quarterly* 5 (Fall 1969): 9–30.

5. Goodman and Burke, *Reading Miscue Inventory.*

6. For a more detailed description of retelling analysis procedures, see Judith W. Irwin, *Teaching Reading Comprehension Processes* (Englewood Cliffs, N.J.: Prentice-Hall, 1986), 167–72.

7. Jeanne R. Paratore and Roselmina Indrisano, "Intervention Assessment of Reading Comprehension," *The Reading Teacher* 40, no. 8 (April 1987): 778–83.

8. Thomas G. Sticht and James H. James, "Listening and Reading," in *Handbook of Reading Research,* ed. P. D. Pearson et al. (New York: Longman, 1984), 305.

9. Donald D. Durrell, *Manual of Directions: Durrell Analysis of Reading Difficulty* (New York: Psychological Corporation, 1980).

10. Sue F. Rogers et al., "A Research View of Clinic Practicum in Reading Education," *Reading World* 23, no. 2 (December 1983): 134–46.

11. Ruth Strang, *Diagnostic Teaching of Reading* (New York: McGraw-Hill Book Co., 1969), 8.

12. Jules Abrams, "Minimal Brain Dysfunction and Dyslexia," *Reading World* 14, no. 3 (March 1975): 219.

13. Ray P. McDermott, "The Ethnography of Speaking and Reading," in *Linguistic Theory* ed. Roger Shuy (Newark, Del.: International Reading Association, 1977), 176.

14. Robert L. Williams, "Misuse of Tests: Self-Concept," *Report of the Tenth National Conference on Civil and Human Rights in Education* (Washington, D.C..: National Education Association, 1972), 17–19.

Suggested Readings

Buros, Oscar K., ed. *Reading Tests and Reviews*, vols. 1 and 2. Highland Park, N.J.: Gryphon Press, 1968, 1972. This index to the Mental Measurement Yearbooks provides a useful reference tool to researching the technical quality of published reading tests.

Dechant, Emerald. *Diagnosis and Remediation of Reading Disabilities*. Englewood Cliffs, N.J.: Prentice-Hall, 1981. Chapter 4 discusses types and severity of reading problems and deals with the characteristics of students with specific types of reading difficulties.

Farr, Roger, and Robert F. Carey. *Reading: What Can Be Measured?* 2d ed. Newark, Del.: International Reading Association, 1986. Chapters 2, 3, and 4 discuss varied means of assessing reading comprehension, word recognition, vocabulary, study skills, and rate. Theoretical concerns are presented, and issues of reliability and validity are addressed.

Goodman, Kenneth S. "Analysis of Oral Reading Miscues: Applied Psycholinguistics." *Reading Research Quarterly* 4 (Fall 1969). Pp. 9–30. This landmark article paved the way for new views of oral reading errors and of the reading process itself.

Hancock, Charles R., William E. DeLorenzo, and Alba Ben-Barka. *Teaching Pre- and Semi-Literate Laotian and Cambodian Adolescents to Read*. Baltimore: Maryland Department of Education, 1983. This helpful publication assists teachers in better serving the needs of English-as-a-Second-Language students.

Harris, Albert J. and Edward R. Sipay. *How to Increase Reading Ability*. 8th ed. New York: Longman, 1985. Chapter 7 discusses the elements involved in a reading diagnosis. Harris and Sipay's book is an important contribution to the field of reading instruction.

Keyser, Daniel J., and Richard C. Sweetland, eds. *Test Critiques*, vols. 1–4. Kansas City, MO: Test Corporation of America, 1984–1987. These volumes examine published tests in terms of their characteristics, uses, and technical aspects. Critical evaluations of their value as assessment instruments are also included.

Lipson, Marjorie Youmans, and Karen K. Wixson. "Reading Disability Research: An Interactionist Perspective." *Review of Educational Research* (Spring 1986). Pp. 111–36. The authors maintain that reading disability research should focus on finding the conditions that enable students to learn rather than look for causative factors. A similar perspective would be useful in reading diagnosis and remediation.

McDermott, Ray P. "The Ethnography of Speaking and Reading." In *Linguistic Theory*, edited by Roger Shuy. Newark, Del.: International Reading Association, 1977. Pp.144–52. This chapter presents an interesting case for the ways in which readers are treated differently. Instances are cited when both communication and motivation are missed, causing certain groups of readers to fail.

Squire, James R., ed. *The Reading Teacher*. (April 1987). This guest-edited issue features thirteen articles focusing on the state of assessment in reading.

EDITORIAL

Cynthia Tomalovitz Bowen

is an elementary supervisor, Baltimore County Public Schools, Maryland.

"I'm going to be the author when I grow up!" Michael would eagerly share with friends and family members. No one was really surprised by that declaration because he was always busily creating picture stories. The illustrations were very well drawn; he used a wide range of color and included painstaking detail. Michael's stories alway contained the necessary elements of quality literature . . . character, plot, setting, theme. As soon as an original story was finished, Michael promptly sought an audience so that he could "read" his most recent creation.

Sometime between Michael's fifth and sixth birthdays, he began asking his eight-year-old sister, Christine, or an adult to write the words of the story on the illustrated pages. He enjoyed his stories and would reread them several times.

The adults who had been with Michael at his daycare center and his kindergarten teacher often commented to Michael's parents about his sophisticated oral language skills. They noticed that he had an advanced vocabulary and frequently spoke in complete and complex sentences.

When Michael entered first grade, he began a formalized, structured reading program. During that time, his behavior as well as his interest in reading began to change. His first-grade teacher noticed that he did not want to participate with the other children in the reading group and began performing silly antics which distracted the other students and caused them to laugh at him. This behavior puzzled his teacher and his parents. Soon he began to demonstrate behaviors at home which concerned his parents; he sometimes acted without thinking, appeared restless and worried, and indicated that he felt he had to be perfect.

Before long, Michael's classroom teacher recognized that Michael demonstrated confusion with discriminating sounds and difficulty with decoding skills. Michael himself recognized that he could not apply the skills that other students had mastered. After careful reflection, Michael's teacher recommended that he be clinically diagnosed. The results of the diagnosis indicated that Michael's verbal ability was above average, yet he was deficient in auditory memory for linguistic sounds. This deficiency was the primary cause for his difficulty in learning to read. It was recommended that Michael's instructional program include visually oriented techniques. This included:

- Using a whole word approach
- Building a basic sight vocabulary of high-frequency words and functional words
- Developing with Michael strong contextual skills

These recommendations were shared with Michael's teacher and parents. As a result of this modification, which his teacher incorporated into his reading program, Michael's interest in and enthusiasm for reading began to return. Michael's parents were especially pleased with the recommendations that were suggested to them. Initially puzzled by the change in Michael's behavior, they had come to understand his frustrations and were now prepared to react appropriately to Michael's needs. As a result of this diagnosis, Michael's needs and strengths were identified, his program was modified for his learning style, and he regained confidence in his ability as an author and reestablished his confidence as a reader.

Cynthia Tomalovitz Bowen

Insights into Remediation

CHAPTER OUTLINE

Guidelines for Remediation
Pitfalls of Remediation

CHAPTER EMPHASES

Effective remediation is based on careful diagnosis.

Remedial programs should seek to guarantee and illustrate success to the student.

The same techniques are used in classroom and clinical remediation.

Several recent research studies have yielded important insights into remediation.

Successful remedial programs require careful planning and skilled implementation.

Remediation of reading difficulties is not based on mysterious techniques that are impossible for the classroom teacher to understand. Rather, remediation is based on sound instructional principles focused on the strengths and needs of the students that have been determined by careful diagnosis. Since remediation calls for skillful teaching, anyone who works in a remedial program should be a skilled teacher who keeps up-to-date by reading and studying.

As previously discussed, there is seldom one cause of reading difficulties; therefore, there is seldom one approach to their solution. The public has often been led to believe the opposite, thereby causing pressure on educators to teach by certain methods which incorporate a little of all known teaching techniques. Instead, remediation should be in direct response to diagnostic findings, necessitating the use of the most suitable educational techniques as solutions to the diagnostic findings. These findings contain information concerning skill strengths as well as needs.

Guidelines for Remediation

Teachers will find remediation most effective if they adhere to the three following guidelines:

- *Remediation must guarantee immediate success.* In the remedial program, initial instruction should culminate in a successful, satisfying experience. In this way, students who have experienced frequent failure in reading begin the remedial program with the attitude that *this* educational experience will be both different and rewarding. Without this attitude, the best remedial efforts are often wasted. Successful learning situations also are assured by directing learning toward those activities that the diagnosis has indicated are the students' strengths and interests. All initial lessons should be directed toward student strengths. As remediation progresses, the time devoted to strengths is likely to decrease. When the students start to ask for instruction in the areas of their weaknesses, changes in instructional strategy can take place. However, throughout the entire program, a large portion of every lesson should be directed to strengths.
- *Remedial successes must be illustrated to the student.* Successes must be presented so that the readers' awareness of them is assured. As students progress, charts, graphs, word files, and specific teacher comments can be used to illustrate successes.
- *Remediation must provide for transfer to actual reading situations.* On some occasions in a remedial program, isolated drill in various areas will be required; however, drill activities should always come from contextual reading material and should always conclude in contextual reading situations. The mastery of all skills takes place best in actual reading situations.

*Students need
individualized
instruction.*

Types of Remediation

Unlike diagnosis, classroom and clinical remediation involves the same teaching strategies. The students need individualized instruction. Instruction is based on sound learning theory and is constantly adjusted to students' responses. While remediation in a clinical setting may be easier because of small group size, the strategies used do not differ. No materials, techniques, or learning theories are reserved for the clinical setting. In fact, the opposite may be true. Many teachers are able and willing to apply skills learned in a clinical setting to their classrooms. Many reading specialists find it useful to conduct remedial efforts without taking the readers from their classrooms. Thus, teachers can easily pick up teaching strategies used by the reading specialist, and reading specialists can often learn from the classroom teacher's teaching strategies.

Implications from Research

The findings of the following six research reports are cause for alarm in considering the plight of students with reading difficulties. Teachers should channel that alarm into constructive use by considering the implications of these studies as they plan remedial lessons.

1. Allington found that poor readers read very little during remedial reading classes.[1] The mean number of words read during a given session was forty-three. He recommends less skill instruction and much more reading time.

2. Clay observed first-graders and found that good readers read 20,000 words during the year and poor readers read 5,000 words.[2] These findings support Allington's, in that poor readers do not get much reading practice. Clay also noted that good readers would correct one error in three, whereas poor readers would correct only one error in twenty. If poor readers made nine errors in a twenty-seven-word passage without correction, it would appear that they were not reading for meaning and practicing poor reading habits.

3. Allington also found that good readers and poor readers are treated differently during instruction.[3] When good readers made oral reading errors, they were interrupted by the teacher 24 percent of the time. Poor readers were interrupted 68 percent of the time. With good readers the interruptions were made at the end of a meaningful unit; poor readers were interrupted at the point of the error. Two implications can be gleaned from these data: good readers get to read more because they are interrupted less; and poor readers, interrupted at the point of error, have difficulty understanding what they read and are not given the opportunity to self-correct.

4. Durkin conducted observational research and found almost no comprehension instruction in grades three and six.[4] Comprehension was assessed but not taught. She also found almost no instruction in the area of study skills. Content knowledge was assessed, but the skills to acquire that knowledge were not being taught. If readers can comprehend what they read, they do well in assessment; and if they cannot comprehend they will do poorly in the assessment sessions.

5. Gambrell, Wilson, and Gantt found that good and poor readers were treated differently in an observational study of fourth graders.[5] Good readers were all reading in material that was very easy (their error rate was 1 in 100 running words). Poor readers were placed in material that was very difficult (one error in nine running words). Good readers were observed reading 57 percent of the time; poor readers were reading only 33 percent of the time. Poor readers spent twice as much time in phonics skill activities as good readers. Finally, good readers were observed to be on task 92 percent of the time but poor readers only 81 percent of the time. These findings may be explained as follows: poor readers are placed in difficult material and sound inaccurate. The teacher therefore increases the skill work, thereby

decreasing reading time. Skill work tends to be meaningless, so the poor readers go off task.

6. A National Institute of Education study involving both reading and mathematics found that time spent on successful learning activities resulted in increased achievement.[6] Time spent on difficult activities that resulted in failure decreased achievement.

As these six studies illustrate, readers with difficulties are experiencing different treatment during instruction which probably contributes to their reading problems. A series of instructional adjustments should be implemented to change the frustrating learning environment to one of success.

ASSURE POSITIVE ATTITUDE. Remedial activities, while based on diagnosis, should concentrate on the interests of students. The sense of self-worth must be developed early. Helping readers realize success with materials that are of interest has tremendous impact. The "I-can't-do-it" attitude quickly turns around to "I can do it." Handicapped readers should not be *talked into* feeling good about themselves; their success experiences should be *realized*. Students should also feel that those success experiences are important. Further, teachers should use materials that highly interest students, such as newspapers, auto magazines, model construction, and cookbooks. One student, reportedly not able to read above the third-grade level, could read football articles in the *Washington Post* with a high comprehension level. The following suggestions can be used as starter ideas.

Remedial activities should concentrate on the students' interests.

1. When a student performs successfully, let him or her teach the activity to another student.
2. Provide rewards for successful performance.
3. Build small group rapport: "We can read—we are worthwhile."
4. Provide teaming situations for successful learning. Let pairs of readers work toward an objective.
5. Make certain the students understand the objectives and know when they have reached them.
6. Keep parents and other teachers informed about successes so that they may reinforce them.

PLAN FOR A BALANCED PROGRAM. Two types of balance make remedial programs effective. First, a balance must be struck between reading narrative material and reading content material. As students see reading skills transferred to content material, they realize that they can be successful in science and social studies activities and that they can achieve overall success in school.

Second, an even balance should be kept between skills and reading. Each skill lesson must result in a successful reading activity. Three steps are appropriate in maintaining this balance.

1. Teachers give the skills lesson.
2. Students practice the skills on an individual lesson.
3. Students do free reading applying the skills.

The research previously cited would seem to indicate that reading time to apply skills should be a major portion of each remedial lesson.

Without these types of balance, remedial instruction can become segmented and distort the purposes for learning to read well. Success in phonics lessons is useless unless those learned skills can be applied in free reading. Teachers need to plan for balance in order to assure a complete remedial program.

ENCOURAGE RISK TAKING. Years of unsuccessful attempts in reading activities tend to discourage students from trying. They risk being corrected, ridiculed, embarrassed, and defeated. If they decide not to try, there is no risk of failure. Remedial lessons must encourage risk taking by:

- Assuring that students are not penalized for inaccurate responses.
- Placing students in material that they can handle with ease.
- Encouraging students to work together toward an answer to a problem.
- Creating a discussion atmosphere during comprehension lessons rather than a teacher-questioning session where only the teacher holds the correct answer (see chapter 10).
- Setting attainable goals for each student; when the goals are reached, the student should be recognized for those successes.

PLAN FOR STUDENT DECISION MAKING. Teachers can encourage students to be enthusiastic toward a lesson by involving them in setting objectives, selecting activities, and participating in evaluation. Many handicapped readers sit through activities designed to improve their reading skills but have no idea what the lesson is designed to teach them.

During orientation activities to a lesson, students should be free to add objectives and question others. Of course, students cannot make all decisions, but they can have input. Generally, students are inclined to put forth more effort once they understand why they are doing an activity.

Allowing students to contract to complete a certain number of activities in a certain amount of time has great impact. The teacher provides a list of possible activities that will satisfy skill drill, skill practice, and free reading requirements. From this list, the students and teacher pick those that are of most interest and appear to be most possible for them. Negotiation is important in contracting. Both the students and the teacher should have input. At times, certain activities are required; at other times, two activities are selected from a list of five. At other times, students may have completely free choice. A form such as Figure 7–1 is useful in deciding which activities are chosen.

Name_____ Date_____

Pick one activity from box 1, 2, 3.
Pick one activity from box 4, 5, 6.
Pick one activity from box 7, 8, 9.
Activity 10 is required.

1. Play initial consonant game.	2. Teach consonants to your partner.
3. Complete skills sheet on consonants.	4. Find words beginning with *s*, *t*, *c*, *b* on page 34.
5. Read story about Pat the Rat.	6. Read aloud with teacher.
7. Read story from book on library shelf.	8. Make display advertising book you are reading.
9. Read aloud with your partner from book of your choice.	10. Participate in ten-minute sustained silent reading.

FIGURE 7–1. A Sample Contract

The student is instructed to self-evaluate by placing a smile or frown in the box beside the activity completed. When all activities are completed, no further work is assigned. The payoff for completing assignments must not be more assignments.

The teacher and students then discuss the quality of the completed activities and plan for the next day's lessons. Activities evaluated positively should be discussed in terms of what made the students feel good about them. Those evaluated negatively should also be discussed. Students should not be made to feel badly about an honest evaluation. Their reactions can be used as clues in future planning. Experience with such contracts shows that many students become increasingly positive about reading; they often ask for more activities, a good sign that reading is becoming interesting and worthwhile to them.

The students then feel very involved with their lessons. They become trusting and enthusiastic. The teacher, always in control, then knows what does and does not interest the students; therefore, better planning results.

CONDUCT TASK ANALYSIS. When students have difficulty with an activity, task analysis can be used as a diagnostic teaching tool. Task analysis allows the teacher to uncover which subskills may be missing in order for the student to complete the given task. Since all students master skills in very personal ways, pat formulas for why a given student cannot respond are of little use. The University of Maryland's reading clinic identifies the following five steps in task analysis[7] by applying the ideas of Ladd.[8]

Step 1   A problem is identified.
Example: A student cannot respond satisfactorily to questioning about the material read, even when reading silently.

Step 2   The teacher determines the strengths and weaknesses the student has in this skill area.
Example: Can read orally with satisfactory accuracy at the fourth-grade level.
Cannot answer literal questions asked from this material.
Can answer literal questions when working at the third-grade level.

Step 3   The teacher forms hypotheses concerning the possible reasons for this difficulty.
Example: The student is not interested in the material.
The passage is too long.
The questions are threatening.
The student does not have a purpose for reading.

Step 4   Through diagnostic teaching, the teacher tests each hypothesis.
Example: For the first hypothesis, the teacher may attempt to determine the student's interest areas and find material at the fourth-grade level in these areas. For the second hypothesis, the teacher may break the passage into smaller parts, asking the questions following each part.

Step 5   The teacher keeps a record of each diagnostic lesson and forms a tentative conclusion to be tested in further instruction.
Example: This student responded well when material was in the area of sports and motorcycles. He also responded better when he jotted down his purposes for reading before he started. Passage-length adjustment did not change his ability to comprehend, and the questions did not seem threatening in this new situation.

Of course, task analysis is a strategy that has been used by good teachers for a long time. However, it can be helpful to formalize the process in this manner so that all can profit from its power as a diagnostic tool.

Task analysis for reading diagnosis proves especially valuable because people do not all learn through the same set of subskills. What stops one person from comprehending a given passage differs from what stops another. And what one person needs as a subskill to read better may well be a subskill that another person does not need. Task analysis provides a highly suitable, flexible strategy for getting at the unique learning styles of each reader.

INVOLVE OTHERS. Teachers must use all possible resources when their students are having difficulty learning to read. The student's problem may best be solved by involving a physical education teacher, speech therapist, parent, psychologist, or family doctor. Even if others do not have suggestions for helping such students, communication channels should be open so that all involved stay informed. Many good instructional programs have become ineffective when members unintentionally work against one another.

Peers can team together with a reader on activities that the reader cannot do alone. They can also help conduct some time-consuming, drill-type activities, so teachers are freed to perform more productive tasks; in this way the peers can also profit from the student's strengths. For example, a certain boy was always the poorest in every activity. He always saw himself as a follower, never as a leader. As a field trip approached, he was taken on a "dry run" to familiarize him with the features of the field trip. He became excited and served as a group leader on the actual field trip. The other children appreciated his leadership and assistance. By getting everyone involved, the teacher can change a student's life from one of failure and frustration to one of success and excitement.

By considering these ideas before starting a remedial program, teachers can make adjustments that provide for a greater chance of success.

THE OLDER HANDICAPPED READER. Secondary school students who encounter serious problems while learning to read require special consideration in planning a remedial program. Materials for instruction and instructional techniques should be selected in terms of appeal to the secondary student. Driver's manuals, job information, consumer education materials, and newspaper articles are examples of appealing materials.

Secondary students who have many unsuccessful experiences tend to be very poor risk takers. They believe that if they do not try, they cannot fail again; of course they fail to realize that they won't learn either. Teachers must plan lessons so that risk taking is encouraged, not punished.

Contracting with these students can also prove effective. The contracts differ from those used with younger students, in that the secondary students are more involved with the decisions made in each part of the contract (i.e., planning, selecting activities, and evaluating). Secondary students with severe reading difficulties can also be excellent tutors for younger students. They take great pride in such roles and obtain excellent results; they probably learn more than the student being tutored. Teachers should also organize instructional activities around problems that the students have identified as important to them. Secondary students can "get turned on to" reading when the learning activities have immediate application in their lives.

Teachers should avoid teaching with the same instructional techniques that have in the past resulted in failure for the student. Specifically, they should:

- Avoid teaching isolated phonics but instead teach students to read for meaning.
- Encourage students to read for retention of ideas, not isolated details.
- Relate reading skills to those academic areas holding the most interest for students.
- Help students recognize that reading is the key to success in school.

While all of these suggestions have application to students of all ages, they have particular application to secondary students with severe reading problems because almost all of these students have been "turned off" to reading somewhere in their school experience. The teacher must therefore work on improving the students' attitude and self-concept by providing successful reading experiences.

Pitfalls of Remediation

The classroom teacher and the reading specialist should consider the following pitfalls that, when not avoided, disrupt the efficiency of many remedial programs.

Fragmented Programs

Remedial programs that focus on the development of skills without providing opportunities for practice and use of the skills generally fail. Students in such programs often develop faulty concepts about the purposes for reading. Similarly, programs that do not provide balance between materials at the independent and instructional levels of the students are limited in their effectiveness. Many packaged remedial programs are seriously fragmented and should only be used if supplements for balance and practice in real reading situations can be provided.

Many well-designed programs are ineffective due to the teacher's compulsion to teach. Involving students in planning, materials selection, purpose setting, and follow-up activities really works. By using contracting, the D-R-T-A, survival reading, and other strategies that involve students, remedial programs stand excellent chance for success.

Teaching to Needs

Constant attention to needs or weaknesses tends to overwhelm students. Every remedial program should be designed to focus on student strengths a large portion of the time.

Oral Reading

Many programs stress oral reading (and often oral reading at sight). Although students should develop fluency in oral reading, and oral reading gives teachers useful diagnostic information, no justification can be found for using it as the major emphasis of the program. Oral reading stresses word pronunciation, an important part of the reading process, but not the ultimate objective. In this chapter, silent-reading comprehension has been stressed. Teachers should be certain that silent reading is a part of every lesson.

Oral reading at sight has no place in a remedial program. Students should always be permitted to prepare for oral reading by practicing silently or practicing orally by themselves. With such preparation, students will be able to produce their best, most fluent oral reading. (Of course, oral reading at sight should be used for on-the-spot diagnosis during remedial programs.)

Illustrating Progress

While often delighted with the progress of their students, many teachers fail to relate this to them. Through contracting, students can understand their progress when each contract is evaluated. Personal progress charts in sight vocabulary development, books read, and skills mastered are effective. Without recognition of success, the students often become discouraged and quit trying.

Sharing Information

When more than one educator is working with a student, a communication system should be developed. Each person should know what the other is doing. Without communication, the student is likely to be exposed to conflicting strategies that serve to confuse rather than help. This becomes very complicated when the student is being tutored outside of the school. In such cases, regular communication from one educator to another is necessary.

Summary

Effective remedial programs focus on the student's self-concept. Strengths must be practiced, recognized, and approved. Students must be decision makers in their instructional activities along with the teacher. All school resources must be used to assist readers in realizing that they can and do read.

Notes

1. Richard Allington, "If They Don't Read Much, How They Ever Gonna Get Good?" *Journal of Reading* 21, no. 1 (October 1977): 57–61.
2. Marie Clay, *Reading: The Patterning of Complex Behavior* (London: Heinemann Educational Books, 1972), 102.
3. Richard Allington, "Are Good Readers and Poor Readers Taught Differently?" (Speech presented at the American Educational Research Association, Toronto, March 1978).
4. Dolores Durkin, "What Classroom Observations Reveal about Reading Comprehension Instruction," *Reading Research Quarterly* 14, no. 4 (1978–79): 481–533.
5. Linda B. Gambrell, Robert M. Wilson, and Walter N. Gantt, "Classroom Observations of Task-Attending Behaviors of Good and Poor Readers," *Journal of Educational Research*, vol. 74, no. 6 (August 1981): 400–05.
6. Carolyn Denham and Ann Lieberman, eds. *Time to Learn* (Washington, D.C.: National Institute of Education, 1980).
7. Robert M. Wilson, "Comprehension Diagnosis Via Task Analysis," *Reading World* 14, no. 3 (March 1975), 178–79.
8. Eleanor Ladd, "Task Analysis," *Reading: What Is It All About?* (Clemson, S.C.: Clemson University, 1975), 68–77.

Suggested Readings

Carbo, Marie. "Research in Reading and Learning Styles." *Exceptional Children*, vol. 49, no. 6 (1983). Pp. 486–94. Presents a review of the literature on the need for designing instruction to the learner's style strengths.

Durkin, Dolores. "What Classroom Observations Reveal about Reading Comprehension." *Reading Research Quarterly* 14, no. 4 (1978–79). Pp. 481–533. A detailed description is presented of the observed behavior of teachers during reading and social studies lessons. This article should be studied by all who are planning remedial lessons.

Gambrell, Linda B., and Robert M. Wilson. *Focusing on the Strengths of Children*. Belmont, Calif.: Fearon Publishers, 1973. Detailed accounts of techniques for focusing on strengths of all students are provided. Ideas for making school enjoyable are included throughout.

Prentice, Lloyd R., Laurie Beckelman, and Phyllis Caputo. *Computer Confidence*. Instructo/ McGraw-Hill, 1983. A resource book for teachers. Includes ideas about the use of computers for instruction, references to clearinghouses, and reference lists of books and periodicals about computers and software.

Smith, Frank. *Understanding Reading*. 2d ed. New York: Holt, Rinehart, and Winston, 1978. The problems of risk taking are discussed in chapter 2 and other chapters. This book is important reading for those who are going to work with students who have experienced large amounts of failure.

Wilson, Robert M., and Linda B. Gambrell. *Contract Teaching*. Paoli, Pa.: Instructo/ McGraw-Hill, 1980. Numerous examples of contract teaching with detailed explanations are included. Record-keeping strategies and reinforcement techniques make this a useful source.

EDITORIAL

Marcia M. Wilson

is a principal in the Montgomery County School District, in Montgomery County, Maryland.

As a classroom teacher, realizing the need to provide for alternatives and student involvement was easy; but identifying an organizational plan that could account for the varying strengths and needs of thirty heterogeneously grouped third graders seemed overwhelming. However, as the time progressed, I was continually unable to deny the frustration I witnessed as many handicapped readers tried and failed with reading, writing, and spelling activities that were too difficult for them. The need for individual students to become aware of and involved in the setting of attainable goals convinced me to try contract teaching.

There are many observations I can reflect upon that have convinced me that contract teaching is a viable and desirable way for teachers to provide for decision making, student involvement, and individually paced instruction, but there is one instance that was so delightful that I'm sure I'll remember it vividly for a long time to come.

I had a class of thirty third graders who were mastering the concept of contract spelling. My class included students from below pre-primer level to ninth grade level. The spelling book issued to me contained twelve words—a number that had proved very easy for some children and totally unreachable to others.

We had passed the stage where children had learned to select, with teacher involvement, those words that they felt they could successfully learn by Friday. We had also talked about various study methods that could help us learn to spell new words, and we were currently experimenting with a limited variety in order to identify those specific techniques that were most beneficial to each individual student.

On Friday, the class was taking the posttest, with each student writing only those words that he or she had contracted to learn. While I was reading the list, I realized that some students, while waiting for me to read a word they had contracted for, had free moments when they could sit back and wait, or look around.

Being familiar with the efforts to copy that can occur if students are frustrated, I immediately asked the students to cover their papers and remember to keep their eyes on their own work area. No sooner had the thoughtless remark left my mouth when one student looked up at me and said, "*Why* would anyone cheat in this room?"

That question caused me to think about and isolate the following changes that were occurring in my room: (1) Being involved in the attainment of a task that was attainable was removing the syndrome of failure and reducing the negative effects of unrealistic competition. (2) The development of an atmosphere where success was possible for all had created an atmosphere where students were encouraging and supportive of one another. (3) Continued experience with success was encouraging students to become risk takers. (4) Involvement of students had developed an awareness of the need for learning as well as a commitment toward learning.

Not only did contracting offer me, as the teacher, a manageable system for offering differentiated learning opportunities, but it proved to be a technique that resulted in a learning climate that was positive and assured success. Had I taken the time to put words to the changes I was witnessing, I might have had a better answer for the boy who asked me, "Why would anyone cheat in this room?"

Marcia M. Wilson

194

Factors That Influence Reading Success

CHAPTER OUTLINE

Readiness Skills or Factors That
Influence Reading Success?
Interest and Motivation
Language-related Factors
Auditory Difficulties
Visual Difficulties
Orientation
The Seriously Disabled Reader

CHAPTER EMPHASES

*Insights can be gained into some of
the difficulties facing poor readers
by looking at the factors that
influence reading success.*
*One key to remediation is attempting
to find ways to interest and
motivate students.*
*Language-related abilities can be
fostered through varied
experiences with outstanding
children's literature.*
*Language differences reduce the
chances that students will take
risks.*
*Auditory and visual skills are best
taught with written passages.*
*When students seem to be disoriented,
teachers should begin by assuring
that the difficulties are not the
result of the learning climate.*

W hy do some children learn to read seemingly effortlessly and, yet, other children struggle, even with a great deal of assistance? There are many answers to this complicated question, but one important factor is that all children do not approach the reading task on an even footing. Some children are considerably advantaged in terms of learning to read.

Learning to read and, later, progressing in reading ability, rely on the quality of instruction the reader receives, as well as on the reader's interest and motivation, degree of language preparedness, and auditory and visual abilities. Readers who are lacking in any of these important areas can learn to read, but they may find it difficult. For this reason, this chapter is devoted to examining the factors that contribute to reading success.

Readiness Skills or Factors That Influence Reading Success?

In many discussions, interest and motivation, language facility, and physical preparedness are referred to as "readiness skills" because they provide important support to underlie beginning reading instruction. It may be, however, that the very term *readiness skills* is misleading for all that it implies. A quick look at some common misconceptions surrounding readiness skills may be helpful.

> *Misconception 1   Children will be unsuccessful in learning to read if they lack any of the recognized readiness skills.* Oftentimes, strengths in one readiness area may compensate for weaknesses in another. Readiness skills are *desirable* but not *necessary* contributors to reading success.
>
> *Misconception 2   Reading instruction should be delayed until children have acquired the readiness skills to proceed.* Readiness skills are more a matter of degree than an all-or-nothing proposition. It would be difficult to say "how ready" a child should be in any of these areas. It is better to ask oneself what type of instruction might be most profitable with a given child.
>
> *Misconception 3   Once a student has begun to read, readiness skills become unimportant.* To the contrary, the abilities that will be discussed in this chapter continue to be important to reading success as students mature in their reading abilities. Students experiencing difficulties in these areas often find their way into remedial programs, even after they have mastered beginning reading.

For all these reasons, from a remedial reading standpoint it is more descriptive to consider factors related to reading success than readiness skills. Many of these factors, such as reading-writing connections and conceptual development, continue to be very important even after students have progressed past beginning reading levels. There are many abilities that good readers possess and that poor readers either lack or fail to use well. By looking at what skilled readers are able to do and how they do it, it is possible to gain valuable insights into the

196

difficulties experienced by poor readers. These insights then can be translated into instructional interventions.

In education, generalizations are often hard to make because so many exceptions to almost any generalization can be found. Nevertheless, from the findings of reading readiness studies of early readers and through other studies that have compared good and poor readers, several trends have emerged.

1. Readers experiencing difficulties are less likely to enjoy reading and to choose to read as a pleasurable free-time activity.
2. Readers experiencing difficulties tend to be less familiar with the conventions of written language (punctuation, grammar, jargon, etc.).
3. Readers experiencing difficulties are also likely to be deficient in listening, speaking, and writing skills as well.
4. The difficulties experienced by some readers may be at least partly attributable to dialect or foreign language interferences.
5. Physical factors such as vision, hearing, and orientation difficulties may cause or contribute to reading difficulties.

Why People Read

There are many reasons why people read, and those reasons can provide teachers with clues to how to motivate readers experiencing difficulties. Research reveals that the reasons people read can be collapsed into two major categories: to gain information and to experience enjoyment. In both of these areas, poorly skilled readers are at a considerable disadvantage.

Reading to Gain Information

There are several ways to highlight the information-gaining aspects of reading in a remedial reading setting. First, readers can be encouraged to use reading to research the answers to questions they pose. Research skills are often neglected in remedial programs, but there are compelling reasons for working with students to research topics of interest. Not only do students gain insights into the information-gaining aspects of reading, but projects may also provide excellent opportunities for teaching useful study skills and strategies that may aid students in their content area studies (social studies, science, etc.).

When readers research topics of personal interest, many important reading and writing skills can also be combined. John, a poor-reading sixth grader, learned a great deal from researching and writing a book about his favorite professional athletes. He had chapters for football, baseball, basketball, and hockey. Each page was devoted to a different athlete and was headed by a picture, followed by a capsule biography, and then a chart with the athlete's records and statistics. John researched his book from varied sources and eagerly reworked each page until he was satisfied. His drafts offered excellent opportunities for proofreading and editing practice that did not appear to John to be "schoolwork" because he wanted others to be able to read his book. Eventually, John's book was added to the school's library collection, and John took a great deal of pride from noting how often his book was checked out by other students.

Functional reading is another important avenue for tapping the motivational potential of information gathering. Functional reading is reading required to perform everyday tasks in the home, community, or workplace. Good readers often take for granted abilities such as reading a menu, consulting a bus schedule, or filling out a job application; but, these reading skills differ markedly from those involved in reading a novel, and readers need to receive instruction in everyday reading areas as well. (Suggestions for functional reading activities are offered in chapter 10.)

Readers also gain insights into the information-gaining aspects of reading when teachers make them aware of the degree to which reading influences their everyday lives. In the morning, students often read a cereal box at the breakfast table, idly read street signs on the way to school, read bulletin boards in the school's hallways as they walk to class, and have countless other casual reading encounters each day. Yet, when many students are asked how much reading they do, they reply that they only read in reading group or when they have to. Remedial readers are often surprised to learn how much information they gain from reading without even being aware of it.

Reading for Enjoyment

Reading for enjoyment starts with reading interest, a powerful force in motivating readers. When readers are interested in what they are reading, they tend to invest more effort and read better. How then can readers' interests be aroused? The short answer is, "By giving them interesting materials to read." Ironically, however, remedial readers often must labor in materials that are decidedly uninteresting. Many commercial materials, especially those designed for skill development, lack interesting content.

Among the best ways to introduce readers to the pleasures of reading are with the varied uses of good children's literature. For younger children, this might involve reading books aloud. Through read-aloud experiences that are later discussed, students develop listening comprehension and recall skills; but more importantly, they come to view reading and literature as personally satisfying. Gambrell and Sokoloski suggest that well-illustrated picture books also offer excellent potential for developing students' oral language abilities. After a book has been read aloud, students may be encouraged to retell the story aided by the book's pictures.[1]

When a book has proved to be especially popular as a read-aloud selection and when the book is not too difficult, students might be encouraged to practice rereading the book themselves. In so doing, the students benefit from having heard how the teacher read the book as well as receive an assist in reading from their familiarity with the storyline. Similarly, teachers report their less-able readers are sometimes helped in reading a selection when the teacher reads aloud the first page or two. Why should that be? In many ways the beginning of any selection is the most difficult because on those pages the characters are first introduced and named, key concepts are first presented, and readers are attempting to activate their prior knowledge.

Mature readers may enjoy finding out more about the authors of some of their favorite books. At times, reading becomes more personalized and interesting when an author's personality and background are revealed. Students come to recognize literature as being written by real people. Better yet, perhaps an opportunity to invite an established children's author to a school may help to launch reading interest.

Other ideas for promoting reading interest include scheduling theme days such as "FIB Day" or "Read-a-T-shirt Day." "FIB" stands for "Friends in Books." On this day students and teachers dress as a favorite character from a children's book of their choice. They bring the book and tell others about their character and why they liked the book. On Read-a-T-shirt Day, teachers and students wear T-shirts to school that feature some sort of written material (appropriate for school, of course). Days such as these help to emphasize that reading can be fun and that not all reading takes place in text materials.[2]

Above all else, students must be granted time and assistance to read for interest and enjoyment without the pressures of book reports. Sometimes called SSR (Sustained Silent Reading) and sometimes SQUIRT (Sustained Quiet Reading Time), these are times reserved for students and teacher to silently read books for pleasure. Many remedial readers have never developed free reading habits because they have lacked opportunities for pleasure reading, and, when students see their teacher reading, there is a valuable modeling effect. The teacher is saying by his or her actions, "I value reading."

Several factors can contribute to SSR success. Students should be given assistance in selecting materials that they not only want to read, but also *can* read. The time allotted for reading should initially be short and then gradually increased. Guests can be invited to participate in reading alongside the students and later tell about the book they were reading. Perhaps the single most important factor, however, is for the teacher to spend the time reading a book simply for pleasure.

Increasingly, educators are recognizing that reading is a language process and, as such, it is inextricably tied to the other language processes of listening, speaking, and writing. What does this mean for remedial reading instruction? It means that "reading instruction" is too narrow a conception. Reading instruction should encompass listening, speaking, and writing instruction as well.

Language-Related Factors

Metalinguistic Awareness

In English, reading proceeds left to right, top to bottom. It consists of words, represented by symbols called letters, and arranged in strings of words called sentences that conform to a wide variety of grammatical rules and conventions. These sentences, in turn, are grouped in paragraphs. Books are always opened from the same side; and, when stories are read, pages are always turned in a precise order. All these intuitive understandings, and more, make up what is referred to as metalinguistic awareness.

Metalinguistic awareness is the reader's understanding of how the language works. As noted earlier, good readers generally have a greater degree of metalinguistic awareness than poor readers; this is one of the enabling abilities that marks them as good readers. Metalinguistic awareness is important from a reading readiness standpoint, but it also has importance in remedial reading instruction. Many readers may be at a disadvantage in respect to early reading instruction because they lack metalinguistic awareness. Sometimes teachers unintentionally contribute to the problem by taking for granted that all students will know what teachers mean when they use specialized jargon associated with reading.

It should not be implied from this, however, that teachers must devote large amounts of time to "teaching" students metalinguistic awareness. The best way to gain these understandings comes from numerous experiences with print in all of its varied forms. Most children begin to develop these understandings in their preschool years while seated in a parent's lap as they watch print as it is being read and help to turn each page. There is no better reading readiness activity than reading aloud to children!

Later, children may "write" scribbled notes to a brother or sister that only they can read (demonstrating an understanding that marks on paper can carry meanings). As children develop literacy skills, these scribbled notes gradually take on more and more characteristics of accepted written prose; however, throughout the early years, children's invented spellings should continue to be encouraged. Simultaneously, parents and older brothers and sisters may model the reading/writing process by writing down dictated messages or stories from the child. An intuitive awareness begins to develop that what is said can be written down and later read . . . that print can carry meaning.

Unfortunately, not all children grow up in literature-rich environments. When children come to school lacking in metalinguistic awareness, teachers should pattern their instruction after some of those first literacy experiences that other children have been fortunate enough to experience. They should read to students and encourage them to write and dictate stories.

Two useful reading activities for encouraging metalinguistic awareness are using big books and predictable books. Big books are books with text and illustrations large enough to be easily shared with a group of children. The teacher may then demonstrate most of the characteristics of early parental lap reading in an instructional setting.[3] As the reading proceeds, the teacher may pause at intervals to involve the children in making predictions about what will happen

---

Predictable Books

Becker, J. *Seven Little Rabbits.* Scholastic, 1973.
Carle, E. *The Very Hungry Caterpillar.* Collins-World, 1969.
Emberley, B. *Drummer Hoff.* Prentice-Hall, 1967.
Garten, J. *The Alphabet Tale.* Random House, 1964.
Ginsburg, M. *My Name Is Alice.* Puffin Books, 1985.
Hawkins, C., and Hawkins, J. *Old Mother Hubbard.* Putnam, 1985.
Keats, E. J. *Over in the Meadow.* Scholastic, 1971.
Lobel, A. *The Rose in My Garden.* Greenwillow, 1984.
Martin, B. *Brown Bear, Brown Bear, What Did You See?* Holt, Rinehart & Winston, 1970.
Parish, P. *I Can, Can You?* Greenwillow, 1980.
Tafuri, N. *Have You Seen My Duckling?* Greenwillow, 1984.
Wildsmith, B. *Toot Toot.* Oxford Press, 1984.

FIGURE 8-1. Predictable Books for Beginning and Remedial Readers. (Many of these authors have written other outstanding predictable books.)

next, and then later, pause to think aloud with the children about the accuracy of their predictions and whether they should be refined. In this manner, children may learn the importance of thinking along with the text as it is being read. The children may also watch the teacher point to words or sentences. They may assist in turning the pages. Or, they may respond to questions such as, "How many *words* are there in this *sentence*? Let's count." In discussions after the reading, students may be encouraged to give their classmates insights into their thought processes by being asked, "How did you know that?"[4]

Predictable books are ones with repetitive language patterns (see Figure 8-1). These books have the greatest effect when they are read many times. As children become more familiar with the language patterns, they are encouraged to join in with the parts they know. There are other important benefits when books are read to children more than once. Martinez and Roser report that repeated read-alouds enhance children's verbalizations about books and also promote a greater depth of understanding.[5] Predictable books are a good means of giving beginning and remedial readers successful, pleasurable reading experiences, and, at the same time, building their metalinguistic awareness.

Oral Language Facility

Listening and speaking abilities underlie reading ability. Through listening and speaking, children develop oral vocabularies and language competence, both of which aid reading. If children have to learn word meanings as well as the printed forms of words, learning to read is difficult indeed. Fortunately, through listening and speaking, most children enter school with extensive meaningful vocabularies. They have also developed intuitive understandings of the grammatical arrangement of the language. This can later provide a foundation for developing contextual abilities. When students lack listening and speaking abilities, teachers can develop them in a variety of ways.

STORYTELLING AND CREATIVE DRAMATICS. One nice way to capitalize on student interest in a favorite story is to follow up the reading by having students reenact the story through either storytelling or creative dramatics. As they invent dialogue and recall the storyline, the students develop many forms of listening and speaking skills.

ROTATING STORY. Rotating stories are introduced by the teacher showing a picture (preferably one with a character approximately the same age as the students) and beginning to tell a story related to the picture. The teacher might introduce characters and setting, and then pose a problem or situation. The picture is passed to one of the students who continues to make up a story. He or she tells as much of the story as desired and then passes the picture to another classmate who continues the story. Eventually, the teacher asks one of the students to try to wrap up the story or retrieves the picture and brings the story to a conclusion.

Rotating stories can provide excellent listening and speaking practice, but when used in remedial settings several cautions should be observed. First, if students do not wish to take part, they should be given the option of merely passing the picture along without saying anything. This keeps shy students from feeling "on the spot." Second, sometimes the opposite thing will happen. One student may talk incessantly without passing the picture along. If this happens, the teacher could gently take the picture back from the student, tell a little bit more of the story, and then pass it along to someone else. Third, sometimes stories can get sidetracked, and the teacher might need to briefly retrieve the picture to breathe new life into the story.

PROJECTIVE DEVICES. Students who lack listening and speaking skills often lack confidence in themselves as speakers. One useful way of making speaking less threatening is to allow students to speak to or through a puppet or toy telephone. Another variation of this technique is to use a radio microphone and have students pretend they are radio disk jockeys or to take the insides out of an old television cabinet and let the students pretend to be on television. Students may also develop their listening and speaking abilities by videotaping a school news magazine or by providing spoken commentary for a videotaped record of a school athletic or arts program.

STRUCTURED LISTENING ACTIVITY (SLA). The SLA is a sequential strategy for developing listening skills that is patterned after the Directed Reading-Thinking Activity (see chapter 10). The steps of the SLA are as follows:

Step 1   Concept Building.
Introduce the story by relating it to the students' prior knowledge.
Discuss important specialized vocabulary necessary for understanding.

Step 2   Listening Purpose.
Suggest some important ideas to help focus the students' listening.
Step 3   Reading Aloud.
Read the story with an emphasis on student interest. Use visual aids and prediction cues interspersed throughout the reading to maintain the students' attention.
Step 4   Questioning.
Discuss the story through teacher-directed questioning.
Step 5   Recitation.
Guide the students through a systematic summary or retelling of the story.

The SLA is based on the premise that because reading and listening are related processes, validated instructional ideas for developing reading comprehension should be possible to adapt to enhance listening comprehension.[6] Research appears to indicate that when young students practice retelling stories that have been read to them, they make gains in the areas of listening comprehension, oral language development, and knowledge of story structure.[7]

Language Interference

When students develop an awareness that their language is different from their peers', they tend to withdraw from oral communication. It's too risky. Everyone has searched for a synonym rather than attempt to use words he or she is unsure how to pronounce. Thus, criticism that usually follows is avoided. Imagine, then, what students must feel who have developed that fear about every utterance they make. If one doesn't attempt oral communication, one won't be criticized. Risk taking is essential, however, for language development. Teachers must develop a climate in which oral communication is enjoyable and rewarding. By reducing the threat of criticism, the teacher increases risk taking and facilitates the use of oral communication. Language difficulties can arise when the student's language does not match the language used in school, is underdeveloped through limited experiential background, or reflects limited conceptual development.

DIALECT LANGUAGE MISMATCHING. Students whose dialect differs from that used in school and in instructional materials are often found in remedial reading classes. Their difficulty lies in attempting to learn to read a language that differs to some degree from the one they speak. How seriously the problem of dialect mismatching affects reading ability is uncertain; however, one may safely assume that it causes a degree of discomfort that, when coupled with other learning difficulties, can interfere with learning to read. Of course, many students with mismatched language do learn to read effectively.

There is nothing so personal as the way a person speaks. Teachers must have a genuine respect for the language that students bring to school. Criticisms of language differences attack not only the students but their families and friends as well. Specifically, teachers should demonstrate acceptance by the following:

1. Respond to language differences without initial correction. Especially in remedial settings, it is vitally important for students to feel secure. Develop a firm relationship based on trust.
2. Respond to what students say and not how they say it. Listen to the ideas that students share and avoid focusing on their dialect to the exclusion of what they have to say.
3. Don't repeat the students' dialect utterances in an effort to call them to the students' attention. Such a strategy is more likely to result in resentment than change. Students will be more likely to respond favorably to instruction when they feel that their language is accepted by their teachers.
4. When students read aloud, accept dialect renderings without comment. If a sentence reads, "I see two dogs," and a student says, "I see two dog," it should be accepted by the teacher without interrupting the reading.
5. When students dictate something for the teacher to write down, it should be recorded exactly as the student dictated it (although words should be spelled correctly). This encourages students to contribute their ideas without fear of failure. Students will also find that they are better able to read something that is written exactly as they said it because it represents their oral language patterns.

Many teachers will probably feel uncomfortable with the above recommendations. They may think that by accepting students' dialect utterances they are shirking their responsibilities to improve students' language. But "improving" is a value-laden term that implies a judgment that the students' dialect is wrong or undesirable. In many everyday social situations, however, the students' dialect will be the preferred way of speaking. With older students, a realistic goal toward which to strive is dialect transfer, not dialect extinction. Instead of trying to eliminate students' dialect, it may be more desirable to equip students with the ability to adapt the way they speak to suit the social situation.

Dialect transfer is based on the notion that, in many social situations (perhaps in the home and community), a student's dialect will be an acceptable and useful way to speak. In other social situations and settings, however, it may serve students well to be able to speak in "more standard English." Employment and educational opportunities are sometimes limited by the way one speaks. Dialect transfer is difficult to promote before students see a need to be able to speak differently.

How can dialect transfer be promoted? It begins first with teachers learning the characteristics of the major regional American dialects spoken by their students so that they can distinguish between poor grammar use and dialect-related utterances. Second, teachers need to give students numerous opportunities to hear and respond to language commonly found in books and used in other segments of society. Once again, reading aloud to students from good literature provides one of the best ways to learn about the connections between oral and written language. The teacher can also serve as a language model by striving to speak precisely.

Later, teachers may wish to distinguish between "school language" and "out-of-school language." Faced with two sentences, students might be asked to identify which one would be more likely to be used by a teacher in school: "I ain't got none," or "I don't have any." Finally, students might attempt to transfer "out-of-school language" to "school language" and vice versa. Throughout, teachers should avoid reference to right and wrong or good and bad.

FOREIGN LANGUAGE MISMATCHING. Many students come to school with a native language other than English. Their mismatch between their native language and the school language may be minimal or nearly total. For many of these students, reading in English represents a frustrating, nonsensical undertaking.

Accurate estimates of the number of bilingual students in this country are difficult to obtain, but one thing appears certain—our national ethnic, racial, and linguistic composition will continue to change. It is estimated that by the year 2010, Hispanics will comprise 14 percent of the total U.S. population.[8] The major bilingual need in our schools today is Spanish/English, but many schools also enroll students with such native languages as Tagalog, Cambodian, Korean, Vietnamese, Farsi, and Urdu.

The degree of difficulty that students encounter depends on their degree of fluency in English and the ability of the school to meet their learning needs. Instructional assistance should be obtained through programs offered by the schools. Clearly, this is very difficult given the diversity of native languages found in some schools. Many principals in metropolitan areas report having more than ten native languages represented in their school populations.

Wherever possible, at the same time they are learning English, students should be given access to interesting books written in their native language. As teachers work with bilingual students, they should remember that those students' lack of English ability does not make them disadvantaged. Their different cultural backgrounds should be viewed as a strength that can enrich the education of their peers. As these students gain English ability, they will be privileged to be fluent in two languages, an enviable position to enjoy in today's multicultural society.

Regrettably, the material and staff resources of many schools are woefully inadequate to meet the needs of non-English speaking students. Several instructional approaches have been found to be useful in working with bilingual students. Teachers might use a threefold approach: (1) enhance students' oral language skills using wordless picture books, (2) develop basic speaking and reading vocabularies using high-frequency, easily pictured nouns, and (3) use a variation of the language-experience approach (see also chapter 9) to bring together listening, speaking, reading, and writing abilities.

Wordless Picture Books

Briggs, R. *The Snowman*. Random House, 1978.
Crews, D. *Truck*. Greenwillow, 1980.
dePaola, T. *The Hunter and the Animals*. Holiday House, 1981.
Goodall, J. *The Adventures of Paddy Pork*. Harcourt, Brace & World, 1968.
Hutchins, P. *Changes, Changes*. Macmillan, 1971.
Keats, E. J. *Skates*. Franklin Watts, 1973.
Krahn, F. *A Flying Saucer Full of Spaghetti*. Dutton, 1970.
Mayer, M. *A Boy, a Dog, and a Frog*. Dial, 1967.
Oxenbury, H. *Shopping Trip*. Dial, 1982.
Spier, P. *Peter Spier's Rain*. Doubleday, 1982.
Ward, L. *The Silver Pony*. Houghton Mifflin, 1973.

FIGURE 8–2. Wordless Picture Books Can Promote Oral Language Abilities. (Many of these illustrators have produced other outstanding wordless picture books.)

WORDLESS PICTURE BOOKS. These books without texts (see Figure 8–2) can be especially useful when students from a variety of linguistic backgrounds are attempting to learn to speak English together. The teacher should show the book to the students two or three times, pointing to different aspects of each picture, and explaining (in the students' native language if possible, otherwise in English) what is happening. Next, students may take turns attempting to narrate the book as they turn the pages. Because the books are able to convey meaning without accompanying explanations, the student narrations need only be as involved as each student is capable. Later, as students acquire more skill, they may attempt to tape record, dictate, or write their accompanying narrations. Because most wordless picture books are written for younger readers, the teacher will have to exercise care in selection and presentation if their use is attempted with older students.

PICTURE NOUNS. Fry has identified 100 nouns that occur frequently in everyday usage and which are easily pictured (see Figure 8–3). These words are arranged into twenty categories, such as People, Transportation, and Clothing, so that students can begin to develop class and meaning relationships between the words that they are learning.[9] There are several advantages to approaching vocabulary using picturable words. They represent concrete objects and therefore are easily learned and remembered. Picture nouns can be readily displayed using wall charts and reinforced through flashcard games and activities. They can also be used to construct rebus stories (combinations of words and pictures) where the teacher can read aloud the connecting text and the students can name the pictures.

COMPREHENSIBLE INPUT PLUS THE LANGUAGE-EXPERIENCE APPROACH (CI + LEA). The language-experience approach (LEA) was developed to harness the language knowledge of native language speakers to teach them to read. Using LEA,

Picture Nouns

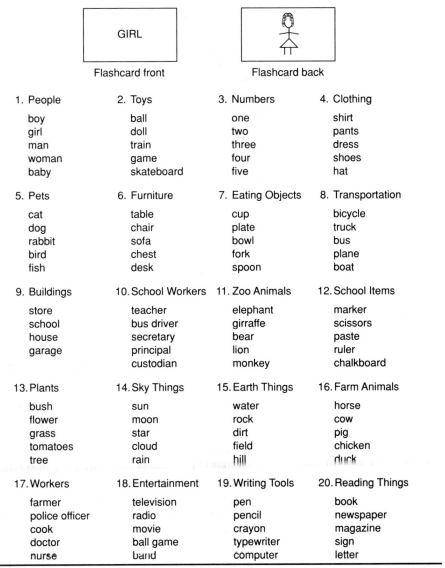

GIRL	
Flashcard front	Flashcard back

1. People	2. Toys	3. Numbers	4. Clothing
boy	ball	one	shirt
girl	doll	two	pants
man	train	three	dress
woman	game	four	shoes
baby	skateboard	five	hat

5. Pets	6. Furniture	7. Eating Objects	8. Transportation
cat	table	cup	bicycle
dog	chair	plate	truck
rabbit	sofa	bowl	bus
bird	chest	fork	plane
fish	desk	spoon	boat

9. Buildings	10. School Workers	11. Zoo Animals	12. School Items
store	teacher	elephant	marker
school	bus driver	girraffe	scissors
house	secretary	bear	paste
garage	principal	lion	ruler
	custodian	monkey	chalkboard

13. Plants	14. Sky Things	15. Earth Things	16. Farm Animals
bush	sun	water	horse
flower	moon	rock	cow
grass	star	dirt	pig
tomatoes	cloud	field	chicken
tree	rain	hill	duck

17. Workers	18. Entertainment	19. Writing Tools	20. Reading Things
farmer	television	pen	book
police officer	radio	pencil	newspaper
cook	movie	crayon	magazine
doctor	ball game	typewriter	sign
nurse	band	computer	letter

Note: Group titles are not Picture Nouns

FIGURE 8-3. Picture Nouns. [From "Picture Nouns for Reading and Vocabulary Improvement," *The Reading Teacher* 41, no. 2 (November 1987). 187. (*Reprinted with permission of Edward B. Fry and The International Reading Association.*)]

students are involved in a first-hand experience that is later discussed and forms the basis for a student-dictated story. The story is recorded by the teacher on the chalkboard or chart paper and then becomes the basis for reading instruction or remediation.

When English is not students' primary language, LEA should be combined with comprehensible input and reinforcement to achieve desired results. Comprehensible input refers to providing students with meaning contexts to acquire new language. These meaning contexts should be concrete and might include large study prints or the wordless picture books and picture noun word cards described above. The teacher should introduce the words and describe them in simple sentences. "A shirt." "This is a shirt." "The boy is wearing a shirt." Students with limited English knowledge benefit from repeated reinforcement of oral language. The teacher should repeat the English sentences many times and invite the students to say them also. Oral reinforcement and comprehensible input are important keys to success. Eventually, the teacher may encourage students to dictate sentences based on the word cards or study prints. "Who has something to tell us about the picture?" These recorded sentences can then be used to teach reading and writing.[10]

Students with limited English abilities have language needs that go far beyond reading instruction alone. They also need to develop their oral abilities, meaningful vocabularies, and knowledge of standard syntactical constructions. If LEA is attempted without comprehensible input and reinforcement, the students' limitations in the other language areas may limit the reading effectiveness of the approach. CI + LEA has been shown to enhance the listening, speaking, and writing abilities of limited-English-proficient students as well.[11]

Underdeveloped Language

As previously noted, reading is a language process. Students experiencing difficulties with reading often have limited oral language abilities as well. Sticht et al. stress the importance of language development in reading by stating that "reading ability is built upon a foundation of language abilities both developed and expressed largely by means of oracy skills of auding [listening with understanding] and speaking."[12] Students from poverty backgrounds in our inner cities and isolated rural areas may have underdeveloped language abilities when compared with same-age peers. These students may appear to lack intellectual ability because they fail to understand situations that are comprehended easily by others. They may lack primary experiences with mountains, lakes, subways, or escalators. Working with these students may require the teacher to simultaneously attempt to develop reading *and* language abilities.

Underdeveloped language is often related to narrow experiential backgrounds and/or restricted conceptual development. In either case, the first prescription for success is acceptance. Every teacher should be urged to view each student as a developing human being. As such, instructional programs should be planned in accordance with where students are, not where teachers would like them to be. Categorizing students under labels or locking them into slow-moving groups indicates a lack of acceptance and is of little educational value. At the same time, expectations of learning rate, learning quantity, and retention ability should be realistic. Programs must be adjusted for these students in order to make use of their strengths. Teachers should use patience, expect gains, and supply rewards for successful performances. Successes must be highlighted; failures must be minimized. Several approaches have been found to be helpful for expanding experiential and conceptual backgrounds.

LANGUAGE-RICH ENVIRONMENTS. When students have underdeveloped language, their needs are best met in a classroom that is rich in language use. Everything that happens during the school day can be discussed. Linking language directly to the students' experiences helps them develop concepts for things they encounter. Trips, pictures, films, drama, puppetry, and audiotapes can be used to develop language experiences. Each experience should be talked about, and one-on-one conversations should be encouraged.

THE LANGUAGE-EXPERIENCE APPROACH. Just as it does for students from different language backgrounds, the language-experience approach assures an approach to reading that is successful, because the concepts that the students encounter are their own.

CATEGORIZING AND CLASSIFYING. Concepts are developed through exercises that require students to place objects in groups. When students categorize things by shape, color, size, or function, they are developing conceptual understanding. Several variations follow:

A. Select the one which doesn't belong.

   peas   corn   hotdogs   beans

   (It is important for students to talk about why they answered as they did. In the above example, a student might have excluded one food because he or she liked to eat all of the others and didn't care for that one.)

B. List four items in each group.

Furniture	Food	Places
____	____	____
____	____	____
____	____	____

C. Place these items into two or more groups that make sense. Be ready to explain *why* you ordered them as you did.

   shoes   red   car   truck   blue   coat   green
   airplane   yellow   boat   shirt   socks

LIST-GROUP-LABEL. Taba proposes an instructional strategy for teacher-led categorizing. It begins with the teacher suggesting a one- or two-word stimulus to serve as the basis for the exercise and writing it on the chalkboard. Ideally, the stimulus should be drawn from the students' reading or from a unit they are studying. The students then brainstorm all the words they associate with the stimulus category as the teacher lists the words on the board. All student responses should be listed, although students may be asked to explain why they associate a particular word with the stimulus. Next, the teacher reads through all the listed words and instructs the students to attempt to group those that "seem to go together in some way" into smaller subgroups. Finally, the students give each subgroup a descriptive label.[13] Some words will not seem to fit well into any single category. Readence and Searfoss suggest establishing a "misfit" category for such words. In order to list a word as a "misfit," the students would have to justify why the word did not belong in any of the other groups.[14]

FEATURE MATRIX. Feature matrices involve students in another form of concept development through categorizing. First the teacher identifies several related terms in the students' reading. These are listed down the side of a matrix chart, and possible features or attributes of the terms are listed across the top (see Figure 8–4).

The teacher shows the students a copy of the feature matrix (without the pluses and minuses), and the students copy it into their notebooks. Then, they try to fill in the matrix by using pluses if the feature applies and minuses if it does not. If the students are not sure about a feature, they can leave it blank. (In the example, David knew that soccer was played with a round ball, but he was not sure how many players are on a soccer team and whether it is played in quarters.)

When all the students have filled in a feature matrix chart, they read the selection attempting to confirm or reject their decisions. As they read, the students are encouraged to change items if they find information in the text that warrants it. Later, the students use their completed charts to fill in a master chart with the teacher.[15] When disagreements arise, the students may attempt to resolve them by reading aloud portions of the text or by consulting other

	Team Sports		
	Periods Called Quarters	Played With a Round Ball	More Than 7 Players
football	+	−	+
baseball	−	+	+
ice hockey	−	−	−
soccer		+	
basketball	+	+	−

FIGURE 8–4. David's Feature Matrix

sources. Feature matrices nicely bring together conceptual development, prior knowledge, language development, and reading.

Some students enter school without the necessary auditory skills to profit from normal instruction. When ignored by the teacher, these auditory skills can remain undeveloped, thus causing considerable discomfort to the struggling reader. For this discussion on remediation, auditory skills will be classified into hearing problems and auditory discrimination problems.

Hearing Problems

While teachers can do nothing to correct hearing problems aside from referring the student to a hearing specialist, they can make temporary classroom adjustments to facilitate a comfortable learning situation by:

1. Arranging the seating so that the students with hearing problems are close to the teacher during group instruction.
2. Standing close to those students' desks during group instruction and increasing their voice volume so that students with hearing problems can hear the instruction. They can also face the students, thereby providing opportunity for lip reading.
3. Creating a "buddy" system. When a student does not hear the teacher or the other students, another student can repeat the information and help that student understand it.
4. When possible, stressing visual learning activities (i.e., reading instead of listening). Instruction for independent work should be written, as should rules, regulations, and announcements. The writing can be on the chalkboard, on chart paper, or in personal notes to students with hearing problems.

Auditory Discrimination

Many students have normal hearing skills but underdeveloped auditory discrimination skills. They experience difficulty distinguishing one sound from another. Their difficulty is likely to be incorrectly identified as speech impairment or trouble with phonics. Because students come to school with most speech skills developed, one would believe that their auditory discrimination skills are also developed. However, for teachers with students who have underdeveloped articulation skills or who are not in the habit of listening carefully, the following suggestions can prove valuable:

1. Request the assistance of a speech and hearing therapist who can work with the students, help diagnose their difficulties or offer suggestions for classroom adjustments.

211

2. Serve as a speech model. Enunciate distinctly and read with articulate speech patterns.

3. Provide exercises that stress gross auditory differences. For example:

> Tell me whether the words that I repeat are the same or different:
>
>> *catch—catch*
>>
>> *big—dog*
>>
>> *many—some*
>
> Tell me whether first sounds you hear in the words that I repeat are the same or different:
>
>> *big—belt*
>>
>> *butter—lettuce*
>>
>> *boy—sail*

4. Gradually provide exercises involving finer auditory discriminations. For example:

> Tell me whether the words that I repeat are the same or different:
>
>> *catch—catch*
>>
>> *corn—scorn*
>>
>> *can—tan*
>
> Tell me whether the first sound you hear in the following words is the same or different:
>
>> *big—pig*
>>
>> *bite—tight*
>>
>> *best—best*

5. Provide exercises that demand longer auditory memory. For example:

> Listen to the first word that I give you. Then tell me whether the following words are the same or different:
>
>> *pig: pig—small—big—pig—dig*
>
> Listen to the first sound in the word I give you. Then tell me which of the following words have the same beginning sound:
>
>> *pig: bite—pick—pencil—dig—picnic*

6. Provide exercises that call for listening for sound in different parts of the word. For example:

> Listen for words that end in the same sound as the word *pig:*
>
>> *dig—ditch—park—twig—dog*

7. Provide exercises that indicate the ability to hear rhyming words. For example:

> Listen to the first word I give you and tell me whether the following words rhyme with that word:
>
>> *cat: rat—sat—pot—pat*

8. Provide a stimulus and ask the student to say some words that rhyme. For example:

> Listen to the first word I give you and tell me some words that rhyme with it:
>
>> *cat:*

Techniques for conducting drill lessons such as these can include placing items on tape and having students do the exercises independently; having an aide or a skilled student read what you have prepared; and calling the students who need such work to you while the others are working independently. These students need daily practice to assist them in developing auditory-discrimination skills. As the skills are mastered, a periodic review should be made. It is also necessary to review the skills prior to developing phonics lessons. Auditory-discrimination skills are also easily developed and reinforced through game activities.

Some students will not respond to these activities due to serious problems in auditory orientation. These students need in-depth training through the cooperative efforts of the reading specialist, classroom teacher, and speech teacher. Phonics instruction should be withheld until a thorough program in auditory sequencing has been completed. These students have difficulty distinguishing initial, medial, and final sounds as they hear them. They also have difficulty associating auditory with visual sequences. Understandably, these are different skills; auditory sequences occur in time and visual sequences occur in space. Because most students come to school with these skills in hand, some teachers assume that all students have them.

**Visual
Difficulties**

As with auditory problems, visual problems also can be grouped into two categories: those dealing with the skills and functions of vision and those dealing with visual discrimination. Numerous students find giving visual attention difficult, either as the result of a physical disability or a developmental lag.

Vision Problems

Visual problems can be adjusted and corrected by vision specialists. The teacher, in the meantime, must work with those students daily. Several suggestions for helping students with vision problems include:

1. Arrange seating so that the reader has the best light, the least glare, and the optimum distance for easy viewing. Those who are farsighted can sit in the back of the instructional area and those who are nearsighted can sit in the front.
2. When writing on the board, use larger letter size than usual.
3. Supplement writing on the board or on chart paper by providing auditory reinforcement.
4. Use the "buddy" system. By working with a student who has normal sight, a student with visual difficulties can seek help when visual difficulties interfere with getting needed information.
5. Stress auditory learning. A student with visual problems may respond better to a phonics approach or to sound reinforcement.

Tracing also helps, for it develops opportunities for reinforcing weak visual skills.

6. Make visual activity periods short. When students show signs of discomfort (e.g., rubbing of eyes and inattentiveness), they should be released from the visual tasks involved in reading.

Adjustments such as these are not the answer to the basic problem but can make learning comfortable for a student.

Visual Discrimination

Difficulties with visual discrimination skills are usually the result of inexperience or inability to attend to the task. In either case, successful experience can usually develop comfort in visual-discrimination skills. The following suggestions can be valuable in developing them.

START WITH THE STUDENTS' LANGUAGE. As students talk, write down what they say. For example, if a student wants to talk about what was seen on the way to school, the following story may develop:

> I saw a big dog. His name was Rex. The dog frightened many of us. But I picked up a stick and scared the dog. Everyone thinks I am very brave. Do you?

Once the story is written, two copies are prepared for each student, one to use for visual discrimination activities and one to save for reading. On the copy that the students can mark, the following activities can be tried:

1. Ask the students to pick words that they know. Write the words on cards and then have them find the words in the story. They do not need to say them, but they do have to match them.
2. Write the letter *s* on a card and ask the students to underline that letter every time they see it in the story.
3. Ask the students to circle all the words that begin with the letter *a* (give them *a* cards).
4. Write a phrase on cards. Have the students find it in the story and draw two lines under it.
5. Ask the students to draw a box around every word that ends with the letter *e*. (Give the students *e* cards.)

From duplicated story copy have the students cut out words and phrases and match them with the story on chart paper. This activity enhances transfer from activities at the seat to activities at the board. Depending on the story, visual discrimination activities can be formulated to help students develop the required skills. Matching, seeing letters in words, finding letters in specific parts of words, and finding groups of the words in a certain order are only a few examples.

By asking the students to do something different in each activity (underlining, circling, drawing a box), the teacher can easily see how well each activity has been completed. As with auditory discrimination, the teacher should start with gross discriminations and move to fine discriminations. For example, beginning with the letter *s* is easier than starting with *d*. Finding a word is easier than finding a letter; finding a letter or a group of letters in a certain position in a word is even more difficult. Discover where the students are in the development of visual discrimination abilities and work from there. Teachers should also provide a stimulus with which the students are to work visually. Auditory reinforcements are fine, but the activities must be visual to visual (i.e., the students see a word on a card and match it with a word on the board).

USE WORD CARDS. Cards on which the students have written words they mastered can be used to develop visual discrimination skills. For example, teachers can ask the students to complete these tasks:

1. Find all the words in their files that end in *e*, like at*e*.
2. Find all the words that end in *ing*, like walk*ing*.
3. Find all the words that have double consonants, like te*ll*.

The suggestions for such activities could be endless, but two points about them are important: (1) teachers are working with visual clues and from words that the students know; and (2) through teaching from strengths, students can develop strong visual-discrimination skills.

PROVIDE A MAGAZINE AREA IN THE ROOM. Teachers should instruct the readers to look through magazines for ads with certain kinds of words (e.g., words about people, words that describe things, etc.). Provide a pair of scissors or some paste, and a place to post these words when found.

USE GAME-TYPE ACTIVITIES. Game-type activities hold considerable merit in developing visual discrimination, just as they do in developing auditory discrimination. For example, teachers can give students a set of cards with letters on them. Then starting with a small group of letters, such as *s,t,* and *w,* they hold up a letter and have students hold up the same letter. Then they hold up two letters and have students hold up the same two letters in the same sequence. Such an activity can gradually increase in difficulty, thus developing the attention to detail and visual-discrimination skills needed for reading. Once the game idea is developed, students can play without direct teacher supervision.

USE NEWSPAPERS TO DEVELOP VISUAL SKILLS. The newspaper is useful because of its availability, its expendability, and its motivational appeal. Students can work at the following activities:

1. Make a collage of all the various forms of a given letter that they can find in advertisements and headlines.

2. Circle all the occurrences of a given letter in the comic strips after a lesson on that letter.
3. Conduct word hunts for words that are in their word banks. Cut them out and paste them on their word bank cards.
4. Find words in advertisements that have unique features and make a collage out of them—for example, all words with ascending letters or that end in *s*.

These and numerous other ideas can be developed from available newspaper supplies and provide motivation in themselves. The students notice that they are working with the same type of material that they see adults use in their homes.

USE COMMERCIALLY PREPARED MATERIALS. Workbook-type activities, spirit duplication master sheets, and pencil-paper activities are commonly used commercially prepared materials. Many such activities start with form identification. For example, five balls are placed on a sheet; four of them are green and one is red. Students are to mark the one that is different. However, such activities should be reserved for only the most severely handicapped and even then seem to be of questionable value in the reading process. Teachers themselves can make materials that are more relevant to the reading process with relatively small commitments of time and energy. Students respond very well to such homemade materials.

When making materials for students to use in visual discrimination activities, several precautions are necessary:

1. Printing should be done very carefully; however, typing is preferred.
2. Printing only should be used on working copies. These copies should contain no art work, photographs, or other distractions.
3. At first, only small amounts of print should be used on a page. Do not smother the reader with too many words and sentences.
4. Make activities short and (if possible) self-correcting. Provide answer keys or models of marked copies.
5. Make the print of beginning activities look like that which the children are accustomed to seeing. For very young children, each new sentence should start a new line. With older students, material can appear in paragraph form. To make the material too much like a preprimer is insulting to older students.
6. Always end the activity by reading the story. If the students cannot read it, read it to them. Always apply the activity to reading for thought by discussing the story and its meanings with the students.
7. When students do well, tell them so. Praise for legitimate successes is important in all drill work, but students should not be praised for incomplete or inaccurate work. Instead, the activity

should be restructured so that students can complete it. Then they can be praised.

Visual discrimination activities should be continued as the students begin to read. Review as well as more advanced activities should be part of the visual discrimination program until students are operating comfortably.

Orientation difficulties are reflected by the inability to visually follow the print in words or sentences. Orientation skills are commonly listed under visual discrimination; however, difficulties in this area seem to be different enough to justify separate classification. Visual discrimination skills are related to seeing likenesses and differences; orientation skills are concerned with the left-to-right controlled visual movements necessary for effective reading.

Orientation

Readers' orientation errors cannot be corrected simply by calling the errors to the students' attention. Remedial procedures for correcting orientation skills are most effective when they help students feel the comfort and success that accompany correct orientation and when they provide practice to extend the skill into a habit. Several specific questions should be addressed in considering orientation problems:

1. What can be done to help students who have difficulty with orientation?
2. Should students be discouraged from finger pointing when they read?
3. How effective are mechanical aids in helping students with orientation difficulties?

Instructional Techniques

Orientation abilities develop naturally in most readers through practice and modeling. Those two principles can be applied to develop instructional approaches. Specifically, the following suggestions are offered:

PROVIDE OPPORTUNITIES FOR WRITING EXPERIENCE. Through writing, students can clearly see the necessity of left-to-right letter formation within a word and word formation within a sentence. Students should be given numerous opportunities to write and to see the teacher writing on the board. Once again, the language-experience approach provides a good opportunity for students to watch the left-to-right progression involved in reading and writing. And when students compose with microcomputers and word processing programs, left-to-right progression is clearly demonstrated.

USE READING IN UNISON ACTIVITIES. Reading in unison has been around a long time, and so, teachers have a tendency to dismiss it as being old-fashioned. For remedial readers, however, reading in unison has several benefits. First, it can build oral reading confidence, because it takes place in a group and individual readers are not singled out. Second, if a reader makes a mistake while reading in unison, often no one else will hear it. Finally, through reading in unison, readers with orientation difficulties can be swept along by those who have developed good reading habits. Before beginning a reading in unison experience, teachers should allow the students to read the selection through silently once so that the students can attend to comprehension and mentally rehearse the reading.

PRACTICE READING ALONG WITH A TAPE RECORDER. Taped stories can provide interesting practice with orientation abilities. Students wearing headphones can listen and read along with taped stories. The students can read either orally or silently, but it is the visual tracking of the text that develops orientation abilities so it is vitally important that the text be easy enough for the student to handle. Commercially prepared tapes are available or teachers may wish to record their own. Sometimes older readers will benefit from recording the tapes to be used by the younger readers. When teachers or students record their own tapes, it is desirable to signal when each new page begins so that students who have lost their place can catch up with the text again.

USE THE NEUROLOGICAL IMPRESS METHOD. This technique was developed initially to be used with individual students, but it can be adapted for group use. When used individually, the teacher sits slightly behind the student and directs the reading into the student's ear. The teacher reads more loudly when the student falters and more softly when the student is reading comfortably and confidently.[16] When used as a group technique, the teacher and students read in unison.

Finger Pointing

Should students be permitted to finger point when they read? In general, the answer to that question would be a qualified "no." Finger pointing has several detrimental side effects. Students who finger point are more likely than other students to read word by word, thereby interfering with reading fluency. They also may be disinclined to look back to reread portions previously read but not understood. Further, finger pointing may hamper reading rate. So, in general, if students do not need to finger point, they should be encouraged to read without doing so.

What about the student who habitually loses his or her place without pointing? That student needs some sort of place-holding assistance, and finger pointing may provide the help this student needs. For such a student, the finger also may help to establish the concept of left-to-right eye movements. Later, perhaps the student can be encouraged to place fingers or thumbs on either end of the line being read to gradually wean the student away from finger pointing.

Some students experience reading difficulties because they tend to be distracted by the print surrounding the line that they are reading. The text seems to "swim" before their eyes. One approach with such a student is to use a line marker that is placed under the line that is being read. This blocks out some distracting influences, those beneath the text. The drawback of using a line marker is the tendency for the student to read line by line. Another instructional adaptation would be to make the student a card with a "window" cut out of the middle that would reveal all of one line and the first three or four words of the next line. Such a card effectively removes the distracting text from both above and below the line *and* helps to minimize the line-by-line reading fostered by a line marker. It also helps to train the student's eyes to sweep down and to the left to begin the next line of reading.

Mechanical Aids

Mechanical aids are available to help students develop orientation skills. Tracking, for example, can be reinforced by the use of the Controlled Reader. Students watch a story from a film paced either a line at a time or by a left-to-right exposure control, which can be regulated for speed. Mechanical aids can help motivate the students to attempt activities that are otherwise rather dull, such as practice to improve reading rate. However, when one considers the costs of such devices and the excitement that can be created with teacher-made materials, it would appear that the use of controlled reading machines in remedial reading is of a seriously limited value. The primary concern is that they place readers in situations that are unnatural. Reading is not a mechanically paced

Skill instruction should always end with silent reading time.

activity that proceeds at a smooth and constant pace; rather, it is a stop-and-go activity where good readers continually adapt their strategies to suit their reading circumstances. Readers stop to use word attack skills and to reread certain passages; they then read quickly through other sections. The notion that all words and phrases deserve the same amount of reading time must be seriously questioned. When mechanical aids are used, they should be followed by practice with normal reading materials without the use of the aid. In such a way, students are assisted in transferring from practice situations to real reading situations.

The Seriously Disabled Reader

Instructional Programming

Some students display serious difficulties involving several or most of the factors influencing reading success. Their perception of the printed page is so distorted that there is little chance conventional reading approaches will be successful. Their difficulties are usually complicated by inability to remember sight words, understand the relationship between letters and sounds, and make any sense out of a passage. Several suggestions are offered for those working with students who have these types of severe difficulties:

1. First the learning climate should be reexamined. Are there any distractions that may be keeping the student from giving full attention to the reading activity? If so, adjustments to minimize those distractions should precede any of the following suggestions.
2. Physical and psychological assessments should be conducted so that problems in these areas can be understood and adjustments made. If no problems are identified as a result of these assessments, the problem lies somewhere in the school program.
3. A school screening committee should gather as much data as possible, including observation of the student during instructional periods. Considering all the resources within the school, the screening committee makes decisions concerning which resources can best assist the student. A plan is implemented, and periodic evaluation of progress keeps the screening committee informed and able to make future decisions.
4. Some schools have special programs for those experiencing serious difficulties. Instructors with special training direct the learning of such students. Often multisensory approaches are recommended for use with students whose learning difficulties are severe. Local college personnel who operate clinics and who work with seriously handicapped readers may be able to offer valuable program suggestions.
5. Means for providing large amounts of individual attention often need to be developed. Teacher aides, parents, volunteers, and peer tutors can assist the teacher. They can assist students as

they work independently from the teacher, work toward keeping them from practicing faulty learning habits, and help them build the sense of self-worth and success that they need so badly.

6. Teachers will need to provide communications with parents. Naturally, parents become anxious about their children's difficulties, and a first impulse may be to either blame the school or the child. Parents need to be kept apprised of measures that are being tried. All too often, parents of these children become easy targets for people who seem to offer easy answers to the student's difficulty. Expensive tutorial programs, often operated to earn profit instead of to help the reader, are easy to find. By helping parents understand the difficulty and the efforts school personnel make, much of their anxiety can be reduced.

Instructional Techniques

Students identified as being severely disabled in reading have failed to learn to read with the usual approaches. When students fail to learn, it is not always because the methods or materials were inappropriate. Sometimes their inability to learn can be traced to the pace of instruction; if given more time the students might benefit from the approach. In other cases, deficiencies in one or more of the enabling abilities may be due to a developmental lag, and the student may eventually gain the requisite abilities. Still other times, however, the methods and materials used with other students may be poorly suited to these students' learning strengths. When this is determined to be the case, alternate means of instruction might be desired. Three of the most often recommended approaches for working with severely disabled readers include visual-emphasis methods, auditory-emphasis methods, and multisensory techniques.

VISUAL-EMPHASIS METHODS. When students appear to have visual strengths accompanied by auditory weaknesses, approaches that maximize those strengths should be considered. Typically, in visual-emphasis methods, students concentrate their attentions on whole word approaches to instruction. This includes building a basic sight vocabulary of high-frequency words (to, and, the, etc.) and functional words (exit, stop, poison, etc.). These basic words are learned through careful presentation and drill. To the degree possible, the teacher should attempt to introduce and practice the words in simple sentences. Students should also work on developing strong contextual abilities as clues to word identification through cloze practice (see chapter 9). The teacher may wish to use word banks and word lists on the classroom wall to reinforce learning and facilitate writing practice. Visual-emphasis methods do not ignore phonics instruction, but it is introduced as needed in the course of whole-word-based instruction.

AUDITORY-EMPHASIS METHODS. Students who have auditory strengths have been found to benefit from instruction that emphasizes phonic sound blending. These approaches usually begin with students learning to identify letter names, then letter sounds, then blend the sounds into words, then place the words into sentences, and the sentences into stories. First words introduced are often small, phonetically regular, minimally different word groups (met, set, pet, bet, etc.). It is "part to whole" learning.

Often these approaches are criticized for being too highly structured and for concentrating too much on single words to the exclusion of meaningful reading. These are valid concerns; however, students who have failed to learn by other methods may respond well to auditory-emphasis methods if they have auditory strengths. If such approaches are used, teachers should attempt to assure that students view the purpose of reading as more than just identifying words.

MULTISENSORY TECHNIQUES. Severely disabled readers who appear to have neither auditory nor visual strengths may benefit from techniques that emphasize each of the senses. These approaches are often described as VAKT (for Visual-Auditory-Kinesthetic-Tactile). They tend to focus on single-word learning and utilize tracing. As the students trace words, they are expected to pronounce them correctly.

There are several variations of multisensory techniques. One of the most popular was proposed by Grace Fernald in 1943.[17] An adaptation of the Fernald method follows:

1. The reader is exposed to a word printed in large, dark letters on a card. (Because these words are usually taken from the reader's experience stories, teachers can assume that he or she knows their meanings.)
2. The reader is directed to trace the word with one or two fingers while saying it. (This tracing procedure is to be repeated until it appears that the reader has mastered the word. The teacher demonstrates as often as necessary when beginning this approach.)
3. After several repeated tracings, the reader attempts to reproduce the word without the copy, again pronouncing it as it is written. Emphasis is placed on the whole word nature of the approach and not on the individual letters.
4. Eventually, students advance to learning words without the tracing step.

Teachers will find several variations of the VAKT technique in the literature. Some prefer that all tracing be done in sand or using sandpaper letters to heighten the touch sensations; others feel that tracing the word in large copy is adequate. Some suggest that the word be printed, providing the best transfer to actual reading. Others prefer that the word be written in cursive to reinforce the flow and connection between the letters. Regardless of the system, the integration of several learning modalities seems to benefit many severely disabled readers. Teachers are cautioned, however, that a VAKT approach should only be employed after other more contextual approaches have failed, because it is extremely time consuming and tends to emphasize single-word learning.

A promising new multisensory technique is the use of hand signs. Signing has been a longtime communication tool of the hearing impaired. Recent work with signing as an instructional technique to teach reading to the hearing students has met with much success. Researchers report that students learn well with the technique and that students say they prefer signing to VAKT for learning new words (see chapter 9).

Summary

Several factors contribute to reading success, and conversely, many students who have difficulties in these areas also have difficulties with reading. Some readers' difficulties may be traced to a lack of interest or motivation in reading-related activities. There are several ways to attempt to reach these students; however, one of the best is by using the motivational power of books. Unfortunately, many remedial programs appear to emphasize skills almost to the exclusion of pleasurable reading.

Reading is a language process, and students may experience language-related reading difficulties. Some may lack metalinguistic awareness. Teachers should not assume all students understand the conventions of printed language and its attendant jargon. Once again, language knowledge is best acquired through varied experiences with interesting books. Other readers may possess underdeveloped listening and speaking abilities. Storytelling, rotating stories, creative dramatics, and puppetry are useful means of enhancing students' oral language abilities. Still other readers may experience some reading difficulties because they are either dialect speakers or come from a foreign language background. For many of these students, the language-experience approach is helpful because it presents these readers with familiar language patterns and experiential content. Language abilities are based on concepts; therefore, classification exercises that build conceptual knowledge may be expected to develop overall language abilities as well.

When students have auditory, visual, or orientation difficulties, those problems may interfere with reading. Teachers need to be aware of these important areas, refer students who appear to have difficulties for further professional help, and make appropriate instructional adjustments to assure reading successes. With seriously disabled readers, a team approach is especially important because these students are often experiencing difficulties with several of the factors that influence reading success.

Notes

1. Linda Gambrell and Carol Sokoloski, "Picture Potency: Use Caldecott Award Books to Develop Children's Language," *The Reading Teacher* 36, no. 9 (May 1983): 868–71.
2. Craig J. Cleland, "The Reading Clinic: Designing a Successful Experience for Students (Pt. 1)," *Reading World* 22, no. 2 (December 1982): 160–62.
3. Charlotte S. Huck and Kristen Jeffers Kerstetter, "Developing Readers," in *Children's Literature in the Reading Program*, ed. Bernice E. Cullinan (Newark, Del.: International Reading Association, 1987), 30–40.

4. Martha Combs, "Modeling the Reading Process with Enlarged Texts," *The Reading Teacher* 40, no. 4 (January 1987): 422–26.

5. Miriam Martinez and Nancy Roser, "Read It Again: The Value of Repeated Readings During Storytime," *The Reading Teacher* 38, no. 8 (April 1985): 782–86.

6. Joyce S. Choate and Thomas A. Rakes, "The Structured Listening Activity: A Model for Improving Listening Comprehension," *The Reading Teacher* 41, no. 2 (November 1987): 194–200.

7. Lesley Mandel Morrow, "Reading and Retelling Stories: Strategies for Emergent Readers," *The Reading Teacher* 38, no. 9 (May 1985): 870–75.

8. Carmela H. Logan, "Integrating ESL/BE and Mainstream Teacher Training," *Educational Horizons* 61, no. 1 (Fall 1987): 41–42.

9. Edward B. Fry, "Picture Nouns for Reading and Vocabulary Improvement," *The Reading Teacher* 41, no. 2 (November 1987): 185–91.

10. Margaret Moustafa and Joyce Penrose, "Comprehensible Input PLUS the Language Experience Approach: Reading Instruction for Limited English Speaking Students," *The Reading Teacher* 37, no. 8 (March 1985): 640–47.

11. Margaret Moustafa, "Comprehensible Input PLUS the Language Experience Approach: A Long-term Perspective," *The Reading Teacher* 41, no. 3 (December 1987): 276–86.

12. Thomas G. Sticht et al., *Auding and Reading: A Developmental Model* (Alexandria, Va.: Human Resources Research Organization, 1974), vi.

13. Hilda Taba, *Teacher's Handbook for Elementary Social Studies* (Reading, Mass.: Addison-Wesley, 1967), chap. 7.

14. John E. Readence and Lyndon W. Searfoss, "Teaching Strategies for Vocabulary Development," *English Journal* 69, no. 7 (October 1980): 43–46.

15. Patricia M. Cunningham and James W. Cunningham, "Content Area Reading-Writing Lessons," *The Reading Teacher* 40, no. 5 (February 1987): 506–12.

16. Paul M. Hollingsworth, "An Experiment with the Impress Methods of Teaching Reading," *The Reading Teacher* 24, no. 2 (November 1970): 112–14.

17. Grace Fernald, *Remedial Techniques in Basic School Subjects* (New York: McGraw-Hill, 1943), chap. 9.

Suggested Readings

Clay, Marie. *Reading: The Patterning of Complex Behaviour.* 2d ed. London: Heinemann Educational Books, 1979. Part 2 of this book discusses early reading skills in detail. Chapter 7 provides interesting reading regarding orientation learning.

Clay, Marie. *Observing Young Readers.* Exeter, N.H.: Heinemann Educational Books, 1982. Clay presents observational research evidence to support her contentions that early natural language explorations are valuable.

Cullinan, Bernice E., ed. *Children's Literature in the Reading Program.* Newark, Del.: International Reading Association, 1987. This multiauthored volume contains a wealth of teaching ideas for unleashing the power of children's literature in the school reading program.

Goodman, Ken. *What's Whole in Whole Language?* Portsmouth, N.H.: Heinemann Educational Books, 1986. This book presents an alternative to a traditional basal reading and skills approach through natural uses of the integrated language arts.

Hall, MaryAnne. *Teaching Reading As a Language Experience.* 3d ed. Columbus, Ohio: Charles E. Merrill Publishing Co., 1981. This book provides a basic background for using the language-experience approach in remediation. Chapter 7 deals specifically with fostering early reading abilities with the language-experience approach.

Hardt, Ulrich H., ed. *Teaching Reading with the Other Language Arts.* Newark, Del.: International Reading Association, 1983. This book will be a valuable resource for teachers who wish to learn more about integrating listening, speaking, writing, and reading instruction.

Lamb, Pose. "Dialects and Reading." In *Applied Linguistics and Reading,* ed. R. E. Shafer. Newark, Del.: International Reading Association, 1979. Pp. 40–50. This thoughtful article examines the relationship of dialects to reading from several different theoretical viewpoints.

EDITORIAL

Gerald L. Fowler

is assistant superintendent for the Carlisle School District, Carlisle, Pennsylvania.

Randy was a very shy first grader. He rarely talked to the other children and often responded to me with gestures rather than words. When he did speak, the sounds were often garbled and the messages limited to one or two phrases. By the end of the first month of school, Randy still seemed bewildered and approached every experience as though it were his first. A referral to our speech therapist came back with the response that Randy had the language capacity of a "two- or three-year-old." My own experiences had shown me that he had no knowledge of letters (names or sounds), few labels for common objects, and limited visual discrimination ability for graphic constructions. Also, Randy was not doing well in the readiness program designed to lead into the basal readers used in our school.

Further background information revealed that he lived with his father and a sister who was a few years older than he. His family was very poor, having few modern conveniences. There were no phones, radios, televisions, or books in his apartment. His father had to leave Randy and his sister alone while he worked. They were given strict instructions to keep the door locked and talk with no one during his absence.

I decided that Randy needed a rich language-oriented program to become a successful reader. I began using the language-experience approach with him. In this way we would begin with the few words he already knew and use them as building blocks in many skill areas. Randy enjoyed this approach. He spent another year in first grade, and four years later I happened to be visiting the school (I had since left) and discovered he was doing quite well in grade five—not the top of the class but well enough to read comfortably in groups and do many of the content-area assignments that required reading.

Gerald L. Fowler

Word Identification

CHAPTER OUTLINE

The Language-Experience Approach
Remediation in Sight Vocabulary
Remediation in Word Attack
Putting It All Together

CHAPTER EMPHASES

The language-experience approach can aid in developing personal sight vocabularies.

Sight vocabulary and word attack activities can be developed from word bank words.

Sight vocabulary and word attack lessons should be short and end with reading in context.

Phonics instruction can be abstract and, therefore, very difficult.

Learning centers can reinforce sight vocabulary and word attack activities.

Some students need a system for attacking unknown words.

The use of signing can reinforce vocabulary retention.

Successful reading requires use of sight vocabulary and word attack skills. Remedial work in these areas should not focus on teaching a large set of isolated words or skills, but rather should concentrate on total comprehension of a reading passage. This chapter will explore remediation in these areas stressing the relationship between word attack activities and comprehension.

The Language-
Experience
Approach

The teacher and reading specialist who are planning remedial activities in the area of sight vocabulary and word attack must understand the language-experience approach. This approach stresses reading as a meaningful, communicative activity. For students who have experienced difficulty reading, an approach that stresses personal meaning has the following advantages:

1. The language-experience approach focuses first and mainly on understanding meaning and then on isolated skill development so that it has more motivational appeal to students.
2. The words used in developing language-experience stories have personal meaning for the students who developed the stories. The teacher can assume that the students have at least one meaning for the words used.
3. The syntax of the stories is familiar to the students who developed them. No strange grammatical structures interfere with understanding.
4. The content of the stories has personal meaning to the students. This assures comprehension and facilitates motivation.

When language-experience stories are used as a basis for remedial activities in sight vocabulary and word attack skills, the lessons should start and end with the words in context so that the students are continuously reminded that all of their effort is toward reading for meaning. The following suggestions can serve as possible techniques for using language-experience stories in developing sight vocabulary and word attack skills.

1. Generate a discussion concerning the experience of a student or group of students. Encourage the students to talk about what they saw or did, how it made them feel, and the meaning the experience had for them.
2. Following free discussion, direct the students to tell a story about the experience. Ask for contributions and write exactly what they say. Always spell words correctly but do not change the contributor's sentence structure. Some guidelines for writing stories follow.

- Encourage all students to contribute.
- In the beginning, use some type of identification for each individual's contribution (e.g., "Donald said, 'I see a big dog'" or "I see a big dog" [Donald]).
- Read what has been written immediately following writing each sentence. Next, have the student who gave the sentence read it; then, the entire group.
- For very young readers, start every new sentence on a new line. For older readers, write in paragraphs.
- Begin with fairly short stories. If the students have more to say, write the story on two pages with only a few lines on each page. Students with serious reading problems can become discouraged with too much print on a single page.
- Have students watch as the story is written. Call attention to the formation of words as they are written.
- As students develop skill with beginning consonants, invite them to help spell words (e.g., "How would I begin the word *boy*?").

3. After the story is written, have the students read it in unison several times.

4. Duplicate the story as soon as possible, making at least two copies for each student. One copy can be placed in a folder to become reading material. The second copy can be used for skill development.

5. Skills can be developed from language-experience stories in a variety of ways. In chapter 8, using language-experience stories to develop visual discrimination, auditory discrimination, and orientation skills was discussed. Skills in vocabulary can be developed using the following methods:
   - Have the students mark all the words that they know. Then have them put several of these words in a private word box or word bank. The students' word banks provide a natural opportunity for meaningful word drills. On the front of the word bank card print the word. On the back write a sentence given by the student using the word.

tiger	The tiger is strong.
(front)	(back)

   - Students can practice their known words in pairs or in small groups. They can match words in their word banks with words in their stories. They can classify words as action words, naming words, people words, words beginning with specific letters, and so on.

- Once a group of words is developed, students can use their word banks to help them with spelling activities. They can use them to build sentences, make crossword puzzles, and in many other activities.
- Add words to the students' banks occasionally. When the word *and* or *the* occurs repeatedly in a story, but has not been chosen for placement in the word banks, call it to the students' attention. Such service words will be needed in future reading and in vocabulary activities.

6. Word attack skills can be developed using the following methods:

- Using word bank words, have students make a collection of rhyming words, e.g., "Collect all words in your word bank that rhyme with *cat*." Then have students share their rhyming words. Write them on the chalkboard and discuss how the words found are the same and how they are different. See if the students can brainstorm to build more *-at* rhyming words.
- Have students search their word banks for all words that begin with a given consonant and share what they have found. See if they can brainstorm to add words that fit.
- Have students search their word banks for words with common prefixes and suffixes and again share and brainstorm.

PIZZA

1. Preheat oven to 425° F.

2. Put pizza flour mix in a small bowl.

3. Add ½ cup very warm water to mix. Stir with spoon until all flour particles are moistened. Then stir vigorously for 25 strokes.

4. Cover bowl. Let stand in warm place for 5 minutes.

5. Using shortening, grease well a 14" pizza pan or a 14"x11" rectangle on a cookie sheet.

6. Lightly spread pizza over the bottom of the pan and ½" up each side.

7. Pour canned sauce over it.

Following direction activities can come naturally from the language-experience approach.

After studying syllabication generalizations, use word bank words to serve as examples and exceptions to the generalization. For example, if the generalization being taught is *vc/cv*, then the students would find words such as *window, picnic, pencil*, and *index* as examples that match the generalization, and a word such as *father* as an exception.

7. Comprehension activities can also be developed from language-experience stories (see chapter 10).

These suggestions in no way cover all the possibilities of the language-experience approach for remediation. Additional specific suggestions are provided under various remedial areas in this and other chapters. Those unfamiliar with the language-experience approach will want to study the books of Hall and Stauffer listed at the end of this chapter.

Remediation in Sight Vocabulary

Sight vocabulary involves instant word pronunciation and word meaning identification. Sight vocabulary study aims at comprehension through decoding and associating a word in context rather than in isolation since word meaning depends on the relationship between the words in a sentence or paragraph.

Remedial procedures will be developed in direct response to the questions asked under the diagnosis of sight vocabulary difficulties. Specifically, those questions are:

1. Does the student miss small, graphically similar words?
2. Do words missed represent abstract concepts?
3. Do word meanings appear to be confused?
4. Does the student know words in context but not in isolation?
5. Does the student appear to know words at the end of a lesson but not the next day?

These difficulties seldom appear alone; rather, they are interrelated. Establishing the answers to these questions helps determine in which areas the interrelationship has taken place so that these areas can be emphasized in remediation. For example, through examination it can clearly be seen that small, graphically similar words are often words with abstract meanings, so dual remedial considerations are required.

Small, Graphically Similar Words

Do the students miss small, graphically similar words or do they falter on words that are obviously different? Quite often, readers will miss small words that have minimal configurational differences (e.g., *when* and *where*) while effectively attacking larger and more obviously different words (e.g., *elephant* and

Christmas). The latter is considered a skill in sight vocabulary, while the former normally shows difficulty in word attack, especially if the words missed are at or below the instructional level. Whichever, the teacher should work from the readers' strengths. If the students can work with words of maximal differences, the teacher should provide more exercises with those types of words, moving gradually to words that are more similar until skill with those words has developed. Then the students should move to words even more alike until skill with words that have minimal graphic differences has been developed.

Ultimately, the student must receive instruction in the discrimination of words that are minimally different. These exercises should be conducted in phrase and sentence form so that the reader realizes that the minimal difference distorts not only the pronunciation but the meaning of the words: "We took the *dig* (instead of *dog*) for a walk." To clarify the similarities and differences in minimally different words, teachers should pull these words from context for study (*dig-dog*). Any exercise, however, should be followed by returning to context.

In the early grades, the teacher may use experience charts to illustrate the need for careful visual discrimination of minimally different words. In these situations, the teacher should take every opportunity to emphasize how words of similar configuration actually differ in both form and meaning, using the reader's own language contributions as examples. For instance, when writing a student's story, the teacher should look for opportunities to demonstrate how certain words look alike or different.

Using words from the students' word banks (i.e., words that are already known) illustrates teaching to strengths. Locating words in the banks that look very much alike, pronouncing them, noting meanings, using them in sentences, and noting how they look alike and different is extremely useful. Attention should be given to differences in all parts of the words—initial, medial, and final.

Programmed materials are available that are particularly adaptable for classroom use in remediation of this skill difficulty. These materials can help the student see differences in words that have minimal graphic differences (e.g., *hat* and *bat*). As an example of these materials, *Programmed Reading* contains a series of exercises through which the reader can develop skill with a minimum amount of teacher supervision (see Figure 9–1). The student must look at the pictures, read the sentence or partial sentence, and use closure to obtain the correct code and message. These exercises progress from the elementary type to complete stories. The forced-choice closure concept, where the reader selects from a limited number of appropriate responses, is maintained at all levels.

The student is reinforced by the appearance of the correct answer after each frame or page, depending on how much material the teacher feels the reader can handle before reinforcement. The skills developed in the workbooks are transferred to reading in prepared storybooks, containing stories with minimally different words. It is unlikely that these materials will satisfy the reader's total reading needs. Programmed materials such as these can be supplemented with the language-experience approach, allowing students to develop their personal word bank of meaningful words.

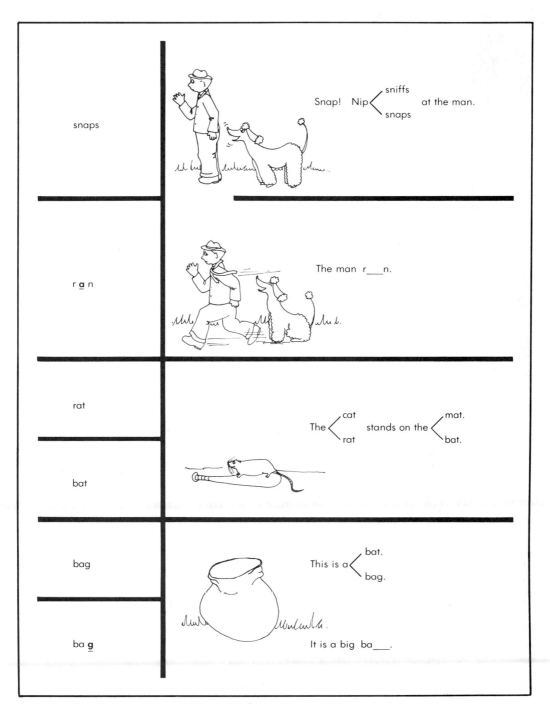

FIGURE 9–1. A sample page of a programmed reader. (*Reproduced by permission from PROGRAMMED READING BOOK 2, Series One. Copyright © 1963 by Sullivan Associates. Published by McGraw-Hill, Inc.*)

A Little Red Hen

A little red hen is in Ben's pen.

Pam looked at the hen and said,

"Can I have the red hen

for a pet?"

Ben said, "If you can get a box

for it, you can have the red hen."

Pam ran and got a red box

with a lid.

She fed the hen and led it

to the box.

The little red hen got into its

little red box.

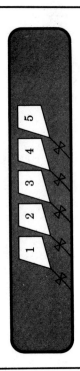

| 5 | The little red hen got into its box. |

| 2 | Pam said, "Can I have the hen for a pet?" |

| 4 | Pam ran and got a box with a lid. |

| 1 | A little red hen is in Ben's pen. |

| 3 | "If you get a box for the hen, you can," said Ben. |

21

Use after page 24 of Unit 5. **Arranging Events in Sequence:** Pupils should carefully read the story on page 22 before doing this exercise. Then have pupils read all of the sentences on this page. Have them find the number 1 and read the sentence that tells what happened first. Then have them decide which event happened next and write the number 2 in the correct box. Repeat for the remaining sentences having pupils work independently. Notice that the last one is done for the pupil. Pupils may copy the sentences in correct sequence on a separate sheet of paper.

FIGURE 9–2. A sample page from a linguistic reader. *(Copyright © 1980 by Merrill Publishing Company. The Merrill Linguistic Reader Catch On, Level C. Reproduced by permission; all rights reserved.)*

234

The linguistic approach can be adapted to almost any type of material, for example, the word banks and programmed materials mentioned previously. The *Let's Read* books and *The Merrill Linguistic Readers* (see Figure 9–2) are prepared linguistic materials for beginning readers and are appropriate for individualized instruction of students with serious reading problems. Both of these approaches have a controlled vocabulary of minimally different words, a controlled initial presentation of words with consistent vowel and consonant sounds, and an absence of pictures so that correct visual perception is necessary for accurate decoding. A similar approach, *The Linguistic Readers*, varies somewhat from these but does maintain the necessity for visual perception of minimal differences. An example of adaptations of *The Linguistic Readers* for instruction is thoroughly described by Botel.[1]

Abstract Concepts

Students often find it particularly difficult to remember words that represent abstract concepts (e.g., *when, these, if, those*). Emphasis in remediation for this type of difficulty should focus on the word as it appears in context since it is from context that these words can be understood. Furthermore, since these words are seldom used in isolation in reading, they should not be taught in isolation.

Once again, experience-story approaches are particularly valuable in developing this type of reading sight vocabulary. Students use these words to formulate their experience stories, allowing a natural opportunity for instruction in the service and function of these words. Although the experience-story approach will probably be used more frequently with younger readers, considerable success with this type of approach has also been found with older students. Experience-story reading allows teachers to determine if words used have meaning for the readers, since they make the contributions. Through these materials, the use and nature of abstract words can be effectively illustrated.

Again, word bank words that carry little meaning of their own (*and, the, of,* and so on) are known to students and can be developed into meaningful activities. For example, using *and, the,* and *of* from a word bank, teachers can ask which word would fit in the blank: bread _____ butter, I see _____ man, and on top _____ the table. The use of such modified closure activities develops skills in the use of abstract words.

Sight vocabulary drills with abstract concepts are most effective when the words are used in phrases (e.g., *in a good spirit*). Prepared phrase cards with the more commonly used word combinations are available in the Dolch game series (e.g., *Match, Basic Sight Cards*).

After a certain amount of sight vocabulary has been developed, students may build sentences from word cards. Here emphasis should be placed on the function of the abstract word as created by the student. With this activity, the unknown word is not placed in a definition situation; rather, it appears in a functional situation—the sentence. Intentional distortions of these types of words in context may be used to illustrate their importance. For example, the text reads,

"*In* the table is a lot of money." It is changed to read, "*On* the table is a lot of money." The students either describe or illustrate how the slight change has affected the meaning of the sentence.

Word games such as *Word Lotto* which use abstract words reinforce words that have been previously learned (i.e., words from students' word banks). Word games are highly motivating and take the drill atmosphere from reinforcement activities. Games such as checkers can be used with words taped on each square. As players move or jump opponents, they are expected to pronounce the words on the spaces involved. Students become so enthusiastic about such activities that they forget they are being drilled.

Confused Word Meanings

Remedial instruction for confusion of word meanings must be based on the following two considerations:

1. Sometimes students, for one reason or another, fail to develop a background of experience that permits them to associate meaning with the word they have pronounced. If this deficiency is chronic, remediation will necessarily consist of experiential language development as well as instruction in sight vocabulary.
2. Although many students know the meaning of a word and can use it in a sentence, they fail to associate the word with the correct meaning, apparently because of preoccupation with word pronunciation. Remedial activities with these students, then, should be in the area of sight vocabulary, where they must be

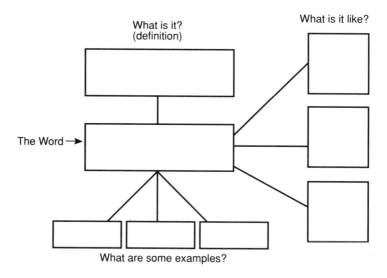

FIGURE 9–3. Word Map Diagram

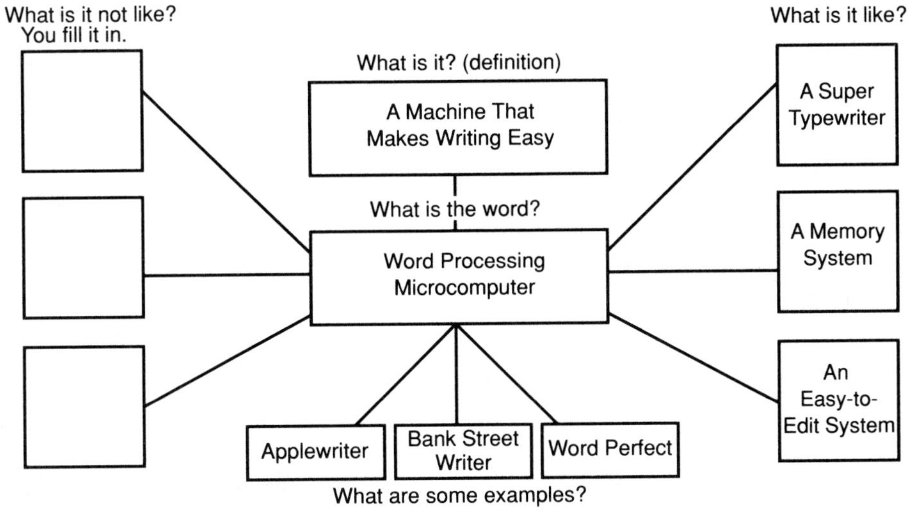

FIGURE 9-4. Word Map Filled In

taught to be conscious of what the word means as well as how it sounds.

As previously stated, every word drill should end with the word in context. In this way the precise meaning and function of the word are best understood; readers with these characteristics must have context emphasized even more precisely. The students begin by reading easy material and demonstrating their knowledge of the words in question by paraphrasing the author's words.

Teachers will often find it useful to establish whether the students know the meaning of a word through definition. If students can give the definition of a word, the meaning of the word as such is not causing the problem; the use of the word in a particular contextual situation is causing difficulty, however. The presentation of the word in various settings is then the appropriate approach to take.

At times, a simple definition does not provide students with enough exposure to a new word to help them to really understand the richness of the word's meaning. Schwartz and Raphael[2] suggest the use of word maps to supply a degree of richness not found in simple definitions.

Their word map expects students to answer the following questions:

- What is the word?
- What is it (definition)?
- What is it like?
- What are some examples?
- Some have added, What is it not like?

The word map might look like the one shown in Figure 9-3.
Filled in, it might look like the one shown in Figure 9-4.

It is obvious that the use of such a word map can greatly enrich the students' understanding of a given word's meaning.

Since students already understand the meaning of the pronounced words, experience stories using the students' own wording again play an important role in remedial efforts. Teachers of elementary school children are urged to provide numerous opportunities for group-experience stories in which an association between the experiences of the group and the words that represent those experiences exists. This presents a golden opportunity to create situations in which students learn from one another. Frequently, students react better to the responses of their peers than to teacher efforts. Two sources of activities to help students develop word meaning skills are Heilman[3] for the younger student and Dale and O'Rourke[4] for the more mature student.

Although frequently not included as a remedial technique, the dictionary can be used to assist older students. Because they know the correct pronunciation of a word in print, they can use the dictionary to find meanings efficiently; consequently, they may develop a habit of consulting the dictionary for unknown words. Techniques for use with the dictionary are discussed in the section "Remediation in Word Attack" later in this chapter.

The *Peabody Language Development Kits* contain programs for numerous language development lessons. Teachers may find this type of program a guide for the entire school year. Among the experiences included with these kits are following directions, brainstorming, critical thinking, memorizing, rhyming, and listening. Pictures, objects, and tapes are used to enrich the child's experiential background.

The *Building Pre-Reading Skills Kit-a-Language* provides the teacher with another program for language development. It consists of pictures through which vocabulary can be stimulated, synonyms developed, and language-experience stories drawn.

For the reader seriously handicapped by the inability to associate the printed word with meaning, the *Non-Oral Reading Series* may contain the requisites for initial instruction. This approach bypasses completely the vocalization of the printed word and emphasizes instead the word's association with a pictured concept. The task is to match the printed symbol with a picture representing the concept for that symbol. This direct association from print to concept minimizes the importance of pronunciation for those who have been overdrilled in it.

Teachers will also find it useful to have the student respond directly through physical activity to such printed word commands as "jump up," and "shake hands." This approach also minimizes vocalization of the printed word, emphasizing again the meaning of the word through student response. The *Nichols Tachistoscope Slides*, developed for this purpose, appear to be effective in establishing the importance of the concepts covered by words.

Collecting words in categories from the word bank can also help stress word meanings. For example, to collect action words, the student must think of word meaning, not just pronunciation. Words that are names of things can be matched with the action words to make short sentences (e.g., *dogs run, ducks*

Placing word bank words on a checker board is an enjoyable drill exercise
for students.

dive, horses jump). Students can look at the sentences they have built to determine which ones make sense, an extremely meaningful activity. In addition,
stimulating students with incomplete sentences, such as "I like to _____ ", makes
the learning more personal and interesting.

Teachers also may use initial sight-vocabulary exercises consisting of
nouns, adjectives, and verbs that can be pictured. The *Dolch Picture Word
Cards*, containing ninety-six of these types of words, may be used. Several
matching games require a student to match a picture with a printed word,
thereby reinforcing understanding of word meaning in a gamelike activity. Such
activities are self-motivating. *Picture Word Puzzles* provide similar reinforcement with children having association deficiencies.

Active participation can be achieved by having students build sentences
from the words that they know. After known words are placed on cards, the
cards are scrambled and the students are asked to build either specific sentences
or sentences of their choosing. The *Linguistic Block Series* can be used in the
same manner by allowing students to fill the blank block with words in their
personal vocabularies.

Meaning in Context

Students who know words in context but not in isolation are indicating that
context aids their reading. By being aware of the function of words in their
language and sentence meaning, these students are demonstrating desirable word

Pupils can build sentences from scrambled world cards.

attack processes. Since most words are encountered in context, this difficulty should not be considered critical.

Occasionally, however, a word must be read in isolation and recognition is crucial (e.g., signs which indicate words such as *Stop, Danger, Women*). Such words should be taught in context, then pulled from context and attention placed on meaning. Since meaning clues seem to aid this type of reader, the stress on meaning should also help. These words should also be pointed out in real life whenever possible. For example, teachers can locate a *Stop* sign and see if students know the word when they see it at a street corner.

Sometimes the student recognizes the word in isolation but not in context. While such cases are rare, some consideration should be given to the problem. Usually this happens when the word has been changed from what students had known. If students learn the word *bank* as a basketball term and then encounter it in the sentence, "I can *bank* on you," they may not understand it. In such a case it would be correct to say that the students did not have the word *bank* as a sight word, so they did not know the word in isolation. Some readers have difficulty with certain types of print. Small print on a crowded page can cause them some confusion. The teacher can encourage these students to frame the word by blocking out all of the other words. If the other words were distracters, the student should then be able to read the word and proceed with reading the passage. However, by starting vocabulary instruction with words in context this problem should not occur.

Learning Not Retained

Students often appear to have mastered words for their sight vocabularies, then the next day cannot recall their meanings. This presents a real problem for teachers, who, thinking that the students have learned the words, plan the next lesson using those words as a base. The students also become confused because they cannot remember those words. The solution for such problems is elusive because several causes may be operating alone or in combination.

PACING. Teachers may be asking the students to learn too many sight words in a given lesson. If so, pacing must be adjusted. In remedial situations, the teacher and the student should negotiate the pace of sight words to be learned. If the teacher feels that a student can learn four words a day and the student says, "I think I can learn three a day," three words should be the accepted goal with an added, "And be certain to learn them well." If this adjustment helps the students remember their sight words, a suitable pace for successful learning has been found. Pace may need to be adjusted daily depending on the difficulty of the words to be remembered (the meanings of *elephant* and *Halloween* are easier to remember than the meanings of *their* and *there*). Teachers should make certain that the students learn what they study.

REPETITION. Another reason for lack of retention may be that the students have not had enough opportunities to encounter the new words. Everyone has thought he or she has mastered something only to find out that it has slipped from memory. Repeated exposure to such information enables clear recall of it. For students who forget easily, teachers should structure extra practice. Games, learning centers, and working with peers can be ways of helping students retain what they respond to initially. Since some students need more exposure to sight words than others, such practice should be individually prescribed.

REVIEW. Still another possible explanation for students forgetting is that the teacher has assumed too much when planning to use the previous day's words as a base for the next day's lesson. A quick review of the materials assumed to have been learned will quickly let the teacher know if the base is solid. If not, a brief review lesson should strengthen the ability of students to recall the sight words so that the base for the next lesson is established.

USING SIGNS. The use of hand signs, developed for communication among hearing impaired persons, has been explored as a possible strategy for reinforcing sight vocabulary with various hearing populations.[5] Many signs are iconic, that is, the signs carry meaning. (For example, the word *children* is signed by miming patting several children's heads, the sign for *up* is pointing up with the index finger, and the sign for *eat* is miming placing food in your mouth with your fingers.) When signs carry meaning, they are easily learned and retained, and they reinforce sight vocabulary in a way that most students find very enjoyable.
    Here is how it works:

1. Show the students the word "eat" on a card.
2. Show students the sign for the word "eat" and have the students make the sign.

Mime right hand feeding the mouth.

3. Pronounce the word and have the students pronounce it as they sign it.

4. Repeat steps 1, 2, and 3 several times.

Teachers who have never taken a sign course have successfully used signing as a strategy to reinforce sight vocabulary. There are many sign books available to assist teachers in making the signs. *The Comprehensive Signed English Dictionary*[6] provides signs for over 3,000 of the most common words. It includes artwork that shows the sign and a written description about how the sign is made. *Signing for Reading Success* (see suggested readings at the end of this chapter) is a booklet that provides signing strategies for use in the classroom with hearing students. These two books should be enough to get teachers started.

In preparation for the lesson, teachers will need to find the sign in the dictionary and practice it a few times. Most teachers feel more comfortable if they can use a sign monitor, a person who knows signs and can check the teacher's signing accuracy. Teachers can follow the four-step process described above. Students are now asked to look at the word, sign it, and then pronounce it. It has been noted that students will sign the word when they see it until they have it mastered, and then they drop the sign step without being told to do so.

Hafer[7] found that learning disabled students retained more sight words when using the signing strategy as compared to the VAKT strategy. She found that it was much faster and that all of the learning disabled students preferred signing over VAKT. Wilson and Hoyer[8] collected data with ten first- and second-grade students over a period of fourteen weeks. During regular instruction, these children averaged a vocabulary retention rate of 69 percent. When using the signing strategy, the retention rate was 93 percent. Knable[9] used signs with adult illiterates in a prison literacy program. He found that (1) the signing helped to reinforce sight vocabulary, (2) the adults enjoyed learning sight words via signing, and (3) the tutors found it easy to use.

Why does the use of signing get such positive results? There might be several explanations.

1. Students view signing as a code, and most students enjoy learning a code.
2. It is multisensory, as is VAKT, but signing is a strategy that can be used with far less instructional time than VAKT requires.
3. It is a strategy that places meaning before word pronunciation. The students look at the word, think about the sign (which usually carries meaning), sign the word, and then pronounce the word. This change of process in word learning might be just what some students need to retain their sight vocabulary.

CONTEXT. Finally, teachers should make certain that the students have learned words in a contextual situation. If the students' word cards have only the word on the front of the card, then sentences using the word created by the students should be placed on the back. If students do not seem to be able to respond to a word, they can turn the card over and see it in a familiar context. In this manner, they can work with word cards without teacher help even when they run into difficulty.

Additional Considerations in Sight Vocabulary

The following aspects of remediation of sight vocabulary problems should be carefully understood by any person conducting remediation in this area:

SKILL SEGMENTATION. Students often see no connection between learning sight vocabulary and reading. Efforts to link sight vocabulary training to actual

Signing can be used as a language-development activity that is fun and highly motivating.

reading situations are essential. Students should be asked why they think they are studying these words. Their verbalization of how sight vocabulary fits into reading helps teachers know how well their students understand the purposes for a given activity.

TELL STUDENTS THE WORD. The teacher will find many situations in which it is advisable to tell students unknown words. Although, normally, teachers should not provide unknown words, they will often find that students are in situations where they simply do not have the skills needed to attack unknown words. In these cases, telling them the word will permit them to move along with the context of the story, focusing attention on those words they have the skills to attack effectively. In such cases, the teachers should not feel guilty about telling students words, nor should they make the students feel this way.

OVERLEARNING. The very nature of sight vocabulary (instant recognition and meaning) implies that it must be overlearned. Overlearning, not to be conducted in isolated drill activities, is most effective when the reader has opportunities to use the word again and again in context. Many remedial efforts fail because they do not provide for overlearning sight vocabulary words in context. Experience stories, trade books, and similar materials are available to facilitate overlearning.

Reinforcing sight vocabulary through the use of word banks exemplifies the concept of focusing on strengths and meets the need for overlearning. Several suggestions for the use of word banks as reinforcers follow:

1. Find all the words that begin like _____ or end like _____ .
2. Find all the words that rhyme with _____ .
3. Find all the words that are one-syllable words or two-syllable words (and so on).
4. Find all the words that are examples of _____ (a given generalization).
5. Find all the words that contain silent letters (or blends or digraphs, and so on).

Similarly, games, either commercially developed or teacher made, make overlearning exciting and fun. Games that follow the pattern of a race track and involve spinning a wheel or rolling dice to move around it can be used. Each block on the race track can require the student to demonstrate a skill: initial consonant substitution, syllabication, or vowel knowledge. Remember that the element of chance enters into game activities; a loss is not a matter of intellectual inability, but luck. Teachers should be certain that this chance factor is obvious to students in all games used for these purposes.

Every remedial session should provide opportunities for the students to read materials of their own choosing. Perhaps as much as 25 to 50 percent of the remedial time can be wisely spent on such activities. Readers become comfortable with words that they will meet over and over again. Overlearning is often interpreted as a drill-and-grill type of activity. Obviously, the more motivating the activity, the less it will be viewed as a chore.

WORD LENGTH AND SOUND LENGTH. Some seriously handicapped readers may look at a word such as *mow* and call it *motorcycle*. These readers have not made an association between sound length and word length. Consequently, they have a slim possibility of making progress in sight-vocabulary development without an intervention program in awareness of sound and graphic relationships. (These lessons should not focus on phonics, but rather on awareness that long-sounding words will appear to be longer in print than short-sounding words.) Instruction is directed to the problem by discussing the problem with the students and then providing exercises with extreme examples (*mow—motorcycle*) and moving toward instruction with minor changes (*mow—mower*).

WORD BOUNDARIES. Some immature readers have difficulty identifying word boundaries even though they sound as though they are reading accurately. Clay reports this type of phenomenon and attributes it to memorization of the passage.[10] The students listen to others and repeat what they have heard. They sound as if they are reading, but they are not. If teachers are concerned that some of the readers are doing just that, they should ask the readers to frame several of the words. If they frame the word *house* as follows, then they show that they do not recognize the boundaries of the word:

I went into (the house to) see Jim.

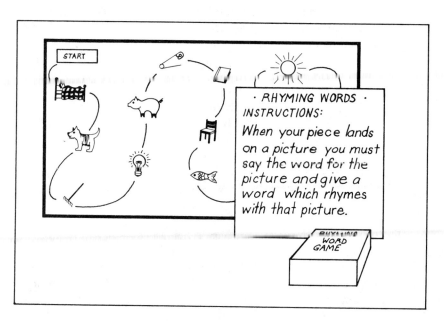

Competitive games enrich otherwise boring phonics activities.

The students should be shown the word *house* on a card and asked to read a sentence. They should be able to find it in the sentence and frame it. In this way, they can learn the boundaries of the words.

Motivation Techniques

The often subtle developments in sight vocabulary should be illustrated to readers so that they may be encouraged by their progress. The following techniques have been found to be particularly helpful:

1. Transferring every lesson to contextual situations illustrates to students that the effort they are making in sight vocabulary is, in effect, making them better readers. Particularly with older students, this in itself is often ample motivation for further improvement.
2. Recording experience stories in booklet form is interesting to younger students because they can see their progress merely by the quantity of the material they have been able to learn to read. The sight vocabulary implications of that quantity can be pointed out if the student doesn't see it.
3. Charts illustrating the goals toward which the student will work in sight vocabulary seem to trigger some students' efforts to perform better. Ultimately, intrinsic motivation should fulfill the function of such charts. Further, these charts should never place one reader in competition with another. Illustrating success through charts must be carefully planned. Objectives must be short term and within the realistic grasp of the student. Charts that emphasize long-range goals can discourage as well as encourage students. During a moon shot, University of Maryland clinicians led their students in a vocabulary development race against the astronauts. The students won the race, and the short-term nature (eight days) of the chart made it worthwhile.
4. Sight vocabulary cards maintained in a file or on a ring illustrate visually to students that they have accumulated a number of useful words through which they can become better readers. These words should not be listed in isolation; rather, they should appear in a sentence with the word highlighted.

Games have been suggested for teaching several of these techniques. These appear to hold a student's interest and to establish a degree of motivation, while assisting the student in developing sight vocabulary.

As has been mentioned, the use of contracts through which students regulate their learning to some degree are of particular value. The completion of a contract is motivation in itself. Of course, specially constructed rewards and motivational devices can be built in. For example, contract completion can result in an immediate reward through free-reading time, praise, and other encouragement.

247

Word
Identification

Word attack skills enable students to pronounce words not in their sight vocabularies and to understand them without teacher assistance as they are used in contextual situations.

Many readers have serious difficulties with word attack skills, so many remedial programs concentrate on them heavily. Consequently, teachers have an abundant amount of material to choose from to teach word attack skills. Also, many approaches to the problem have been recommended in the professional literature. With this wealth of information, teachers can easily overemphasize instruction in word attack skills. Heilman proposes, "The optimum amount of phonics instruction that a child should receive is the minimum amount he needs to become an independent reader."[11] Following such advice should lessen the possibilities of overemphasis. Another danger related to word attack instruction is that it often occurs in isolation away from context. Students often fail to see the purposes for such lessons and interest lags. Teachers should end all word attack lessons in context so students can see how what they have learned has helped them to read better.

In light of the research on good and poor readers, reading specialists and classroom teachers should assure all readers ample time to practice reading. They should especially remember this as they develop lesson plans in word attack skills.

In the discussion on the use of criterion-referenced tests in chapter 3, teachers were warned against testing too many objectives. Some programs that accompany CRTs lock students into learning a specific set of subskills prior to moving to the next level. Since these subskill lessons seem to concentrate on word attack skills, this area presents the greatest problem. Different students need different amounts and types of phonics instruction. Teachers should take care to avoid use of programs that lock students into specific learning sequences. Remedial programs in word attack should be designed to foster independence in reading, not mere proficiency in word attack drills.

Because various methods exist for attacking words not known at sight, educational focus should be on word attack skills that assist the reader in attacking words most efficiently in terms of time and most consistently in terms of application. Once overlearned, efficiency in word attack should have the same aims as efficiency in sight vocabulary (i.e., to decode the word and associate its meaning instantly to the context in which it occurs).

As indicated in the diagnosis chapters, word attack falls into three major categories: phonics clues, structural clues, and contextual clues. Dictionary skills, a fourth category of word attack that normally is not considered a remedial necessity, need development in remedial programs at times.

**Remediation
in Word
Attack**

Discovery Technique

Teachers must assume that most students referred for remedial help have had instruction in word attack skills. Since those skills have not been mastered, the teachers can conclude that previous instructional efforts have failed. Therefore, part of the reason for failure in learning word attack skills must be attributed to the instructional technique. Throughout this section, the discovery technique will be mentioned as a solution to specific problems.[12] A brief review of the discovery technique and some of its possibilities are included as a preface to the discussion of remediation in word attack.

1. Present words that contain the visual clues desired for instruction. For example (using known words):

    index   *picnic*   *pencil*   *chapter*

2. Direct the students to observe visually the patterns in the words. For example:
    - Place a *v* above each   v v
      vowel.   index
    - Place a *c* above each   vccv
      consonant between the vowels.   index
    - Divide the word into   vc cv
      syllables.   in/dex

3. Have the students form generalizations in their own words. For example, one student may say, *"vc/cv"*; another might say, "When you have *vc/cv* divide between the *cs*" concerning these patterns and this syllabication. Any appropriate response is acceptable. Teachers should avoid forcing their own wording on the students.

4. Have the students turn to material that they are reading to collect words that fit the pattern. For example, refer to a specific page in a book on which there are five words that fit the pattern. The students may also find words in their word banks that fit the pattern.

The major advantages of the discovery technique include the active response of the students, acceptance of their generalizations, and the impact that results from forming a generalization through the use of visual clues. Teachers may choose to vary the approach at times; in fact, Botel suggests that steps 3 and 4 be reversed. Other variations may include a discussion of exceptions to the generalization; help in beginning the wording (e.g., "When a word contains the pattern . . ."); and activities directed from word lists to determine the ability of the students to discriminate the visual pattern. Although the discovery technique takes more time than simply telling the students, the lasting effects are extremely valuable.

Remedial efforts in the area of phonics will deal with the questions asked after diagnosis.

1. Does the student appear to not use graphic cues?
2. Does the student attack small words accurately but not large ones?
3. Does the student seem to know sound-symbol relationships but seem unable to use them during reading?

Although in diagnosis the skills of phonics have been delegated to one of three precise areas (letter sounds, syllabication, and blending), the remedial program should combine these areas for instructional purposes. The functional use of phonics skills involves the reader's ability to divide the word into syllables, sound the letters, blend the sounds into a recognizable word, and check the derived pronunciation in the context from which the word was taken.

Auditory discrimination skills are essential to successful phonics instruction (see chapter 8). However, with seriously handicapped readers, any phonics instruction should start with auditory discrimination activities. Teachers should make it a policy not to assume prior learning in this area.

Phonics instruction is the most abstract, and therefore most difficult, element of language students must learn. Lessons, therefore, should be short, detailed, and related to some contextual situation.

GRAPHIC CUES. Does the student appear not to use graphic cues? Which graphic cues are used accurately? For each student, the teacher should have a list of all known strengths in phonics. This information has been accumulated during oral reading testing and specific phonics testing. All phonics lessons should start with these strengths. As new skills are mastered, teachers should adjust the list of strengths for each student. In this way, the teacher always has an accounting of each student's phonics knowledge.

Teachers should also make a plan for instruction. Plans should include the approach to be used to teach the skills, methods for practicing the skills, and procedures for using them.

PLANS FOR TEACHING THE SKILL. Teachers must decide whether to teach phonics from whole words or in isolation. In either case, the major decision concerns which approach best suits the student's strengths. Both will call for providing ample opportunity for all students to demonstrate their skills rather than their weaknesses, and the suitability of either approach will depend on the following:

1. The teacher's familiarity with a given technique combined with the availability of materials and results obtained through their use. Although teachers generally work best with familiar tech-

niques and materials, new methods and ideas should not be overlooked. Inflexible and inappropriate teaching can result from the failure to adapt. Teachers should be as objective as possible in assessing the materials and techniques that can be used most effectively.

2. The student's previous experience and reaction to that technique. If, after good instruction, a student fails with a given technique and develops a negative attitude toward it, another approach may be more desirable.

By using these two factors to help make decisions about what approach to use, no doors are closed. It must be remembered, however, that working from known words has a distinct advantage since instruction is related to something already meaningful to the students.

Students should be alert to the idea that each time they decode a word, the sounds that are uttered should be associated with a meaningful concept. Techniques must be used to facilitate this alertness in each phonics lesson. The students may be required to put the pronounced word in a sentence, or the teacher may present words in which classification is possible (e.g., things done at school or names of animals). In either case, attention is called to the fact that the pronounced word has meaning as well as sounds.

Several approaches for instruction are outlined here.

1. *Discovery technique.* In phonics instruction the discovery technique is used to help students develop an awareness of the consistent sound-symbol relationship. The teacher starts with visual and auditory stimulation:

   Let's read these words:

              see   sit   sox   sun

   Listen carefully to the first sound in each word.
   They all start with the same sound. Let's hear it.
   With what letter does each of these words start?

   Once the students have an awareness of the relationship between the letter *s* and the sound it represents, the teacher has several choices:

   Look in your word banks and see how many words you can find that start with the letter *s*. Pronounce these words and see if they all have the sound that *see, sit, sox,* and *sun* start with.

   Look in your book on page ___ . There are three words that start with *s*. Find them and let's see if they start with the sound we hear at the beginning of *see, sit, sox,* and *sun.*

   Or, I'll give you some word endings. You place the *s* sound in front and let's see which ones make real words:

              s-and   s-at   s-im   s-oz

Tempo is important. These steps can be dragged out to a point that makes instruction boring. Teachers should make this instruction snappy and move to the generalization step:

Let's all try to say in our own words what we have learned today.

Teachers should check each effort and help students clarify the generalization. A student may write, "When a word starts with the letter *s*, it will start like the word *sat*." At this point, instruction is over and students go into a practice activity.

2. *Word families.* Many students develop excellent word attack skills quickly through the use of word families and initial-consonant substitution. After some instruction on the initial sounds, words can be built quickly.

You know the initial sounds that the letters *t, s, f,* and *p* represent. This word ending is *-at.* Put your consonant in front and see how many make real words:

t-at   s-at   f-at   p-at

Attention is placed on two aspects of reading in these activities: initial-consonant substitution is easy and quick; and when students pronounce words they should always make a check to be sure the word has meaning for them. Other word families such as *-in, -and, -et* can also be used. Teachers should control the pace so that students are not overwhelmed, but keep it moving in a snappy, interesting way.

3. *Speech-to-Print Phonics.* A commercially prepared program that uses parts of all of these techniques, *Speech to Print Phonics*, has been used with success. The program features learning several sounds, applying them through substitution, checking for meaning, and using repetition. These materials can be used with groups or individual students.

4. *Cloze.* Cloze techniques, which were discussed in the diagnosis chapters, can also be used for phonics instruction. Students can be given sentences with parts of words left out and attempt to insert the correct part so that the sentence will make sense.

The __oy hit the __all.
The dog   it the man.
We had __ean soup for dinner.

In a teacher-directed activity, the teacher can ask the group for the letter that should go in the blank in order for the sentence to make sense. The teacher then inserts the correct letter. For individual practice, a similar set of sentences can be developed so the students insert the correct letters themselves. This adds the element of writing the letters, which is reinforcing.

As skill with one sound is developed, other sounds are added, making the activity one that requires more discrimination.

> The ___oy baked a ___ake.
> Mary ___aught the ball.

These activities can be started as teacher-directed and lead to individual performance.

5. *Word-bank words.* Teachers should use the students' reading sight vocabulary to develop phonics lessons. Use word bank words to:
   - Collect all words that begin or end with the same sound
   - Collect rhyming words
   - Collect words with the same vowel sound and place them in long-sound and short-sound groups

Once these collections are made, teachers should help the students draw generalizations about the sounds represented by the letter under investigation. Students will find words with letters that do not fit the generalizations; use these to discuss the exceptions to generalizations.

City, cell, and *cycle* are exceptions to the K (hard) sound of c because they are followed by *i, e,* and *y*. Teachers can have the students find other words using the letter c followed by either *i, e,* or *y*. Do they fit this exception to the K (hard sound) generalization?

Practice sessions allow students to work with what they have learned.

If none of the instructional techniques prove effective, the teacher is encouraged to employ task analysis techniques. Since all learners respond in terms of their uniqueness, it may be that some logical explanation exists for a reading difficulty. Teachers should examine students for what they are able to do; specifically they should see if students can:

1. Respond to initial, final, medial letters.
2. Recognize familiar parts in unknown words.
3. Know the meaning of the words read to them.
4. Find the word in a dictionary.
5. Distinguish sounds when words are read to them.
6. Respond to a word when it is placed in context.

From such a list of observations, strengths and instructional needs can be recorded.

PRACTICING LEARNED SKILLS. Practice sessions allow students to work with what they have learned so that they can gain a degree of comfort with the skill. The following are suggestions for practicing learned skills:

1. *Games.* Teacher-made or commercially developed games can be used to let students practice what they have learned. *SRA Word Games, Phonics We Use Learning Games, Vowel* and *Consonant Lotto* are examples of packaged kits that are available. After instruction, students play those games that contain the skills they have learned. Teacher-made games, although time consuming to construct, can be made to relate directly to the skills of a given lesson.
2. *Learning centers.* Self-directed activities that relate to skills learned can be made available. Small groups or individual students can work through centers, practicing their new skills. Centers can be either self-correcting or activities can be checked by the teacher. They generally deal with topics that interest students to add an attention-getting dimension. An example of a learning center activity is given in Figure 9–5.
3. *Tutoring.* As soon as a teacher determines a skill to be mastered, the students should be allowed to teach the skill to someone else. It does not matter if the other person knows the skill or not. By practicing teaching a skill that has been recently learned, the student plays the teacher's role. Students enjoy it and learn from it.
4. *Worksheets.* Some workbooks contain highly useful activities for follow-up practice. *Phonics Skilltests, Phonics We Use,* and *Working with Sounds* are a few of the many commercial materials available for practice sessions. Teachers should pull out the pages as they are needed rather than overwhelm the students with the entire workbook at once.

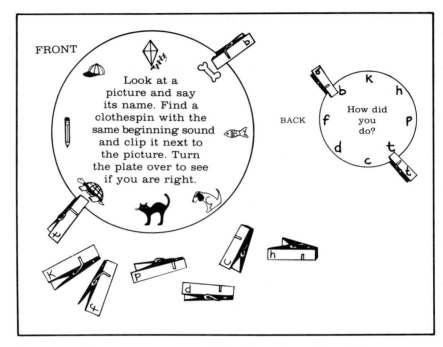

FIGURE 9-5. A learning center using clothespins and a cardboard plate provides manipulative activities. Note that the center becomes self-correcting when students turn the plate over.

Teachers should try to make practice sessions short and interesting. By paying attention to the students as they practice, teachers can prevent frustration. If the practice activity is too difficult, it should be adjusted so that the students experience success and are not practicing mistakes.

USING LEARNED SKILLS. After instruction and practice, students should have opportunities to use their new skills in reading. Each remedial session generally should end with a period of silent reading to show the students that the reason for their effort is to make it possible for them to read on their own. Once they get this idea, these reading periods are valued by the students.

ATTACKING SMALL AND LARGE WORDS. Many students use phonics to attack short words that they do not know at sight, but cannot effectively transfer this use to longer words of more than one or two syllables. This results from a lack of effective means to break these longer words into shorter, more easily decoded parts. Thus, teachers should teach students general rules of syllabication. The instructional level of the students will help the teacher determine the specific generalizations to be taught. However, the following three generalizations are essential for all students in learning the syllabication of words.

1. *The vowel-consonant-vowel generalization.* When a word is structured v-c-v, syllables are usually divided between the first vowel and the consonant.

v cv

over = *o/ver*

However, vowels that are followed by the consonants *r*, *x*, or *v* are an exception to the v-c-v generalization: the *r*, *x*, or *v* is grouped with the preceding vowel.

vc v

carol = *car/ol*

vc v

taxi = *tax/i*

vc v

river = *riv/er*

2. *The vowel-consonant-consonant-vowel generalization.* When a word has the structure v-c-c-v, syllables are usually divided between the consonants.

vc cv

picnic = *pic/nic*

However, blends and digraphs are treated as one consonant.

v c v

achieve = *a/chieve*

3. *The consonant-le generalization.* When a word ends in the structure consonant plus *-le*, those three letters form the last syllable.

c-le

ankle = *an/kle*

For students who fail to understand syllabication after learning these generalizations, teachers should use the Fernald technique,[13] modifying it to require students to pronounce each syllable as it is traced.

Once the word has been dissected, either through syllabication or through actual sounding of each letter of the syllable, the students must be able to blend these sounds to obtain a pronunciation with a meaning. When difficulty with blending arises, the student must be given ample opportunity to obtain a feeling for blending by dividing known words into syllables and blending their sounds to come up with a meaningful utterance. Blending sounds and syllables is an inherent part of each lesson in which the student learns the sound or divides the word into syllables.

Several phonics approaches simplify the problem of blending and pronunciation by teaching the sounds as units rather than isolated pronunciation. In the following case, for example, the sound *b* will be taught in the initial position as it relates to the various short vowel sounds: *ba, be, bi, bo, bu*. This then is immediately substituted in word-building exercises:

bad   beg   bit   boss   but

INABILITY TO USE SOUND-SYMBOL RELATIONSHIPS DURING READING. Sometimes a student knows sound-symbol relationships but seems unable to use this knowledge during reading. This common difficulty often leads to isolated skill practice; however, the emphasis should be on application of learned skills in contextual reading.

One cause of this difficulty may be that students have learned many phonics subskills and are confused about which ones to use. Of course, different skills should be used in different situations. For example, rhyming elements are useful when they are recognized. When they are not, attention to the initial sound may be most helpful. If phonics instruction is taught with techniques for use, then application may occur. For example, the *Speech-to-Print* program does this. Once the sound-symbol relationship is learned, the students are asked to use their new skill in a substitution activity that focuses on the use of context as well as the new phonics skill.

Another cause of this difficulty is that many students learn far too many phonics subskills. Lesson after lesson on the many variations of the vowel sound-symbol relationships can lead to confusion. Smith states that there are far too many rules for the vowel sound-symbol relationships for most young students to master.[14] In one count he came up with 106 vowel rules. Excessive instruction in subskills can lead to a distorted view of reading and a confused reader.

Still another cause may be that initial failure with phonics instruction has created a lack of risk taking while reading. Botel suggests that sound-symbol relationships be taught through the syllable approach.[15] It is easier to learn and blend and it is closer to meaning. This approach involves teaching high-frequency syllables (*-at/-ate, -an/-ane, -ad/-ade*, etc.). He lists all possible combinations.[16] Then the reader substitutes initial consonants and consonant blends to develop a word attack system.

Structural Clues

Deficiencies in the ability to attack compound words are generally not too serious because students can easily be taught to pronounce words if they know the parts. If they do not know the parts, they probably have an inadequate sight vocabulary. Although prefixes cause more difficulty than compound words, the fact that they are at the beginning of the word, usually a separate, easily pronounceable syllable, and concerned with a meaning that directly alters the base word makes them easier to learn and causes less difficulty in remedial reading. However, in the case of suffixes, where these three factors are often missing, many students experience difficulty. It is with suffixes that the service of the base word is most likely to change, even though a precise difference in meaning is not evident. Note in the following words that when the suffix is removed the base word's spelling and configuration is distorted, causing an additional complication in the study of suffixes:

| run | running | runn-ing |
| hope | hoping | hop-ing |

The discovery technique is again suggested for its advantage is making students generalize structural patterns from known words.[17] This technique is equally applicable to difficulties with prefixes, suffixes, or compound words. In teaching decoding and interpretations of the prefix *un*, for example, it may be best to follow a procedure similar to this:

1. Present the word *happy* in a sentence such as *John is happy in school.*
2. Change the word to *unhappy: John is unhappy in school.*
3. Have the students discuss the difference in meaning.
4. Present several oral words in a similar manner.
5. Have the students generalize by answering the question, "What does *un* generally do to the meaning of a word to which it is prefixed?"
6. Collect word patterns of this type and see if they apply to the generalization.
7. Note that *un* has a sound that is consistent and that it changes the meaning of the words to which it is attached.
8. As the students read, their attention should be directed to words prefixed with *un*. They should determine if these words fit the generalization.

Word wheels that contain the base word can be made easily: as students move the wheel, they add either a prefix or a suffix to the base word. Suggestions for these can be found in Russell and Karp's *Reading Aids through the Grades.*[18] The teacher is cautioned in the construction of such reinforcement devices to be certain that the students know the base word and to be alert to the spelling changes that occur when the suffix is added. Prepared exercises of this type are found in materials such as the *Classroom Reading Clinic*. In this kit, word wheels on which base words are altered by prefixes and suffixes provide ready-made reinforcement exercises.

PRACTICE. Practice activities for structural skills do not differ from those that follow phonics instruction. Games, learning centers, tutoring, and practice sheets are appropriate here also. For older students, *Tactics in Reading* and *Basic Reading Skills* provide mature activities for practice.

USING LEARNED SKILLS. The reading time provided at the end of practice sessions is important for the students to develop the understanding that all of these activities have one purpose—to make reading a more enjoyable and successful experience.

Context Clues

Authors provide context clues by redundancy in their writing and through deliberate attempts to help the reader. Readers pick up on those clues through the use of their knowledge of syntax, semantics, and punctuation. Just how does a reader gain these skills for use in reading? Probably the best way is to read a great deal and read all types of material (fiction, content, newspapers, poetry, and magazines). Obviously seriously handicapped readers find this difficult because very little material is suitable for them to read for practice. Teachers should examine students' reading to determine if they ignore syntactic, semantic, and punctuation cues to uncover whether they have problems with context clues.

IGNORING SYNTACTIC CUES. Students who make substitutions but use the correct part of speech in the substitution are telling their teachers that they understand the language but cannot read the exact word. Those who substitute the incorrect part of speech are telling their teachers the material is so strange to them that they cannot make use of their language knowledge. The teachers' very first task is to make adjustments in material to determine if the students continue to misuse syntactic cues on easier material or material that is of higher interest to them. If adjustment of materials eliminates the problem, practice in reading should be provided in that type of material.

If students continue to substitute incorrect parts of speech, direct instruction in simple closure activities is appropriate. Students may be asked to discuss which word may fit in this blank:

Mary has a _____ baseball bat.

Answers such as *new, big, large, small, green, yellow,* and *nice* can be accepted. Teachers and students should discuss why they fit; then other parts of speech can be eliminated, and the practice can continue. Students enjoy this open-ended type of response and can quickly become aware of the syntactic cues that our language offers.

IGNORING SEMANTIC CUES. If students substitute words in reading that do not distort meaning, they are on their way to being successful readers. However, if they distort meaning with their substitutions, they are missing the ideas of the author. Teachers must first adjust the materials to see if easier materials and materials of more interest can correct the errors. Such adjustments almost always work. If the concepts or technical vocabulary are too complex for students, they stand little chance of using context effectively. Smith talks of readers using prediction as a technique to develop awareness of meaning.[19] For example, teachers read these sentences to the students:

The team had their high scorer under the basket. The score was 96–94 with three seconds left. Jim thought, "Wow, what a *(blank)* game!"

Then ask, "What words would fit in the blank and what words would be wrong? Why?"

The same types of activities can be used in silent reading. Let groups of students work together to determine which word can be used and why. Authors provide semantic cues in all types of reading.

Some commercial materials may assist the teacher in providing many experiences of this type. *Using the Context* provides numerous activities at various grade levels.

For mature readers, teachers can use newspaper articles and words that can be supplied. Students are excited about such adultlike reading and quickly understand how the use of context clues is more than a guessing game.

IGNORING PUNCTUATION CUES. Punctuation errors are often due to the frustration level of the material rather than failure to observe punctuation. Therefore, specific attention to punctuation marks in reading will be useless. Time will be spent more wisely on other skill areas with materials of the proper level. However, if the error is due to lack of knowledge about the use of punctuation marks, instruction is needed.

Reading in unison is an effective, subtle way for students to obtain a feeling for the function of punctuation marks. Following group oral reading, the students' attention should be called to the fact that punctuation marks have different functions and call for different inflections. Listening to good oral reading on a tape recorder will make readers aware of the need to observe punctuation marks in their reading materials.

Opportunities for students to follow the teacher's reading to observe effects of punctuation also may prove helpful. Intentionally distorting the punctuation, the teacher can ask students to explain what happens to the author's ideas. When used sparingly, this technique works well with those having trouble hearing their own punctuation errors.

When readers have difficulty using punctuation it is almost always because the materials are too strange or too difficult. Teachers should make certain that practice activities always involve appropriate materials that reduce frustration.

Use of Dictionaries

Dictionary skills are indispensable for word attack. Students with reading problems may benefit from dictionary instruction. Work in programming has produced two publications that may be of use in remediation, *Lessons for Self-Instruction in Basic Skills* and *David Discovers the Dictionary*. These programs have an individualized approach requiring minimum teacher supervision for the student to acquire the skills necessary to use the dictionary.

Teachers should provide a dictionary for every reader. When word at-tack problems occur, students should use the dictionaries. The skills needed are quickly formed and lead the readers to independent dictionary use. Of course dictionaries require the use of alphabetizing skills and locating skills, but these can easily be taught and readers can gain self-esteem from the independence that results.

Putting It All Together

As discussed in the phonics section of this chapter, some students seem to know their subskills but have difficulty using them. More instruction with subskills is obviously not the answer; other explanations must be found.

One possible explanation is that instruction was not followed by oppor-tunities for the use of the newly learned skill. Through disuse, the skill gradually becomes weakened and eventually lost. Each lesson must be followed by reading practice, and in some cases it may be well for that practice to be monitored by the teacher so that the transfer of the skill to reading can be verified.

Another explanation may be that the students have received conflicting advice about how to use their new skills. One teacher may suggest starting with the initial consonant, another may suggest using a dictionary, and parents may tell them to spell the unknown word. While many readers withstand such con-flicting advice, some poor readers can become thoroughly confused.

Teachers should help students establish a minimal strategy for attacking unknown words. All teachers working with the students agree to the strategy and use it consistently with them. Parents and librarians are also informed of it and use it. In this way, the student is seeing that what is learned in reading classes is carried over in other areas of school and even at home. The strategy that any group of teachers would develop should relate to what they stress dur-ing instruction. The following is an example of such a strategy:

When you come to a word you do not know, use this technique.
1. Read on and look for clues.
2. Frame the word.
3. Try the first sound.
4. Divide the word into smaller parts.
5. Consult the dictionary or ask someone.

Here the students are asked to use context clues first, configuration clues sec-ond, phonics third, syllabication fourth, and then either use a dictionary or ask someone for help. Teachers should then teach each of these strategies. Students have cards they can refer to with the strategies written on them. They can use these for bookmarks. Teachers post the strategies in each room and the media center, send a copy home, and emphasize the strategy in every lesson. In this way, the students get the idea that what they have worked so hard to learn has application for reading.

Using a minimal strategy does not limit those students who have more skills that they can use. It simply gets the readers started on the road to in-dependent reading using word attack skills.

By far the strongest motivation to students for studying word attack skills is being able to see how this knowledge enables them to become more independent readers. It is essential, therefore, for students to be put in the situation of transferring learned skills to context in every lesson if possible. Game-type activities, as suggested, make reinforcement of these skills more informal and pleasurable.

The discovery technique has motivational appeal, especially to some of the older students who need work in word attack. Generalizing the concepts of word attack with a minimum of teacher supervision usually becomes a highly motivating situation.

Graphic illustrations of progress usually help motivate students. Teacher-made materials designed to illustrate established goals and the students' achievement within their scope and capabilities are effective motivating devices too.

Programmed materials with immediate feedback contain inherent motivational appeal. These materials, designed to reinforce, correct, and alter incorrect responses, establish situations in which the reader eventually will be successful—a desirable outcome in all types of remedial programs.

Summary

The remedial techniques used in the area of vocabulary deficiencies, whether sight vocabulary or word attack, are based on diagnostic findings. Once these deficiencies are determined, educators have a variety of remediation approaches from which to choose. Starting with those that they believe will serve most adequately, educators remain alert during instruction to the possibility that the original approach may need to be modified as instruction continues.

Constant awareness of the value of incorporating skill activities into contextual situations is the responsibility of both the teacher and the reading specialist. Continued drill, without well-developed transfer opportunities, is of little value.

Notes

1. Morton Botel, *Forming and Re-forming the Reading/Language Arts Curriculum* (Washington, D.C.: Curriculum Development Associates, 1975).
2. Robert M. Schwartz and Taffy E. Raphael, "Concept of Definition: A Key to Improving Students' Vocabulary," *The Reading Teacher* 39, no. 2 (November 1985): 198–205.
3. Arthur W. Heilman, *Smuggling Language into the Teaching of Reading*, 2d ed. (Columbus, Ohio: Merrill, 1978).
4. Edgar Dale and Joseph O'Rourke, *Techniques of Teaching Vocabularies* (Palo Alto, Calif: Field Educational Publications, 1971).
5. Joanne Greenberg, McCay Vernon, Jan Hafer DuBois, and Jan C. Knight, *The Language Arts Handbook* (Baltimore: University Park Press, 1982).
6. Harry Bornstein, Karen L. Saulnier, and Lillian B. Hamilton, *The Comprehensive Signed English Dictionary* (Washington, D. C.: Gallaudet University Press, 1983).
7. Jan C. Hafer, *The Effects of Signing As a Multisensory Technique for Teaching Sight Vocabulary to Learning Disabled Students* (Ph.D. diss., University of Maryland, 1984).
8. Robert M. Wilson and Judy Hoyer, "The Use of Signing As a Reinforcement of Sight Vocabulary in Grades One and Two," *Yearbook of the State of Maryland International*

Reading Association, 1985 (College Park, Md.: State of Maryland International Reading Association, 1985), 43–51.

9. James Knable, "The Effect of Signing for Teaching Sight Vocabulary to Incarcerated Adults" (Ed.D. diss., University of Maryland, College Park, Maryland, 1988).

10. Marie Clay, *Reading: The Patterning of Complex Behaviour* (London: Heinemann Educational Books, 1972), chap. 6.

11. Arthur W. Heilman, *Phonics in Proper Perspective,* 4th ed. (Columbus, Ohio: Merrill, 1981), 22.

12. Morton Botel, *How to Teach Reading* (Chicago: Follett Publishing Co., 1968), 64.

13. Grace Fernald, *Remedial Techniques in Basic School Subjects* (New York: McGraw-Hill Book Co., 1943), pt. 2.

14. Frank Smith, *Understanding Reading* (New York: Holt, Rinehart & Winston, 1978), 140.

15. Morton Botel, *Forming and Re-forming the Reading/Language Arts Curriculum* (Washington, D.C.: Curriculum Development Associates, 1975).

16. Ibid., 36–42.

17. Botel, *How to Teach Reading,* 40.

18. David H. Russell and Etta E. Karp, *Reading Aids through the Grades* (New York: Columbia University Press, 1951).

19. Frank Smith, "The Role of Prediction in Reading," *Elementary English* 52, no. 3 (March 1975): 305–11.

Suggested Readings

Botel, Morton. *How to Teach Reading.* Chicago: Follett Publishing Co., 1968. In chapters 3 and 5 of this well-written book, Botel presents the "discovery" and "spelling" mastery techniques for use in sight vocabulary and word attack lessons. The teacher will find this a practical guide to developmental and remedial activities.

Burmeister, Lou E. "Usefulness of Phonic Generalizations." *The Reading Teacher* 21 (1968): 349–59. This article reviews the research on phonics generalizations. Reading this review is essential prior to working with children in a program that concentrates on the use of phonics.

Clymer, Theodore. "The Utility of Phonics Generalizations in the Primary Grades." *The Reading Teacher* 17 (1963): 252–58. This article discusses how functional the generalizations commonly taught to children are in terms of the number of times the generalizations hold true and the number of words to which they apply.

Coley, Joan, and Linda Gambrell. *Programmed Reading Vocabulary for Teachers.* Columbus, Ohio: Merrill, 1977. This book presents the basic knowledge a teacher must have to work with students in the area of sight vocabulary. The material is presented in programmed format.

Forte, Imogene, Mary Ann Pangle, and Robbie Tupa. *Center Stuff.* Nashville, Tenn: Incentive Publication, 1973. This book contains a useful collection of ideas for developing learning centers on many topics.

Fries, Charles C. *Linguistics and Reading.* New York: Holt, Rinehart and Winston, 1963. One explanation for the linguistic involvement in teaching reading can be found in this book. For those who have difficulty understanding the linguist, this book is a good introduction. Teachers of handicapped readers must acquaint themselves with the works of the linguists.

Greenberg, Joanne et al. *The Language Arts Handbook.* Baltimore: University Park Press, 1982. This book presents a case for the use of finger spelling and signing as reinforcers in language arts instruction and includes many specific lesson suggestions.

Jan C. Hafer and Robert M. Wilson. *Signing for Reading Success.* Washington, D.C.: Gallaudet University Press, 1986. This booklet provides information for teachers on the use of signing and finger spelling for instruction in sight vocabulary, phonics, language arts, and drama as well as in classroom management. It also contains a summary of some of the research that has been done with signing with hearing students.

Hall, MaryAnne. *Teaching Reading As a Language Experience.* 3d ed. Columbus, Ohio: Merrill, 1981. This book presents basic information for teachers concerning the nature and uses of language experience as an approach to reading instruction.

Heilman, Arthur W. *Phonics in Proper Perspective.* 5th ed. Columbus, Ohio: Merrill, 1985. Heilman has combined an assessment of the place of phonics with a survey of the skills to be taught; he has also included examples and appropriate word lists. The educator who works with handicapped readers will find this book indispensable in working with phonics.

Lee, Dorris M., and R. V. Allen. *Learning to Read through Experience.* New York: Appleton-Century-Crofts, 1963. A combination of philosophy and techniques, this book is a must for those who plan to work with seriously handicapped children. This approach will be of particular value with many children, and the book will provide the educator with a thorough background from which to work.

Stauffer, Russell. *The Language-Experience Approach to the Teaching of Reading.* New York: Harper & Row, 1970. Chapters 1, 2, and 3 discuss the theory and uses of language-experience approaches. Chapter 10 discusses special uses of language experience, including clinical cases.

Waynant, Louise R., and Robert M. Wilson. *Learning Centers . . . A Guide to Effective Use.* Paoli, Pa.: Instructo, 1974. This volume provides numerous ideas about the construction and use of learning centers. Those who want to use learning centers in remedial programs will find this book useful.

Wilson, Robert M., and MaryAnne Hall. *Programmed Word Attack for Teachers.* 4th ed. Columbus, Ohio: Merrill, 1984. This book presents basic knowledge about word attack needed by teachers for instruction. The material is presented in a programmed format followed by self checks that enable teachers to demonstrate their knowledge of word attack skills.

EDITORIAL

Geneva J. Wagner

is a Chapter 1 Reading Specialist in the Bradford Area School District, Bradford, Pennsylvania.

Students who experience reading difficulties need instruction in one or more of the following areas: the enlargement of sight vocabularies, the development of word attack skills, and the improvement of comprehension skills. Because of the problems they have encountered when attempting to read, many of these students have developed negative attitudes toward reading. In order to improve the attitudes of their students, teachers need to implement instructional techniques that make reading enjoyable and meaningful. One technique I have found to be successful is an adaptation of the language-experience approach.

Before students enter our Chapter 1 program, they are given a variety of informal tests as well as a standardized test. The information obtained from these tests is used as a basis for instruction and remediation. Of course, additional information is obtained as the teacher works with the students. One of the informal tests that we use with second-grade students is the Dolch Word List. Each student is asked to read the words aloud. The teacher keeps a record of the words the student did not know as well as all misread words. Once the teacher knows what words each student needs to learn, steps are taken to teach those words.

Four of my second graders needed help in learning the Preprimer Dolch Words. I made a list of the words each student needed to learn on individual index cards. Some of the words were missed by several students, and some of the words were missed by only one student. We then examined the words on each list and discussed topics that would enable us to use everyone's words in a single story. Because this was a group activity, each student received help on the words he or she had missed as well as reinforcement on the words missed by others.

The students dictated the story, and I recorded it. Throughout the process, the students had to learn to compromise; we could not use every idea that was suggested. Because it was a story involving action, we discussed what ideas were the most realistic and why. Some of the students had fewer words to use, so they were free to offer suggestions as to how the others could incorporate their words. Much of the story involved dialogue; therefore, we made sure each student made an equal number of conversational statements. By the time everyone's words had been used, our story had developed into a play, even though we had not started with that goal in mind.

Using a word processor, I typed the story on the computer and made a copy for each student and myself. We decided that all students would read the dialogue they had contributed, and I would be the narrator. Using a fluorescent highlighter, I marked each student's speaking parts. We then practiced reading our parts aloud. A discussion of the need to read with expression followed. When the students were able to read fluently and with expression, we decided where in the room each set of actions would take place. Finally, we dramatized our story. Looks of pride were evident as the students placed the stories in their folders.

As a result of this experience and many other positive experiences, I am convinced of the power of the language-experience story in the development of word attack, sight vocabulary, and comprehension skills. Adaptations in this approach, such as the one I have discussed, serve to add variety and to increase student motivation. Students experiencing reading difficulties need to experience learning techniques which are interesting and which apply reading to daily life.

Geneva J. Wagner

Comprehension Development

CHAPTER OUTLINE

About Comprehension
Instructional Approaches
Instructional Strategies
Specific Remedial Comprehension
  Activities
Extended Remediation
Remediation for the Culturally
  Different

CHAPTER EMPHASES

*Comprehension should be taught as a
  personal process.*
*Instructional approaches should reflect
  what teachers know about
  comprehension.*
*Instructional strategies can be used
  with any approach.*
*Materials for instruction should be
  interesting and relevant.*

To understand reading comprehension, it may be useful to begin with a discussion of what is currently known about it. Reading comprehension is a complex skill that is difficult to discuss because it is so deeply rooted within each individual reader. Nevertheless, there are several things that have emerged from recent comprehension research that can help to guide instruction. This chapter begins with a series of short statements about reading comprehension. Next, comprehension-enhancing approaches and strategies are presented. After the midchapter summary, the discussion shifts to an examination of specific comprehension activities that parallel the various areas identified in comprehension assessment. The chapter ends with a look at the extended remediation areas of reading speed, distractibility, reluctant readers, and culturally different students.

About Comprehension

Comprehension is so complex that very little is known about how each student processes information. In recent years, many scholars have developed theories about how the process seems to work and researchers are now busy attempting to evaluate those theories. The following points about comprehension seem reasonable and have implications for instruction:

COMPREHENSION IS PERSONAL. Smith focuses on the personal nature of reading.[1] Reading comprehension is influenced by the sum total of experiences and knowledge that readers bring to the printed page. Students who possess strong background in a subject area will be at a considerable comprehension advantage when called upon to read a passage about that subject. Further, because readers differ in their prior knowledge and experiences, each person's reading interpretations will also differ. Ability to comprehend is also influenced by reader strategies. Comprehension is personal because readers differ in the ways they construct meaning from text.

COMPREHENSION REQUIRES PREDICTING. Students participate in comprehension through the active process of predicting. They must anticipate what is coming and then check to see if their predictions are correct. Risk taking is obviously involved in predicting. Frequent inaccurate predictions make the process risky. This, in part, explains why people enjoy reading about matter in which they have considerable prior information and shy away from matter in which they are not knowledgeable. Prior knowledge helps them make accurate predictions so less risk is involved in the activity.

COMPREHENSION MUST BE PRACTICED. Allington suggests that students need to read a lot to develop successful comprehension.[2] However, data indicate that readers experiencing difficulty in reading often have less time to practice reading, spending more time in skill-development activities.[3]

COMPREHENSION INVOLVES MORE THAN ANSWERING QUESTIONS. Durkin reports that most classroom teachers stress comprehension assessment activities, such as question asking, to a greater extent than instructional activities.[4] Questions primarily *assess* rather than *teach* comprehension. Many have challenged the use of teachers' questions as a learning technique.

COMPREHENSION NEEDS ORGANIZATION. Teachers should construct lessons so that students build on their previous knowledge. If students are expected to respond just to questions or to unrelated bits of information, comprehension will be negatively affected. Organizing information shows students how knowledge they already have filed away can be associated with new concepts to develop more accurate schemata about a subject. As students increase their understanding in this manner, reading becomes more meaningful.

COMPREHENSION REQUIRES ATTENTION TO TASK. If readers are inattentive, comprehension becomes impossible. Boredom, difficult material, incorrect student expectations, and distractions can take students off task, creating a setting inconducive to comprehension. Everyone remembers reading a page only to realize that they haven't absorbed its content; they were thinking about something else when they should have been concentrating on what they were reading. In such cases, no comprehension takes place. Thus, classroom teachers should be sensitive to signs that a student's mind is wandering so that this problem can be quickly corrected.

COMPREHENSION INVOLVES PRODUCT AND PROCESS. The student's comprehension products may fail to provide us with useful insights into the processes that they used to produce them. Therefore, the comprehension process cannot be evaluated solely by examining products. For example, fluent, accurate oral reading does not necessarily indicate good comprehension, nor does answering all of a teacher's questions. While these types of products are encouraging indicators that comprehension has occurred, they do not give us full information about the readers' processes.

COMPREHENSION REQUIRES ACTIVE MONITORING. Comprehension is enhanced when students continually assess their understanding of what they are reading. When students lose the gist of what they are reading—either at the sentence level or at the paragraph level—they should be aware enough to stop and look back to try to regain understanding. Comprehension monitoring appears to be a behavior more readily exercised by good readers. Many poor readers keep on reading even after they have lost the meaning of a sentence or passage. Students become better readers when they become aware of how well they are comprehending.

Instructional Approaches

The selection of instructional approaches should reflect the information about reading comprehension just discussed. Instructional approaches that seem to fit this knowledge include the directed reading-thinking activity, the problem approach, the language-experience approach, and nonquestioning approaches.

The Directed Reading-Thinking Activity (D-R-T-A)

Stauffer has developed an instructional strategy that focuses on the teacher's role in directing reading as a thinking activity.[5] This strategy can be used with a large group of students or can be adapted to individualized instruction. The steps include the following:

1. Identify purposes for reading
2. Guide students in adjusting reading rates with different purposes and materials
3. Observe reading
4. Develop comprehension
5. Provide fundamental skill training activities[6]

Stauffer's D-R-T-A emphasizes the student's place in the learning process. His rationale includes a list of assumptions about what students can do. The student is personally involved in each step of the lesson; the teacher is seen as a member of the group, not as the authoritarian figure. For example, in identifying purposes, the students are taught to make observations about the materials, set their purposes, then read to satisfy those purposes. The teacher is on hand to guide and assist but not to dominate. When the students' purposes do not fit the information in the passages they are reading, the teacher helps them reset their purposes using what they have already read.

This approach is personal and draws on the prior knowledge of the students. It involves the act of reading and encourages attention to task. The students are continuously organizing and reorganizing new information so that it fits with their prior knowledge. Prediction and hypothesis setting take the place of direct teacher questions.

The Problem Approach

By making students responsible for the direction of their learning, the problem approach encourages student task-oriented behavior. Brigham and Pilato list the following essential steps to this approach.[7]

1. Ask students what they would most like to learn about. Then record responses on a chalkboard in the students' language. (Use silence and an expectant attitude to stimulate responses; try for at least one idea from each student.)

2. Ask students which ideas seem to go tog
   include others, and which are different fr
   gradual organization processes of the gro
   sets of general topics and individual ques
3. Ask students what they wish to learn ab
   and the reasons for their choices. Take v
   and priorities.
4. Ask students if they have additional que
   choice topic, thereby breaking the main
   subtopics.
5. Copy the master plan from the board ar
   off. Use this material for reading the nex
   such as "Is this what you decided to do?
   do it?" "Are there ways in which you m
   "How might these ideas be stated more
6. Assign a committee of three to five stud
   subtopic.
7. Have each committee elect a chairperson, a recorder, and
   perhaps a spokesperson for liaison with the rest of the class and
   the instructor. These positions may be rotated.
8. Chairpersons lead committees in developing resource plans.
   Questions are arranged in logical sequence. New questions are
   elicited and placed in sequence. Committees develop lists of
   resources to consult. Questions are assigned so that each student
   is responsible for exploring one or more questions individually,
   and perhaps one question with help from other students.
9. Each committee should have its own planning-record folder with
   copies of each item for each member. At the beginning of each
   meeting, work is reviewed by going over the notes of the
   preceding meeting. These notes have been taken by the recorders,
   typed exactly as they were written, and duplicated by the
   teacher. Included are the purposes, accomplishments, evaluation
   of the meeting, and any remaining questions.
10. Resource lists are expanded and resources tapped. Often this will
    require skills in letter writing, telephoning techniques, interview
    methods, and field trip planning.
11. Each committee decides what data it will use and in what form.
    Eventually it must decide on a format for presenting its findings
    to the class. This format may consist of a mock television news
    report, a videotape production, a model or construction project,
    a role-playing skit, or a slide and audiotape project. After a
    format is selected, the presentation is given.
12. The whole class evaluates each presentation after it is given,
    using these questions:
    • What have we learned?
    • Was it worth learning? Why?

How might we use what we learned?

What additional questions do we have?

• What was the best thing about the way the ideas were presented?

These steps demonstrate to students the interdependence of purpose, planning, oral and written language communication, thinking, doing, and evaluation. All planning steps are recorded, as are all activity steps. Gradually, planning and implementation are integrated toward student-meaningful outcomes.

At each stage, thinking-language-organizational skills are developed *as* (and *only* as) students evidence a specific need for them. Skills are not developed at the instructor's convenience but only as obvious student readiness occurs.

In all of these steps, students are asked to use and develop a wide range of thinking-language skills in an oral situation as a basis for their application in reading and writing activities. They are required to be active, responsible participants in the instructional situation.

With the problem approach the student is involved in a personal discovery of meaning. The student is the discussion maker, active learner, and organizer of information. The teacher serves as a resource for the students.

The Language-Experience Approach

The language-experience approach (see chapters 8 and 9) may be the most effective method of assisting many students with comprehension difficulties. After sharing a common experience (field trip, filmstrip, science experiment, etc.), the students develop a story that the teacher records. (Older, more skilled students may write the story themselves.) Comprehension of meaning is assured because the story is in the students' words and concerns a recent experience. Stories can be collected and saved for future reading and comprehension skill extension. Some skill extension activities may include the following:

1. Developing suitable titles for the story
2. Discussing the feelings of various persons in the story
3. Adding a creative ending to the story
4. Changing a part of the story to alter the outcomes
5. Checking to determine if the events as given by the students are in sequential order in terms of what actually happened

As with the D-R-T-A and the problem approach, the language-experience approach is a personal approach to comprehension. It directly involves the students' prior knowledge and provides resource materials for successful reading practice.

Nonquestioning Approaches

The following approaches rely on instructional techniques other than teacher questioning to aid students with comprehension difficulties.

COMMUNICATION WITH THE AUTHOR. Students can write to the author of a story to obtain information such as why he or she wrote the book, what research was done to write the book, or details about his or her life.

ADD OR CHANGE ENDINGS. Stories may have surprise or expected endings. Students can write or dictate new endings and have fun sharing them.

DISCUSSION OR DEBATE. Controversial issues in a story or book can be discussed or debated. Students can attempt to determine the validity of a given action based on their prior knowledge or their research of the topic involved.

COMMUNICATION WITH A STORY CHARACTER. Various students can take the part of the story's characters. Other students can interview them, write them letters, question their activities in the story, or ask them to act out their part. These and other nonquestioning activities facilitate comprehension development without questioning. The students respond in a personal manner through a variety of organizational strategies. The teacher or reading specialist can pick one approach and follow it or combine approaches. This decision will probably be based on the student's age and interest, comfort with a given approach, and the materials available for instruction.

Teachers may select from various instructional strategies when using each of the approaches discussed. These may be used with any approach, used some days and not others, and used with some students and not others. These should be used to help provide variety in instructional lessons.

**Instructional
Strategies**

Developing a Setting for Questioning

Students answer questions in two situations. One is a recall situation in which the reading materials are not available to the students. The other is a locate situation in which students can use the reading materials to locate answers to questions. Many regular classroom activities have stressed the recall situation, which involves not only reading comprehension but also memory abilities.

However, remedial lessons should focus on locating skills. Students need to be allowed to use the reading material either to find or verify their answers. Students can answer about 30 percent more questions when locating than when recalling. Since remedial lessons should focus on strengths, locating is desirable. Students have probably read the materials if they can locate the answers. By stressing locating instead of recalling, students are encouraged to learn how to use reading materials. They begin to see books as resource materials that can be reexamined and consequently develop mature reading skills.

Most people maintain some type of professional or personal library in their homes because they enjoy the privilege of rereading something that was of interest or because they need to locate information that has slipped from memory. After reading an interesting story in a book or the newspaper, people do not want to be expected to remember details.

Adjusting Materials

Materials for instruction are usually chosen by the teacher. If the materials are too difficult or uninteresting they should be replaced. Instead of trying to force students through such materials, the teacher should be aware of ways to adjust the materials or get different ones. Many students who are experiencing difficulty in comprehension are working in materials so difficult that they cannot possibly achieve success. By expecting them to practice reading in difficult materials, teachers create a situation in which poor reading skills are encouraged. Inaccurate, nonfluent reading can be learned and reinforced when materials are too difficult. In such situations, attention to meaning becomes difficult because too much attention is given to figuring out words. Read-along books, wordless books, and high-interest, low-vocabulary books should be acquired for these students. (A materials section is included in appendix B. Teachers should become familiar with these and other materials so that selections can be made for various students. Other materials may need to be rewritten to reduce either concept load or vocabulary difficulty.)

Providing Wait Time

Rowe's work discussing wait time should be considered by all teachers, but particularly by those working with handicapped readers.[8] Rowe found that teachers tend to give very little wait time, that is, the time between asking a question and calling for an answer. One second was the average wait time. By training teachers to wait for three seconds or longer, Rowe found that student responses increased and were more complete.

Rowe also found that the amount of time between the student's answer to a question and the teacher's response to the answer was very short. When teachers waited after a student responded, the student tended to expand the first response, and other students tended to interact without teacher interruption. By providing wait time after asking questions and before responding to answers, students are allowed time to think and form their responses as well as to elaborate on them.

Most teachers find applying wait time in their classroom difficult. Many are so accustomed to constant discussion and rapid-fire question-and-answer sessions that silence seems unnatural. Yet effective use of wait time can be learned if practiced. Students should know that they will be given more time than usual to answer a question. Teachers should allow three to five seconds and then note the increased quantity and quality of student responses.

Using Task Analysis

Task analysis has special application to reading comprehension. It can lead teachers to make appropriate adjustments when students become overwhelmed in a comprehension lesson and are unable to respond. Teachers should determine what the students do and what seems to be the difficulty. They hypothesize several adjustments that might improve the learning situation and check out each one through diagnostic teaching; then they alter their instructional plan.

Task analysis has been most useful when severe comprehension problems are encountered. The following example illustrates this:

Problem

Warren cannot recall literal details when reading in text material at an eighth-grade readability level.

Strengths

Warren can read orally with relative accuracy at eighth-grade level (IRI).

Warren can respond to about 20 percent of literal questions at eighth-grade level after silent reading (IRI).

Warren can respond to 90 perent of literal questions at sixth-grade level (IRI).

Warren appears to try hard to comprehend what he reads.

Hypotheses

Warren will:

H1. Respond if material is more interesting.
H2. Respond if permitted to locate the answers to literal questions at eighth-grade level.
H3. Respond if passages are shorter.
H4. Respond if made aware of purposes for reading.

Hypothesis Testing

H1. Obtain materials at the eighth-grade level with a variety of interests, let Warren select one to read, then check comprehension.
H2. Pick a passage that Warren can read aloud accurately and ask literal questions in a locate situation.
H3. Divide a passage into three parts, asking questions between each part.
H4. Prior to reading, discuss the purposes for reading with Warren.

Results

Hypothesis testing indicates that Warren responds successfully to situations 1 and 2, but that 3 and 4 seem to make no difference. An instructional plan is then drafted.

Instructional Plan

Instruction is adjusted by either allowing for self-selection or by encouraging the locating of answers, or both. If Warren responds successfully over time, then task analysis was useful in this setting. If he continues to have difficulties, the task analysis is repeated and new hypotheses developed.

Using Pupil Questions

When using questioning strategies, teachers often do all of the work. They decide what is important, form a question, and make sure they have an answer. By using student questions, teachers involve students in those important steps. Students come to the comprehension session prepared to ask, not answer, questions. They can ask questions of the teacher or other students. They should be able to justify their answers and locate them in the passage from which the questions are derived. Students in the question-asking role increase their attentiveness and enthusiasm, while demonstrating that they comprehend the passage.

Interestingly, students tend to ask the types of questions that they hear from their teachers. And they tend to respond to the answers to their questions in the same manner in which their teachers respond when they ask questions. If a teacher does not like the type of question students are asking, his or her question-asking and answer-responding techniques should be reevaluated.

Using the InQuest Procedure

InQuest stands for "Investigative Questioning Procedure." As proposed by Shoop,[9] it is a comprehension strategy that encourages students to actively ask and answer questions as they read. It is recommended for students in third grade and up.

InQuest can be used with story selections that the teacher either reads aloud to students or with ones they read for themselves. It involves interrupting the reading at selected intervals and conducting an impromptu news conference based on the story characters and events. One student is assigned to assume the part of a major character, and the other students become investigative reporters who interview the character. Through the questioning and the answers given, the students develop fuller understandings of their own reading comprehension. They also tend to read more thoughtfully.

Shoop suggests that good student questioning is a skill that a teacher might have to carefully cultivate. She suggests that teachers might wish to show students a videotape of a national news conference or a "60 Minutes"-type interview to give them an idea of what is involved. She also recommends that students critique their own questions and answers to gain greater insights into good questioning techniques.[10]

Developing Personal Outlines

Outlining is an effective way to organize a passage's important material. All too often, however, outlining activities are another of those "right" or "wrong" experiences that are so frustrating to students who are already having difficulty being "right." Personal outlining for a reading-comprehension lesson could involve steps like the following. Start by eliciting from the students which ideas they think are important or interesting. Such a start on a comprehension lesson tends to create a thinking atmosphere instead of a testing one. The teacher is encouraged to accept all suggestions, noting them on the chalkboard. Some may be quite divergent from the message in the passage, but it is important to know

*Personal outlining
helps the students
elicit which ideas they
think are important or
interesting.*

what the various students gather as the important message. Each idea is recorded without comment. After several ideas have been suggested, the students are encouraged to pick the one they think is really most important. The opportunity to change one's mind is likely to enhance the thinking process.

Next, pairs of students who agree about the important idea are formed. Their task is then to go back through the passage to find support statements or proof for their idea. A format sheet such as the following should be provided:

1. (Important idea)
   a. (Support)
   b. (Support)
   c. (Support)

This procedure can be repeated in long passages of several paragraphs where there may be several important ideas. Students can then discuss or otherwise share their efforts. Aside from giving students practice in the important skill of outlining, this approach has several advantages:

1. The locating of literal facts has a purpose—the purpose selected by the students.

2. Students learn to locate swiftly and accurately since the location is specified.
3. On-task behavior is promoted since students are working in areas of their choice.
4. Poor choices for what is important are clearly illustrated to students since they have difficulty finding support for them.
5. Students accustomed to this approach perform well in literal comprehension activities that may follow.

Throughout this activity, students are encouraged to paraphrase instead of using the exact words of the author. Those reading above the second-grade level can work effectively in this manner and learn to direct themselves after four or five lessons.

Personal outlining combines the notion that reading comprehension should be personal and that it should result in some type of organization of the material.

The transfer of this type of comprehension activity to a system of report development is clear. Now the students go to the library seeking certain information for a report. They read the materials, decide what is most important, go back to the material and seek support for their important ideas. When they come back to their classroom they can read their report, talk about it, and write paragraphs about each important idea.

Using Semantic Webbing

As previously noted, when students are assisted in cognitively organizing something that they read, their comprehension is enhanced. Semantic webbing is one of several related strategies that aid students' organization of text. Known variously as structured overviews,[11] graphic postorganizers,[12] story frames,[13] semantic maps,[14] think-links,[15] and semantic webs,[16] each differs somewhat from the others but all help students to see the overall organization of a piece of literature.

FIGURE 10–1. A Pre-reading Semantic Web. *(From "Highlighting Issues in Children's Literature through Semantic Webbing," by Craig J. Cleland,* The Reading Teacher, *March 1981. Reprinted with permission of the International Reading Association.)*

*Semantic webbing
encourages active
student involvement.*

Semantic webbing can be used in both prereading and postreading settings to enhance comprehension. A semantic web such as the one in Figure 10–1
might be used to help students to activate their prior knowledge and gain an
overview of what they will read. In the example, the students are alerted that
the story will unfold in three major episodes or events. After the story is read,
the teacher may use the semantic web to guide a student discussion of the events,
filling in the web as the discussion evolves. Figure 10–2 shows a semantic web
completed by a group of second-grade students following the reading of *The
Terrible Thing That Happened at Our House* by Marge Blaine.[17] Semantic webs
need not be this involved, and color-coding the parts of a web can aid students
to identify them more readily. Often teachers use words written on the stems
of a semantic web to lessen the number of circles and to simplify the visual
design. Other variations of semantic webs include caterpillar or spider bodies
with story parts written along each leg.

Semantic webs can be found in many different forms being used for many
different purposes. Initially, teachers will want to guide the formation of semantic webs on the chalkboard, chart paper, or an overhead transparency. Later,
when semantic webbing is more familiar to the students, they may be encouraged
to complete their own semantic webs.[18]

Using Story Grammar Questions

Story grammar questioning helps students understand the organization of a
story's basic elements. Instead of asking questions about unrelated story events,
story grammar questions focus on text organization.[19] The questions help stu-

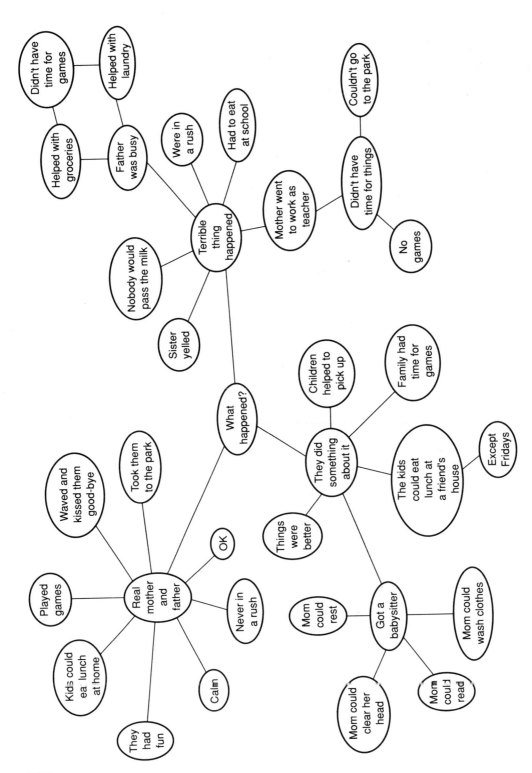

FIGURE 10-2 A Post-reading Semantic Web. *(From "Highlighting Issues in Children's Literature through Semantic Webbing," by Craig J. Cleland, The Reading Teacher, March 1981. Reprinted with permission of the International Reading Association.)*

dents realize the important organizational factors of the story: setting, initiating events, reaction, action, and consequences. Example questions might be:

- *Setting:* Where and when did this story take place?
- *Initiating events:* What caused the children to become startled?
- *Action:* What did the children do?
- *Reaction:* What did their parents do?
- *Consequences:* In what way were the children rewarded for their behavior?

The use of story grammar questions is an alternative to using questions which focus on mental processing. Instead, these questions focus on the story's major events and, as such, represent a holistic approach to story comprehension.[20]

Story grammar questions assist in the development of a schema for story structure. Using this schema while reading stories in the future can enhance comprehension.

Encouraging Retelling

This strategy involves retelling stories or portions of stories. Retelling is a personal reorganization of the parts of the story that made an impact on the students. One may ask students to retell parts of the story that were most interesting, parts that were most important, funny parts, or sad parts.

On short passages students may be encouraged to retell as much as they can. On long passages, chapters, or books, the retelling is usually centered on only part of the reading.

Retelling is open ended. The students do what they can do. Prompting can aid retelling. Such comments as "Who else was at the scene of the accident?" or "Why do you think she did that?" can help students recall the complete incident.

Retelling can be done in groups or on an individual basis. In groups, retelling has a sharing effect when each student retells his or her favorite part. Discussion can follow each retelling to make it more like a real-life sharing experience.

Some teachers are reluctant to use retelling strategies when they are working with groups of students because it requires most of the group to merely listen while one student is retelling. Teachers might wish to vary the technique by having students retell in pairs or into a tape recorder. Teacher aides or parent volunteers also can serve as listeners for retelling activities.

Encouraging Student Writing

Reading and writing are mutually related and beneficial processes. Students experiencing reading comprehension difficulties will benefit when teachers encourage them to write for others. As they write, students should be encouraged to talk about what makes reading enjoyable and comprehensible for them. And, in the process of writing, students will learn about how syntactic (word arrangement) and semantic (meaning) features of the language are related to reader understanding.

For many poor comprehenders, the type of writing that they are required to do most often consists of filling in blanks, circling answers, copying sentences, and practicing spelling and handwriting. Of course, all of these activities may be shown to have a place in the overall scheme of things; however, students benefit most when they engage in "real writing"—stories and other extended pieces of writing that others will want to read.

Publishing their written work gives students a valuable writing perspective. As they write for others, students develop a sense of audience. They learn to ask themselves, "Who will be reading my work and what would interest that reader?" They may also wish to collaborate with classmates to receive reactions or get suggestions on editing or proofreading. Not all writing may warrant publishing, and students should begin to make critical judgments about the quality and appeal of their work. Some writing activities include student-authored books, short story collections, greeting cards, advertisements, telegrams, and newspapers.

Once students have written something that someone else would enjoy hearing, they might read it aloud to others in the Author's Chair, a special chair exclusively reserved for student read-alouds. Before and after the readings, the audience may ask questions of the writer and gain shared insights into the writing process. Most of all, the reader gains a sense of self-importance as the other students listen supportively to his or her story. Another idea for celebrating students' written achievements is to feature a different student each week on an Author of the Week bulletin board, complete with the student's picture, list of published works, and copies of favorite writing.[21]

The comprehension benefits of student writing can be considerable. As students write, they must use their prior knowledge and organize their experiences. They also grow in their knowledge of written language characteristics as they apply their language knowledge to the task of written communication. And, at its heart, writing requires students to actively construct meanings.[22]

Encouraging Repeated Reading

Rereading passages can have positive effects on fluency and understanding. A history student will read and reread several times an account of a Civil War battle. Such rereading develops a permanent memory of the sequence of events. Educators are often reluctant to have students reread materials because they fear it will bore them. But, if the material is interesting and worth remembering, then rereading is not only advisable, it is essential. Repeated readings can be done orally or silently, depending on the purpose for the reading. Students often enjoy repeated readings and are proud to demonstrate their reading proficiencies to their teachers, parents, and peers.

Think-alouds offer students the opportunity to hear what a mature reader is thinking while reading. Davey details the process as follows.[23] As the teacher is reading a difficult passage aloud he or she thinks aloud about the strategies to be used in the difficult parts. For example, the teacher reads the title and makes a prediction or describes a picture made in the mind concerning an event. By modeling reading strategies, students see the thought processes involved and will do the same.

Encouraging Look-Backs

As they read, students should be continually monitoring their understanding. When they realize they do not understand something previously read, they should be encouraged to look back in the text and selectively reread the portion that they failed to comprehend. Although this may sound like common sense, Garner notes that many students (particularly poor readers) fail to do this because they have the mistaken idea that looking back is "cheating." It has been found that students can be taught to actively monitor their comprehension and use look-back strategies when comprehension breaks down.[24] In the process, comprehension abilities are enhanced.

Midchapter Summary

Four approaches have been detailed that can be used individually or in combination, each of which reflects what we know about comprehension. Then fourteen instructional strategies were suggested for use with any of the approaches. Interest is sometimes maintained when a strategy is used for awhile, then set aside for the use of another, then used again. Each has its strengths and limitations, so it is not recommended that an entire remedial comprehension program be developed through the use of only one approach or strategy.

As in other skill areas, specific remediation in reading comprehension will be discussed in terms of the questions asked as a result of a diagnosis:

Specific Remedial Comprehension Activities

1. Do larger units of material seem to interfere with comprehension more than smaller units?
2. Do difficulties occur with some types of comprehension and not others?
3. Does the student have difficulty using locating skills?
4. Does the student have difficulty reading content material? Why?
5. Does the student fail to comprehend most of what is read?

When a comprehension difficulty exists there will probably be no one answer. For example, the student having difficulty with locating skills will likely have difficulty in reading content materials also. Thus, teachers should continue to look at reading as a complex process, keeping in mind that single solutions are unlikely.

Units of Materials

Improving reading skills depends on the student's ability to respond to printed units of increasing length. In diagnosis, teachers can easily note whether the reader's comprehension is limited basically to sentences, paragraphs, or larger units. In these cases the student is not able to recognize the relationship between units of varying sizes and the flow of ideas created by the author.

All remedial approaches must start at the instructional or independent level. When the difficulty lies in unit size, the instructional level should be geared to the largest unit each student can handle effectively. Using the D-R-T-A, teachers can help students set objectives for reasonable amounts of material. Students quickly become aware of the amounts of material they can handle and learn to set objectives accordingly.

The paragraph appears to be a reasonable starting place, usually containing one major idea and some supporting details. Teachers should help students understand paragraph structure through identifying the topic sentence.

Several companies publish reading series that feature short, interesting selections of a page or two in length followed by comprehension questions. These materials are designed to be highly motivating yet easy to read. Because they are relatively short, students can read them at a single sitting and teachers can easily adapt them to a variety of uses. When the questions that follow the reading selections are in multiple-choice or true-false formats, one way of adapting the materials is to have the students try to answer the questions *before* reading the selection and then read to confirm, reject, or refine their predictions. Students can also try to write their own questions to accompany a reading selection. When paragraphs are numbered in the margins, locating practice can be easily designed. Students can be asked a question and then given the number of the paragraph in which the answer can be found—a real time-saver for beginning instruction.

Teachers can also adjust the amount of material included in experience stories. If a long story is dictated, the teacher can place it on two or three sheets, making parts 1, 2, and 3. Students can respond to each part and then finally to the entire story.

USING NEWSPAPERS. Teacher-made materials can be developed easily to help students handle large quantities of material. For example, a television guide from the Sunday newspaper can be used to help students handle varying amounts of printed material and to respond to tasks of varying difficulty. Students can be asked questions such as these:

- What show is offered on Channel 4 at seven o'clock on Tuesday evening?
- What sports programs are offered on Saturday?
- Select four movies you would like to watch during the week.
- What shows are featured at eight o'clock each day?
- Schedule your own television watching for the week for an hour each evening.

LEARNING ACTIVITIES. Newspaper articles, classified advertisements, telephone yellow pages, cookbooks, shop manuals, catalogs, encyclopedias, and dictionaries can be developed into lessons similarly by starting with a specific activity requiring minimum reading and moving toward extended activities requiring considerable reading. Students in remedial programs can relate easily and enthusiastically to materials such as these, even though they may tend to be uninterested in reading. Some of these types of materials contain very small quantities of print and are therefore ideally suited for students who have difficulties with larger units.

Difficulties with Some Types of Comprehension

Teachers use questions to determine the student's ability to respond to comprehension activities. Teachers can gauge student strengths and needs by the type of questions they ask. The type of question and its response need careful consideration prior to discussion of remedial activities. All too often, the type of question asked in commercially prepared materials is designed to obtain specific facts from the story where students demonstrate only literal understanding. When working with groups of students, questions at the literal level can be asked of the entire group at one time. Using Durrell's idea of every-pupil-response cards, all can quickly respond to literal questions. Each reader, for example, has two cards, one stating *yes* and the other *no*. The teacher can select five or ten important details from the story and ask questions calling for a *yes* or *no* answer. Cards with names of story characters, dates, and numbers that indicate choices in multiple-choice questions can also be used. The teacher notes all of the responses; if answers to any questions are incorrect, reading is redirected or questions reformulated. Literal understanding can be checked in a short period of time, allowing more time for interpretive and problem-solving questions and activities. While literal comprehension is extremely important, the time normally allocated for it is disproportionally large.

When interpretive questions are asked, the reader is expected to respond by paraphrasing the ideas of the author. Such questions as the following may be asked:

- In your own words, state the most important idea of the story.
- How would you summarize the author's major point?
- Why did the major character lose his temper?

Interpretation requires the readers to draw on their experience to interpret the author's words. Although interested in accurate interpretation, the teacher must not have a preconceived statement of the answer. Readers interpret in the best way they can and their efforts must be accepted. If students' answers contain inaccuracies, they have either read incorrectly or have inappropriately applied their experiences. In either case, inaccuracy calls for reteaching rather than criticism.

When questioned at the problem-solving level, students are expected to think beyond the story's content and apply either critical- or creative-thinking skills to the author's ideas answering questions such as the following:

Creative

- What would you have done if you were Jim?
- Can you think of a better ending for the story?

Critical

- Did Jim make good decisions? Why?
- What reasons can you give for Father's actions?

Obviously, questioning at the critical- and creative-thinking levels calls for openness on the part of the teacher. When the teacher asks critical questions, the students must understand the author, must be able to interpret the author, and must apply their experiences in order to analyze what has happened. The students' answers may differ from the one that the teacher has in mind and still be accurate. If student reasoning is unclear, probing questions help students seek alternatives.

In creative thinking, any answer given is considered acceptable and correct. Students tend to enjoy creative activities and, when their answers are accepted, tend to become more creative. For example, a group of students is asked to think of a new title for a story with the idea of making the story into a television show. They are told that the title should attract attention. They usually start with rather traditional titles but soon open up as they see the teacher accepting all of their responses.

The teacher's responses to the students' efforts are perhaps even more important than his or her questions. Accepting, probing, reteaching, and making reading activities exciting for students depend on the teacher's attitude toward the responses they give. Students also will learn to accept and value varying peer responses as they see the teacher accepting them.

Three types of comprehension are considered in remediation: interpretive comprehension, literal comprehension, and problem solving.

INTERPRETIVE COMPREHENSION. Strategies for developing interpretive comprehension skills can be developed through some of the following suggestions.

Closure activities can be used as excellent means of helping students develop awareness of interpretation. Given a cloze activity such as the following, groups of students can see how many words they can fit into the blank and still have the sentence make sense. Doing this calls for awareness of the meaning of the rest of the sentence.

Mike is a *good* football player.

Later, a full sentence can be provided, and students can add words that do not necessarily change the sentence's core meaning.

Pat is a good tennis player.
Pat is a *tremendous* tennis player.

Using brainstorming, glossaries, or dictionaries, students add enhancing words to build many sentences without significantly changing the meaning of the sample sentence.

After experience stories are written, the teacher can write a paraphrased version of the same story. Students match the specific section of the teacher's story with their own. Once that skill is developed, students can work in teams, paraphrasing their own stories.

Since interpretation involves the ability to relate one's thinking to the author's, the first step of the D-R-T-A, identifying purposes for reading, will need emphasis. Reading purposes will stress such activities as summarizing, reading between the lines, and determining the main idea instead of reading for details or facts. The first step of the D-R-T-A is also the place for building a background for the story. Pictures, discussions, film-strips, and motion pictures may be used to assure that the students have experiences with the story's concepts. At other times, simply using several of the terms in the story and discussing situations using those terms assists the students when they encounter the terms in the story.

Building a story into a motion picture or play by identifying the three most important scenes and then formulating a selling title motivates students while subtly stressing the main idea. Several interested students can become involved in developing a play or a movie from the story. Then other students perform the roles without reading lines from their books. Interpretation using paraphrasing, inferring, and selecting the main idea will be essential. Many students demonstrate such skills in unique ways; for example, they may make a comic strip from a favorite story by creating both comic pictures and captions. Of course, a teacher's acceptance of such efforts is the key to encouraging students to continue trying.

Analysis of the topic sentence in a paragraph can also develop interpretation skills. The topic sentence contains the main idea. By stating the topic sentence in their own words, the students are exhibiting an understanding of the main idea and of paraphrasing. An independent activity can involve matching cutout topic sentences with appropriate paragraphs.

Open-ended questions that ask students to summarize a written passage can be developed. Performances on these are acceptable at many levels of refinement. For example, a summary can be a word, phrase, sentence, paragraph, or several paragraphs. Summaries can be either written or oral and can be either drawn or acted out. By changing the activity, teachers can maintain student interest while continuing to develop the same skill.

Students can learn from their peers if they are grouped so that readers having difficulty paraphrasing can work with those who are good at it. They can work in teams of two or three to answer a teacher's question. By teaming students carefully, every student will be able to make contributions to the final product. Pairing students does not encourage independence, but it often helps students overcome frustration, hopelessness, or uncertainty. Teaming also assists in making students active, rather than passive, learners.

With older students, questions can be written (such as multiple-choice questions) relating to the story's content but changing the author's wording. In such cases, teachers paraphrase the way they ask questions. The student's task then matches the paraphrased idea to the author's idea. Thus, students see that the same idea may be expressed in several different ways.

Sometimes a simple probing question can be helpful. For example, if a student answers with the precise words of the author, the teacher can respond, "Yes, that is correct. Now let's try to think of other ways to say the same thing." If the author has written, "The general led a successful charge," the teacher may suggest that the students attempt to say the same thing using another word for *successful* or *charge.*

When inferences are stressed as an interpretive skill, the teacher must be aware of two types of inferences: one the author provides intentionally and one the reader develops. For example, some authors lead the reader to a conclusion without actually stating it. Since inferring involves "reading between the lines," the teacher should talk with students about it in exactly those terms.

Elements such as mood, time, danger, and happiness are often only implied by the author. Questions such as "How do you think the player felt after the game?" "When in history did the story take place?" and "Would you consider the people to be in danger?" are examples of questions that stimulate students to infer. Each question can be followed by probing, "What did the author say to make you think that?" The probing activity helps students clarify their own thinking and understand how others have reacted to the same story they have read.

Cartoons can be used in activities designed to teach paraphrasing, obtaining the main ideas, and developing inference skills. For example, using three or four cartoons on the same subject, the teacher can have groups of students write captions for the cartoons and then let other groups try to match the captions with the pictures. Such an activity can be developed at many levels, all of which can be highly motivating.

When students have severe difficulty interpreting written material, the teacher should start with picture interpretation; this entails helping the student look at pictures that have story possibilities in terms of what appears in the picture and then moving to interpretation. For example, the teacher can ask, "How do you think the children feel?" "How is that street different from the street you live on?" and "Make up a title for the picture." Once students have skills in picture interpretation, these responses should be developed into experience stories.

When a reading specialist draws experience stories from pictures, both literal understanding and interpretation responses should be developed. To modify the language-experience approach in order to develop interpretation, students can be asked to change a sentence without changing the meaning, change a word without changing the meaning, identify the sentences that describe the picture and those that interpret the picture, and discuss the main ideas. By moving from pictures to language-experience stories, reading specialists can make a natural transition from vicarious experiences to reading.

The next step is interpreting stories written by others. Perhaps groups of students can write stories about the same picture. These stories can be compared using the same questions asked in individual picture interpretation. When students are successful with the stories of others, they indicate that they are ready to start with other printed material.

LITERAL COMPREHENSION. Literal comprehension calls for the student to locate or recall specific facts or sequences from a passage. All literal comprehension should involve a situation where students are permitted to locate answers in the passage, not requiring recall from memory. Since a fact or sequence question has a right or wrong answer, the students have no options in a recall situation but to know or not to know the answer. However, when permitted to locate, if they do not remember the answer, they have a way to find it. The comprehension strategy suggested at the beginning of the interpretive section is also very useful in helping students become aware of how to find important facts in a story.

Pointing out the important information via italicized print, boldface type, information repeated for stress, and illustrated information highlights clues to important details to be remembered. Perhaps more subtle but equally useful are clues that words contain. Descriptive adjectives, proper nouns, action verbs, and the like all call attention to those types of details that should receive more careful attention, as in the following sentence:

The *large house burned* in the middle of the *night.*

Most basal material is designed to develop understanding skills. The classroom teacher using basal materials first must be certain that the student is working at the appropriate level and then select those lessons that appear to be most useful.

Understanding sequences causes considerable difficulty for many students. When this skill is deficient, students are limited in their ability to handle content-type materials and to fully appreciate reading of longer units. The thought processes needed involve perceiving groups of items that are related in time (i.e., one comes first, then the next, and so on). Initially, students must obtain sequencing practice from such activities as following oral directions, doing independent work from oral and written instruction, or discussing events from a story that has been read to them by another.

To help students develop sequencing ability, teachers normally start with a sequence of two events and advance to more involved sequences after this is understood. For example, teachers can begin with two events that are clearly representative of the beginning and ending of a story. When the students can sequence with two events (i.e., when they can tell which one came first), a third event, then a fourth, can be added. Starting with many events to sequence tends to smother readers with choices and does not lead to effective sequencing.

Placing comics taken from the Sunday newspaper in sequence is a motivating technique for teaching sequences. Teachers should start with obvious sequences and move toward more subtle ones. Comics that are cut apart and pasted to cards are quite durable. Numbers on the backs of the cards indicating the sequence make the activity self-correcting. A teacher can build many sequence activities from comics in a short time and with little expenditure of school funds. Teachers can also develop sequence activities from newspaper headlines. Students can read the headlines and place the events in order. They can also match the headlines with newspaper pictures that they have placed in sequence.

Some experience stories can be cut into parts. When experience stories are stimulated by photographs taken during a trip, the photos can be arranged in sequence and topics can be written for each picture. Students can then arrange the parts to make a sequential story.

Directing the students' attention to sequencing words or clues that authors use for emphasis is usually valuable. Items that are numbered, steps in a process, dates, the mention of time, and the use of sequence words (e.g., *afterwards, before, during*) are all indications that the author feels the sequence of events is of particular importance.

Developing students' consciousness of sequence often is done best by more subtle means. Teachers may attempt to direct students to the idea of making a movie in which three or four scenes are to be produced by asking, "In what order should the scenes occur so that the audience will understand the story?" Many teachers have successfully used the technique of asking the students to retell the story. However, teachers should realize that the reader who is deficient in the sequencing skill may experience considerable difficulty in telling the story in sequence and may relate the details indiscriminately instead. In such cases locating sequential events is preferred.

Although initial instruction in this area should be conducted at easy reading levels, teachers should eventually move to the instructional level because the student is most likely to see the necessity for concentration in order to reach desired goals there. There are many commercial materials available that build literal understanding (see appendix B). Students should not be drilled in materials without immediate teacher follow-up to evaluate and redirect, because continued failure causes materials to become burdensome and uninteresting. By correcting errors immediately, the teacher enhances the likelihood of reinforcing correct responses. Of course, it is usually better to provide answer keys so that students can check their own work. When they check their own answers, reinforcement possibilities increase. They are more involved in the appropriateness of their work; their responses are reinforced immediately; and they can look for the correct answer when they cannot figure it out from the question asked. Self-correction is a highly desirable activity for students and saves teachers considerable time.

Experience stories in which the student is asked to explain how to do something (such as build a model airplane) and then is directed to sequence the steps can serve as excellent starting points to teach sequencing. When possible, the teacher can obtain funds to purchase car, ship, or airplane models and help students see the importance of sequences by working with them in constructing models using the sequential directions on the box.

PROBLEM SOLVING. Students usually are not thought to need remedial assistance if their only difficulty is in problem solving. However, problem-solving activities should be considered necessary and valuable in remedial situations. Such activities involve the reader in a reaction to the author's message. The reaction takes either a critical or creative form. A critical reaction calls for convergent-thinking activities where the author's ideas are challenged, defended, and evaluated. Creative reactions call for divergent-thinking activities where the author's ideas form a base from which new ideas can be developed.

When students set their own purposes, their choices frequently involve problem solving. They want to know how to use a piece of equipment, or they want to challenge the author's ideas. Such choices should be encouraged as a demonstration of mature thinking.

Newspaper reading is a natural activity for problem-solving lessons. Generally, the headlines are stated so that the students either wonder what the problem is or what the solution is. The articles also lend themselves to scanning, since they are generally written from the most important to the least important facts. Students can be encouraged to take sides on issues and find support for their sides in news articles and editorials. Students' views can be developed more fully if the teacher asks questions such as the following: "Do you agree with the author's position?" "Is the story true?" "Were the people justified in doing what they did?" Each of these questions can be followed by other questions such as "Why?" or "Why not?"

Problem solving can also be stimulated by allowing students to work in pairs or small groups. In groups, students get a chance to try out their thinking without committing themselves to a specific viewpoint. Problem-solving skills are often refined through give-and-take discussions.

Students often see problem-solving activities that are related to content subjects such as history as highly relevant. This gives the classroom teacher an opportunity to use content materials as reading instructional materials. Thus, the students are helped in two school subjects at once. This technique also prepares students for lessons focusing on materials that they have difficulty reading.

With picture interpretation, problem-solving questions are asked about action pictures (e.g., "How would you feel if you were there?" or "What do you think will happen next?"). As students develop skill in responding to problem-solving questions concerning pictures, they can create language-experience stories. Once several groups of students have worked on the same picture, stories can be compared, read, and discussed.

The teacher can use very easy reading material to help students develop problem-solving skills. With older students, newspaper advertisements and television commercials help stimulate problem-solving thinking. The teacher can ask students what the material is really saying with questions such as, "What words are used to influence the reader or listener?" "Is the ad truthful? Why or why not?" "How would a competitor rewrite this ad?"

Role playing is also useful for students who have difficulty reacting to reading creatively. They can be encouraged to respond creatively through materials such as *Teaching Reading through Creative Movement*, which consists of records with voice, music, and stories, for students to act out. As students become freer in creative expression, they can react to many things that they read. After the creative expression, discussions about why they feel the way they do make a logical transition to creative discussions.

Difficulty Using Locating Skills

Locating information is a learned skill. It does not help handicapped readers much simply to allow them to use the book to answer questions. Instead, some systematic instruction is necessary, coupled with large amounts of practice.

If teachers start with materials that highly interest students and the objective of trying to obtain literal information, the chances of success are enhanced. Record club memberships, cooking instructions, and local map reading are the kinds of material that can get students accustomed to locating information before paragraph-size passages are introduced.

In longer passages, students should be encouraged to think first about whether the information needed is in the front, toward the middle, or at the end of the passage. Considerable time can be saved if students do not start searching in the beginning for information that occurs toward the end of the passage. The mental set for locating can be developed. Instead of trying to recall details, the student tries to get the flow and direction of the passage so it is easier to locate specific information.

Personal outlining provides an excellent means for teaching locating skills. With this strategy, students will be locating information that has already been deemed important. They can locate information for topics of interest in the library and in other types of resource materials.

Real-Life Reading File Folder materials have been developed to help students locate information using the types of materials they are likely to encounter in their daily lives. These materials stress the importance of using prediction strategies, critical reading, and vocabulary development, as well as locating strategies. Materials are classified according to the skills of following directions, obtaining information, and reading labels and forms. They are suited to students reading on the third-, fourth-, fifth-, and sixth-grade levels (see Figure 10–3).

Newspaper activities are also useful in developing locating skills. A sports article about an important baseball game can be used to have students locate the reason for the high score. Obviously, every word in the article is not important to accomplish this objective. Students can be taught to skim through the article to get the important section or can locate the box score and determine which players were responsible for the scoring. In fact, all sections of the newspaper can require skimming to locate important information. The American Newspaper Publishers Association publishes and distributes (free of charge) a bibliography of the best materials available for using newspapers in an educational setting.[25] Wilson and Barnes present ideas for teachers to use local newspapers for the development of a variety of comprehension skills, including the locating of information.[26]

Difficulty Reading Content Material

Many students seem to read satisfactorily in reading classes but are not able to read content materials. One problem here may be that the content and readability of the materials are too difficult. Another may be that students find success when working under teacher direction and difficulty when working alone.

Teachers should first consider the readability of the material which the students cannot comprehend. Often extreme differences in readability exist between the books used in reading class and those used in content areas. Content-area books often are written at a level much higher than graded reading books. On an informal basis, the teacher should note the differences in the size of the print, the length of sentences, the number of difficult words, and the concept difficulty. If any of these factors varies noticeably from the reading class materials, the problem is probably in material difficulty. Yoakham,[27] Spache,[28] and Fry[29] present readability formulas that may be used to obtain a grade level of readability, although they do not evaluate the concept load of the material. The cloze procedure also has been developed to enable teachers to determine the ability of the student to handle materials; it will indicate the ability to handle concepts, as well as word and sentence structures. Taylor claims it is of value in determining readability.[30]

The clozure technique can give teachers insights into the abilities of students to read required textbooks. It involves these steps:

1. Select at random several passages containing about 100 words each.
2. Retype passages, leaving out every fifth word. (Authorities differ on which words to omit, but the fifth has been found to be

BIKE SHOP

Sometimes, when we can't repair things ourselves, we must take them to a repair shop. Most repair shops present the customer with an invoice when the work is done. An invoice is an itemized bill for goods and services.

Look at this invoice from Bill's Bicycle Shop.

INVOICE 5386

BILL'S BICYCLE SHOP
101 Main Street
Anderson, South Carolina
385-9360

Sales and Service

Name: _Shirley Carter_   Date: _1/3/80_

Address: _109 Edner Road._   Phone: _389-4290_

Anderson, S.C.

Services Requested: _Repair back fender and replace chain._

QUANTITY	MATERIALS USED	PRICE	AMOUNT
1	chain	3.50	3.50
1 sm. can	red paint - #303	2.50	2.50

DATE	WORK PERFORMED	HOURS	RATE	AMOUNT
1/5/80	Straighten fender & paint.	2	3.80/hr.	7.60
	Replace chain.	½ hr.	3.80/hr.	1.90

Work performed by:

David Caley

X _____

Signature — The above work completed satisfactorily
All services guaranteed for 30 days after completion.

Sales Tax	.18
Total	15.68

Use this page with duplicating pages Bike Shop 1 and Bike Shop 2

Published by Instructo/McGraw-Hill, Paoli, Pennsylvania 19301 Copyright © 1980 Instructo/McGraw-Hill, Inc.   No. 8511

FIGURE 10–3. Sample of a Locating Skill Lesson from *Real-Life Reading.* *(Copyright © 1980 by Instructo/McGraw-Hill. Reproduced by permission; all rights reserved.)*

It looks like this bicycle needs some repair work. If you read and answer the following questions carefully, you will learn about invoices and repair expenses.

Write your answer in the space provided.

P 1. How do you think the bicycle might have been damaged?

Any reasonable answer is acceptable.

P 2. Can you list two advantages of taking a damaged bike to a shop instead of trying to fix it yourself?

It might look better afterwards.

It might last longer.

It might be safer to ride.

Or any reasonable answer.

L 3. Bill's Bicycle Shop is located at _____

101 Main St., Anderson, S.C.

L 4. The telephone number for Bill's Bicycle

Shop is _____ 385-9360 _____.

L 5. Where was the bicycle taken for repairs?

Bill's Bicycle Shop

L 6. What services were requested?

Repair back fender and replace chain.

L 7. Who requested the repairs?

Shirley Carter

L 8. On what date were the repairs requested? 1/3/80

L 9. On what date were the repairs made?

1/5/80

C 10. Who made the repairs? David Caley

C 11. How much did it cost for 1 hour of labor?

$3.80

Published by Instructo/McGraw-Hill, Paoli, Pennsylvania 19301 Copyright © 1980 Instructo/McGraw-Hill, Inc.   No. 8511

Bike Shop 1

FIGURE 10-3 (continued)

295

effective.) As a rule, neither the first word in a sentence nor proper nouns should be omitted. An example of a clozure test on easy material would appear as follows:

It was an exciting day. Nancy was anxious to _____ her birthday party this _____ . She had invited some _____ from her room at school. She _____ that they would all _____ able to attend.

Have the reader read the incomplete sentences, filling in the missing words. To "cloze" properly, the student must know the words and understand the concepts, thereby anticipating the author's ideas.

As teachers gain familiarity with the clozure technique, they will find it valuable in determining whether a book is appropriate for a given student.

Bormuth has found that a clozure test score of 38 percent right is approximately equal to a regular test score of 75 percent right.[31] Therefore, as a rule of thumb, clozure scores below 40 percent right should be regarded as danger signs for that student with that material. Either instructional adjustments are needed or easier material must be used for instruction. (For limitations of the 40 percent criteria, review chapter 5.)

Reading problems in understanding content materials usually do not become pronounced until the student has reached the fourth grade. It is at this point that content reading becomes a regular part of the school program and the student with study skill problems is clearly handicapped.

STRATEGIES TO ASSIST STUDENTS IN READING CONTENT MATERIAL. The teacher should use the D-R-T-A with content area materials. Students who fail to see the need for attacking unfamiliar materials must be directed in the same manner used in reading class. Each step of the D-R-T-A must be used carefully in the development of skill in reading content materials, gradually permitting students to guide themselves through the steps.

Older students may find it beneficial to follow a specific study technique in reading content materials. Several of these are available, the most prominent being SQ3R (survey, question, read, recite, review).[32] The effect of this type of technique is the same as a D-R-T-A except that students are to apply it to their studies without supervision. Independence in reading content material is the desired objective of this strategy.

Activities in which the students organize and classify ideas are useful in remediation. Students who cannot read in the content areas usually have difficulty with outlining skills. Beginning with completed outlines of material recently read, the teacher illustrates the method of following the author's train of thought. An outline format is then presented for students to complete, followed by simple outlining of clearly organized material with little or no direction from the teacher. The *Reading for Meaning* workbooks, designed for the intermediate and secondary grades, have practice exercises to develop students' abilities to organize material through a gradual exposure to outlining techniques. The *SRA Organizing and Reporting Skills Kit* has individualized exercises that gradually introduce the concepts of notetaking, reporting, and outlining.

When teaching notetaking skills, teachers might find it helpful to teach students to use the one-word note technique. After taking notes from a book or lecture, the students write a one-word note in the margin. That one word should denote the essential meaning of the section. When preparing for writing or examination, the location of the one-word note helps students quickly locate the section that needs to be reviewed in their notes.

The ability to follow directions has a direct relationship to the ability to perform in study situations. This skill depends on students' abilities to follow the sequence and organization of the author's thoughts, as well as their abilities to obtain the main idea. The *Specific Skills Series* (e.g., Using the Context, Locating the Answer) includes sets of intensive exercises in following directions at the various grade levels. Once the ability to follow directions is mastered, remedial sessions should provide opportunities to practice this concept at regular intervals.

Teachers can use many activities to help students develop mastery of following directions. As has been suggested, the use of model cars, ships, and airplanes helps a reader realize the importance of following directions carefully. Reading the directions on the box and following them step by step to completion can be a highly useful reading and learning experience. If students cannot read all of the instructions, they should work in pairs, helping each other. Learning centers can be developed to help students follow directions. Using pages from telephone books or newspapers, students can be instructed to follow direc-

Using newspapers, students can be instructed to follow directions ranging from simple to complex.

tions ranging from the simple to the complex (e.g., find a phone number; find a phone number and address; find the phone numbers of three dentists and give their names, get their addresses, and determine which lives closest to your home).

Another SRA study aid, the *Graph and Picture Study Skills Kit,* is designed to be adapted to any subject area. These materials are useful in developing a type of reading often overlooked in remedial programs. The *Be a Better Reader* books provide specific suggestions for study in the major content areas, particularly for older students. The *Study Skills Library,* which provides specialized instruction in developing the same type of concepts, is useful with younger students. Individualized for clinical use, these materials can serve a highly useful function with students who are deficient in study skills.

Adaptation of the language-experience approach to content subjects has been very effective.[33] Four teachers agreed to work with students in the seventh grade who had serious reading problems. They taught mathematics, science, social studies, and English through the language-experience approach and were pleased to find that these students could learn the content when the materials were presented in a personalized, readable manner. Reading specialists can work with classroom teachers to develop skill in presenting material and information to the students without using texts (e.g., lecture, discussion, tapes, films, pictures, demonstrations, experiments); in drawing students' verbal expressions of what they have learned; in writing language-experience stories based on the students' contributions; and in developing reading and content skills from the written stories.

Reading specialists also can help content teachers rewrite materials that are too difficult. Basically rewriting involves cutting sentence length, eliminating complicated sentence structures, and reducing word difficulty through the use of synonyms.

Herber suggests several teaching strategies that are useful in helping students in the content areas.[34] He suggests that teachers use study guides to assist students in content reading. Study guides help students understand content objectives; guide students in using specific text materials to understand its organization; and assist them in using that material to meet the stated objectives. He suggests the use of small-group instruction to encourage risk-taking behavior and suggests that such groups contain a range of achievement levels so that students can learn from one another.

Bruner and Campbell recommend studying book parts so that students can use the book organization to their advantage.[35] Lessons on the use of the table of contents, the index, the glossary, and the appendixes are recommended. They also recommend lessons that help students use maps, graphs, pictures, and cartoons to assist comprehension.

When students have great difficulty with content reading, paired learning can prove helpful. Two students work together to accomplish the content objectives. This has a double effect. First, the student having the most difficulty feels that learning is possible and that help is available. Second, the helping student experiences the satisfaction of being able to help someone else and learns more in the process, since it is often through teaching that one gains a more thorough understanding of the material to be learned.

Failure to Comprehend Most Reading

For the student who does not respond to even the most simple comprehension checks, remedial techniques are difficult to apply because starting places are hard to determine. However, teachers must change any materials that cause the students difficulty; continued use of these materials cannot be defended. For these students, the level of the material must be easy, the interest of the material must be high, and the quantity small.

Intensified use of experience stories permits teachers to start with relatively easy, interesting material of as small a quantity as desired. Again, students are directed to demonstrate an understanding of the experience stories, which, because they contain their own concepts, can usually be done without difficulty. Once a feeling for this type of activity is developed, the student is exposed through the D-R-T-A or the problem approach to easy, interesting printed material.

Placing the student in reading situations that call for action and reaction is often successful. Signs, posters, and flash cards calling for reaction are developed from the opportunities that appear daily in and out of the classroom. Several publishers have released series that actively involve readers in making decisions as they read through adventure stories. At the bottom of each page or two, the reader is asked a series of questions. "Will you go into the cave? If so, turn to page 23. If not, turn to page 32." These materials often prove to be so motivational that students will read them again and again.

Vocabulary exercises requiring students to respond nonverbally to printed symbols have considerable usefulness here. The *Nichols Slides* (or similar activities) can be used by starting with very simple, direct commands and progressing as students develop the skill (e.g., start with words such as *sit, stand,* and *jump* and go to more complicated word combinations such as *stand and sing now* or *jump three times*). With these students, drill activities without contextual emphasis certainly should be discontinued.

Several techniques have been developed to encourage students to respond to reading in rather nontraditional ways. One involves the use of creative movement to display understanding of a story that has been read to or by the students. Materials entitled *Teaching Reading through Creative Movement* have been successful with seriously handicapped readers.

Another approach to eliciting student response is the use of popular music. A phonograph, records, and lyrics set the stage. Students listen to the music and sing along. When the music is over, the meaning of the lyrics is discussed. Rereading is done to verify opinions. Older students seem to respond well to remediation involving music as the motivator.

Reading which involves essential information for survival in society has also been used effectively. For example, students need to be able to read driver's manuals and job applications. *Real-Life Reading* materials are particularly useful because they are written at low readability levels but contain highly motivating content such as understanding skateboard rules, how to earn money, and using a television guide. These materials can be used in teacher-directed lessons until the students feel comfortable enough to work on them independently or in pairs.

Extended Remediation

The problems students encounter related to speed of reading and distractibility can become instructional concerns.

Reading Speed

Slow reading speed often causes students to give inappropriate responses. In such cases, when students have been asked to read a selection (ample time must be allotted) and to answer several questions, their comprehension responses appear to be unsatisfactory because they have not completed the material. Upon careful examination, it is often found that they have responded properly to those questions related to the material that was read and have missed those concerned with material not read. Teachers must question why the students are reading slowly. If they are having difficulty breaking the written code, activities designed to increase reading speed are useless. The same is true if they are struggling with unfamiliar concepts. However, some students read slowly because they have applied oral reading speeds to silent reading, lack concentration, or do not know how to vary their reading speed. In these cases, some remedial instruction may be helpful.

Readers who have developed slow reading speeds should first be placed in reading material that is both easy and interesting. Teachers should attempt to assure that difficult words will not slow or stop reading. The second step is to be certain that the students are reading for personally set purposes. Purposeless reading is bound to be slow. Teachers can use the first step in the D-R-T-A for purpose setting. Then they can help readers read for those purposes using skimming techniques. The newspaper can provide excellent material to teach skimming skills. Purposes are set according to what is known from the headlines, pictures, or prior information. Students will find the time needed for reading will vary with the type of purpose set. At times, it will be useful for the teacher to set the purposes and permit a limited amount of time to find the answer. This is often best done after the material has been read silently. Readers can be asked a question and then asked where they remember seeing the answer in the passage. They quickly get the idea that one need not read all of the words in the passage to obtain a specific answer. As flexible rates are developed, students can begin to use those various rates in specific settings.

Prepared materials are available for students to use for practice exercises in reading within certain time limits. The *SRA Laboratories* have rate-building exercises in which the student must read and answer the question in three minutes. The student should be started with rate-building exercises at very easy levels. The emphasis here is on efficiency in relatively easy high-interest material. The *Standard Test Lessons in Reading* also have the three-minute time limitation. In the remedial session, the three-minute time limit will often need to be adjusted. Since there is no rationale for the three-minute limit, teachers should allow more time for those students who need it. Time should be monitored, however, and the students should be encouraged to complete the work accurately and as swiftly as possible.

Other available exercises are designed to motivate improved time performance by emphasizing such reading-rate measures as number of words read per minute. In remediation none of this emphasis should be stressed without equal or greater emphasis on the quality of comprehension that accompanies the rate. The *Better Reading Books* are an example of this type of material to be used with older students, providing personalized charts for easy motivation to better speed and comprehension.

Charts and graphs that illustrate the students' progress are always helpful. These should be constructed so that each student can note small gains in improved rate, so that comprehension is charted as well as the reading rate, and so that the goals are realistically within reach. If students reach the graph's goal quickly, the teacher simply makes a new graph, again with easily reached goals. All such charts are maintained as private information.

Distractibility

A teacher must look for the reason why students become distracted. Perhaps students find the material so boring that everything else seems more interesting by comparison. In these cases, the purposes for reading may be adjusted or different materials can be used. However, some students are distracted by the classroom surroundings. Everything is asking for their attention—other students, learning centers, bulletin boards, artwork, and the teacher. In these cases, several suggestions are offered:

1. Distractible students should be placed so that others' actions are no more distracting than necessary. In the classroom, this would normally involve a front corner seat.
2. Remediation with distractible students should not be conducted in physical surroundings in which pictures and other distracting objects are prominent. In clinical situations, a plain room where a student's total efforts can be directed to the book should be used initially. In the classroom, distractible students should take their reading instruction in an area of the room that lacks extensive decoration.
3. When distractibility is recognized as a serious limitation, it is often helpful to use books that contain a minimum of pictures,

thus permitting students to focus attention on the print and the skills necessary to read it.

4. Distractible students will need to have skill exercises in shorter duration periods. They should understand that their entire attention will be expected for a short time, after which they may move to another activity and return to reading skill activities later. In the clinic, varying activity as much as possible is helpful. Unfortunately, such adjustments are difficult and at times impossible in the classroom because they disrupt the activities of the other students. The classroom teacher, however, should provide a variety of activities and at least refrain from punishing students for distractibility over which they have no obvious control. In the more extreme cases, students should run, jump, and play actively in other ways between their periods of reading-skill activities. Opportunities should be used to get them to be active in as well as out of class. For example, the teacher could have them come to the chalkboard for some of their work and let them pass out materials to others, thus providing them with opportunities to release some of their energy. In this way, their tensions become relaxed, and they become more receptive to the required silent work at their seats.

5. Students who are easily distracted generally enjoy a program that has as much consistency as possible. When they can anticipate an interesting routine, they are more likely to be able to concentrate on it to its completion. In rare instances, continued distractible behavior, even after adjustments have been made, calls for medical referral. These students may be demonstrating symptoms of behavior that need medical attention.

6. Closed-captioned, prime-time television programs, where words appear on the screen to communicate the events being shown, can provide an excellent means for reaching distracted students. This process, developed by the National Captioning Institute, requires a decoder which makes hundreds of hours of television programming with captions available each week. Although originally intended for use by the hearing impaired, hearing students who had been unable to concentrate on book reading are captivated by captioned television.[36] (See chapter 12 for a complete explanation of captioned television.)

The Reluctant Reader

Most students experiencing reading difficulty are reluctant to engage in reading activities. However, the term *reluctant reader* as used in this section refers to those students who have the necessary skills for reading but are reluctant to use them. These students need to see reading as a rewarding experience. In every

*Learning centers are
excellent for providing
students with inde-
pendent learning
activities.*

lesson, they should be reading for purposes that they feel are important. Drill-
type activities should be held to a minimum, and purposeful reading should
be increased.

First, these students need to see that free reading is an activity the teacher sees as worthwhile. Therefore, free-reading opportunities should occur periodically in all classrooms. *Free reading*, in this case, implies reading that is
not followed by question-and-answer periods, and reading in which the students
choose their own materials. As students develop the understanding that free
reading can be fun and worthwhile enough to take school time, gradual attitude
changes will likely be noted.

Developing a willing attitude toward reading obviously depends on the
availability of books. The reluctant reader must have books available for free
reading in the classroom and school libraries, and at home. There is little chance
to develop attitudes and habits that favor reading when books are difficult or
impossible to obtain. School administrators should note that attempts to be
thrifty by cutting appropriations for classroom and school libraries make
teachers unable to encourage the reading habit.

Learning centers that provide students with opportunities for selecting the
materials they are going to use, for pacing themselves, and for correcting their
own work have been used with considerable success with the reluctant reader.

Teachers should use every opportunity to promote free reading through
the use of peer group recommendations. Students who have read interesting
books and want to share them with others can often create more interest than
the teacher can. Sharing may be done through brief, voluntary, oral reports;
through a classroom card file including the name of the book and the reasons
that the student enjoyed it; or through a school book fair where interesting books
are displayed.

The teacher can develop interest by reading to the students from books which contain stories and ideas of interest but which would be too difficult for them to read themselves. Teachers who read children's books are able to provide book summaries to develop interest in new books as they appear in the library. Teachers can also influence attitude toward reading by showing enthusiastic interest in their own personal reading.

Teachers may find published book reviews and booklists to be useful. Two periodically updated publications that contain recommended books for children include *The Read-Aloud Handbook*[37] and *A Parent's Guide to Children's Reading.*[38] Reviews of new children's books can be found in *Booklist* and in *The Horn Book Magazine.* Another source of good, new children's books is "Children's Choices." Published in each October issue of *The Reading Teacher*, these are capsule reviews of books deemed noteworthy by regional teams of school-age children. Through the use of such resources, the teacher can also recommend books to parents that would be appropriate gifts. Teachers should encourage parents to consider a book a valued, highly desirable gift.

Often reluctant readers are hesitant to select a book that is threatening in terms of volume. Perhaps due to pressure from adults, the readers have developed an attitude that taking a book from the library commits them to read the book from cover to cover. The teacher, of course, must discourage this attitude, for everyone has been in situations where, after starting a book, they feel no desire to finish it. Nevertheless, too many false starts tend to discourage students from sampling brief portions of books prior to selecting the books from the library. Two materials that let students sample books are *The Literature Sampler* and the *Pilot Library.* Both of these provide the teacher with a guide to a book's readability and the interest factors involved with it.

Extensive use should be made of book series that, while maintaining high interest, have low vocabulary levels and provide interesting reading. Without books to reinforce the skills that are being developed in remediation, the chance for transfer of these skills is seriously limited. Table 10-1 lists high-interest, low-

TABLE 10-1. High-interest, Low-vocabulary Books

Series	Vocabulary Level	Publisher
About Books	2 to 4	Children's Press
All About Books	3 to 6	Random House
American Adventure Series	2 to 3	Wheeler
Bucky Buttons	1 to 3	Benefic Press
Cowboy Sam	1 to 3	Benefic Press
Dan Frontier	1 to 3	Benefic Press
Deep Sea Adventure Stories	1 to 3	Harr Wagner
Dolch First Readers	1 to 2	Garrard
Interesting Reading Series	2 to 3	Follett
I Want to Be Books	1 to 3	Children's Press
Sailor Jack	1 to 3	Benefic Press
The Monster Books	2 to 4	Bowmar

vocabulary books that have been used effectively in classrooms and clinics. Books such as these are inexpensive and readily available.

Free reading may be permitted in materials such as the *SRA Reading Laboratories* and *The Reading Skill Builders*. When they are used for free reading, students should not be required to answer questions or to do the vocabulary exercises. Of course, selections should be at a recreational reading level.

Other types of material that can be used with reluctant readers are those classified as survival or functional reading materials. Throughout the discussions on remediation, attention has been called to the types of materials that students need to read in order to function and survive in our society. These materials have strong appeal and are relevant and essential.

Survival materials include such items as medicine labels, danger signs, road signs, and warning notices. Students who cannot read these types of materials are in danger in day-to-day life. Their chances of survival in society are enhanced when remedial instruction includes these types of materials and the skills needed to read them. Functional reading materials include such items as newspapers, menus, employment forms, and phone books. If students are unable to read such materials, their ability to function in society is seriously limited.

Originally, survival and functional reading programs were being recommended for only the seriously handicapped reader. Today, however, these programs are recommended for all readers as an important part of the reading program. In many schools, they are developed in learning-center format, and students use them throughout the year.

In remedial programs, survival and functional reading materials are especially important. For seriously handicapped readers, the entire remedial program can be developed around such materials. Older students with serious reading problems especially profit from survival and functional reading programs. Sight vocabulary, word attack, and comprehension activities are drawn from the materials. Experience stories supplement the materials. Lists of words such as the Essential Driver's List and the Essential Vocabulary List are used.[39] Such programs encourage the readers, and they often ask for instruction beyond the survival and functional programs.

Students' interest and reading needs are surveyed. For example, a group of students may be about to obtain learner's permits for driving a car. All types of materials related to driving can be collected. The students can bring their driver's manuals and car maintenance manuals to the lessons, and instruction can be directed toward the understanding of such materials. Actual automobile trips can be planned during which students use their learned skills.

One elementary school developed boxes of actual materials needed to function or survive in society. One box included medicine bottles; another contained boxes, cans, and bottles from the grocery shelf; another held all types of maps. Students picked the area of concentration they wished to pursue and immersed themselves in the activities. The Wilson and Barnes book listed in suggested readings at the end of this chapter describes many survival and functional reading activities.

The use of closed-captioned television is another motivating way to reach the reading needs of these students. As discussed earlier, closed-captioned television increases attention to task and provides students with a common experience with which to relate the drama on the television screen.

Remediation for the Culturally Different

Some students come for reading instruction with experiential backgrounds that are quite different from other students and from their teachers. These students might come from foreign countries and thus do not have adequate command of English since English is not their native language. Not only do these students have a problem with language, but they also might have trouble relating to the customs and values of American society. Another group of students have lived in our culture and speak English but come from an environment that limits their ability to relate to the language and customs of school. The approach to reading comprehension instruction with both of these types of students must start with language to which they can relate.

The language-experience approach is therefore a logical starting point. Using their own experiences as language for reading comprehension instruction eliminates most of the obstacles of learning for these students. Their skills with English and their personal experiences can be put into print and they will be able to relate to the printed message in a personal way. By providing common experiences through community field trips, science experiments, cooking activities, and games, their language experiences can be extended and developed into additional printed experience stories. When moving from language-experience stories to book reading, the selection of reading materials is very important.

The work of Hancock, DeLorenzo, and Ben-Barka[40] provides numerous useful suggestions for teaching reading to refugee children. They suggest starting with the language-experience approach. This source is rich with suggestions, commercial materials, references, and an important list of "do's and don'ts" for working with ESL students.

Several programs are available for language skill development. The *Peabody Language Development Kits, The Visual-Lingual Reading Program,* and *Building Prereading Skills Kit-a-Language* can be used. *The Language Master* can also facilitate language and concept development. Written words and a picture representing those words can be placed on the cards. The teacher then orally records the word on the tape that appears on the bottom of the card. The students run these cards through the machine, seeing the word and the picture while hearing the word read.

Summary

By selecting approaches for teaching comprehension that reflect what is known about comprehension, one can enhance the chances of a successful program. With these approaches, a variety of instructional techniques can be developed that will make the lessons interesting. Specific activities that are based on information that was obtained during the diagnosis are often needed. By using high-interest materials with all instructional strategies, teachers can keep interest high, help students achieve success in large quantities, and assure positive student attitudes.

1. Frank Smith, *Understanding Reading* (New York: Holt, Rinehart & Winston, 1978), 67.
2. Richard Allington, "If They Don't Read Much How They Ever Gonna Get Good?" *Journal of Reading* 21, no. 1 (October 1977): 57–61.
3. Linda Gambrell, Robert M. Wilson, and Walter N. Gantt, "Classroom Observations of Task-Attending Behaviors of Good and Poor Readers," *Journal of Educational Research* 74, no. 6 (July/August 1981): 400–04.
4. Dolores Durkin, "What Classroom Observations Reveal about Reading Comprehension Instruction," *Reading Research Quarterly* 14, no. 4 (1978–79): 481–522.
5. Russell G. Stauffer, *Teaching Reading As a Thinking Process* (New York: Harper & Row, 1969).
6. Ibid., 12.
7. Bruce W. Brigham and Virginia H. Pilato, "A Heuropractice Strategy in Adults: A Psycho-Educational Procedure for Teaching Handicapped Adults," *Journal of Exceptional Adult Education* (Fall 1982): 7–11.
8. Mary Budd Rowe, *Teaching Science As Continuous Inquiry* (New York: McGraw-Hill, 1973), 242–66.
9. Mary Shoop, "InQuest: A Listening and Reading Comprehension Strategy," *The Reading Teacher* 39, no. 7 (March 1986): 670–74.
10. Ibid., 673.
11. For more information, see Richard P. Santeusanio, *A Practical Approach to Content Area Reading* (Reading, Mass.: Addison-Wesley, 1983), 39–42.
12. For more information, see Joseph L. Vaughn and Thomas H. Estes, *Reading and Reasoning Beyond the Primary Grades* (Boston: Allyn and Bacon, 1986), 167–70.
13. For more information, see Gerald L. Fowler, "Developing Comprehension Skills in Primary Students Through Use of Story Frames," *The Reading Teacher* 36, no. 2 (November 1982): 176–79.
14. For more information, see Joan E. Heimlich and Susan P. Pittleman, *Semantic Mapping: Classroom Applications* (Newark, Del.: International Reading Association, 1986).
15. For more information, see Frank Lyman, Charlene Lopez, and Arlene Mindus, *Elementary Language Arts Guide* (Clarksville, Md.: Howard County Board of Education, 1977), 47–60.
16. For more information, see Glenn Freedman and Elizabeth G. Reynolds, "Enriching Basal Reader Lessons with Semantic Webbing," *The Reading Teacher* 33, no. 6 (March 1980): 677–84.
17. Marge Blaine, *The Terrible Thing That Happened at Our House* (New York: Four Winds Press, 1975).
18. Craig J. Cleland, "Highlighting Issues in Children's Literature Through Semantic Webbing," *The Reading Teacher* 34, no. 6 (March 1981): 642–46.
19. Marilyn W. Sadow, "The Use of Story Grammar in the Designing of Questions," *The Reading Teacher* 35, no. 5 (February 1982): 519.
20. Ibid., 521.
21. Don Graves and Jane Hansen, "The Author's Chair," *Language Arts* 60, no. 2 (February 1983): 176–83.
22. John D. McNeil, *Reading Comprehension: New Directions for Classroom Practice*, 2d ed. (Glenview Ill.: Scott, Foresman and Co., 1987), 163–64.
23. Beth Davey, "Think Aloud—Modeling the Cognitive Processes of Reading Comprehension," *Journal of Reading* 27, no. 1 (October 1983): 44–47.
24. Ruth Garner, *Metacognition and Reading Comprehension* (Norwood, N.J.: Ablex Publishing, 1987): 113–15.

25. Merrill F. Hartsorn, ed., *Newspapers in Education, Bibliography* (Reston, Va.: American Newspaper Publishers Association, 1983).
26. Robert M. Wilson and Marcia M. Barnes, *Using Newspapers to Teach Reading Skills* (Reston, Va.: American Newspaper Publishers Association, 1975).
27. Gerald A. Yoakham, *Basal Reading Instruction* (New York: Prentice-Hall, 1955), app. 1.
28. George Spache, *Good Reading for Poor Readers* (Champaign, Ill.: Garrard Press, 1968), chap. 4.
29. Edward B. Fry, "Fry's Readability Graph: Clarifications, Validity, and Extensions to Level 17," *Journal of Reading* 21, no. 3 (November 1977): 242–51.
30. W. L. Taylor, "Cloze Procedure—A New Tool for Measuring Readability," *Journalism Quarterly* 30 (Fall 1953): 415–33.
31. John R. Bormuth, "Comparable Cloze and Multiple-Choice Test Comprehension Scores," *Journal of Reading* 10, no. 5 (February 1967): 295.
32. Francis P. Robinson, *Effective Study* (New York: Harper & Row, 1961).
33. Robert M. Wilson and Nancy Parkey, "A Modified Reading Program in a Middle School," *Journal of Reading* 13, no. 6 (March 1970): 447–52.
34. Harold L. Herber, *Teaching Reading in the Content Areas*, 2d ed. (Englewood Cliffs, N.J.: Prentice-Hall, 1978), chap. 4.
35. Joseph F. Bruner and John J. Campbell, *Participating in Secondary Reading* (Englewood Cliffs, N.J.: Prentice-Hall, 1978), 53–62.
36. National Captioning Institute Research Report 83-6, Falls Church, Va., 1983.
37. Jim Trelease, *The Read-Aloud Handbook*, rev. ed. (New York: Viking Penguin Books, 1985).
38. Nancy Larrick, *A Parent's Guide to Children's Reading*, 5th ed., rev. (Philadelphia: Westminster, 1983).
39. Corlett T. Wilson, "An Essential Vocabulary," *The Reading Teacher* 17 (November 1963): 94–96.
40. Charles Hancock, William DeLorenzo, and Alba Ben-Barka, *Teaching Pre- and Semi-Literate Laotian and Cambodian Adolescents to Read* (Maryland State Department of Education, 1983).

Suggested Readings

Carin, Arthur A., and Robert B. Sund. *Creative Questioning and Sensitive Listening Techniques*. 2d ed. Columbus, Ohio: Merrill, 1978. Carin and Sund illustrate how teachers' questions help and hinder learning and learners.

Cook, Jimmie E., and Elsie C. Earlley. *Remediating Reading Disabilities*. Germantown, Md.: Aspen Systems Corporation, 1979. This book presents thousands of ideas for enriching instruction beyond the basal series. Chapter 9 focuses on numerous suggestions for making comprehension meaningful and interesting.

Devine, Thomas G. *Teaching Reading Comprehension: From Theory to Practice*. Boston: Allyn and Bacon, 1986. This book contains much useful information related to how students comprehend and how to assist them to comprehend better. Chapters 4 through 8 present specific comprehension-enhancing strategies.

Irwin, Judith Westphal. *Teaching Reading Comprehension Processes*. Englewood Cliffs, N.J.: Prentice-Hall, 1986. The author presents comprehension instruction as an active and personal undertaking. Many useful strategies and approaches for extended remediation are included.

McNeil, John D. *Reading Comprehension*. 2d ed. Glenview, Ill.: Scott, Foresman and Company, 1987. The author examines the implications of schema theory for reading instruction. Chapter 3 discusses the student as questioner, and chapter 10 addresses reading/writing comprehension connections.

Rowe, Mary Budd. *Teaching Science as Continuous Inquiry*. New York: McGraw-Hill, 1973. Wait time is presented in detail. Every teacher working with readers experiencing comprehension difficulties should be familiar with Rowe's research and recommendations in relation to wait time.

Stauffer, Russell G. *Teaching Reading As a Thinking Process.* New York: Harper and Row, 1969. Stauffer provides rationales and procedures for use of the D-R-T-A. Any student not familiar with the D-R-T-A is referred to this source.

Wilson, Robert M., and Marcia M. Barnes. *Survival Learning Materials.* York, Pa.: College Reading Association, 1974. This book presents a rationale and many ideas for developing survival and functional learning materials.

Wilson, Robert M., and Linda B. Gambrell. *Reading Comprehension in the Elementary School.* Boston: Allyn and Bacon, 1988. This book includes numerous strategies for enhancing comprehension.

EDITORIAL

Joetta Palkovitz

is a supervisor for the Washington County Public Schools in Maryland.

Andy, Bruce, Charlie, Danny, David, and Dwight were twelve-year-old seventh graders who were having difficulty reading material intended for their grade level. These students were very reluctant to engage in any type of reading activity. They possessed strengths in the areas of decoding, literal comprehension, and group participation. They exhibited weaknesses in the areas of higher-level comprehension skills, organizational skills, and study skills, as well as on-task behavior and self-concept as readers.

After examining and taking into consideration the strengths and weaknesses of the group, it was decided to employ the Problem Approach in order to involve the students actively in an instructional situation. The group decided they wanted to learn first about the various jobs and responsibilities involved in running a fast-food restaurant. Next it was decided that the best way to obtain the information was to contact a fast-food restaurant and arrange for a tour and a question-and-answer session with the manager. After the visit to the restaurant, the students summarized and demonstrated what they had learned by setting up their own fast-food restaurant. Various jobs with corresponding responsibilities were undertaken by each member of the group. Students from other classes were invited to visit the "restaurant," "purchase" food items, and ask questions pertaining to jobs, responsibilities, etc.

The students experienced successful instructional situations using this approach in that they were able to bring their experiential background and prior knowledge to the task in order to provide a resource of information. By being active participants involved in directing their learning, the group of originally very reluctant readers gained a new enthusiasm for reading through the Problem Approach. Their self-concepts as readers, on-task behavior, higher level comprehension skills, organizational skills, and study skills continually improved with each successive use of the approach.

Joetta Palkovitz

Assessment and Planning for Handicapped Students

CHAPTER OUTLINE

Historical Injustices to Handicapped
Students
Procedural Safeguards
Special Considerations for Diagnosis
Special Considerations in Remediation
Areas of Potential Difficulty

CHAPTER EMPHASES

*Teachers should know about
procedural safeguards that aid
handicapped students.*
*Working with handicapped students in
both diagnostic and remedial
capacities requires special
consideration of their unique
learning needs.*
*Many of the same approaches and
techniques that are used with
students in the regular classroom
may be adapted for use with
handicapped students.*
*Teachers should exhibit positive
attitudes when working with
handicapped students to aid them
in achieving their fullest potentials.*

T he past decade has brought about sweeping changes in the ways handicapped students are viewed and educated. Handicapped individuals are being recognized as having the potential to make significant contributions to society if given the proper opportunities. These opportunities include the right to a free and appropriate public school education and the chance for many of the handicapped to be educated right beside their nonhandicapped peers. These important reforms have been brought about through the efforts of many individuals and advocacy groups who have encouraged far-reaching federal and state legislation aimed at serving handicapped students' educational needs.

These new and valuable rights have brought with them several attendant responsibilities which classroom teachers and reading specialists must share. Increasing numbers of handicapped students who previously were educated in self-contained special education classrooms are now being placed in regular elementary and secondary classrooms. This shift has required the regular classroom teacher to become increasingly involved in the education of many (although by no means all) handicapped students. Faced with this new challenge, the classroom teacher needs to acquire an added measure of knowledge and awareness of how to best meet the unique social, emotional, and learning needs of handicapped students.

Often the reading specialist is also asked to play an active role in designing and implementing an educational program for the handicapped student. Even if the reading specialist has minimal personal contact with the student, he or she may be called on to help with placement decisions and to serve as a resource person to the classroom teacher in selecting methods and materials to use with the student.

Teachers should have an awareness of the unique learning needs of individual students and understand the desirability of designing an instructional or remedial program which maximizes opportunities for personal success. For the handicapped student, however, such considerations take on even greater significance. Effort should be made to focus on these students' strengths to provide a viable means of highlighting what the students are able to do, rather than what they cannot do. This may, in turn, pay off in increased dividends to student self-esteem and academic attitudes. As students begin to feel better about themselves as learners, they often invest more effort in their remediation and become, in effect, partners with their teachers in their education.

In preparing to work with handicapped students, professionals must be aware of pertinent legislative safeguards that have been enacted to protect handicapped students' rights. Although much legislation in the seventies and eighties has focused on the rights of the handicapped, perhaps the most far-reaching federal acts were Public Law 93–380 passed in 1974 and Public Law 94–142 passed in 1975. Although certain provisions of both laws have been widely debated, they have been generally praised as valuable advances in promoting educational opportunities for handicapped students between three and twenty-one years of age.

Historically, the handicapped student has suffered from discriminatory treatment by the educational community. Although much of this discrimination was thought to be in the students' best educational interests, students were often placed in special programs using questionable criteria and kept in those programs even when their educational needs were not being met. The following specific injustices made legislative intervention necessary.

Exclusion from the Educational System

In the past many severely handicapped students in the community were excluded from an appropriate education due to a lack of facilities. Tragically, many of these students failed to reach their fullest potentials and were educated in the living rooms and bedrooms of their homes without benefit of the special methods and materials that a special class or school might have provided. Others were placed in private physical care institutions by their parents at great expense, yet they too often failed to receive an appropriate education because it was considered beyond the scope of a physical care facility.[1]

Placement without Parental Consent

Until recently, students were placed in special classes and programs when the school officials determined that such a placement was in the students' best interests. Although on the surface this practice might appear to be well within the schools' proper expertise and province, an unbiased examination of the record indicates that certain special-class placements in the past were made for administrative convenience. Not requiring parental consent allowed few opportunities to challenge the appropriateness of a student's special-class placement.

Identification Based on a Single Assessment

Past inequities have resulted from a student being identified as handicapped by inadequate or inappropriate means. At times, students were being identified as handicapped due to their poor performance on a single test. Perhaps the most prevalent and striking example of this practice was the use of a single intelligence score to justify placing a student in a class for the mentally retarded. When one examines the reliability and validity data for some intelligence tests, the injustice of single instrument assessment becomes obvious.[2]

Difficulty Returning to the Regular Classroom

Compounding the seriousness of special-class or program placement based on a single test score, students, once identified handicapped, often never had the

315

opportunity of "testing out" and returning to the regular classroom. Another factor which tended to retain students within the special education system was the decelerated pace of most classes for the handicapped and the different nature of the academic curriculum. Because of this slower pace and lack of opportunity to return to the regular classroom, many placements which should have been relatively short, such as some placements of emotionally disturbed children, became permanent instead.

Disproportionate Percentages of Minority Students

An examination of enrollment logs twenty-five years ago reveals that minority students were enrolled in special education programs at an unnaturally high percentage compared to the percentage of minority students in the general school population. This was due, in large part, to the testing instruments that were being used to identify students for special education services. Many of these tests contained items which were racially or culturally discriminatory. Furthermore, some of the standardization populations on which the test norms were based were not representative of the students in the schools in which the tests were being used.[3]

Classes Not Suited to Students' Needs

Sometimes students in the past were placed in classes that were inappropriate for them, such as the placement of cerebral palsied individuals who, despite average or above-average intelligence, were placed in programs for the mentally retarded. Such placements often sadly resulted in these students becoming educationally retarded by default.[4]

Segregation of the Handicapped

For many years, self-contained special education classes and schools were the dominant and preferred system for educating handicapped students. A growing realization developed, however, that many handicapped students were much the same as their nonhandicapped peers. Routinely placing handicapped students in self-contained special classes denied handicapped students the social, emotional, and academic benefits of being educated along with their friends and neighbors.

Procedural Safeguards

Although some unjust practices of the past still remain, today the handicapped are protected by certain procedural safeguards through recent federal and state legislation. In assisting in the education of handicapped students, classroom teachers and reading specialists should be cognizant of the laws which have been designed to aid the handicapped. A brief overview of some of the requirements and procedures these laws mandate follows.

Free and Appropriate Public Education

A free, appropriate, public education that includes special education and related services must be provided for all students. This education should be designed to meet students' special needs and provide safeguards for the rights of handicapped students and their parents. It should also provide for periodic evaluation of special programs to assure their effectiveness.

Categories of Handicapped Students

Children are considered handicapped if they have been identified as mentally retarded; hearing impaired or deaf; speech impaired; visually impaired; seriously emotionally disturbed; orthopedically or other health impaired; deaf-blind; multihandicapped; or specific learning disabled and because of their impairments need special education and related services. The last category, specific learning disabled, will naturally include many students experiencing serious difficulties learning to read. Reading specialists, however, must be prepared to be involved with the assessment and instruction of all handicapped children.

Evaluation and Placement Procedures

Assessment of a student believed to be handicapped should be comprehensive and multidisciplinary. It should assure that diagnostic procedures are appropriate to the student's suspected impairment and that the student is subsequently correctly identified as being either handicapped or nonhandicapped. This provision has particular significance in the case of students believed to be specific learning disabled. Because the existence of a specific learning disability is difficult to establish with certainty, a wide variance has emerged in the number of students identified as being learning disabled in different school districts and states.[5] A clearer definition of specific learning disabilities is needed to assure that students are appropriately identified.

Assessment procedures should also be designed to be as fair as possible. Testing materials and procedures should be selected and administered so that they do not reflect cultural or racial discrimination. Multiple criteria and tests should be used so that no single instrument determines a student's placement or program.

At times, evaluation of a student suspected of having a disability will be undertaken by a multidisciplinary team. This is an excellent approach to evaluation since various professionals bring different perspectives to the decision-making process. If a team cannot be involved in the assessment, however, the diagnostician must take particular care to investigate varied causes, contributing factors, and approaches when considering student difficulties.

Parental Participation and Consent

The past ten years have witnessed tremendous gains in the rights afforded to parents of handicapped children. Parents now must be notified in advance of proposed changes in their child's educational placement. Such notification must be made in the parents' native language. If desired, parents may have access to records pertaining to their child's evaluation, performance, and placement.

When a local educational agency recommends that a student receive a change in his or her educational placement that requires special education or related services, the student's parents must consent to the placement. If the parents do not approve of the change, they may seek an independent evaluation or request an impartial due process hearing where they may challenge the proposed placement. Students who do not have parents to represent their interests in placement decisions (as in the case of students who are wards of the state) are entitled to have surrogate parents appointed to speak for them. The surrogate parents should not be members of the educational system that is recommending the change.

Individualized Education Program

An individualized education program (IEP) will be developed for each handicapped student. The IEP is developed from the results of the multidisciplinary assessment. It should reflect the cooperative efforts of a variety of persons including the following:

- The student (where appropriate).
- The student's teacher.
- One or both of the student's parents.
- A special education professional.
- Other individuals who can contribute to the process.

IEPs take many different forms in various educational agencies, but all IEPs must include the following:

- A statement of the student's present levels of educational performance.
- A statement of annual goals as well as short-term instructional objectives.

- A statement of special education or related services to be provided as well as the extent to which the student will participate in regular education programs.
- The projected dates for initiation of services and the expected duration of those services.
- Appropriate objective criteria and evaluation procedures and an annual evaluation to determine whether the objectives are being achieved.

An IEP must receive a review no less than once a year and must be in effect and approved by the parents before special education and related services can be provided (see Figure 11-1).

Educational agencies and teachers must make good faith efforts to assist students in achieving the IEP's objectives and goals. However, neither school officials nor teachers may be held legally responsible if a student does not achieve the growth expected.

Least Restrictive Learning Environment

Many people mistakenly equate the terms *least restrictive environment* and *mainstreaming.* The least restrictive environment requires that handicapped students be taught along with their nonhandicapped same-age peers as far as it is reasonably possible. For most handicapped students this will mean that they should be mainstreamed into the regular classroom for at least part of the school day. Clearly, however, mainstreaming is inappropriate for some handicapped students. When placement options exist for these students, they will be best served by the placement that is the least segregated from the regular school population.

Although acceptance of the least restrictive environment has brought about many positive social and emotional benefits for both handicapped and nonhandicapped students, the classroom teacher must remember that a handicapped child who has been mainstreamed will still need certain instructional adjustments in order to profit from regular classroom instruction. Success or failure in understanding this fundamental principle can often be the difference between success and failure for the mainstreamed student.

Careful preparation and data interpretation are necessary in arriving at an accurate and comprehensive reading diagnosis. In the case of a handicapped student, however, the difficulties of diagnostic assessment are often complicated by the presence of the student's handicap. In undertaking the handicapped student's diagnostic reading assessment, attention should be given to the following special considerations.

**Special
Considerations
for Diagnosis**

Individual Education Program

Child's Name *Margi Emory*

School *12ᵀᴴ St.* Grade *5*

Date of Program Entry *Nov. 3, 1989*

Long-Term Goals:

1. *Develop comprehension in 2² reader.*
2. *Develop word attack system.*
3. _____

Summary of Present Levels of Performance

Comprehends well in 2' reader
Knows all initial consonants
Knows many rhyming syllables
Does not attack unknown words

Short-Term Objectives	Specific Ed. or Support Services	Person(s) Responsible	Percent of Time	Beginning and Ending Date	Review Date(s)
1. Margi will use non-questioning activities to further develop comprehension skills.	classroom	classroom teacher	5	Nov. 3, 1988 - April 1, 1989	April 1, 1989
2. Margi will substitute initial consonants to -AT, -IN, and -ING to form new words	Title I Resource	Title I Resource Teacher	5	Nov. 3, 1988 - March 1, 1989	March 1, 1989

Committee Members Present

Mrs. Bowen - Principal
Mrs. Emory - Parent
Mr. Fowler - Teacher
Mrs. Dayhoff - Title I Resource
Mr. Czarnecki - Vice Principal

Parent Approval ✓ Yes __ No

Louise Emory
  signature

Objective Evaluation Criteria:

  1. Reading comprehension evaluation by vice principal.
  2. CRT now in use in school for initial consonant substitution.

CONFIDENTIAL INFORMATION:

Percent of Time in Regular Classroom _____

Placement Recommendation
  Grade 5, Mr. Fowler

Committee recommendations for materials, techniques

use initial consonant substitution with Durrell Speech to Print Phonics. Use non-questioning strategies - Wilson, p. 312

FIGURE 11-1. An Example of an Individualized Education Program (IEP)

The reading specialist should know details about the student's handicapping condition prior to assessing the student's reading performance. Diagnostic and remedial decisions may depend on the severity of the student's handicap. Clearly, certain instruments and procedures that may be used in assessing a student with moderate visual impairment will be inappropriate in assessing a legally blind student. For this reason, the diagnostician would do well in many cases to request a medical or clinical summary of the student's handicapping condition. This may also spare the student from duplicating previous testing. By knowing about the student's handicap, the reading specialist will be in a better position to judge the effect of the handicap on the student's reading performance. For remedial purposes it will be useful to judge how much of a student's poor performance is attributable to the effects of a handicap (which is often not likely to change) and how much of that poor performance may be due to other factors such as inappropriate instruction or a negative attitude (which might be successfully overcome in a remedial setting).

Prior to testing a handicapped student, reading specialists should explore the range and scope of remedial alternatives that will be available should the student be found to need remedial attention. Prior knowledge of available remedial alternatives may aid in diagnostic decision making about such things as which diagnostic lesson to try and the relative importance of the student's behaviors in both group and individual situations. Knowledge of the student's handicap will assist in making a thorough diagnosis.

At the outset of the actual evaluation, the diagnostician should establish rapport with the student. Handicapped students, perhaps more than their nonhandicapped peers, need to feel relaxed and secure in the testing session. Depending on the nature and severity of the handicapping condition, the student may have undergone a great deal of prior assessment and feel frustrated, hostile, or embarrassed about the prospects of further testing. Therefore, so that accurate and effective diagnosis can take place, the reading specialist should conscientiously seek to relieve any apprehension that the student may bring to the diagnostic situation.

One novel method of establishing rapport with students is to begin assessment with a diagnostic lesson instead of ending it with one, as is commonly done. These diagnostic lessons can be aimed at the students' strengths or interests. This method may be best suited to handicapped students because of the large amount of diagnostic information that is available about them from previous assessment. When the reading specialist is confident that the handicapped student is at ease and is eager to perform to the best of his or her ability, the evaluation may proceed.

Reading assessment of the handicapped student, as with other students, should include formal and informal testing, direct observation in group and individual settings, and student self-assessment. The reading specialist should resist the natural temptation to rely on his or her favorite instruments. Such a practice can be especially misleading when working with handicapped students. Often such students perform poorly in certain conditions but do well in other situations. (For example, a hearing-impaired child can perform poorly when questions are asked orally but do well when responding to signed questions.) Reading specialists should limit the amount and duration of testing to that which is necessary to arrive at reliable hypotheses. Testing which goes beyond that point is superfluous and may only serve to fatigue and frustrate the student.

While administering a test the diagnostician must avoid giving subtle or overt hints. People often feel sympathy or pity for a handicapped student and, while such feelings may be natural, the reading specialist should be on the guard against conveying these feelings to the student or allowing them to taint the test's outcomes. Diagnosticians should remember that the student's interests are best served when the diagnostic findings are as accurate as possible.

Often placement decisions will be based on diagnostic assessment results. For the handicapped student, extremely important decisions, such as the likelihood of success after mainstreamed placement, may depend largely on the reading specialist's accuracy in evaluating the student. Diagnosticians should be able to defend the reliability and validity of the tests that they use. They should also have evidence that each test is a useful assessment instrument for students with specific handicaps. (For example, an auditory discrimination test would not be useful for assessing a deaf student.) Diagnosticians must also be able to demonstrate that a test is not culturally or racially biased. When data are derived from questionable testing instruments, misplacement may result. Correct placement is the responsibility of every individual who is involved in developing an IEP. These individuals share the further responsibility of making far-reaching goal-setting decisions based on their diagnostic recommendations. In order to make these recommendations the reading specialist must be knowledgeable, skillful, and well-prepared.

Subskill assessment is routinely used by some professionals, but it can lead to misplacement if all aspects of the reading process are not assessed. For example, it was once reported that a visually impaired student had severe weakness in several of the visual discrimination skills. When the student's oral reading skills and silent-reading comprehension were assessed, the student was found to be reading above grade level and up to potential. Upon further evaluation the student was found to be doing well in reading class where the teacher considered him a good student. Using a visual discrimination subtest to evaluate a student with visual impairment seems logical; however, in this case, the student had overcome those deficiencies despite an inability to perform on a given test. Had the total reading behavior not been assessed, this student would have been inappropriately placed in a program to improve visual perception.

Other subskill evaluation instruments can lead to similar misevaluation. For example, some readers cannot perform well on phonic subskill tests, yet they can read without difficulty. Others may not do well with auditory discrimination tests yet also have no difficulty reading. Total reading performance must be assessed along with specific subskills.

Diagnostic assessment of the handicapped student should focus on strengths, although traditionally it tends to concentrate on weaknesses. Within the IEP, strengths can be reported within the section devoted to the student's present levels of functioning.

Looking at the handicapped students' strengths becomes even more important considering the fact that many teachers view handicapped students in a negative light. Teachers need to ask what reading skills a hearing impaired student has developed, or be certain of how well a mentally retarded student reads. As strengths are identified and communicated to student, parents, and teachers, a new view of the student's capabilities emerges. In some cases this will be the first notation in school records regarding a handicapped student's strengths. When the IEP is developed, program adjustments for a student's strengths will be just as important as those adjustments made because of weaknesses. By emphasizing the student's capabilities, the student is granted a sense of self-worth, and the parents are infused with a feeling of hope rather than despair.

Diagnosis of the handicapped student should be continuous. Again, although continuous diagnosis is important for all students, it has particular significance for the handicapped student for a number of reasons. First, some initial diagnostic findings may be incorrect. Without continuous reassessment, these erroneous findings can lead to misguided instructional efforts and unrealistic academic goals. Second, many handicapped students can be expected to make smaller and less dramatic gains than other students; continuous diagnostic assessment can aid the teacher not only in redirecting instruction, but also in demonstrating gains to the handicapped child. All students like to do well, and continuous diagnosis can provide a way of bolstering a student's self-concept. Finally, continuous diagnosis can help the reading specialist adopt a more prescriptive approach to remediation—something every handicapped student needs.

Not all handicapped students will require remedial work in reading. Many handicapped students have disabilities that do not affect reading growth (such as the orthopedically impaired). Other individuals may be performing at levels equal to their abilities despite having a handicapping condition which might be expected to inhibit reading (such as some visually impaired students). When a remedial program is indicated, however, the following special considerations may help to guide the handicapped student's instructional program.

**Special
Considerations
in Remediation**

Beware of Labels

Because they are often identified for special services, handicapped students bear labels. Labels are an unfortunate by-product of federal and state funding systems which dispense monies to school districts based on the number of handicapped students (by category) that they report. While labels appear to exist out of administrative necessity, classroom teachers and reading specialists should exercise restraint in using labels. Research has shown that labels create anxiety and negative expectations on the part of teachers.[6]

When teachers are told that a given student is disabled, they tend to lessen their expectations for the student; the student, in turn, tends to achieve only up to those lowered expectations. Labels also tell little about a student's specific strengths and weaknesses and even less about instructional approaches that may prove successful with the student. This is primarily because labels are general and because students within labeling categories tend to be heterogeneous. For example, as much variation exists among the behaviors and abilities of learning disabled students as exists among so-called average students.

Reject Failed Methods and Materials

No single method can be expected to prove successful with all handicapped students or even with all students having the same disability. Nevertheless, teachers sometimes appear determined to defend the use of one specific method or material for handicapped students, even when it does not appear to be meeting with satisfactory results. Perhaps this tendency is due to the mistaken idea that because an approach has been developed and recommended for handicapped students, it will be universally successful. This can be a common outgrowth of labeling. If one method fails with a student, teachers should keep trying others until the student meets with success.

Set Realistic Goals

Realistic goal setting plays an integral part in any successful reading program. However, with handicapped students, effective goal setting takes on an even higher priority. If teachers set remedial goals too high and then fail to adjust them, the handicapped student will fall short of those goals, causing additional harm to his or her feelings of self-worth and ambition. On the other hand, if goals are set too low, some students will achieve up to those goals and no farther. One of the most difficult aspects of teaching is the ability to set goals that will challenge students to work to their highest capabilities but which are not unattainable.

Adapt Instruction

Many of the same approaches and techniques that are used with nonhandicapped students in the regular classroom may be adapted for use with their handicapped counterparts. Frequently, the teacher will need only to make some special accommodation for the student's disability. (For example, the language-experience approach might be used successfully with a blind child if the stimulus experience is one which can be perceived through the four senses he or she can use, and if the story is transcribed into Braille.) Teachers must remember that their overall objective is to make program adjustments so that a disability does not handicap the student or that an existing handicap can be minimized.

Present Reading As "Making Sense"

Reading involves "making sense" of printed materials; yet a close examination of many remedial programs for handicapped students might lead one to conclude otherwise. In many programs for mildly mentally retarded students, for example, students spend the majority of instructional time attempting to read single words and parts of words. Many programs for the learning disabled emphasize word recognition drill to eliminate reversal difficulties even though attention to meaning might be a more prudent approach to reversal difficulties.[7] In reading, emphasis should be placed on obtaining meaning. Teachers should make every effort to help students see reading as a meaningful process.

Maximize Resource Efforts

A mainstreamed handicapped child often requires the resource services of two or three specialists. And, while such a multidisciplinary approach may be the best way to meet the student's educational needs, problems can arise when services are duplicated, approaches are counterproductive, and time is lost from the regular classroom. In an effort to minimize these difficulties, some schools have scheduled regular multidisciplinary staff meetings to discuss ways to coordinate the special services required by handicapped students. In these team meetings, diagnostic findings can be reviewed so that the group can determine how a student should be placed to minimize the time he or she must spend outside of the regular classroom. In many cases the resource person is asked to assist the student within the student's regular classroom. Team meetings can also be used to coordinate the student's remedial program so that all team members are kept informed of what each member is doing.

Unfortunately, personnel with little reading training often must provide reading instruction for students with multiple handicaps. Since such personnel may have limited understanding of the reading process, they may tend to rely on commercial materials that focus on subskill development. The reading specialist may want to offer suggestions for approaches and strategies that reflect a more complete understanding of the reading process.

It would be better, of course, if the reading specialist were assigned the responsibility of developing and implementing the reading portion of the IEP. The instructional program needs to be coordinated with the classroom teacher who is responsible for most of the other instruction. As in all instructional programs that remove students from the classroom, the IEP's effectiveness is related to the coordinated effort of all involved.

Use Support Systems

Placing one or more handicapped students in a regular classroom often creates additional demands on the time of an already busy classroom teacher. Fortunately, assistance for the classroom teacher is available in a variety of forms.

Resource personnel within the school provide one avenue of support for the classroom teacher. Special education teachers, adaptive physical education teachers, school counselors, reading specialists, and nursing personnel all have training with special students. These professionals are usually delighted to help and can aid the classroom teacher with useful suggestions and advice.

Within the classroom, the teacher can take advantage of student resources. Learning pairs and peer instruction provide two excellent ways of involving students in working with handicapped classmates. Allowing students to work on activities in pairs lets them help each other. Paired learning is especially important when students are working independently from the teacher. Peer instruction allows students who have mastery of a skill to help others learn it. Sometimes to learn a skill it takes an extra two or three times through a process. The student can be strong in one area and not in another, so that different students can be peer instructors at various times. Further, teachers should remember that handicapped students can serve as effective peer instructors just as well as nonhandicapped students. (For example, a deaf child can teach other students to sign.) By looking for handicapped students' strengths, teachers will find areas in which they can be the helper.

Two final potential sources of support can be sought from community volunteers and parents. People with special skills or with extra time can help in the classroom for a portion of the day. They may assist a handicapped student who needs individual attention in order to complete some activities. Some communities have been very successful in organizing retired people to assist in neighborhood classrooms. Parents are another often untapped resource. Parents are usually eager to further their children's education and respond with enthusiasm when they are told how they can help.

Areas of Potential Difficulty

Recent changes in the ways handicapped students are educated have created some situations that many teachers may find difficult. These difficulties can result in teacher frustration and discomfort. A discussion of a few of those areas follows.

Lack of Services While Awaiting IEP Approval

Since the IEP must be approved before special educational services can begin, a waiting period at the start of the school year may force the student to remain in an inappropriate placement. Although regulations exist to expedite the placement process, at times this waiting period can become quite extended. Teachers will need to provide instruction during the waiting time. They should assess strengths, help handicapped students feel comfortable in their classrooms, and plan programs that are practicable. They should also seek suggestions from reading specialists for materials and methods of instruction.

Planning for
Handicapped
Students

Lack of Teacher Training

Regular classroom teachers are usually not trained to work with specific types of handicapped students. Teachers should ask for in-service programs, resource assistance, and recommendations for materials and procedures. In these cases, teachers should not feel inadequate when asking for help. As teachers strengthen their teaching skills with the handicapped, their frustrations will diminish.

Lack of Time

Teachers have reported that they feel that they lack time to help their regular students when they must individualize programs for handicapped students who have been placed in their classroom for portions of the day. Teachers often feel pulled in many directions. Teachers should ask for additional help to relieve them of this time problem. They can use one or more of the resources mentioned earlier in this chapter so that they will have more time.

Distorted IEP

Teachers may be asked to implement an IEP in which the reading section is distorted. This usually occurs when the IEP lists objectives in terms of subskills. Teachers should make note of the difficulties in implementing the IEP and ask that it be reassessed. Observations can be made regarding the frustration that results when the student tries to complete the activities. These frustrations may relate to inappropriate materials or the lack of time to help the student feel success with the IEP's objectives. Once it is clear that the suggestions and goals in the IEP are inappropriate, a team meeting can be called to reassess the program.

Class Size

Special class sizes are sometimes controlled by national, state, or local rules and regulations, although most regular classroom sizes are not. As handicapped students find increasing opportunities to participate in these regular classes, some attention should be given to class size control. If this is not done, classroom teachers will likely come to resent the additional responsibilities placed on them without an adequate support system needed to make the delivery of those responsibilities a reality.

Summary

Federal legislation has permitted sweeping changes in the ways that schools educate handicapped students. Legislation alone, however, cannot assure change. Sincere effort must be made by all who come in contact with handicapped students on a day-to-day basis to realize the potential that exists within the law. The two greatest obstacles to positive change in educating handicapped students appear to be money and attitude. Legislation can provide money, but the educators working with handicapped students must approach their task with the desire to explore the limits of what each of these students *can* do.

Advances have already been made in the ways handicapped students are being educated. Increasing numbers of students who formerly were enrolled in self-contained special classes are now taught in classes with their peers. This serves to break down the barriers of fear and aversion that have plagued the handicapped student in the past. Furthermore, some handicapped students are discovering that they are not as handicapped as they once thought themselves.

Of course the picture is not all positive. Many students have handicapping conditions that make a regular classroom placement inappropriate. Misunderstanding and harassing of the handicapped still exist. The problems mentioned in this chapter are not yet solved. New priorities for the handicapped must be set and funding systems must be adjusted. But happily, handicapped students are now finding a new type of schooling waiting for them.

Notes

1. Edward L. Meyen, *Exceptional Children and Youth* (Denver: Love Publishing Company, 1978), 12–18.
2. Ibid.
3. Sterling L. Ross, Henry G. DeYoung, and Julius S. Cohen, "Confrontation: Special Education Placement and the Law," in *Contemporary Issues in Special Education*, ed. Rex E. Schmid, Judee Moneypenny, and Ronald Johnston (New York: McGraw-Hill Book Company, 1977), 26–28.
4. Lloyd M. Dunn, "An Overview," in *Exceptional Children in the Schools*, ed. Lloyd M. Dunn (New York: Holt, Rinehart and Winston, 1973), 43–45.
5. Beatrice F. Birman, "Problems of Overlap Between Title I and P.L. 94–142: Implications for the Federal Role in Education," *Educational Evaluation and Policy Analysis* 3, no. 3 (May–June 1981): 5–19.
6. Bob Algozzine and Laura Stoller, "Effects of Labels and Competence on Teachers' Attributions for a Student," *The Journal of Experimental Education* 49, no. 3 (Spring 1981): 132–36.
7. Stanley L. Rosner et al., "Dealing with the Reading Needs of the Learning Disabled Child," *Journal of Learning Disabilities* 14, no. 8 (October 1981): 436–48.

Suggested Readings

Ballard, Joseph. *Public Law 94-142 and Section 504—Understanding What They Are and Are Not*. Reston, Va.: Council for Exceptional Children, 1977. This book uses a question-answer approach to assist one in understanding PL 94–142 and Section 504 and provides detailed information and suggested additional references.

———. *Education for All Handicapped Children*. Washington, D.C.: National Educational Association, 1978. This publication uses a case study approach to examine the impact of Section 504 and PL 94–142 and provides both positive and negative reactions of teachers, parents, and other school officials.

Gearheart, Bill R., and Ernest P. Willenberg. *Application of Pupil Assessment Information.* 3d ed. Denver: Love Publishing Company, 1980. This text provides useful explanations of technical aspects of testing instruments and short descriptions of many tests used by professionals who evaluate students with handicaps. It also suggests means by which diagnosis and remediation can be linked in an IEP.

Meyen, Edward L. *Exceptional Children and Youth.* Denver: Love Publishing Company, 1978. Chapter 1 presents an informative overview of recent changes in the field of special education. This text includes "Resource Guides" at the end of each chapter which suggest excellent source materials on a variety of topics.

National Educational Association. *A Teacher's Guide to PL 94-142.* Washington, D.C.: National Educational Association, 1978. This guide uses a situation-response approach to explain some of the major implications of PL 94-142 and tackles controversial as well as legal implications. It may be reproduced for teacher use.

Rosner, Stanley L. et al. "Dealing with the Reading Needs of the Learning Disabled Child." *Journal of Learning Disabilities* 14 (October 1981): 436-48. This interesting and provocative article presents the need for attending to the cognitive and affective needs of the learning disabled student when designing instruction. The authors question the use of several prevalent practices.

Wallace, Gerald and Stephen C. Larsen. *Educational Assessment of Learning Problems: Testing for Teaching.* Boston: Allyn and Bacon, 1978. This well-researched book presents informal and formal assessment techniques in a wide range of pertinent skill areas. The authors emphasize the need for active classroom assessment as a base for meaningful instruction.

EDITORIAL

Paula M. Summers
is a teacher of learning disabled children for Intermediate Unit No. 17 in Wellsboro, Pennsylvania.

Ricky began having learning as well as behavioral difficulties during his kindergarten year and was subsequently referred for psychological testing at the age of six and a half. Because of his lack of success in acquiring the reading and math readiness skills needed for a first-grade placement, it was recommended that he participate in a transitional first-grade program for the following school year. Once again school success eluded this child, and another psychological evaluation was performed to determine an appropriate placement for the ensuing year. Recurring difficulties included poor perceptual memory, visual-motor developmental lag, distractibility, and short attention span. Compounding these problems, Ricky was also beginning to exhibit severe behavioral problems. Recommendation for his third year in school included placement in a program for learning disabled (LD) children to address his academic needs with mainstreaming into first grade for nonacademic subjects as well as participation in science and social studies experiences.

As Ricky's LD teacher, I began by reviewing the psychological reports, interviewing his previous teachers and having conferences with his mother. It became evident that distractibility and poor self-control were the key inhibitors in Ricky's earlier classroom experiences. Teachers complained that Ricky was unable to complete any tasks without direct supervision. The teacher needed to remain beside Ricky, pointing to each new item to be completed.

Assessment of skills at the beginning of the school year showed that Ricky had acquired readiness level skills and was ready to begin first-grade work. I decided to utilize the reading program currently implemented in the first-grade curriculum, with additional supplemental materials available to reinforce the more difficult-to-acquire subskills.

I made a point of observing Ricky's behaviors as well as performance very closely those first couple of weeks. I noticed that his biggest obstacle to learning appeared to be an inability to block out extraneous stimuli. This included anything from regular classroom activity to focusing on a single item on a worksheet of multiple items. I immediately took several measures to counteract these obstacles. Ricky's desk was rearranged so that he was facing a wall and in close proximity to me, and this was done in such a way that Ricky would view it as a privilege, not as punishment. I began cutting his worksheets in half along with giving him a ruler or marker to block out other work and minimize distraction. I set up a sticker chart posted on the wall in front of him with each assignment that needed completion written down with blank squares to be filled in with stickers as each task was finished. At the end of the week, these stickers would convert into points that could be spent in the class store, and the sticker chart went home for additional praise and prominent display. These measures had great impact on the amount and quality of work Ricky was completing.

I also arranged a conference with his mainstreamed teachers, all of whom had worked with Ricky the previous year in the areas of art, music, and gym and were apprehensive over behavioral difficulties. I shared with them my findings and made recommendations to each of them conducive to their classroom settings. These included such things as having Ricky sit at a smaller table in art class with only one other child (rather than with ten at a larger table) and placing Ricky at the front of the classroom in music class so that his field of vision was limited to a child on each side and the teacher. The gym teacher began giving Ricky

"special helper" privileges to enhance self-esteem. We also sent a sticker booklet with Ricky to each of his classes so that teachers could acknowledge a good work day. These stickers also converted to points for store purchases.

By mid-year Ricky was successfully completing his work assignments. This eliminated the need for reinforcing each completed task, and the sticker charts were phased out. We are well into the second half of the school year now, and Ricky is discovering the pleasures of learning for the sake of learning. Ricky is proud that he is doing the same first-grade work equally as well as his classmates. His mother is thrilled that he is beginning to enjoy school for the first time in his school career.

Although Ricky still needs the structure of a resource room setting with an individualized program, I have no doubt that he will accomplish the necessary compensation skills needed for successful participation in the regular classroom in the near future.

Paula M. Summers

Technology
in the
Reading
Program

CHAPTER OUTLINE

Microcomputers
Captioned Television

CHAPTER EMPHASES

Although microcomputers are most often used for drill-and-practice, there are many other valuable classroom uses that can support reading diagnosis and remediation.

Word processors can help student writers to view writing as a process.

As microcomputer technology evolves, teachers can expect that it will assist them in many new and exciting ways.

Captioned television is a motivational and successful tool for working with readers experiencing reading difficulties.

333

F or many years, reading teachers have looked to educational technology to help their students. Many have used tape recorders, overhead projectors, filmstrip projectors, and a variety of reading pacing machines such as controlled readers and tachistoscopes. All these technological aids have been helpful with some students. Usually, the least expensive have been the best received because of low budgets and a degree of uncertainty about their overall effectiveness; therefore, tape recorders and overhead projectors were commonly used.

In recent years, two relatively new technologies—microcomputers and captioned television—have been added to reading teachers' choices. This chapter will discuss the potential benefits of these technologies for reading teachers.

| Microcomputers | *Adapting to Rapid Change* |

Until relatively recently, teachers failed to recognize the potential represented by microcomputers to change the ways they have traditionally provided services to their students. Today's teachers find themselves in the midst of a technological revolution that is announcing microcomputer innovations almost weekly. A 1987 study found that the number of microcomputers in U.S. elementary and secondary schools increased by 18 percent between 1986 and 1987. It was also reported that in 1987 approximately 44 percent of schools nationwide had a full-time computer coordinator, a position that would have been hard to find ten years previously.[1] Faced with such rapid change, many teachers have become understandably anxious and skeptical; however, when properly approached, microcomputers represent a powerful force to energize both classrooms and clinics.

There is more to come. O'Banion states that "in the coming decade, computers will provide opportunities for student learning . . . that cannot be imagined at this moment."[2] Ironically, this statement represents both the best and worst features of technology. At its best, technology can enable teachers to do exciting, previously impossible, new things in their classrooms. This remains the largely untapped potential of microcomputers to influence education. Unfortunately, most early classroom computer applications merely satisfied themselves with displaying programs on a video screen that mirrored traditional worksheets and workbooks.

There is also the human factor to be considered. A natural tendency exists to fear the unknown. The microcomputer field is even more threatening to some because it is an area in which many students possess more knowledge than their teachers. Once initial fears are resolved, however, teachers often become enthusiastic converts. Heffron described the stages of computer acquisition as fear, followed by awe, pleasure, confidence, complacency, pride, and anticipation for what will come next.[3] However, even teachers who already use microcomputers find it difficult to keep pace with the breathtakingly rapid changes in the field while balancing their other classroom responsibilities. Without updating, today's innovation rapidly becomes yesterday's outdated and obsolete program.

An Overview of Current Reading Uses

Microcomputers are used in a wide variety of applications to support teaching by classroom teachers and reading specialists. Kinzer suggested that the following five broad categories, developed by Luehrmann and expanded by Goldberg and Sherwood, may provide a helpful way to describe reading related computer use: learning about microcomputers; learning from microcomputers; learning with microcomputers; learning about thinking with microcomputers; and managing learning with microcomputers.[4]

LEARNING ABOUT MICROCOMPUTERS. Students initially need to be introduced to computers and begin to develop necessary skills to work with them. This is often referred to as "computer awareness" and "computer literacy." Students must understand the uses of computers in society as well as learn more mundane matters such as turning on the machine and caring for computer diskettes. Ideally, both regular classroom teachers and reading specialists should possess the requisite knowledge and skills to contribute to students' overall computer literacy.

LEARNING FROM MICROCOMPUTERS. There are presently two major means of learning from microcomputers—drill-and-practice programs and tutorial programs. The major factor which distinguishes drill-and-practice programs from tutorials is the ability of the software program to teach a concept. Drill-and-practice programs provide reinforcement of previously taught skills; tutorials introduce new skills. Formats resembling video games are often the basis for drill-and-practice programs. Other software programs allow teachers and students to design their own crossword puzzles, hangman games, word finds, and concentration games for vocabulary practice. Sentence combining and cloze generating software can increase student abilities to see relationships between the syntactic and semantic systems of language (such as Sentence Combining published by Milliken and M-SS-NG L-NKS: Young People's Literature published by Sunburst Communications). Jones, Torgesen, and Sexton found that students using a computerized spelling program increased in decoding skills as well as in decoding speed.[5] Tutorials, on the other hand, may assist the teacher to move students ahead independently by introducing new concepts and skills. The best of these programs are branched to enable students to receive extra explanations and examples of concepts that they find difficult. Branched programs offer the additional advantage of enabling students to quickly move ahead past skills and concepts that they already know. Many remedial readers report that they enjoy the infinite patience of microcomputers to repeat concepts in a variety of ways without making any negative judgments or comments.

Microcomputers can be helpful tools in comprehension development.

LEARNING WITH MICROCOMPUTERS. Simulation programs represent interesting learning approaches where students must solve real-life situations posed by the computer. In the process, students must use information supplied by the computer to make decisions. Immediately thereafter, the students receive feedback concerning the consequences of the decisions they make. In order to be successful in the programs, the students must think and make good choices. As they read and think through their options, some simulation programs allow students to use electronic notepads and record notes directly on the screen. Later, those notes can be outputted through the computer printer for a teacher to see.[6] Although many simulation programs present social studies or science situations, several companies are beginning to market simulation programs in reading. Typically, these programs require students to read stories to decision points and then decide what the characters in the stories should do (such as Story Tree published by Scholastic). Besides being motivational, such programs help to emphasize the personal, active nature of reading comprehension. One drawback of some simulation programs may be the difficulty of the reading required to complete the simulation exercise. Rude suggests that perhaps students would benefit by working on simulations in pairs or teams so that less able readers may be assisted with the reading demands of the program.[7] Lemonade Stand and Oregon Trail are two popular simulation programs published by MECC which also have public domain versions.

LEARNING ABOUT THINKING WITH COMPUTERS. As previously discussed, students develop thinking skills through simulation programs, but they may also gain insights into thinking processes by learning computer programming languages. This is one of the more controversial areas of microcomputer instruction.

Teachers are divided on the necessity of programming for students, but most agree that computer programming develops students' problem-solving abilities. Programming languages that are most appropriate for early development of thinking skills include BASIC and LOGO. Software programs are also beginning to be developed that help students to better organize what they read or write (such as Think Tank published by Living Videotext).

MANAGING LEARNING WITH COMPUTERS. Microcomputers are assisting teachers in managing many aspects of reading instruction. Readability checks, once done laboriously by hand, can now be performed instantly by the microcomputer. Readability software programs (such as Readability Analysis Program published by Random House) can also help to alert the teacher to potential difficulties associated with a particular book or passage. Does it have an unusual number of polysyllabic words? Are the words in the passage fairly common or obscure? All this information, which previously was very tedious to obtain, can now be quickly accessed. Microcomputer spreadsheets can assist teachers with record keeping and filing functions. Other computer programs are available to create certificates, cards, posters, cartoons, and banners to spice up the reading classroom (such as Print Shop published by Broderbund, Certificate Maker published by Springboard, and Create with Garfield!: Deluxe Edition published by DLM). There are even software programs to assist teachers with interpreting miscue analysis. Currently, word processing is the most widely used application of microcomputers to manage learning.

Word Processing

Most teachers will want to use the word processing capabilities of microcomputers for reading and writing instruction. Word processing programs have become very "user friendly," or easy to use. They have menus and special instructions to guide users who do not have much background in computer use.

Word processors can aid student writers in a variety of ways. In writing, the process a writer uses to arrive at a finished document is important. Word processors encourage students to view writing as a process of successive drafts and numerous revisions. Elbow suggests that writers avoid trying to write slowly in order to arrive at a finished product on the first draft. He notes that when writing is approached in this manner, writers come to think of their original words as "cloyingly precious,"[8] thereby resisting any later changes. Word processors can help to change this common tendency. They permit ease of editing and revision. No longer is there a need to rewrite entire sections when a writer wishes to revise a document; the changes can be made in seconds. A writer who finds an error on page two of a twenty-page paper merely enters the correction, and the remaining eighteen pages automatically adjust to the change. Word processors also allow writers to move words, sentences, or paragraphs from one section of a paper to another section. In the past when a writer realized that something would look better somewhere else in a paper, the temptation existed not to make the changes because of the extra work that would be involved. Today, writers who use word processors can submit a paper that is exactly as they wish it to be.

There are other technical capabilities inherent in word processor use. Word processors allow the writer to center material without counting or guesswork; they also create right and left justified margins. There are also software programs that will check each word in a paper against an extensive dictionary, identifying those that do not appear in the dictionary, and suggesting correct spellings for misspelled words. Bank Street Writer III published by Scholastic is a word processing program with its own built-in thesaurus and spelling checker. One area that is also becoming increasingly popular is "desktop publishing." Many word processing programs are including capabilities to create many different type styles and attractive graphic aids, illustrations and displays (such as GraphicWriter published by DataPak and A-Plus: The Homework Solution published by Savant). Not only does writing become easier for students, but they can also publish stories, books, and classroom newspapers that have a professional look.

Writing and reading have always been intertwined. Word processing highlights the reading-writing connection. One might read before writing in order to have something about which to write. Once written, stories must be read and reread to edit and revise. Finished copies may be produced from a printer for the student and classmates to read. Some software programs effectively model the reading-writing connection by assisting students in generating written stories from motivational situations presented on the microcomputer (such as StoryBook Starters published by Mindscape). Explore-a-Series by Collamore/D.C. Heath is an interesting approach to reading/writing. With this software, students begin by reading a fictional story; then, on a computer they can make changes in the story as they "page" back through the story episodes.

Word processing can be used to develop language-experience stories, creative writing, book reports, and other writing needs. If more than one copy is needed, most printers will print multiple copies. There is no need to wait for language-experience stories to be typed and duplicated. Each student can receive a personal copy in a few seconds. Microcomputers also offer excellent storage capabilities for student-developed word banks. New words can be easily added and alphabetized; previously entered words can be instantly called up.

In just the few years that microcomputers have been available in schools, their price and size have decreased significantly. Weighing less than ten pounds, some portable, battery-powered "laptop" microcomputers have greater computing power than full-sized models of eight years ago. These powerful units offer truly versatile word processing performance. At Mansfield University, a portable microcomputer was used to assist classroom note taking for a student who was learning disabled in writing. A fellow student was recruited in each class to take lecture notes directly into the microcomputer. At the end of each class period, two copies of the notes were printed—one for the notetaker and one for the learning disabled student. The note taker further agreed to serve as a study partner for tests (a natural collaboration as both students were studying from the same set of notes). The notes were found to be far easier to read than handwritten notes, and both students benefited from the partnership.

Word processing has additional benefits. Teachers can prepare and store lesson plans, tests, worksheets, letters, and professional reports more easily than ever before. When teachers use microcomputers to help them in their daily work, the modeling effect is significant. Students will be more likely to approach microcomputers positively if they see their teachers using them. Just as teachers set a positive reading example by being readers, teachers can also be positive role models of microcomputer use.

Guidelines for Selecting Software

The market is currently flooded with software programs, a few of them excellent, some of them good, and too many of them fair to poor. The big problem is how to select software materials without the opportunity to examine them. Most companies, fearing illegal copying, will not release examination copies; once a sealed package is opened, it cannot be returned. Some software companies provide sample portions of programs that contain enough of the program for potential buyers to evaluate its usefulness but not enough to encourage copying. Another way to preview software is to attend computer shows advertised in local newspapers and computer journals. Because competition in the computer field is great, many software publishers send representatives to these shows as a means of letting teachers see and try software before purchasing it.

Many school districts maintain software lending libraries for their staffs. These centrally located facilities house software selected by computer coordinators. These staff personnel attend computer shows and read software evaluation reviews published in trade journals. They screen the programs and attempt to obtain the best programs available. These professionals also may be able to assist teachers in preparing backup disks to ensure against accidental damage in handling an original disk.

At times, software catalogs provide enough information so that previewing is not needed; however, catalog descriptions attempt to portray programs in the best possible light, and even major weaknesses may not be readily apparent without the opportunity to run the program. The old caveat emptor, "Let the buyer beware!" is certainly good advice in the software market.

Teachers who are charged with the responsibility of screening and ordering their own software may wish to consult published reviews in educational computer journals. *Classroom Computer Learning, Electronic Education, The Chime Newsletter, Tech Trends, Electronic Learning,* and *The Computing Teacher* all regularly publish reviews of new educational software programs. Teachers may also wish to personally evaluate software programs by reviewing copies at regional centers before making a purchase to see if the programs adequately address their students' needs.

There are numerous checklists to assist teachers wishing to evaluate software programs. Balajthy proposed a thorough fifty-five-question checklist for evaluating reading software which divided questions into the following six categories:

1. "Is the program educationally valuable?"
2. "Is the program easy to use?"
3. "Does the program make maximum use of the computer's capabilities?"
4. "Is the program user-proof?"
5. "Is documentation provided in hard copy?"
6. "What assurance of program quality is there?"[9]

With remedial readers, one of the largest drawbacks of many programs is the inflexibility of the program to be adapted to individual students' needs. Other programs may present too few practice exercises. In still other programs, the number of words presented on the screen at a single time may be overwhelming to the poor reader.

Because one of the criticisms directed at microcomputer usage is that it discourages social interactions, teachers may wish to consider the degree to which a program encourages or permits cooperative learning. Computer use need not be a solitary activity. Many teachers attest to the spirit of shared problem solving and achievement that they have witnessed when students have worked together on certain programs, sharing their insights, triumphs, and disappointments.

Recent and Future Developments

The preceding sections have described the most common current microcomputer applications; however, the microcomputer is an emerging technology, and a great deal of its power is yet to be tapped. Much of the excitement surrounding the new microcomputer technology relates to developments that enable teachers to do things previously only dreamed about. What follows are several recent and future innovations that seem to offer particular promise to the remedial reading field.

THREE AND ONE-HALF-INCH DISK. The development of a new, smaller, and more durable disk capable of storing even more information than before has ushered in a new generation of less expensive, lighter, and smaller microcomputers. Three of the largest educational computer vendors, IBM, Tandy, and Apple, have moved toward the smaller disks for their school-marketed hardware.[10] Many industry analysts predict a gradual phaseout of the larger five-and-one-quarter-inch floppy disk. These new machines are designed to maximize screen size while minimizing the machines' "footprints" (the amount of space they require on a desktop).

COMPUTERIZED DIAGNOSTIC TESTS. For years, physicians have used software programs to aid them in making more reliable diagnoses. Recently, software packages have been released to aid teachers conducting a reading diagnosis. One of the first was CARA (Computer Assisted Reading Assessment) published by Southern Micro Systems. It is expected that more and more reading assessments will be developed that appear in computerized formats.

Microcomputer-administered assessments offer several advantages over conventional paper-and-pencil tests. Henk suggests that reading inventories of the future might utilize microcomputers to monitor readers' eye movements, brain functions, voice patterns, neurological activities, and other physiological variables. Computer-aided assessments could also consider such previously untapped factors as reader interest, look-back strategies, and prior knowledge.[11]

A new approach to reading diagnosis that appears to have great potential is computerized adaptive testing. Computerized adaptive tests based on item response theory tailor the reading test to the abilities of the individual test taker. Traditional paper-and-pencil tests require able readers to wade through numbers of too-easy items. Conversely, less able readers often become frustrated by hopelessly difficult test items. In each case, the accuracy of the assessment is damaged. Students take computerized adaptive tests at computer terminals. The computer presents the directions, practice items, and a randomly selected first item. Based on the student's response to the first item, a second item is selected for that student from out of a larger item pool. The student's answers to the first two questions determine the third item presented, and so forth. The result is a challenging test for each test taker; the more able student receives a more difficult test than the less able student, but both tests are appropriate to their individual abilities. Efficiency is another advantage offered by computerized adaptive tests. It appears likely that computerized adaptive tests will be able to measure as accurately as traditional paper-and-pencil tests with far fewer test items. What once required an eighty-item test, might now be possible with a twenty-item test.[12]

TELECONFERENCING. Teleconferencing uses portable microcomputers linked to a central source by a telephone modem. In many ways, they resemble electronic bulletin board services and are often referred to as BBS's. Users can use an on-line BBS in one of two major ways. They can either call in and type a message that is stored in the system for others to retrieve and read later, or they can hold "real-time" conferences with other users. During real-time conferences, users seated at microcomputers in different locations, that are linked through the BBS, can carry on conversations that appear directly on their screens.[13]

Teleconferencing holds promise for both reading teachers and students. Teachers can use the service to swap ideas and obtain advice on professional issues of interest. Students can use a BBS to establish electronic pen-pal relationships with a degree of control and anonymity that the shy or less able student may appreciate. Initially, the poor reader may wish to submit bulletin board material that has been carefully composed and proofread. Later, with greater confidence and keyboarding skills, the student may choose to attempt real-time conferencing.

In many communities, local BBS's are being established, greatly reducing telephone costs. However, if a school has toll-free agreements, the larger national services like American Peoplelink, CompuServe, Delphi, and The Source offer capabilities that are hard to match. Each of these services charges a per-hour fee, however, and many schools may find the fees prohibitive unless costs come down.[14]

DATABASES. A database is a form of computer filing system that can efficiently provide rapid storage, search, and retrieval of large quantities of information. The program that accesses the information is often referred to as a database manager. The user can search and call up any combination of cross-listed information and then have that information reported in a variety of different forms (charts, tables, lists, etc.). Databases enable students to seek the answers to complicated questions, particularly those involving relationships among several variables, much more quickly and efficiently than with print materials.[15] For example, using traditional materials, it would be extremely time consuming to attempt to answer a question such as the following: "Since World War II, which three European countries have had the highest gross national products and what are their principal industries?" Such a question would be relatively easy to research by using a database manager. Increasingly, it can be anticipated that computerized databases will be the research and study tools of choice. Many of the major computer software companies currently market databases.

INTERACTIVE VIDEO. Ask ten computer experts what emerging school technology they are particularly excited about and five may answer, "Interactive video." This exciting new technology combines microcomputer access capabilities with the visual and audio quality of videodisc players. Current interactive video applications are primarily of two types, archival and tutorial,[16] although as with other aspects of technology, novel applications are emerging all the time.

Archival programs allow students to request and view motion pictures, still photographs, and text of selected topics. They are capable of creating, in effect, video encyclopedias that permit students to read, view, and hear information about a broad selection of topics. From a remedial reading standpoint, the potential exists for archival programs to enhance students' understanding of what they read through vicarious experiences that build their background knowledge.

Tutorial programs typically intersperse text and questions throughout "video chapters" viewed by students. By using the interactive video medium, realistic depictions far exceeding standard computer graphics are possible. Miller and Gildea, who experimented with using the motivational power of popular motion pictures, such as *Raiders of the Lost Ark*, to create contexts for vocabulary learning, reported gains in vocabulary learning when students could request information concerning word meanings in one or more of three forms: definitions, illustrative sentences, and picture form. In this fashion, students were able to self-select the presentation system that best suited their personal learning styles.[17]

READING PROSTHESES. Although they bear little resemblance to classroom microcomputers, reading prostheses are included in this section because they use computer technology to address reading difficulties. The Kurzweil Reading Machine (KRM) is an example of a reading prosthesis, or artificial reading device.[18] Originally developed for the blind and resembling a compact photocopier, the Kurzweil Reading Machine is capable of reading books aloud at sight. Students merely place a book with the text side down on the glass plate on top of the machine and key in appropriate commands on a Braille-coded keyboard. The KRM is programmed with 2,500 pronunciation rules and produces artificial speech that includes natural intonations and pauses.[19] The optical sensors in the computerized machine visually scan the lines of text, and a voice synthesizer produces a spoken facsimile. Users can vary the rate that the material is read, request to have words or lines reread, or have unfamiliar words spelled. Since its initial development in 1974, the KRM has become increasingly smaller and less expensive. A recently released new generation of the device called the Kurzweil Personal Reader is the size of a small suitcase and only weighs about 20 pounds. In the years to come, it might be expected that the KRM and other computerized reading prostheses like it may significantly help many severely reading disabled students.

Benefits and Cautions

It may be helpful to think of a computer as a powerful and versatile tool. Any tool works best in the hands of a skilled, careful user who knows the purposes for which the tool is best suited. On the other hand, damage and frustration can often result when an unskilled novice indiscriminately tries to use a tool for unintended purposes. If a carpenter tried to use a hammer to saw a piece of wood in two, eventually the job could probably be accomplished, but the result would be far from satisfactory. In such a case, the carpenter would receive the blame, not the hammer. When it comes to educational computer use, too often the computer has been blamed for a poor result when, in reality, the computer was inappropriately used by a teacher.

For the teacher of reading, the computer offers the opportunity to aid students in several ways. Some of the major advantages of diagnostic and remedial reading microcomputer applications include the following:

1. *Active involvement.* When students perform computer-presented tasks, they are required to be active participants in their learning.[20]
2. *Risk taking.* Many microcomputer software programs encourage students to make personal choices and observe the outcomes. When students program with LOGO, they often make and then test hypotheses.

3. *Demonstrated progress.* Some microcomputer programs track students' progress and illustrate gains.
4. *Continuous feedback.* As students work on a microcomputer program, they receive feedback at multiple points regarding their performances.
5. *Improved writing.* Studies with word processors suggest that when word processor use is combined with instruction in revising, students write more and revise more.[21] Gains were found to be proportionately greater for low-achieving students than for able learners.[22]
6. *Attitudinal gains.* Many remedial readers report that microcomputer tutorial and drill-and-practice programs help make learning fun and that word processors give them greater freedom and success as writers.
7. *Time on task.* MacArthur, Haynes, and Malouf found that a group of learning disabled students were on task 76 percent of the time while working with computer learning, but a comparable group were on task only 57 percent of the time while working with traditional pencil-and-paper activities.[23]

In the past, critics of microcomputers have tended to focus on two problems associated with educational microcomputer use—software of questionable value and the tendency for some teachers to use microcomputers as substitute teachers. Although those criticisms are often deserved, the best way to assure that computers will be used properly is for teachers to have a clear understanding of both the reading process and computer capabilities.

Captioned Television

For many television programs, captions are available that present written interpretations of the audio portion of the programs. To see those captions, one must either have a special television set or have a tele-decoder that permits the viewer to see the captions on any television set. (See the picture on p. 347.)

Captions were developed for the hearing impaired population who, prior to captioning, were unable to fully enjoy or understand television programming. A hearing able individual can gain some insights into the barriers to understanding encountered by the hearing impaired population by turning off the sound and attempting to watch the evening news. Those portions missed by the viewer will seriously interfere with understanding because listening plays an integral role in television "viewing."

Captions provide hearing impaired people with some input into the audio portion of the program. One should remember, however, that as helpful as captions are, they only provide partial information concerning the audio portions of a presentation. For example, they cannot reproduce music or voice intonations that play an important part in many programs.

Captions are "closed" because of the concern of some television executives that captions might interfere with hearing people's enjoyment of television; thus, the term *closed-captioned television.* Many programs are closed-captioned and indicated as such by a message on viewers' television screens. The message usually reads, "This program is closed-captioned for the hearing impaired." Or, it might show CC, which is a signal to hearing impaired people that they can see the captions if they use their decoders. At times, the following symbol is used to designate a closed-captioned program:

Benefits of Closed-Captioned Television for Remedial Readers

What does closed-captioned television have to do with remedial reading instruction? More than one might think! In 1983, captioned television was used in the University of Maryland reading clinic with interesting results. Students in the clinic attempted to read television captions as they watched, using the same expression as the actors they were viewing. It was found that reluctant readers willingly watched captioned television programs and, in the process, improved in oral reading fluency. An unexpected additional benefit was that the students also made gains in sight word knowledge.[24]

A 1985 study, funded by the U.S. Department of Education, studied the effects of captioned television on hearing impaired and learning disabled hearing students to determine if those two unique populations could benefit from lessons taught with captioned television. The study found closed-captioning to be effective with both groups.[25] Teachers and students also reported enthusiasm for the techniques.

Why did instruction with captioned television work so well with poor readers? Several possible explanations exist. First, using closed-captioning, students are exposed to meaning through the visual images before the written code is presented in captioned form. Meaning and understanding come first and the written message is a logical follow-up. In this way, it seems to have similar advantages to the language-experience approach. However, in this situation *all* students have exposure to the same prior knowledge through the use of the television drama. They also gain prior exposure to the essential vocabulary through the captions combined with audio portions of the program. It seems to provide a rich, multisensory medium for vocabulary learning.

Second, closed-captioned lessons prove to be very motivating. Because television is of major interest to many students, why not make it a learning experience as well? It has been recognized for some time that interested students tend to stay on task longer and learn more easily. Disinterested students do not stay on task as well and have difficulty learning effectively.

Third, for hearing students, closed-captioned presentations are a multisensory activity. That is, the drama, sound, and captions combine to create multiple stimuli to enhance learning possibilities.

Fourth, of course, it is novel and innovative. Students involved in the projects asked if they were really learning while watching television. In one school, a remedial reading teacher was using closed-captioned television with her students. When word reached the other students in the school, there was immediate interest on the part of the students and teachers to see what it was like. Schedules were adapted so that all could see what was going on and the response was very positive.

Finally, closed-captioned television has some positive factors that are most evident on the personal level as witnessed by this report from a University of Maryland reading clinician:

> Mary was initially extremely inhibited and would not communicate anything. She had little confidence in her reading ability and did not participate with others. When asked to read aloud, she would barely whisper and hesitated when asked any type of question.
>
> After having watched captioned television three different times, Mary was observed to be absorbed in the captioning and read aloud (very loudly). It seemed that her confidence was increased to the point that she was proud of her fluency and wanted others to know about her success.
>
> We reminded all children to read "not so loud" but Mary could not be stopped. Mary continued to read in a *loud* voice. In the days following this experience, Mary continued to communicate with me and even wanted to read a book to me![26]

The annual clinic follow-up survey revealed that Mary, who had formerly been assigned to a Level-3 special education placement, was no longer in need of those services and was reading with an average grade-level reading group in her regular classroom. Her teacher and parents reported that she was cheerful, outgoing, and happy; she had even joined Girl Scouts. Of course, Mary had received a lot of other educational experiences that contributed to her confidence and achievement gains. However, it appeared that the three days in reading clinic using closed-captioning was a pivotal experience when Mary suddenly realized that she "could" read and be proud of it. Once Mary was started on the path to reading confidence, her teachers and parents capitalized on her positive experiences and maintained the momentum.

Necessary Equipment

Teachers can get involved with closed-captioned lessons with a minimum of expense and special equipment. All that is needed is a regular television set (color preferred) and a tele-decoder. Tele-decoders cost under $200 and represent a one-time expense. After the tele-decoder is purchased, there are no other charges. The tele-decoder is hooked up to the television set in similar fashion to a video cassette recorder (VCR) and closed-captions are then available free of charge for the hundreds of hours of commercial broadcasting each week that are closed captioned. Some teachers may wish to save programs on a VCR. If so, they

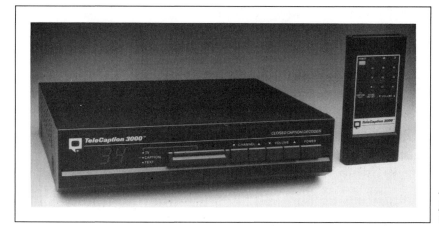

*A tele-decoder can
provide words on the
television screen.*

should ask their district media consultant about relevant copyright laws. In general, copyright laws permit teachers to tape off-air shows and use them two times for instructional purposes. After forty days, recorded shows must be erased.

Using Closed-Captioned Television in Reading Instruction

Closed-captioned television can be used like any other instructional material. The only thing that changes is the medium through which students receive the printed word. That is, instead of the printed pages of books, students using closed-captioning read words printed on their television screens. One might choose to do the following instructional activities with either a book or with a captioned television program:

1. Preview the show (book).
2. Select vocabulary to be introduced.
3. Assist students in purpose setting.
4. Show the program (read the book).
5. Initiate discussion and other types of comprehension activities.
6. Initiate rereading—either by reproducing scripts from the captions or by showing the program a second time without sound.
7. Initiate follow-up activities that seem appropriate. Examples of follow-up activities include discussions of vocabulary usage, discussion of cause and effect, creation of different story endings, and/or related readings from books on similar topics.

Does the above sequence sound familiar? Of course it does. These are the same activities that teachers use every day in textual materials. There is no need for greater preparation for captioned television lessons than for more traditional instruction with books.

Teachers have found that the use of short (very short) segments of shows works best. Five- or ten-minute segments carry enough meaning for the instruction to be useful. One teacher used a thirty-second segment of "Ripley's Believe It or Not." It contained thirty-three words, so it was easy to make scripts for follow-up instruction.

Experience has shown that it is best to use programs in which the captions are as close as possible to the audio portions. Shows of a documentary nature such as "3–2–1 Contact" contain captions that are much closer to their audio than do dramas requiring dialogue. Of course, documentaries also provide useful educational content as well. "Sesame Street" and "Ripley's Believe It or Not" work well for the same reasons. One should not worry too much about the level of the program; the motivational aspect of closed captioning takes care of many of those concerns. At a recent in-service program, "Sesame Street" was used to introduce teachers to closed captioning. When the television set was turned off before the program was over, some of the teachers complained. They wanted to see the end of the show and read more captions.

Teachers report that it seems best to use captioned television as a supplement to instruction. They report that using closed captioning two or three times a week seems to get better results than does daily use. Further research is needed to determine optimal classroom viewing patterns.

Security is an important consideration. Tele-decoders look like VCRs and may be prime targets for theft. Teachers will want to make sure that televisions and tele-decoders are well secured when not in use.

Teachers should preview programs before using them in school. Many programs on broadcast television contain depictions of violence, sex, drugs, and other topics that make them inappropriate for in-school usage. Because of their content, a surprising number of late afternoon and prime-time programs are unsuitable for instructional use.

Summary

In the hands of teachers who understand their advantages and weaknesses, microcomputers and closed-captioned television possess potential to empower teachers and evoke enthusiasm in students. Because of the speed with which the technology field is evolving, however, even the most conscientious teacher can become overwhelmed. Teachers should ask themselves how they can best take advantage of today's technological aids to instruction.

Microcomputers are the most widely growing recent technological innovation. Although most present reading applications of the microcomputer are for drill and practice, microcomputers can serve many other useful functions. Students can develop computer literacy skills, learn new reading skills, work through simulation programs, develop thinking skills, and write and edit with greater ease. Teachers can take advantage of microcomputer programs that compute readability, make posters and cards, print certificates and banners, and keep records. One particular area of microcomputer promise is word processing. Many students report that they prefer writing with a word processor to writing with pencil and paper because of the greater freedom it gives them to compose, edit, proofread, and print their written work. One of the difficulties of using microcomputers for instruction is selecting quality software. Teachers need to critically examine software because some commercial products on the market are decidedly lacking in technical and educational quality. Although the future of microcomputer development is difficult to predict with certainty, it appears that three-and-one-half-inch disks, computerized diagnostic tests, teleconferencing, data bases, interactive video, and reading prostheses are among the promising innovations of the future.

Closed-captioned television was originally developed for use with the hearing impaired, but it has been found to have benefits for poor readers as well. It represents a multisensory reading approach that is motivational for many students. It also channels students' existing interest in television into learning directions. As the twenty-first century approaches, teachers of reading will increasingly benefit from the educational power of technology to promote learning.

Notes

1. Scholastic, Inc. "Educational Techology 1987: A Report on *EL*'s Survey of the States, "*Electronic Learning* 7, no. 2 (October 1987): 39–57, 83.
2. Terry O'Banion, "Innovative Partnerships Assist Community Computing Programs," *Technological Horizons in Education* 14, no. 10 (June 1987): 56.
3. Kathleen Heffron, "Literacy with the Computer," *The Reading Teacher* 40, no. 2 (November 1986): 152–55.
4. Charles K. Kinzer, "A Five-Part Categorization for Use of Microcomputers in Reading Classrooms," *Journal of Reading* 30, no. 3 (December 1986): 226–32.
5. Kathryn M. Jones, Joseph K. Torgesen, and Molly A. Sexton, "Using Computer Guided Practice to Increase Decoding Fluency in Learning Disabled Children," *Journal of Learning Disabilities* 20, no. 2 (February 1987): 122–28.
6. Kathlene R. Willing, "Computer Simulations: Activating Content Reading," *Journal of Reading* 31, no. 5 (February 1988): 400–09.
7. Robert T. Rude, *Teaching Reading Using Microcomputers* (Englewood Cliffs, N.J.: Prentice Hall, 1986), 42–43.
8. Peter Elbow, *Writing with Power* (Oxford: Oxford University Press, 1981), 39–46.
9. Ernest Balajthy, *Microcomputers in Reading and Language Arts* (Englewood Cliffs, N.J.: Prentice-Hall, 1986), 44–45.
10. Holly Brady, "Tandy Fills Out Its 1000 Line," *Classroom Computer Learning* 8, no. 1 (September 1987): 26–29.
11. William A. Henk, "Reading Assessments of the Future: Toward Precision Diagnosis," *The Reading Teacher* 40, no. 9 (May 1987): 860–70.
12. Harold Wainer, "On Item Response Theory and Computerized Adaptive Tests," *Journal of College Admissions* 27, no. 4 (April 1983): 9–16.
13. Linda Roehrig Knapp, "Teleconferencing: A New Way of Communicating for Teachers and Kids," *Classroom Computer Learning* 7, no. 6 (March 1987): 37–41.
14. Ibid., 40–41.
15. Fay Wheeler, "The New Ready-Made Databases: What They Offer Your Classroom," *Classroom Computer Learning* 7, no. 6 (March 1987): 28–32.
16. Judy Salpeter, "Interactive Video: The Truth Behind the Promises," *Classroom Computer Learning* 7, no. 3 (November/December 1986): 26–34.
17. George A. Miller and Patricia M. Gildea, "How Children Learn Words," *Scientific American* (September 1987): 94–99.

18. Leo D. Geoffrion and Olga P. Geoffrion, *Computers and Reading Instruction* (Reading, Mass.: Addison-Wesley, 1983), 150–51.

19. Richard M. Restak, "Smart Machines Learn to See, Talk, Listen, Even 'Think' for Us," *Smithsonian* (March 1980): 48–57.

20. Julie S. Vargas, "Instructional Design Flaws in Computer-Assisted Instruction," *Phi Delta Kappan* 67, no. 10 (June 1986): 738–44.

21. Colette Daiute, "Physical and Cognitive Factors in Revising: Insights from Studies with Computers," *Research in the Teaching of English* 20, no. 2 (May 1986): 141–59.

22. David W. Dalton and Michael J. Hannafin, "The Effects of Word Processing on Written Composition," *Journal of Educational Research* 80, no. 6 (July/August 1987): 338–42.

23. C. A. MacArthur, J. A. Haynes, and D. B. Malouf, "Learning Disabled Students' Engaged Time and Classroom Interaction: The Impact of Computer Assisted Instruction," *Journal of Educational Computing Research* 2, no. 2 (Summer 1986): 189–98.

24. Patricia S. Koskinen, Robert M. Wilson, and Carl Jensema, "Closed-Captioned Television: A Tool for Reading Instruction," *Reading World* 24, no. 4 (May 1985): 1–7.

25. Department of Education, *Using the Technology of Closed-Captioned Television to Teach Reading to Handicapped Students* (Washington, D.C.: Performance Report for DOE grant #G-00-84-300677, 1987).

26. National Captioning Institute, *Two Pilot Projects Which Used Captioned Television to Teach Reading to Hearing Children* (Falls Church, Va.: National Captioning Institute, Research Report 83-6, 1983), 6.

Suggested Readings

Balajthy, Ernest. *Microcomputers in Reading and Language Arts.* Englewood Cliffs, N.J.: Prentice-Hall, 1986. This book provides a thorough overview of microcomputer applications in the reading program. Balajthy assists the reader in making informed professional decisions concerning the uses of microcomputer technologies.

Blanchard, Jay S., George E. Mason, and Dan Daniel. *Computer Applications in Reading.* 3d ed. Newark, Del.: International Reading Association, 1987. The authors discuss the varied uses of microcomputers in school reading programs. Recent innovations are surveyed, and predictions about future uses are made.

Heller, Rachelle S., and C. Dianne Martin. *Bits 'N Bytes About Computing: A Computer Literacy Primer.* Rockville, Md.: Computer Science Press, 1982. This is a beginning book about computers, what they can do for us, and how they can affect our lives. These authors also produce the *Bits 'N Bytes Gazette*, a periodical newsletter for children.

Koskinen, Patricia S., and Robert M. Wilson. *Have You Read Any Good TV Lately?* Falls Church, Va.: National Captioning Institute, 1987. Teachers interested in suggestions for the use of captioned television as a medium for reading instruction will find this booklet helpful. Lesson suggestions are based upon several years of study with various groups of hearing and hearing impaired students.

Koskinen, Patricia S., Robert M. Wilson, and Carl Jensema. "Closed-Captioned Television: A Tool for Reading Instruction." *Reading World* (May 1985). Pp. 1–7. This article overviews closed-captioned television uses and suggests factors that contribute to its success in teaching reading.

Rude, Robert T. *Teaching Reading Using Microcomputers.* Englewood Cliffs, N.J.: Prentice-Hall, 1986. Readers desiring an easy-to-read, introductory-level discussion of varied reading-related microcomputer topics will find this book useful.

Strickland, Dorothy S., Joan T. Feeley, and Shelley B. Wepner. *Using Computers in the Teaching of Reading.* New York: Teachers College Press, 1987. The authors discuss the microcomputer as tool, tutor, and tutee. Chapter 8 provides an especially interesting discussion of issues and trends in microcomputer use.

EDITORIAL

Gordon B. Browning

*is supervisor of Pupil Services
for the Kent County Public Schools in
Maryland.*

If I have learned only one thing in the many years I have spent in public education it is this: each child is unique. Although I have often read about the "average student," I have yet to meet one. Each child comes to school with a background of experiences and a set of abilities and interests that is not exactly like any other. Although that makes teaching so very interesting, it also makes teaching extremely difficult, as we are charged with taking each child at his or her current level of performance and leading that child as far as we can in the limited time we spend together.

Basal textbook series and limited time combine to make it difficult for the teacher to address individual differences. In a single class period at the secondary level, for example, there is not time to provide two minutes a day to each student. Things are better at the elementary level as the student and teacher remain together for a greater portion of the school day, but there is never enough time to challenge and encourage the quick learner or to assist and motivate the reluctant one.

The great hope for technology is that it may provide the time we need. The arguments continue to rage over the cost of technology, but those of us who labor in the trenches have a more pressing concern. We seek a way to provide extensive repetition and practice for the student who is unable to grasp the material as quickly as his or her classmates and to provide an individualized presentation to the student able and eager to progress beyond his or her peers.

The vast majority of students will learn well without technology. American schools do a superior job with most students. It is to those who do not fall within the norm—the reluctant reader and the gifted learner—that technology offers the greatest potential. It is to the teachers of those students that technology offers the most assistance.

I have seen gifted students develop their skills at drawing inferences and understanding relationships as they worked with language arts software. I have seen them spend hours with simulation software learning ecology, economics, chemistry, sociology, and long-range planning skills. I have seen them write their own programs to address their specific concerns yet such activities would have been difficult for the classroom teacher to provide prior to the advent of computers in the school.

Handicapped students have profited from technology as well. Adaptive devices have made learning easier for the physically impaired. Through the use of voice synthesizers, Braille writers, and alternative communication devices, such as communication boards and adaptive switches, students who would have been denied such basic activities as reading, writing, and communicating can now interact with those who are not physically challenged.

The reluctant reader has, I believe, the greatest untapped potential to profit from technology. Several studies have demonstrated the effectiveness of the computer with poor readers. The computer offers a way for the poor reader to break the cycle of poor performance and teacher expectation of continued poor performance. For most students, the computer is highly motivating, increasing active learning time. For the reluctant reader, it is doubly so. The computer's ability to never "lose its temper" with students has been frequently praised by teachers and students alike. Its

ability to "do it over and over until we get it right" provides a sufficiency of practice opportunities, and its ability to reward good performance without demeaning those efforts that are less than acceptable makes us all wish we could always be so kind. Reluctant readers need that!

Not every student will do better with a computer than without one. Some may even do worse. Not every teacher will find the computer a useful piece of classroom equipment. Not every school district will consider the computer a cost-effective investment. For those who do, the potential for student achievement and for the development of positive attitudes toward learning will more than offset the cost involved in making technology accessible.

Gordon Browning

Evaluation of Diagnostic, Remedial, and Resource Programs

CHAPTER EMPHASES

The remedial program must be continuously evaluated.

Evaluation of remedial programs should be made on the basis of student change.

Educator evaluation should be included in the remedial program's evaluation.

I nstruction that has been determined effective to diagnose the strengths and needs of students stands a good chance of succeeding. Upon completion of such a remedial program, students are likely to be improved readers. The educator must determine what changes have taken place and assess the extent of those changes. Many questions need to be answered in an effective evaluation of a remedial program, such as the following:

1. Has performance in reading improved?
2. Has attitude toward reading changed?
3. Has reading become a chosen free-time activity?
4. Could more have been accomplished with more efficient diagnosis?
5. Was observed progress attributable to the remedial program?
6. Have parents noticed behavior changes?
7. Did observed changes occur in areas stressed in the remedial program?
8. If the program was conducted outside of the classroom, has the classroom teacher been able to build on the progress made there?

These and other questions should be studied and answered. Naturally, not all of them apply to every situation, and some are more difficult to answer than others. For example, if a student made great gains during a remedial program that was designed to supplement what the teacher was doing in the classroom, to what does one attribute the progress? Maybe the teacher made important adjustments in instruction and is responsible for the student's improvement, or maybe it was from an effective remedial program; more than likely, it was some combination of the two.

Guidelines for Effective Evaluation

The following guidelines, applicable to all education, have particular application when evaluating the effectiveness of remedial reading programs.

Evaluation Should Have a Broad Base

Ample allowance must be made for factors such as improved medical attention, relaxed home pressures, and reaction to both negative and positive diagnosis. If a student has been provided with glasses as a result of a physical screening, a proper evaluation of the tutoring program must give consideration to the effect of the glasses as well as to the instruction. In an examination of clinic cases at the University of Maryland, for example, it was found that students referred for inadequate visual screening performance made better progress (as a group) if the parents followed the referral advice than students whose parents did not follow referral advice. Apparently, attention to the visual needs of these students had an effect on the progress they made. The appropriate importance to be attributed to each factor in evaluation is extremely difficult and, at times, impossible to determine.

357

Evaluation of
Diagnostic,
Remedial, and
Resource
Programs

Evaluation Should Be Continuous

Continuous evaluation is crucial to effective instruction. It involves many of the same processes as diagnosis (i.e., an evaluation of the student's skill development and reading effectiveness). Evaluation of past performance should be considered diagnosis for future instruction; therefore, evaluation should be continuous.

Evaluation Should Be Objective

Objective measures of performance should be used in an effort to control bias. One often reads evaluation reports that state that "the teachers and students were enthusiastic about the progress that had been made." Although enthusiasm is a highly desirable factor, it cannot be the sole basis for evaluation of program effectiveness. However, nonobjective evaluation techniques are certainly valuable and are not to be precluded by this guideline.

Evaluation Should Be in Terms of Established Goals

It is sometimes desirable and natural for considerable progress to be noticed in areas for which instruction had not been planned. Such progress, however desirable, must be considered secondary to the program's goals. Teachers must be cautious about claiming credit for attitude change, for example, unless the program included attitude change in its objectives.

Student Self-Evaluation

Student evaluation of remedial progress and remedial programs should not be overlooked. Students often render insights toward remediation that elude educators. Teachers should seek student self-evaluation and program evaluation, and they should use these in evaluating remedial programs.

Pupil–teacher conferences can be used for self-evaluation. If students feel that they will not be penalized for their honesty, many can provide accurate, useful statements concerning their feelings about how they have done in their remedial sessions, or about their reactions to specific materials and techniques. Questionnaires also can be used in student evaluation. Questions concerning how they feel they have performed in terms of specific objectives, the portions of the program they enjoyed most and least, and the changes they would recommend may be included. Finally, contract evaluation can be used for self-

A major goal of the remedial program is to strengthen good attitudes toward reading, school, and self.

evaluation. Such evaluation occurs immediately after the contract is completed so students can evaluate their own work honestly.

Change in Student Behavior

The teacher's first concern is the program's effect on student behavior. Basically, four areas of changes are open for observation in student behavior: attitude, reading behavior, test results, and school performance.

Attitude Changes

If students enter remedial programs with poor attitudes toward reading, school, and themselves, one of the remedial program's major goals would be to improve those attitudes. Data for justification of attitude change are readily available. Behavior in class, willingness to attend to reading tasks, choice of reading for free-time activities, willingness to discuss ideas obtained from reading, and willingness to be helpful to others (perhaps as a tutor) are all useful indicators of attitude changes.

Following remedial sessions at the University of Maryland reading clinic, parents are petitioned for information on changes they have noticed. The most frequent change noted is that the student is now reading. "He picks up the newspaper and actually reads it." "She reads road signs and billboards now as we drive down the road." Such comments show that the students are happy

359

Evaluation of
Diagnostic,
Remedial, and
Resource
Programs

to display their reading skills and see themselves as readers. Information can be obtained from students as well as parents to assure the reliability of the responses. The inherent danger of interviews and questionnaires is the tendency for respondents to maintain a "halo" effect. Therefore, the interview or questionnaire should be structured to avoid pointing to obviously expected responses.

Classroom behaviors provide readily observable indications of students' attitudes. Observation in the classroom, when systematically approached, gives teachers the advantage of examining student behavior in real-life reading situations rather than having to make judgments about students based solely on paper-and-pencil tests. Miccinati and Pine suggest the use of running commentaries; shadow studies which note student behavior at fifteen-minute intervals; checklists; and anecdotal records.[1] One way to assess reading attitudes with any of these methods would be to note how a given student uses Sustained Silent Reading (SSR) time in the classroom. What is the student reading? What percent of the time is the student engaged in on-task behavior? How long does it take the student to settle down and begin reading? The systematic observation of the answers to these and other questions may shed some light on the nature of the student's reading attitudes.

Reading attitudes may also be assessed with an attitude scale. A paired scale requires a student to express a preference between two stimulus objects, activities, words, phrases, or pictures. A pairing instrument which uses pictures to assess the reading attitudes of primary-age children is Askov's Primary Pupil Reading Attitude Inventory.[2] A summated rating scale requires a student to respond to a statement along a five-point continuum which ranges from *Strongly Agree* to *Strongly Disagree*. The Heathington Primary Attitude Scale and the Heathington Intermediate Attitude Scale are examples of summated rating scales.[3]

Reading Behavior Changes

During remedial activities, teachers should keep records of reading behavior changes which indicate what skills in reading the students display that they could not display when the program started. These data will be available if teachers collect them as instruction proceeds. Evaluated contracts can be a source of such data. Informal, teacher-made check tests can be administered when the teacher feels that some students have developed a new skill. Teachers are more receptive to a discussion of reading behavior changes of their students than to a discussion of test score improvement. The changes in reading behavior can be readily used in the daily classroom reading program.

Behavior changes can be noted and recorded best through some type of systematic observation procedure. By establishing a list of kinds of behavior desired and by observing students periodically with the use of a checklist, the frequency of that behavior can be recorded. If such behavior were observed two times in twenty observations at the beginning of a program and eighteen times out of twenty observations later in the program, then one can start to talk specifically about that behavior change. Casual observations, however, are very difficult to quantify.

One useful means for teachers to gain insights into a student's reading behavior change is to keep a record of the nature and amount of a student's independent reading. It might be expected that, if significant changes are occurring in a student's skills and attitudes, those changes will be reflected in the student's independent reading habits. The teacher should be cautioned, however, to not merely look for the student to select more difficult books to read. In many cases with remedial reading students a positive step is reflected when they select *easier* reading material. This is because so many poor readers self-select books on the basis of pictures, covers, topics, and so on, and end up selecting books that are too difficult for them to read independently.

Test Results

By diagnosing from test answers, posttesting can provide some information about student progress in a remedial program. But the problems are almost great enough to discourage much reliance on pre-posttest results.

First, the results that report gains in reading levels are impossible to interpret in terms of reading behavior. For example, a report indicating that a student gained four years in reading comprehension tells nothing about the student's actual reading behavior. Second, gain scores are notoriously unreliable. On many tests, a difference of one or two items can make a large gain score. Third, it is difficult to obtain two forms that are truly equivalent of any test. When different forms are used, it is difficult to determine whether noticed gains are the result of the remedial program or the test form that was used.

When educators use test results to evaluate remedial programs, they should use teacher-made criterion-referenced tests (CRTs), containing numerous items for each objective, to assure maximum reliability. Some examples are:

1. Word lists taken from reading materials at various levels can be used to measure gains in word recognition.
2. Paragraphs followed by carefully constructed questions taken from materials of varying reading levels can assist in measuring gains in reading accuracy (when reading orally) and in comprehension (when reading silently). By structuring the reading tasks, insights can also be gained into both recall and locating abilities.
3. Skill quizzes constructed by teachers to assess students' abilities to perform in the areas of given instruction can be used to measure skill development. Such information is useful for the teachers who will work with the students next. The information is reported in terms of reading behavior and can be interpreted further if desirable.

361

Evaluation of
Diagnostic,
Remedial, and
Resource
Programs

TABLE 13-1. Use of Criterion-Referenced Tests for Pretest and Posttest Evaluation of Comprehension

	Response to Interpretive Questions			
Student	*Passage Level*			
	Grade 5		*Grade 6*	
	Pre	Post	Pre	Post
Brook	70%	100%	50%	80%
Jennifer	80%	100%	60%	90%
Andrea	60%	90%	40%	70%

Table 13-1 illustrates how CRT pre-post evaluation can be used to evaluate one aspect of comprehension performance. Each student made impressive gains.

Performance in School

For those students who have been removed from the classroom for remedial assistance, the ultimate evaluation of the success of the program is in terms of how well they do when they return to the classroom. Feedback from the classroom teacher is one source of information; grades earned are another.

Teachers can be interviewed or polled through a questionnaire to discuss observed changes in classroom behavior. If the students improve behavior in small groups out of the classroom, the teacher must be certain that those changes carry over into the classroom setting. If not, then the program should be adjusted either in the classroom or for more extended remediation out of the classroom.

Grades are another way of looking at classroom performance; however, many variables that influence grades cannot be evaluated by grades alone. Over a long period of time, the grades in Table 13-2 seem to tell us that Nancy was doing poorly prior to remediation and has done much better since remediation.

These changes, however, cannot necessarily be attributed to the remedial program. Perhaps fourth grade represents the year in which a difficult personal

TABLE 13-2. Earned Grade Record Over Time

Student's Name	*Nancy*				
Subject			*Remediation*		
	Grade 2	*Grade 3*	*Grade 4*	*Grade 5*	*Grade 6*
Reading	D	D	C	B	B
Language	C	C	C	B	B
Spelling	D	F	D	C	C

situation was resolved in Nancy's life. Or, perhaps Nancy experienced a positive change in attitude related to school. In the case of an individual's grade improvement, teachers cannot attribute the change directly to the remedial program. However, if most of the students enrolled in the program showed similar gains, this might indicate that the program was having a positive effect.

Ways to Interpret Gain Scores

Bleismer suggests methods of using gain scores regardless of the severe limitations they have for interpretation.[4] These interpretations of gain scores create some interesting problems when one is attempting to evaluate a remedial program through gain scores.

Grade-Level Improvement

Bleismer, in citing three basic postremediation evaluation techniques, calls this a simple pretest and posttest comparison. If a student enters a remedial program reading at 4.5 grade level and leaves the reading program at 5.5 grade level, a teacher can conclude that the student has gained 1.0 years in grade level. Obviously, the adequacy of the test instrument used to determine grade-level performance limits this aspect of evaluation. It does not account for the student's chronological or mental age increase or for changes that would have occurred without remediation.

Reading skill performance as compared to grade level is of particular interest to both the classroom teacher and the principal because it has much to do with the student's placement in a particular room and within a class.

Reading Potential

Evaluation of reading potential attempts to determine whether students are working up to expected levels. Bleismer calls attention to the fact that potential (mental age) will change with age and that estimates must be adjusted for effective evaluation.[5] Regardless of a student's grade-level performance and ability to perform in an assigned classroom, growth up to potential is generally considered a desirable goal of remediation. In Table 11-3, if Jim has an estimated potential of 5.0 and a reading level of 3.0, his working development is lagging behind his mental development by 2.0 years. If, after a semester of work, this reading level rises to 4.2, his potential will have to be reestimated before growth can be measured.

Note that in Table 13-3 Jim's reading potential increased as he grew older, thereby lessening the apparent effect of the difference in reading grade-level changes. Remedial sessions accelerated his growth over his potential by 0.4 years (found by subtracting the differences). Reading potential techniques will be of more interest to the reading specialist than to the classroom teacher or the parent. One major problem with using potential as a standard occurs when remedial

TABLE 13-3. Comparison of Potential and Achievement

363

Evaluation of
Diagnostic,
Remedial, and
Resource
Programs

Student's Name	*Jim*	
	January	May
Potential	5.0	5.8
Reading	3.0	4.2
Difference	2.0	1.6

efforts are being made to improve skills related to these measures of potential. In those cases, potential will be misleading if used as a standard. For example, if a remedial program includes opportunities for language development, opportunities of potential improvement are also included. Such programs actually have resulted in considerable improvement on language-related tests of intelligence.

Past Performance

Evaluation of skill improvement in terms of students' previous performance rates is of some advantage with older students. Bleismer recommends that the identifiable variables be controlled.[6] Suppose that Judy (see Table 13-4) has completed six years of school and has scored at a grade level 4.6 before remediation is begun. This indicates an average gain of 0.6 years of reading skill for each year in school ($4.6 - 1.0 \div 6$). (Note that 1.0 must be subtracted, as all children start with a reading level of 1.0 [the zero month of first grade].) If she obtained a reading level of 5.5 by the end of one year in remediation, the gain would be 0.9 years of skill in one year ($5.5 - 4.6 = 0.9$). Yet she is not reading up to grade level and may not be reading up to expectations. She has not progressed even one full year under intensive remediation. Nevertheless, improvement is greater than it has been in the past, thus indicating that the remedial program is profitable to her.

Note that the gain of 0.9 years is greater by 0.3 years than could have been expected from the average of previous efforts. While of interest to the reading specialist and the classroom teacher, the rate of improvement during

TABLE 13-4. Comparison of Current Achievement with Past Achievement

Student's Name	*Judy*		
Years in School	Average Yearly Gain Before Tutoring	Gain During Year of Tutoring	Growth Attributed to Tutoring
6	($4.6 - 1.0 \div 6$) = 0.6	0.9	0.3

Evaluating students' previous performance rates is particularly useful with older students.

remediation is little consolation to the student or the parent, especially if the student remains limited in classroom performance.

Evaluation of past performance is limited by the unlikely assumption that the past performance was evenly distributed. However, with older students who have significant reading deficiencies, this method of evaluation may provide the most useful indication of student progress.

Limitations

All the evaluation techniques suggested here are limited by the instruments being used to make comparisons. Standardized tests are inherently unreliable and cause notable gains to be suspect due to the error factor of the measuring instrument. As noted in chapter 3, grade-equivalent scores are especially susceptible to misinterpretation. Misinterpretation of grade-equivalent scores has become so widespread that the Delegates Assembly of the International Reading Association has adopted a resolution urging test publishers to eliminate grade-equivalent scores from their tests.[7] If teachers use standardized tests, standard scores provide a better means for reporting student performance. Teachers should also remember that standardized tests may not measure the skills that formed the remedial objectives for a particular student. Furthermore, it may be that the standardization population may be mismatched with a teacher's group of remedial students. Thus, standardized tests should usually only be used to indicate gains with groups of students; informal tests can be used to measure the gains of individual students.

Two other problems occur when evaluating with standardized tests. First, all standardized tests contain error in their measurement; the amount of error makes score changes possible by chance. Therefore, small gains in standardized test scores over short periods of time cannot be considered highly accurate. Second, students may *regress*. If a group of students were given a standardized test today and then readministered the same test a week later, low-scoring students would, by chance, tend to improve their scores (scores would tend to move toward the mean), while high-scoring students would decrease their scores (scores would tend to move toward the mean). This phenomenon has obvious implications in evaluating the reading performance of students who have been initially referred for special programs in reading due to their low performance on a standardized test.

365

Evaluation of
Diagnostic,
Remedial, and
Resource
Programs

The educator's efficiency is difficult to evaluate and is, therefore, less likely to receive the evaluation efforts that student growth receives. Educator efficiency in programs should be evaluated in the following areas.

Educator Efficiency

Adequacy of Diagnosis

Because of emphasis placed on the proper use of diagnosis and the time spent in accomplishing it, it can validly be included in evaluation. Educators must determine whether diagnosis has uncovered a student's remedial strengths and needs effectively and precisely. Furthermore, they must decide that the diagnosis, while not overextended, is complete enough to cover the areas of the students' skill development. When there is a failure to evaluate in all areas, inefficiency will likely develop in remedial sessions. At times, teachers use tests that, for them, appear to supply essential information for a diagnosis; however, upon closer examination, these tests do not provide any information that could not be determined more readily by other diagnostic techniques.

Adequacy of Remedial Approach

As educators become accustomed to working in remediation, specific approaches often develop into standard procedures with all students. The resulting error here, unless there are constant attempts at evaluation, is that diagnosis is disregarded, since a given remedial approach is used with all students. For example, if all students were to be tutored through the use of the language-experience approach, diagnostic conclusions are not used to determine the remedial approach. Through evaluation of remedial approaches, the educator is led to develop the variety of effective approaches prescribed by the students' diagnostic strengths and needs.

Adequacy of Remedial Techniques

Similar to the difficulty of not selecting adequate remedial approaches, using a prescribed technique with all students regardless of the remedial approach is equally limiting and should be avoided through careful evaluation of remedial techniques. For example, a graph to illustrate progress will not motivate all students in all remedial techniques. The evaluation of techniques will save time in remediation and lead the educator to those techniques best suited to the students' strengths and needs.

Adequacy of Remedial Materials

As educators become familiar with the manuals and contents of the variety of materials available in remediation, they are likely to select and use those that appeal most to them. This action is appropriate when these materials are selected after an evaluation of their effectiveness; however, if they are selected on the basis of familiarity alone, their adequacy should be evaluated. As the flood of materials continues, the educator will need to be involved with more material evaluation.

In addition to the materials' appeal, educators need to consider the appropriateness of the level of materials. As stated throughout this text, students experiencing difficulties in reading must be placed in materials which they can handle with ease. The single indicator of a successful remedial program is when students are reading fluently and with ease. The press to move these students to more difficult materials usually only results in frustration for students and teachers alike.

A variety of techniques are available to assist the educator in the various aspects of evaluation discussed here. The teacher can and should consult with other teachers; ask for help from a reading resource person in the school or district; read evaluations of materials in the professional literature; talk with students about books they like and dislike; conduct studies using certain materials with one group of students and other materials with another group; examine the activities required by the materials and compare them to objectives for the remedial program; and give students choices of materials to use, observing their consistent selection of one over another.

Single-subject experiments have a long history in psychology and psychiatry but have been used infrequently in education. The appeal of studying the effects of an intervention on one subject over a period of time holds considerable merit in evaluating educational innovation.

Recently, considerable attention has been given to using single-subject research ($N = 1$) to evaluate the effects of schooling on individual students.[8] Adapted from case study research, single-subject research is an acceptable, maybe even preferred, way to study individuals.

In $N = 1$ research, subjects serve as the controls, and baseline data are collected over a period of time. Once a pattern of behavior is observed and

367

Evaluation of
Diagnostic,
Remedial, and
Resource
Programs

that behavior stabilizes, an intervention is introduced. The effects of that intervention are also observed over time in the same manner that baseline behaviors were observed.

The advantages of $N = 1$ studies are:

1. Data are collected over time. One unusual behavior is not compared to one intervention behavior, but many data points are used.
2. The subject becomes the control in the experiment.
3. Specific interventions can be isolated and studied in detail.
4. These studies, when replicated, provide convincing evidence of the effects of an intervention.

As with other types of evaluation, much rests on the validity of the dependent variable. Therefore, natural school evaluation techniques should be used (e.g., the number of sight words learned in a lesson).

Adequacy of Total School Efforts

If requested, the reading specialist should be able to conduct an evaluation of the total school efforts in the area of diagnostic and remedial reading. Assuming that the reading specialist is acquainted with research design and controlled experimentation techniques and has the ability to interpret research data, there is little reason for not using such techniques. Burg et al. present an evaluation model that consists of the following four major stages: (1) Needs assessment; (2) Program planning based on the needs assessment; (3) Formative evaluation, including implementation evaluation and progress evaluation of students in the program; (4) Outcome evaluation, both in terms of skills and attitude.[9] To be effective, evaluation must be as broadly based as possible and involve students, parents, classroom teachers, reading specialists, support staff, and administrators. The evaluation should also be based on the stated goals of the reading program and not on the evaluation team's subjective impressions. Some schools involve college or university consultants in chairing the evaluation effort because of the particular expertise of these people and because evaluation conducted by people from outside the school is less likely to reflect bias.

Adequacy of the Resource Role

If the reading specialist functions in a resource role, that role deserves careful evaluation also. How one functions on screening committees, in teaming situations, in helping teachers try new ideas or materials, and when conducting staff development sessions are examples of areas that may be included.

Reading specialist self-evaluation, classroom teacher evaluation, and supervisor evaluation can all be included. Questionnaires, observations, and teacher requests for assistance can be used to compile an evaluation report.

The resource role is of major importance (see chapter 15) and therefore should receive a most objective and careful evaluation. If ignored, a real possibility exists that one may go on performing functions that are not valued by others and are thereby ineffective. For example, a reading specialist may develop a newsletter each month that highlights new materials that have arrived in the school. If, upon evaluation, the reading specialist finds that no one reads the newsletter, then another form of communication about new materials should be developed. To continue with the newsletter would be a waste of effort because it has proven an ineffective way for informing teachers of new materials.

If teachers do not value the resource role and would prefer that the reading specialist work more with students, a reevaluation of the activities in that resource role needs to be undertaken. Discussions with staff and supervisors may facilitate a better use of the reading specialist's time and efforts. For example, one may find that classroom teachers really appreciate the efforts to facilitate the use of new materials by way of demonstrations but they do not value the half-hour-per-week staff development sessions on classroom management. Reevaluating the staff development sessions would then be in order, and a possible increase in the demonstration of new materials may be useful.

Adequacy of Districtwide Reading Programs and Personnel

While evaluating individual teachers and schoolwide reading programs is highly desirable, districtwide reading programs and personnel should also be evaluated. This type of evaluation is usually initiated by supervisory personnel on central office staffs. Various school personnel can be surveyed with a questionnaire that lists the program objectives or with sampling interviews. The questionnaires or interviews can provide data regarding the number of teachers or students serviced and an indication of their perceived effectiveness. By obtaining that information from teachers, reading specialists, and school-based administrators, the central office staff has data that can be used for school board decision making, public relations, and for central office staff meetings.

Summary

Evaluation should be carefully planned for all remedial programs. To make valid comparisons, pretesting and noting behavior prior to remediation are essential. To evaluate student success in a remedial program, teachers should be expected to use assessments of attitudes, reading skills, test performance, and classroom performance. To assure professional growth, teachers should continuously evaluate their own effectiveness in both diagnosis and remediation.

Notes

1. Jeannette L. Miccinati and Mary A. Pine, *Observing Students' Reading Skills* (York, Penn: College Reading Association, 1979), 11–34.
2. Eunice N. Askov, *Primary Pupil Reading Attitude Inventory* (Dubuque, Iowa: Kendall/Hunt Publishers, 1982), 6.

369

Evaluation of
Diagnostic,
Remedial, and
Resource
Programs

3. Betty S. Heathington, *Heathington Primary Attitude Scale* and *Heathington Intermediate Attitude Scale* in *Teaching Reading*, ed. J. Estill Alexander (Boston: Little, Brown and Company, 1983), 365–68.
4. Emery P. Bleismer, "Evaluating Progress in Remedial Reading Programs," *The Reading Teacher* 15, no. 5 (March 1962): 344–50.
5. Ibid.
6. Ibid.
7. Delegates Assembly of the International Reading Association, "Misuse of Grade Equivalents," *The Reading Teacher* 35, no. 4 (January 1982): 464.
8. Alan E. Kazdin. *Single-Case Research Designs* (New York: Oxford University Press, 1982), chap. 1.
9. Leslie A. Burg et al., *The Complete Reading Supervisor: Tasks and Roles* (Columbus, Ohio: Merrill Publishing Company, 1978), 101–11.

**Suggested
Readings**

Anderson, Scarvia and Samuel Ball. *The Profession and Practice of Program Evaluation.* San Francisco: Jossey-Bass Publishers, 1980. The authors present educational evaluation as a foundation for program improvement. This comprehensive book examines the match between evaluation purposes and evaluation methods. Chapter 8 discusses ethical responsibilities in evaluation.

Burg, Leslie A. et al. *The Complete Reading Supervisor: Tasks and Roles.* Columbus, Ohio: Merrill Publishing Company, 1978. Several of the chapters of this book are of interest from an evaluation perspective. In chapter 6, a model for evaluation is discussed. Chapter 8 surveys observational techniques for measuring teacher performance, pupil-teacher interaction, and pupil behaviors. The book closes with a discussion of evaluation as it applies to in-service staff development.

Farr, Roger and Robert F. Carey. *Reading: What Can Be Measured?* 2d ed. Newark, Del: International Reading Association, 1986. The book takes an objective but critical look at evaluation instruments used by reading personnel in schools and clinics and provides guidelines for research applications in reading assessment. These authors have made a significant contribution with this updated edition of a 1969 classic.

Kazdin, Alan E. *Single-Case Research Designs.* New York: Oxford University Press, 1982. A thorough discussion of methods for using single-case research. Techniques for conducting such research, an argument in favor of these types of designs, and a discussion of the advantages and limitations of single-case research are included. If teachers want to conduct this type of evaluation they should study a book such as this

Maginnis, George. "Evaluating Remedial Reading Gains." *Journal of Reading* 13, no. 7 (April 1970): 523–28. This article discusses several of the inherent problems involved in evaluating remedial reading. Maginnis presents several positive suggestions for avoiding those problems.

Miccinati, Jeanette L. and Mary A. Pine. *Observing Students' Reading Skills.* York, Penn.: College Reading Association, 1979. In a fifty-two-page monograph, the authors present a rationale for classroom observation, suggest methods for employing observation in a systematic manner, and give illustrations of practical applications of observational techniques in classroom settings. The publication is a very useful and informative guide to observational techniques.

Smith, Richard J., Wayne Otto, and Lee Hansen. *The School Reading Program: A Handbook for Teachers, Supervisors, and Specialists.* Boston: Houghton Mifflin Company, 1978. Evaluation is discussed as an integral part of effective program development in chapter 7 of this text. The authors make the point that educational decision making is most sound when based on objective and reliable evaluation.

EDITORIAL

Marianne Pfeiffer

is a principal for the Howard County Public Schools in Maryland.

Edith was a second-grade student. Informal diagnostic testing done by her classroom teacher at the beginning of the school year indicated that she had not retained many of the reading skills she had been taught during first grade. The classroom teacher asked me as the school reading specialist to conduct further assessment of Edith's reading.

Word recognition and silent-reading comprehension scores from an Informal Reading Inventory suggested that she would probably be most successful in a basal of a lower readability level than the basal she had apparently "finished" in the spring of first grade. Further assessment showed that Edith had strengths in word meaning and use of context cues but showed weaknesses in word recognition, word attack, and silent-reading comprehension.

A review of Edith's cumulative folder showed that she had progressed steadily through all the first-grade readers but that skill testing conducted at the end of each reader showed "fragile" growth with progressively more skill deficiences.

A conference was held with Edith's mother, Mrs. Hensley, to discuss starting Edith in a corrective reading program. Mrs. Hensley shared great concern about Edith's progress in reading and feelings about school. Mrs. Hensley stated that during her preschool years Edith had been a happy, relaxed child who greatly enjoyed singing or putting on skits for an audience. Now she was shy and withdrawn around adults. Mrs. Hensley also shared that during her preschool years Edith had enjoyed being read to or looking at books but that she no longer was interested in either.

Edith began receiving corrective reading help in addition to her classroom reading instruction. The classroom teacher and I tried to build on Edith's strengths using reading material we were sure Edith could successfully read. Each time we had a conference with Mrs. Hensley we shared careful documentation of Edith's reading "successes." Mrs. Hensley often requested reinforcement activities to use at home, and we supplied her with many games and activities which we hoped would be enjoyable as well as reinforcing.

In March at a report card conference, Mrs. Hensley, the classroom teacher, and I all agreed that Edith had made substantial progress in reading since the fall. We discussed Edith's strengths in the areas of word recognition, word attack, literal and interpretive comprehension, and study skills. We were all obviously pleased with the conference, but before Mrs. Hensley left she shared one "problem."

It seemed that at home in the evenings Edith didn't want to leave the books she was reading to do reading games and activities with her mother.

Mrs. Hensley probably didn't anticipate the look of shock that was on my face. Had we really failed to communicate to Edith's mother that the overall goal of the year's classroom and corrective reading instruction had been to help Edith become a "reader"? As flashes of previous conferences went through my mind I sought evidence that we had not forgotten to verbalize our goal. I felt relieved as I remembered fragments of conversations in which we had discussed Edith's attitude toward reading as well as how we planned to help her realize and use her reading strengths. Possibly our failure came in not clearly defining the term "reader." I then remembered suggested book lists and discussion concerning allowing Edith to read books of her own choice. As I concluded that at no one point had we lost sight of our goal, I also realized once again the importance of continuous evaluation which keeps not only the day's objective, but the overall goal, in our minds and in our verbalizations. Parents and students can only assume that what we verbalize is what we consider important.

Later I reflected on one more lesson I had been retaught during this conference—the importance of student self-evaluation. Mrs. Hensley, the classroom teacher, and I had been concerned about Edith's initial negative attitude toward reading. As we saw the change in Edith's attitude and reading ability we should have been more sensitive to and supportive of Edith's image of herself as a "reader." If we had been more attuned we might have realized that Edith had a more efficient and possibly clearer perception of the situation than we did. She recognized her reading strengths and she was enjoying putting these into use. It seemed that she realized the goal of the year's activities had been for her to become a reader and, when not encumbered by adults, a reader was precisely what she was.

Marianne S. Pfeiffer

Parental Roles

CHAPTER OUTLINE

Parental Roles in Diagnosis
Parental Roles in Remediation
Pitfalls in Parental Cooperation

CHAPTER EMPHASES

*Parents and teachers can form
effective partnerships to remediate
student reading difficulties.*

*Parents are in the best position to help
when they are kept informed
concerning students' needs and
successes.*

*The things that parents say and do
help to shape students' opinions
both about reading and themselves
as readers.*

*Parent training programs can be
effective keys to parent
involvement.*

D**on't worry, we'll handle it"** is quite often the only suggestion that some teachers offer parents who are seeking ways to help their children with reading difficulties. Today, such advice is inappropriate and will likely fall on deaf ears because parents increasingly are involving themselves in their children's education. As the educational level of our adult population rises, as the emphasis on education for success in life continues, as education continues to be examined in the public press, and as commercial exploitations of parental concerns expand, teachers must help parents assist their children with reading. It is imperative that educators seek the ways parents can be most helpful in terms of the educational goals that they have established.

On the other hand, without proper guidance, parents may "help" their children in inappropriate or harmful ways. For example, uninformed parents often attempt to motivate their children through comparisons with brothers, sisters, or playmates. More often than not, undirected parental activity merely compounds the child's dislike of reading and actually interferes with progress in a remedial program.

Parental anxiety is likely to mount as a child's progress in reading declines.[1] When children sense parental anxiety, reading difficulties can become compounded. Parents must have their concern and anxiety channeled into useful, helpful educational activities. Teachers should not just tell parents not to worry but establish a role for them through which they can be most helpful.

Parental anxiety can easily be increased when parents read articles about dyslexia and believe their children to be its victim. The term *dyslexia* is commonly misused and often excites parents without cause. Teachers should discuss specific reading difficulties and avoid using terms that carry little meaning and serve only to excite parents.

Clinical and classroom diagnostic and remediation situations inherently demand that the parental role vary. The difference in roles is generally one of degree; the very nature of clinical situations demands that parents become more actively engaged in their child's remediation. In this chapter, as parental roles in diagnosis, remediation, and prevention of reading difficulties are discussed, suggestions are given to both the classroom teacher and reading specialist for directing parents toward useful activities. However, teachers and specialists should remember that all parents may not be able to perform all of these roles.

Parents teach their children to walk, talk, and do numerous other activities required to survive in society. Educators rely heavily on the ability of the parents to teach their children these skills. When they do not fulfill this responsibility, parents leave their children ill-equipped for progress in school. As the children develop difficulties in reading, educators logically call on their first teachers, their parents, to assist in any way that will be useful. The suggestions that follow, then, are based on the following beliefs:

1. Parents can help.
2. Parents often know best what makes their children react most effectively.

3. Children want parental support and assistance and strive to please their parents through school success.
4. Without parent-teacher teamwork, success with readers experiencing severe difficulties will be unnecessarily limited.
5. When directed toward useful roles, parents are usually willing to follow the advice of educators.

Except for the classroom teacher, parents most likely will be the first to recognize that their children are not making satisfactory progress in developing reading skills. Although the classroom teacher may fail to observe signs of frustration in a student, one can be certain that such awareness will not escape parents for long. The responsibility for the intitial identification of the reader's difficulties, in such cases, often falls to the parents. Parents should be directed to observe their children in reading and call to the educator's attention any of the following symptoms of frustrated reading:

1. Avoidance of reading.
2. Inability to complete classroom assignments or homework.
3. Inability to discuss with parents material that he or she has just read.
4. Habitual difficulty in attacking unknown words, especially if the difficulty is noticed after two or three years of schooling.
5. Word-by-word, nonfluent oral reading, especially when he or she has practiced this reading silently before reading it orally.
6. Complaints from the child of visual discomfort in reading periods of fifteen minutes or more.
7. Inability to complete real-life reading activities that should be understandable for a child of that age.

By directing the educator's attention to specific symptoms such as these, parents may identify reading difficulties before they become serious enough to necessitate the more formal types of reading diagnosis and remediation. Upon receiving observations such as these from parents, the educator should conduct as much diagnosis as necessary to find the nature of the difficulty.

Parents may become overly anxious while observing their children for these symptoms. Parents whose children do not have reading difficulties should be aware of this, just as other parents need to know the nature of their children's reading difficulties. In this way, needless anxieties can be relaxed, thus creating better learning situations.

Many schools involve parents in each step of the diagnosis. Permission is requested before assessing the student's reading achievement. Results are discussed with parents, and parents are involved with screening committees that seek the most appropriate resource assistance for the student. In cases involving handicapped students, parent signatures must be obtained to place the student in an optimum learning environment. Public Law 94-142 requires parent signature and provides for parental appeals when they disagree with the placement of their handicapped child.

Another important role of parents in diagnosis is to supply information in support of or in conflict with the tentative hypotheses that have been established in classroom diagnosis or initial screening techniques. The parents' role in clinical diagnosis, then, is to supply supporting observations concerning their children's work in school, attitudes toward reading, and physical well-being. Without this information, which is frequently obtainable through either questionnaires or interviews, the reading specialist is likely to err in making judgments based on relatively short exposure to the children. It is generally more effective to obtain information from parents after tentative hypotheses have been reached, lest the parents' opinions tend to bias the examiner.

Parents have complete responsibility for the follow-up in areas in which referral has been made. Parents have the right and responsibility to attend to the physical and emotional needs of their children, and teachers usually expect the parents to take children to vision specialists, neurologists, psychiatrists, and other specialists.

As parents become involved in the diagnosis, they should also be consulted concerning the findings. Perhaps nothing is more frustrating to parents than to know that their child has undergone extensive study, yet they have not been consulted about the findings. However, making diagnostic conclusions available to parents is far more than a courtesy because quite often parents must enact the suggestions for alleviating the problem. At times, when parents become involved in the process, their child will make almost immediate progress and no longer need remedial intervention from the school.

In clinical settings when a diagnosis of a student has been conducted, the parents should be informed in detail of the results. In the past, parents didn't receive a full report with test scores because it was thought they could not interpret those scores and might misuse them. Consequently, parents were making inferences from vague descriptions that were far more serious than were indicated by the case. Today educators suggest that parents get a full report of any diagnosis, including test scores. In this way, parents are not left with vague descriptions of their child's performance. Parents are today sent the same report sent to the schools, discussing every aspect of diagnosis, including test scores, their interpretations, and the recommendations for remediation.

Parents appreciate this openness. They feel fully informed, and they know what information is going to the school. They can follow up on the report with a parent-teacher conference. Naturally, instances will occur when a parent may abuse such information and go to the school with an "I told you so" type of comment. In general, however, far less abuse occurs when parents are fully informed than when they are partially informed.

Parental Roles in Remediation

For parents to have any role at all in remediation, they must have a general understanding of the educational goals set by the person conducting the remediation. This is not only ethically appropriate but reaching the goals is far more feasible when the parents are effectively involved. The first task, therefore, is to inform parents of realistic goals and of the general approaches to be used in attaining these goals. These goals should be short range and easily attainable so that the child, the parent, and the educator all can see clearly that progress is being made. Of course, this will necessitate contacting the parent as the goals are readjusted and as progress in reading skills is made. Again, contacts with parents are most effective when they occur in consultation sessions.

The most appropriate role for parents after they understand the program is to provide situations in the home whereby the skills learned in remediation can be reinforced. Although reinforcement activities may be time consuming, parents should recognize the necessity for providing reinforcement opportunities. Specifically, this work involves parents in the following actions:

1. Providing a quiet, comfortable, and relaxing place for reading in the home.
2. Providing a planned time during the day when the household becomes suitable for reading: the television is turned off; other members of the family pursue reading interests; and a pleasant attitude regarding this time is created.
3. Assisting the child with material that is difficult in either word pronunciation or sentence and paragraph meaning. One of the parents should always be available to help the student but must not "breathe down the child's neck." The parent (while reading something of personal interest) simply may be in the same room and available to the child, if needed.
4. Assisting the child with follow-up exercises that are sent home after a remedial session. The parent must understand that the child is learning a skill and will probably not be perfect in these attempts. Neither the classroom teacher nor the reading specialist will send material home for practice unless there is relative assurance that it can be completed with some satisfaction. However, instances will arise when, regardless of the care taken, the child will take home materials that are too difficult to read without assistance.
5. Being available when the child needs an audience or when a discussion is desired following either oral or silent reading. Parents should display interest in what the child has read, thus permitting a sense of having done something that pleases the parents.
6. Providing the praise and reward for demonstrations of skill development. Since the materials sent home for practice should allow the child to demonstrate reading strengths, positive reactions from parents can do much to help the child feel good about being a reader.

These activities should be conducted in cooperation with the reading specialist or the classroom teacher; specific activities should be developed by these educators in terms of the goals that already have been explained to the parent.

Furthermore, teachers should demonstrate these techniques to parents. Illustrating how effectively the recommended suggestions actually work with their child builds the parents' confidence in the recommendations.

Parents should understand what *not* to do as well as what to do. Depending on the educational goals, the educator should anticipate the types of problems likely to arise and direct the parents away from them. One way in which the educator can avoid a potential problem is to assist parents in channeling their natural desire to help their child into constructive activities. If a parent feels his or her child has a great deficiency in phonics skills, for example, the educator should be informed and the parent provided with an explanation of when that skill will become a part of the program. Furthermore, it should be made clear that no matter how great the temptation to have the child "sound out" the word, it is the parents' job to tell the child unknown words until the sounding skill is approached remedially. These examples relate to phonics. Although it is in this area that most parents feel most anxious, it is the area in which they generally do the poorest job of assisting educators. As a general rule, therefore, parental attention should be directed away from instruction in phonics, while opportunities are provided for the parents to notice their child's development in reading through carefully prepared home assignments. Once again, children demonstrate their strengths to parents through such activities as reading orally an experience story that they have mastered, drilling for five minutes on the word cards they have mastered, and discussing exciting problem-solving activities that they worked on in school.

Another parental role in remediation is obtaining books for the children to read. Normally, the educator will supply the first books from materials available in the remedial program; however, since the supply of books is often limited, parents can be encouraged to assume responsibility for obtaining books. The educator, in this case, will supply the parent with a list of appropriate books for the child to read at home, asking the parent to obtain these books from libraries, friends, bookstores, and the like. Consideration for the level and the interest factors of available books should be evaluated in the recommendations made to parents. Teachers may want to recommend books to parents near the child's birthday or at holidays so that books can be included on gift lists. More than simply supplying the child with a book, such activity develops the attitude that a book is something of considerable worth because it is given as a special gift. Parents should also assume the responsibility for taking their children to the library on a regular basis, where children experience book self-selection and develop the library habit.

Parents commonly want to supplement the efforts of the remedial program with commercially available materials. Unless these materials are in accordance with the educational goals that have been established and unless the educator knows of the materials and can recommend their appropriateness for this child, they should be avoided. By placing parents in the teacher's role, unsuitable commercial materials may involve the parents to a degree that is unprofitable for them, the child, and the educational goals for which they all are striving.

Parents can become involved in two more ways. First, seminars that are designed to help parents understand the nature of their children's reading difficulties and to help them understand the approach in remediation can be conducted. These seminars often include the involvement of public school personnel such as principals, reading specialists, and supervisors so that parents can obtain answers to their concerns about all areas of their child's schooling. The seminars can reduce a lot of unnecessary anxiety.

Further, parents can become instructional material constructors. Many parents bring their children to the reading clinic and wait for them instead of going home and coming back. Teachers can ask them if they would like to help. Clinicians can leave plans and materials for the construction of games, centers, or posters, and the parents can develop the materials. The parents can personally deliver the materials to the clinician and stay to observe them in use. This process will increase parental understanding of the remedial program.

While parents need to know their role in helping to correct their children's reading difficulties, it is even more desirable for them to know what they can do to head off reading difficulties before they have a chance to develop. Next to the classroom teacher, parents can do more to prevent the development of difficulties than anyone else. Sometimes teachers will face parents who are not

Next to the classroom teacher, parents can do more to prevent difficulties from arising than anyone else.

anxious about their children's lack of success in reading. When unconcerned, parents are less likely to seek assistance even if it becomes necessary, thus implying to the children that they do not care. Each school and each teacher should take every opportunity to present preventive information to parents. Programs during Education Week, PTA meetings, individual conferences with parents, and notes sent to the home may be used to help parents prevent the occurrence of reading difficulties.

The following suggestions are designed to inform parents of activities that diminish the possibility that their child will develop poor reading habits and skills. They should be recommended by educators only when appropriate. No attempt is made here to supply a formula that will work with equal effectiveness with all parents.

PHYSICAL CARE. Parents who desire to avoid the complications involved with failure in school (in reading, particularly) should examine their children's physical needs. A visual examination prior to entering school and every other year thereafter is excellent insurance of proper vision. An annual physical examination with follow-ups that are recommended by the family doctor eliminates the necessity of waiting until symptoms of physical disability become so apparent that they interfere with school success. Many physical difficulties go unnoticed until failure in school is so acute that remedial programs are inadequate to handle them. For example, if children have refused to read for years because of visual discomfort, they have a void of reading experiences for which, at times, it is impossible to compensate.

A quick look around any classroom makes it apparent that many children come to school without proper rest. Since most teachers consider the first period of the morning the most effective instructional time, children need to be awake and alert. Parents who need suggestions concerning the amount of sleep their children require should consult the family doctor.

Along with adequate rest, children need a substantial breakfast. Children who go without breakfast, fighting hunger long before lunchtime, are incapable of efficient use of school time. Recommendations for minimum breakfast requirements are readily available; however, when in doubt, parents should consult the family doctor. If parents send children who are physically sound to school, they have a greater chance to succeed.

EMOTIONAL CLIMATE. Children who are secure, loved at home, and understood will experience little interference with school success. Parents can implant an attitude that learning will be fun and, though difficult at times, always worthwhile. They can develop such an attitude by incorporating (1) no threats for failures in school (e.g., withdrawing television privileges); (2) no promises for success in school (e.g., paying for good grades); (3) respect and confidence in the teachers; and (4) interest and enthusiasm for what is being accomplished in school. Parents should avoid criticizing the school and its teachers in front of their children. As parents, they have a right to voice their objections, but they should do so to the school authorities and teachers rather than to the children. When children have the attitude that the school is weak and the teachers are incompetent, learning difficulties are compounded. Furthermore, parents can be directed to avoid as much as possible directly or subtly comparing their children to peers and siblings. The reaction of a child who is striving to do as well as another student is seldom positive or desirable. More concern should be demonstrated over each child's ability to perform as well as possible; performance that matches a sibling's should not be the goal adopted to satisfy parents.

SETTING AN EXAMPLE. All parents usually strive to set a good example for their children. In reading, that example can be one of reading for enjoyment. Children who from their earliest years notice that both parents seem to enjoy spending portions of their leisure time reading can develop a favorable attitude toward reading before entering school. Some leisure reading may be done orally for the children or for the family. All oral reading should be accomplished with as much skill as possible; therefore, parents should first read silently all materials that they plan to read orally. Often parents are inclined to discontinue oral reading as soon as their children develop skills in reading; however, oral reading by parents should continue. Parents should take every opportunity to read to children the books that are of interest to the children but that are too difficult for their present reading skills. Children who come to school with family leisure reading experiences have definite advantages in learning to read because they realize the wonders that reading can unlock for them.

Some parents have found success with a daily silent reading time. All family members read for ten to twenty minutes. They read materials of their choice for their own enjoyment. Such sessions provide additional models of reading for fun.

PROVIDING LANGUAGE EXPERIENCES. Parents are to be encouraged to use every opportunity to widen their children's language experiences. Through such activities as reading to children, taking them on trips, and discussing events with them, situations are created in which language can be developed through experiences. Parents should be encouraged to lead children into discussions that will add listening and speaking vocabulary words to the experiences. It is, of course, the listening and speaking vocabularies upon which the reading vocabularies hinge. Parents miss opportunities to help their children by failing to discuss trips and experiences with them. Trips about which little is said are not necessarily useless, but all parents should be encouraged to reinforce experiences with language experiences relating to them. For example, during a trip, parents can let children help read maps, menus, and road signs; they can take photographs and discuss them later; and they can help children write captions to be placed on the backs of photographs. Alerted to the potential of structuring language experiences, parents can learn to use them more effectively.

REGULATING OUT-OF-SCHOOL ACTIVITIES. Parents who permit their children to do as they wish with all out-of-school time indicate their lack of concern for their children's well-being. First, parents must understand that a full school day takes a good bit of concentration and is mentally fatiguing. Therefore, children should be exposed to opportunities after school for active, expressive free play. Outdoor play, which physically releases children, is desirable when possible. Second, the school program relies on the interest and excitement that can be developed by the teacher and the materials from which the children are learning. Therefore, unusually large amounts of television viewing may interfere with the school program. After five hours of murder, passionate love, dancing girls, and comedies, children are not likely to fully appreciate a program that features the elementary school band or a story in the first-grade reader that must be geared to a limited reading vocabulary. Although no formula is prescribed, teachers might suggest limiting children to an hour of television viewing an evening. Of course, parents cannot expect children to sit in the living room and not watch the shows that the parents are watching. This suggestion, then, implies that television viewing for the family should be restricted, especially during school days. Parents should also be encouraged to understand the need for children to accomplish home assignments and have some quiet time. Quiet time, of necessity, involves the entire family.

FOLLOWING ADVICE. Parents must be encouraged to follow the suggestions of school personnel in matters concerning the education of their children. The greatest difficulty in this respect is when parents consider the age at which children should enter first grade and the decision to have students remain another year in a given grade. Each school system has its own method for determining whether children are ready to profit from first-grade instruction. When, after careful consideration, the school advises parents to withhold a child from first grade for one year, parents should carefully review the reasons behind such a recommendation and abide by the school's decision unless they have some compelling evidence that the school is in error. Parents should remember that educators have the best interests of students in mind, too, and that the school often has a more objective perspective of the child's level of skills and maturity. Confrontations between parents and the school often create needless student anxiety and result in some students being placed in school programs for which they are not ready. Scores of children with reading difficulties are victims of early entrance against school advice.

School advice in connection with the retention of children generally receives parental concern that is passed directly to the children. Educators not only want the parents to comply with this advice but to embrace it with enthusiasm so that children feel they have not let their parents down. Unfortunately, in our pass-or-fail system, other children create a negative connotation of retention that will, unwittingly, create some disturbance within the children. Retention need not be compounded in the home by parental anxiety. To start with, parents can refer to retentions as "repeating a year" instead of "failing a year." Perhaps the time is near when retention in school will not be marked by failure to be promoted at the end of the year. All children should be on a program of continuous progress, making it realistically impossible for each retention to occur. Continuous progress involves an educational program in which each learner starts each year in terms of the points that instruction ended the preceding year. In the final analysis, it is the present system, not children, that creates retentions. Many schools have instituted continuous progress programs, much to the satisfaction of parents, children, and teachers.

REINFORCING LEARNED SKILLS. As discussed under "Parental Roles in Remediation," skills learned in school can be reinforced by understanding parents in the home. Home reading situations should always end pleasantly with children feeling satisfied. Parents who cannot control their anxieties and tempers should avoid working with their children at home. When children read orally to anxious parents, difficulty frequently arises regardless of the care teachers have taken to make sure that the children can read the books that have been sent home.

In practical terms, when children come to unknown words, parents should tell the children the words. If they miss them again, they should be told again and again. Words missed with regularity should be noted and sent to the teacher for analysis of the type of error and the necessary instruction. However, parents are seldom satisfied with this limited role; thus, the following course of action is suggested. When children miss words time after time, the parent should print the words carefully on cards. When the reading is finished and the story has been discussed, a few minutes can be spent glancing over these cards. As the words are pronounced, the children should be asked to use them in sentences, which should be written on the back of the cards with the target words underlined. Preceding the next reading session at home, a little game-like drill can take place in which the children read the sentences and the unknown words.

Obviously, numerous attempts at parental cooperation go astray, creating more harm than good. Educators must be alert to these pitfalls and, when signs of their appearance occur, use alternate approaches to parental participation.

Pitfalls in Parental Cooperation

LACK OF CONTACT. Perhaps the worst pitfall teachers make is not contacting parents. Since parents will assume roles, they will best be taken in terms of the school's program. Parental contacts should be periodic, calling for follow-up sessions to reinforce parental behavior. All too often, one parental conference is considered sufficient to meet the need for parental involvement. However, this is untrue. In a six-week summer program, for example, three formal parental conferences and numerous informal conferences are needed to assist parents in becoming effective helpers.

UNDERESTIMATING PARENTAL LOVE. Even those parents who appear to be unconcerned love their children. However, parental love easily can be misdirected. For example, some parents criticize the school in attempts to make their children feel more comfortable. When schools ignore parental love, this can result in a lack of cooperation between parents and educators. As has been suggested, sending the children home with activities that will permit them to demonstrate their strengths to the parents gives parents opportunities to demonstrate their love for their children with positive reinforcement.

NEEDLESS ANXIETY. Many parents confront educators with considerable anxiety. They are afraid, frustrated, and upset. To make such parents useful partners, educators need to work with them to overcome these feelings of anxiety; overanxious parents find it extremely difficult to work with their own children in any activity. When conversing with parents, the educator should listen to what they have to say—really listen and postpone judgments. Extra care should be taken to make activities for such parents as positive as possible. As parents start to relax and gain confidence in the school's program, they can become more helpful partners.

ONE PARENT. Educators often are forced to settle for the reactions and opinions of only one of the child's parents. Teachers must avoid this pitfall, for children act to please both parents. Therefore, every opportunity should be made to involve both parents, even if a home visit is required to attain this end. Often after talking with the other parent, teachers have reversed their opinions of the home and the learning climate. Due to the large number of single-parent homes, involving both parents in school programs may be impossible. Teachers should be alert to these situations to avoid causing embarrassment to one-parent families.

FAILURE TO FOLLOW UP. When a remedial program is finished, the parents deserve a summary of the results. Unless parents receive a final report, they may continue with remedial activities that are no longer appropriate. The summary, therefore, should include specific recommendations for future parental roles concerning the children's changing needs.

ASSUMING THE TEACHER'S ROLE. Sending workbooks home so that parents are placed in a teacher's role is seldom useful and often harmful. Educators must clearly see the difference between the parents' role as reinforcer of learned skills and the educator's job of developing new skills. Workbook activities provide too many teaching situations for most parents to handle well. However, if children have worked in a skill activity successfully in school, allowing them to demonstrate that success to their parents should be encouraged.

OVERREACTION TO INFORMATION IN THE PRESS. Newspapers and magazines often carry articles about some aspect of reading: "Scores are down"; "Be sure your school is using this approach"; "Your child's diet can affect learning." These and other such topics build anxiety. Teachers should help parents obtain as much information as possible before reacting to such articles. The information in the article may be true but inapplicable to a certain school or to their child. The information in the article may be a distortion that needs clarification. And, at times, the information may be inaccurate, requiring that correct information be supplied.

TRAINING FOR PARENTS. Today's parents likely will have training sessions available to them. These sessions are usually designed to inform parents about reading and offer suggestions on how they can help their children at home.

Many administrators are inviting parents to teacher in-service sessions. Those administrators feel that parents should know what training teachers are getting and what innovations are being suggested. By informing them in this manner, educators avoid misinterpretations.

Some reading clinics offer classes for parents of children who are attending the clinic. They inform the parents about their objectives, their procedures, and the anticipated outcomes of the clinic experience. They talk about how reading difficulties get started and how they can be corrected. They offer strategies for parents to use when they need to contact school personnel about their children and offer ideas that parents can use at home. Attendance at such classes is excellent, and responses are enthusiastic.

Parents serve as aides and volunteers in many schools. As such, they get two types of training. They attend workshops and seminars designed to instruct them in their role in the school, and they get on-the-job training from the teacher with whom they are working. Frequently, parents are enrolled in graduate classes, not working for a degree, but simply becoming better informed.

Many colleges now offer courses designed for parents who are interested in helping their children. Parents are interested in knowing about the reading process, about how reading is taught in school, and about how they can help at home. In almost every instance parents state that they have been working with their children and that they intend to continue to do so. An educator's best action is to provide parents with enough information so that what they do at home can be as helpful as possible.

Summary

Educators must evaluate the student's home situation and make specific recommendations as to which roles are most appropriate for parents to enable them and educators to work as a team. All parental roles should be in keeping with the educational goals that the remedial program is attempting to accomplish. When parents are not actively involved, needless limitations are placed on the educator's effectiveness. Assuming that most parents are going to help their children with reading, educators must direct their efforts toward the most useful purposes.

Notes

1. Robert M. Wilson and Donald W. Pfau, "Parents Can Help!" *The Reading Teacher* 21, no. 8 (May 1968): 758-61.

Suggested Readings

Burmeister, Lou E. *Foundations and Strategies for Teaching Children to Read*. Reading, Mass.: Addison-Wesley Publishing Company, 1983. Chapter 5 focuses on ways in which the community, the school, and individual teachers can get parents involved in developing the reading abilities of their children. Included are examples of activities, letters, and fliers that have met with success in promoting parental involvement.

Gambrell, Linda B., and Robert M. Wilson. *Twenty-eight Ways to Help Your Child Be a Better Reader.* Paoli. Pa.: Instructo/McGraw-Hill Book Co., 1980. Practical suggestions are offered to parents so that they can work with their children. Suggestions take little time and do not interfere with school curricular activities.

Landau, Elliott D. *Creative Parent-Teacher Conferences.* Salt Lake City, Utah: E. D. Landau, 1968. This work presents guidelines for various types of conferences with which educators are confronted. It offers specific suggestions to make conferences effective.

Oliastro, Louis A. *Parents Teach Your Child to Read.* Uniontown, Pa.: LIZ Publications, 1979. This seven-page booklet provides information for parents about how to use photographs of their children's experiences as a basis for language development. As the children talk about the pictures, the parents record the story. These personal stories with pictures are then used for reading instruction.

_____. *The Reading Teacher* 23, no. 8 (May 1970). Through twelve articles featuring the role of parents in reading activities, this entire issue of *The Reading Teacher* focuses on parental roles in reading education.

_____. *The Reading Teacher* 33, no. 8 (November 1980). Three articles by Joan Raim, Nicholas Criscuolo, and Anne Auten, provide interesting ideas about involving parents in school reading programs.

Trelease, Jim. *The Read-Aloud Handbook.* New York: Penguin Books, 1985. The author urges parents to encourage the reading development of their children by reading aloud to them on a regular basis. Suggestions are given for effective reading aloud and an annotated bibliography of more than 300 titles offers a wealth of excellent read aloud books.

Wilson, Robert M., and Donald W. Pfau. "Parents Can Help!" *The Reading Teacher* 21, no. 8 (May 1968): 758–61. This article summarizes a study in which parents were asked how they helped their children at home. Children were grouped as below-average readers and above-average readers. Those children receiving most parental assistance at home were the below-average readers.

EDITORIAL

Leanne Stephen

is Chapter 1 Reading Supervisor in the Northeast Bradford School District, Rome, Pennsylvania.

Learning to read is one of the most important skills a child must accomplish. It is important that parents take an interest in and support their children on whatever level they are reading. They must encourage them to do their best so that growth and development in reading will be built upon successful experiences.

In our elementary school, we feel that active parental participation in the child's education is fundamental to student achievement. When parents are involved in their child's education, studies have shown that the learning process is improved. As the child and parent work together, the child develops a positive self-image and is then free to confidently develop his or her abilities and interests to their fullest capacities.

Parents often ask, "What can I do to help my child learn to read?" In response to this query, our school actively and continually promotes activities to encourage parental involvement. Parents play a critical role in their child's reading skills development, and this necessitates that we must provide parents with programs and activities that will supply them with the tools to be effective partners in the learning process.

This past year, through our Chapter 1 program, we became involved with such a program, which is structured, individualized, nongraded, and supplemental to the child's Chapter 1 school reading program, and is designed for parents of elementary students in grades two through six. The program is designed to increase Chapter 1 parents' understanding of the reading process and to promote a cooperative learning partnership between parent and child. Parents are presented with specific strategies and materials to reinforce and strengthen their child's word recognition and comprehension skills. These skills are developed through the use of letter tiles (which helps children focus on details in a word and develop a visual memory of the word), through questioning, looking for detail in pictures, and reciprocal questioning about material read. These are specific strategies that can be used in the home to reinforce the child's reading progress.

Groups of fifteen parents and children meet for six one- and one-half-hour sessions with a reading specialist. During the first half-hour of each session, the reading specialist introduces and models one reading strategy to the parents. This reading strategy will be used for the week. While the reading specialist works with the parents, the children are working with teachers who introduce them to the same strategy. The second half-hour, the parents practice this strategy with their child under the supervision and direction of the reading specialist and teachers. In the final half-hour of the session, the reading specialist answers questions from the parents and provides follow-up suggestions for the parents to use with their children, while the children once again work with the teachers. The parent and child then practice this strategy at home during the week.

This program is evaluated by informal student surveys administered before and after the program. The surveys are given to all Chapter 1 students whose parents participated in the program, as well as to a random sample of Chapter 1 students whose parents did not participate in the program and who meet the criteria requirements of a one-to-one match of grade level. Also administered during the final session of the program is a parent evaluation form that covers items such as the parents' assessment of their ability to work with their child and parents' increased understanding of the reading process. Parents may also add any comments they may wish to make about the program.

The success of the program is evidenced through such parent comments as "The program works very well for a child that needs to build self-confidence" and "When I work with this program, my child and I share quality time."

This is an excellent program that provides parents with the tools to be effective partners in the learning process. By working together with parents, we are providing children with the support that will nurture their very best efforts in school.

Leanne Stephen

Professional Roles

CHAPTER OUTLINE

Professional Responsibilities
The Reading Specialist in the School
    Program
The Classroom Teacher in the School
    Program
Out-of-School Programs
Accountability
Legal Responsibilities
Be a Reader

CHAPTER EMPHASES

*The classroom teacher and reading
    specialist should work together to
    decide a student's reading
    placement.*
*Reading specialists should plan their
    schedules to be able to work with
    all types of students.*
*Teachers must know the legal
    ramifications of their actions.*
*Teachers should model desirable
    reading habits to influence
    students.*

Public concern over school reading programs continues to grow. Newspapers, magazines, radio, and television focus public attention on the strengths and weaknesses of reading programs. Professional concern about reading is reflected in the large number of reading journals being published and in the extensive amount of reading research published each year. Public and professional concern has resulted in pressures on school systems to produce better readers and to supply more reading support programs. Unfortunately, such pressures occasionally create more problems than they solve. Hastily developed programs may emerge, inappropriate materials may be incorporated, personnel with questionable qualifications may be hired, and too many duties may be placed on personnel already employed. Therefore, consideration of professional responsibilities and roles may help both the teachers and the administrators who are planning reading programs.

Professional Responsibilities

"Am I qualified to help students having difficulties with reading?" "How will I be able to start a program in my classroom?" "To whom should I look for help?" These are questions educators ask when they realize that many students with reading difficulties could be helped by establishing special reading services. Prior to implementing programs, however, teachers must understand their professional responsibilities in establishing remedial programs.

The Student

Regardless of the type of program or the competency of the person conducting it, consideration first must be given to the student who is to benefit from the program. Educators are professionally responsible for directing students toward those programs that seem to be best designed for their needs. Referral need not reflect negatively on educators if they decide that they cannot assist the student as well as another can; rather, this action credits them. Clearly, many educators feel threatened when they become aware that they cannot help certain students. To call for outside help may seem to indicate a lack of competency. However, the diagnosis and correction of many reading difficulties cannot possibly be handled by any one person. Consequently, to call for assistance when it is needed is a sign of professional maturity.

Cooperation

As mentioned in previous chapters, diagnosis and remediation are programs that cannot be conducted without full cooperation from all persons involved with the student. Programs that are conducted in isolation limit the ability to offer the student a complete program. Therefore, programs should not be instituted without thorough communication with the student's parents, classroom teacher, and other resource personnel.

Referral

When possible, all referrals—medical, psychological, and psychiatric—should be made prior to remediation and formation of program procedures. It is inefficient to start a remedial program without consultation when a student demonstrates symptoms of difficulties in these areas. All conclusions should be considered tentative until verified by appropriate professional assessment. Even then the final effectiveness of a diagnosis is only confirmed during instruction. The educator does not refrain from working with these students; however, the full efficiency of remedial programs normally will not be realized without referral reports.

When considering the role of the reading specialist, the school screening committee becomes important. As discussed previously, the screening committee consists of teachers, administrators, specialists, and sometimes parents or students. The committee works to bring the most appropriate school resources to assist the teacher with students who are experiencing difficulty with their learning activities.

Qualification

In an attempt to avoid confusion, the term *reading specialist* has been used throughout this book to describe any reading professional who is not currently teaching within the regular classroom and who has responsibility for the developmental or remedial reading program within a school. There exists, nevertheless, considerable confusion within the field regarding the terms used to designate reading professionals. The terms *reading specialist, reading consultant, reading supervisor, reading teacher,* and *reading tutor* appear to be defined differently within various states and school districts. Nowhere does this confusion appear to be greater than in the case of the *reading specialist.* A study undertaken by the Evaluation Committee of the International Reading Association reveals that the term *reading specialist* appears to have become both a generic and a specific term. In some cases, reading professionals are designated as *reading specialists* after completing a certificate program which bears that name. In other cases, teachers refer to themselves as reading specialists due to the nature of the job that they hold in the schools.[1] It is the professional responsibility of the school administration to assure that reading specialists who are engaged in remedial and resource roles within their schools have the necessary training and state certification to do their jobs properly.

Code of Ethics

When remediation is conducted outside the classroom, the educator is professionally responsible for avoiding casting unwarranted reflections of inadequacy on the school program, particularly to parents. However, if the school program is suspect, the educator is professionally obligated to consult appropriate school personnel in an effort to remedy the deficiency. (See the Code of Ethics approved by the International Reading Association in appendix E of this book.)

Guarantees

An educator can seldom guarantee specific outcomes of specialized reading services. Many variables may influence a student's performance in reading. To offer guarantees to parents or school officials is clearly unethical. What can be offered, however, are the best services of the personnel who willingly perform carefully conducted evaluations.

The Reading Specialist in the School Program

Program Suggestions

The following suggestions are designed to assist reading specialists assume the role that will best suit the needs of the schools for which they are responsible and the students within those schools. A reading specialist may assume responsibility for more than one of these program suggestions, for they are frequently related.

DIAGNOSIS. As discussed in chapters 2, 5, and 6, clinical diagnosis is a major responsibility of most reading specialists. The reading specialist conducts the diagnosis and prepares the recommendations with directions for remediation. Many reading specialists feel that they can be very useful to the classroom teacher through diagnostic services, because classroom teachers often lack the specialized knowledge and skills required in clinical diagnosis.

REMEDIATION. Often the job responsibility of reading specialists involves working instructionally with students. The following strategies have been used effectively in working with students.

1. Some reading specialists find working with students in the classroom to be advantageous. The classroom teacher works with some students and the reading specialist with others. Communication problems are diminished as both the teacher and the specialist have opportunities to learn from one another. By working in the classroom, the reading specialist has the opportunity to work with all types of readers. Such a strategy can also be a means for training a classroom teacher to use a new technique.

For example, one principal places the reading specialist in first grade for an hour every morning. The specialist works with students, referred by the classroom teacher, using the signing technique with students having difficulty developing sight vocabulary. Working one to one, the reading specialist reinforces the words the students select to learn from their language-experience stories.

2. Other reading specialists prefer to work with the students outside of their regular classrooms. They establish a learning environment that is different from that to which the students are accustomed. Distractions are lessened, and students feel honored by such attention. This strategy usually calls for the reading specialist to work with small groups of students who have similar strengths and needs. One reading specialist has set up a rich learning environment and accepts students referred by classroom teachers on a contract basis. The students may come one day for a little reinforcement, or they may come on a regular basis.

3. In order to serve as many students as possible, some reading specialists establish miniclinics.[2] A small group of students comes for a short time period to develop a specific skill. For example, a teacher may have seven third graders who are having difficulty locating information. A miniclinic can be set up for two weeks, one hour a day, for these third graders. At the end of the clinic, the students are evaluated; the evaluations are shared with the teacher; and a new miniclinic can be developed for other students with different needs.

Most reading specialists will find it useful to use some combination of these three strategies with students in remedial situations. One reading specialist works during the morning with students who have been identified as having serious difficulties with reading, while afternoons are composed of the following activities:

1. She conducts miniclinics. All types of readers attend these various miniclinics, including some gifted and talented students.
2. She conducts diagnosis when it is needed.
3. She meets with each team in the school during its planning time at least once a week.
4. She schedules time when she will be available to work in classrooms with teachers. At times she works with students and at other times she works with the teachers.

This type of scheduling allows maximum use of various skills. It also keeps the reading specialist from getting bogged down with one type of activity all day long. All students view the reading specialist as a helpful person in the school, not just those who are experiencing difficulty with reading.

PLANNING. Planning with teachers so that students' educational programs are coordinated can be an important part of the reading specialist's responsibilities. In schools where teachers work and plan in teams, the reading specialist should make efforts to be a part of every planning session. If a unit on space is being planned, then that unit can be incorporated into the instruction being conducted by the reading specialist. The reading specialist may also take the initiative of coordinating the schoolwide reading program.

CLINIC DIRECTOR. In larger school districts, a particularly skilled reading specialist may direct a reading clinic in an attempt to serve severely handicapped readers. Clinics usually are established in buildings to which the students can be brought for help. As director of the clinic, the reading specialist may assume all of the roles discussed in this chapter, as well as the administrative functions of the clinic, supervision of staff, and the communication between clinic and classroom.

IN-SERVICE EDUCATION. Occasionally, the reading specialist will find it worthwhile to conduct in-service programs with classroom teachers. Through demonstration, discussion, and consultation with authorities, teachers gain insights into effective methods of working with readers experiencing difficulties. In these situations, the specialist's responsibility is to inform teachers who have a common lack of understanding in certain areas. Reading specialists do not need to view in-service programs as formal, day-long training sessions. In addition, although releasing teachers from classroom time for in-service programs is desirable, it is not always necessary.

Reading specialists can form many successful strategies involving small amounts of time. They can prepare informational notes on recent developments

Teachers and reading specialists should coordinate educational programs for students.

in reading and pass them on to teachers. Any teacher interested in more details can contact the reading specialist. For example, the reading specialist reads an article on wait time and shares the idea in a note to the staff, or the specialist receives some new information about oral reading diagnosis and shares it with the staff. At times, one relatively modest idea has a better chance of being implemented than do ideas that require major changes and considerable training of the teachers.

Some reading specialists have developed fifteen-minute modules for inservice programs. These modules deal with a single concept and include handouts, transparencies, and materials for implementation. The specialist announces which modules are available, and interested teachers sign up for the modules of their choice. At a designated time, the teachers meet and the module is presented. Discussion follows, and the teachers decide whether they want to try the new idea. They also may decide they would like to try it but would need some help from the reading specialist during the initiation of the idea. Examples of some of these short modules are:

1. Helping teachers develop maze tests from one of their books.
2. Showing teachers a way to develop note-taking skills with their students.
3. Discussion of the meaning of test results from a diagnostic session.
4. Sharing a new material that has come to the school.
5. Discussion of a position taken by a reading authority in a recent article.

At times enough interest is generated in one of these short sessions that teachers ask for more information on that topic.

RESOURCES FOR CLASSROOM TEACHERS. Many reading specialists find their training best suits them to serve as resource people to the classroom teacher. Instead of working with students outside the classroom in diagnostic and remedial activities, resource teachers can aid the classroom teachers in various ways:

- *By helping with diagnosis.* Test administration, scoring, and interpretation can be conducted as a team, thus permitting the classroom teacher to learn diagnostic skills.
- *By helping in the classroom with students who are experiencing difficulty.* Planning and team teaching special lessons as well as offering continued support to help the teacher better handle students with reading difficulties allows for teacher development as well as providing service to students.
- *By obtaining materials for the teacher.* Instead of keeping reading materials in a reading room, the reading specialist can bring needed materials to classroom teachers and help them use them effectively. The resource specialist may obtain materials that the

teacher requests and may recommend new materials for certain situations. Resource specialists can also suggest professional materials such as books, pamphlets, and articles.

- *By planning with the teacher to develop effective instructional goals.* The classroom teacher, using the knowledge and skills of the reading specialist, can develop better plans for instruction.
- *By evaluating program effectiveness.* By applying research and evaluation skills, the resource specialist can assist classroom teachers in looking objectively at their reading programs, modifying portions of the programs that appear to be weak, and assisting them in emphasizing portions of the programs that appear to be strong.
- *By interpreting for teachers the reading research that may have application for the classroom.* As a result of their own reading, attendance at conferences, formal course work, and discussions with their colleagues, resource specialists should stay alert to the most recent trends, research, methods, and materials in reading remediation.

Generally, resource personnel should be assigned duties that will allow them freedom to work effectively with teachers. They should not be assigned to evaluate teachers. They should not set policies that teachers must follow, nor should they force themselves into situations where the teachers do not want their assistance.

SUMMER SCHOOL. An increasingly large number of schools are establishing summer programs for students who have not made adequate progress during the school year. Reading specialists often will be responsible for such programs, with particular emphasis being placed on screening and selecting students who are to be assisted. In addition, they may be responsible for selecting teachers who will be involved. The financing of these programs, while normally assumed by the school, may to a small extent be supplemented by a nominal fee paid by the parents. Such a fee stimulates a more serious attitude toward the work required in the program. Summer programs may make it possible for students to remain in the classroom during the year, thereby providing them the fullest opportunity to benefit from the classroom program. Of course, students with serious reading deficits cannot always profit from summer programs alone. To avoid the stigma of failure that is often attached to such programs, summer facilities can be developed for good readers as well. All types of readers can then be involved, making it no disgrace to attend a summer reading program.

PUBLIC RELATIONS. Public relations duties, which include PTA meetings, conferences with parents, and home visits, may fall to the reading specialist. At such meetings, the school's reading program can be explained, questions answered, and misinterpretations corrected. The reading specialist can take advantage of the suggestions mentioned in chapter 14 when provided with opportunities to meet the public.

399

Professional Roles

SUPERVISING TUTORING. Many schools conduct tutoring programs to facilitate the learning of certain children. Tutors can be volunteers from the community, older students, teacher aides, and peers. To be effective, these programs need careful organization and supervision. These tasks often fall to the reading specialist since much of the tutoring is done in the area of reading.

A tutor handbook has been developed to help teachers plan, organize, and implement a tutoring program (see the suggested readings at the end of this chapter). It includes suggested instructional activities which are appropriate for tutors.

TRAINING PARAPROFESSIONALS. As paraprofessionals become more available for reading assistance, the job of training those persons will fall on reading specialists. The better paraprofessionals are trained, the more useful they will be. A model program for such training has been developed in Prince Georges County, Maryland. Hundreds of paraprofessionals are trained and supervised by reading specialists as they work with classroom teachers to help individual students.

All schools are being encouraged to consider the maximum use of such personnel to assist overburdened teachers. Reading specialists will need to consider the many duties that paraprofessionals can perform and develop training programs to make their work as effective as possible.

Pitfalls for Reading Specialists

Programs developed by reading specialists are not without potential difficulties, especially for those with little experience. Certain pitfalls can be encountered in establishing reading programs. Anticipating these before beginning such a program may relieve reading specialists of frustrating situations that can ultimately cause considerable difficulty.

OVERLOADING. Reading specialists often assume responsibilities that overload them to a point of ineffectiveness. First, they should not be expected to assume all the roles that have been suggested in this chapter; rather, they should start where they can be most effective and slowly expand as they see opportunities. Second, in the diagnostic and remedial role, they cannot be expected to carry the same student load as a classroom teacher. The very nature of the clinical situation precludes large groups. When overloaded, the reading specialists' effectiveness will be limited unnecessarily.

INADEQUATE HOUSING. Teacher's rooms, damp basements, and even worse locations have been relegated to the reading specialist to conduct diagnostic and remedial programs. Assuming that a program is worthwhile, the school administrator must make provisions for a well-lighted, comfortable, nondistracting environment for the students and the teacher. To be most effective, housing considerations should be built into the basic plans for the program's development.

SCREENING. Final responsibility for determining which students can be helped most effectively must be left to the reading specialist. Without diagnosis, a given classroom teacher is likely to select the least intellectually able student for remedial attention, when intellectual ability alone is not a sufficient criterion for program enrollment. Reading specialists should provide for the screening of all referred students yet retain the right to reject any student who they feel cannot profit effectively from the established program. They will have to reject temporarily those students who add to the tutoring load, creating class sizes that cannot be taught effectively. Interschool relations may be strained unless clear-cut procedures are established concerning the final responsibilities for identifying students to be accepted in the reading specialist's programs.

One such procedure involves the screening committee that contains all of the resource personnel available in the school, as well as the principal. The reading specialist makes recommendations regarding reading placements to the committee. Others provide their input and a decision is made.

THE IMAGE. Specific efforts should be made to avoid the reading specialist's image as the educator who works with failures. As previously suggested, reading specialists should work in the classroom, participating in all types of programs for readers. Such adjustment will help the students assigned to them relax their anxiety about their abilities. It will also prevent specialists from getting a distorted opinion of the school's reading program. (This occurs easily when one works hour after hour, day after day, with only the shortcomings that a given system has produced.) Working with teachers in the classroom also aids reading specialists in maintaining perspective, especially concerning the difficulties teachers may have working with specific students in large groups.

Another aspect of image is related to the way teachers view reading specialists. Reading specialists should be treated as part of the teaching staff, assuming their share of teacher special chores such as bus duty or playground duty. They should attend all teachers' meetings and, in general, do what teachers do. If the image is developed that the reading specialist gets special treatment, rapport with the teaching staff will suffer.

DEMONSTRATIONS. Normally, demonstrations are requested when teachers are uncertain of how to use a new technique or material. Traditionally, the demonstrator replaces the teacher and thereby becomes ineffective. Demonstrations should be conducted with the classroom teacher as a participant. Specifically, the classroom teacher plans the lesson with the reading specialist; the classroom teacher teaches portions of the lesson; the classroom teacher remains in charge of the class; and the reading specialist assists in planning and executing the lesson. As soon as is practical after completing such lessons, the classroom teacher and the reading specialist should discuss what happened and how it can be applied to an everyday situation.

Using techniques such as these removes teachers from the passive, observing role and places them in an active, participating role. Teacher behavior is more likely to be modified with such an approach.

This procedure does not rule out the use of a demonstration when it is appropriate. For example, if a new material is provided and no one knows how to use it, it would be appropriate for the reading specialist to prepare a lesson for others to observe.

Program Participation

Classroom teachers participate in school programs with readers in several ways. An understanding of the possibilities may assist each teacher to serve most effectively.

CLASSROOM DIAGNOSIS. As teachers develop skill in the techniques of classroom diagnosis, they are likely to find themselves assigned to students who are in need of this service. The best teachers will perform this type of function as an ongoing part of their teaching program. The administrator should not overload teachers since excessive numbers of weak students obviously will hamper their efforts with all students assigned to them. Classroom teachers will provide additional input to screening committees when sharing the information from a classroom diagnosis.

CLASSROOM REMEDIATION. Teachers should work to develop successful readers using their remediation skills. The following strategies are useful for teachers working with readers experiencing difficulties in the classroom setting.

1. With flexible skills grouping, teachers can establish skills groups for specific purposes; when the purpose is accomplished, the group is disbanded and a new group is formed. If ten students need instruction on the use of initial consonant substitution, then a skill group is formed. As students gain the skill, they leave the group.
2. Using small bits of time when all other students are occupied, teachers can provide the reinforcement necessary for practice sessions to be successful. For example, such time can be used to review a lesson taught the day before or to go over the student's sight words.
3. Some administrators arrange for released time for teachers with skill in remediation. This time is set aside so that small group instruction can take place without distracting the entire class. The

benefit of such arrangements on student progress has been well worth the administrative inconvenience.

4. Some teachers find a few moments before and after school useful for that little bit of extra instruction and attention that makes so much difference to students.

5. Most of what has been discussed under remediation can be incorporated into the regular reading lessons being taught. For example, the regular lessons can focus on locational skills and strategies if students need practice locating information.

Classroom teachers will find combinations of these strategies effective in conducting classroom remediation.

TUTORING. Having developed skills in diagnosis and remediation through either in-service programs or formal course work, many teachers serve as tutors in school-established programs. The teachers' activities in these programs are usually supervised by the reading specialist and are directed toward the instruction of individuals or small groups.

DEMONSTRATION. When teachers are particularly skillful in either classroom diagnosis or remediation, other teachers should observe them. Observations may be made during afterschool programs or through released time. To foster positive feelings about their teaching competencies, teachers should be permitted to evaluate their own strengths and to offer their rooms for observations. Reading specialists can assist classroom teachers in identifying their strengths and urge them to offer their talents for the benefit of their colleagues.

PUBLIC RELATIONS. All teachers have the responsibility of interpreting the school's program to parents. Those who have studied the program more thoroughly may assist in events such as the PTA in order to illustrate the program's features clearly to parents. Parents may accept the classroom teacher in this role better than they do the reading specialist because they know that the classroom teacher works with their children each day.

Pitfalls for the Classroom Teacher

Like reading specialists, classroom teachers also must be alert to several pitfalls in their roles.

OVERLOADING. Teachers who are skilled in diagnosis and remediation may become overloaded with poor readers. Ultimately, overloading is detrimental to effectiveness with these children. Even when using free periods, short sessions before and after school, Saturdays, and summers, many good teachers need more time to do an efficient job. In addition, teachers must regulate their time so that relaxation and recreation are part of their daily schedule. Their major responsibility continues to lie with the whole class and the education of all students assigned to them. Thus, overloading should be avoided.

REPLACEMENT. Some teachers contend that they do not need to work with students in reading if the students are working with the reading specialist. This position is difficult to defend. The reading specialist should only supplement and reinforce what the classroom teacher does during regular instruction. The students who need extra help should be learning from both the classroom teacher and the reading specialist in a planned cooperative program.

SHORTCUTTING. Attempting to diagnose without using the suggestions in chapters 2, 3, 4 and 5 leads to inadequate classroom diagnosis. However, after limited experience, classroom teachers can start to modify and refine these suggestions to use in classrooms and to suit the needs of their students. After several diagnostic efforts, teachers will realize that their students are all proficient in some areas and that study in those areas is not essential in classroom diagnosis. However, this does not justify excluding major portions of classroom diagnosis.

COOPERATION. Regardless of negative feelings toward the total school reading program, all teachers should work as team members to help students. Gross distortions of the school program in an effort to satisfy personal philosophies of teaching reading must be avoided when they interfere with the overall school objectives. By cooperating and attempting to convince the school of the need for basic changes, teachers will better serve their students. Needless to say, discord within the school should remain within the school and not become a topic for community gossip.

CONTINUED STUDY. As changes occur in the field of reading, teachers must continue to study. Some find studying educational periodicals useful. Specific reference can be made to the journals of the International Reading Association,[3] the National Council of Teachers of English,[4] the College Reading Association,[5] and the National Reading Conference.[6] These organizations are striving to keep teachers informed of developments in the reading field. Other teachers prefer in-service workshops and institutes; still others prefer formal course work in the colleges and universities. Of course, most teachers seek a suitable combination of methods.

Many teachers lack important contemporary knowledge in the ever-changing field of children's literature. As stressed throughout this book, reading skills and reading attitudes go hand-in-hand. Teachers need to have current knowledge of children's books, yet, a study by Wendelin, Zinck, and Carter notes that many pre-service and in-service teachers are woefully outdated in their knowledge of current children's literature.[7] Teachers should establish a personal reading plan that will keep them informed of changing developments in this field.

Out-of-School Programs	Many educators take part in out-of-school programs designed to assist readers who are experiencing difficulties. Some find themselves teaching in these programs; others have parents asking them for their opinions of the programs; and still others find these programs to be interfering with the school's educational objectives. A brief look at the nature of some of these programs may assist the educator in making decisions concerning them.

Examples of Programs

TEACHER-EDUCATION CLINICS. Many teacher-education institutions operate reading clinics to educate teachers. Students who are brought into these clinics for assistance are generally diagnosed and tutored by teachers doing advanced work in the reading field. Normally, the costs for services in teacher-education clinics is small since the programs are not expected to pay for themselves. These programs' effectiveness generally relates to the effectiveness of the clinical supervision that the teachers receive and the prerequisites for entrance of college students into clinical courses.

Some teacher-education clinics limit themselves to diagnosis, while others include remediation. Although the thoroughness of each program varies, they generally follow the guidelines of clinical diagnosis and remediation presented in this text and can be considered reliable.

PRIVATELY OPERATED CLINICS. A variety of privately operated clinics are usually available in large population centers. Designed for financial profit, these clinics generally charge fees much higher than those charged at teacher-education clinics. The effectiveness of these clinics is clearly limited by the personnel and materials available for diagnosis and remediation. Referrals to this type of clinic should be made only after acquaintance with the personnel and the philosophy of the clinic. Private clinics should work with the schools. Unless cooperation is achieved, the effects of privately operated clinics are limited.

PRIVATE TUTORING. Programs designed by private tutors are generally restricted by the proficiency of the tutor and by the materials available for precise diagnosis and remediation. These private tutoring programs are most effective with readers who are experiencing mild difficulties in reading. Many excellent, well-qualified private tutors perform highly satisfactory services; unfortunately, others cause more harm than good. Private tutors are obligated to work closely with the school, which involves the students in an instructional program every day. No justification can be found for programs that do less. Referral should be based only on a personal evaluation of effectiveness.

COMMERCIAL PROGRAMS FOR PARENTS. Often advertised as panaceas, programs that place parents in teachers' roles assume that all readers have a common deficiency and that instruction with a given technique can be done without diagnosis.

Unless the educator is familiar with the program's contents and unless a diagnosis has been conducted to pinpoint the remedial area, these programs are not recommended. All such programs are not inherently bad; some of them are well designed and have been used with considerable success. The educator must study them closely. An assessment should also be made of each parent's suitability as a teacher.

TEMPORARY PROGRAMS. Several private companies have organized short, intensive programs designed to send materials and instructors into schools and industry to improve general reading skills. Many of these are well designed and taught excellently; others are not. The long-term gains of such programs must be questioned, and these companies should be willing to answer questions and submit research concerning these programs so the educator can evaluate their relative worth.

OUTPATIENT PARENTAL INSTRUCTION. Several clinics have been established to diagnose children and train parents to conduct remediation. Amazing results have been reported with this technique; however, the long-term gains need evaluation. Outpatient clinics usually handle large numbers of children and usually request periodic return for reevaluation and retraining for the parents. Since the programs are outpatient in nature, their overall costs are not great, although the per-hour cost may be high. These programs are generally designed for children with specific disabilities and usually should follow referral from medical personnel, psychologists, psychiatrists, or reading professionals.

Pitfalls of Out-of-School Programs

The basic limitations of each out-of-school program have already been mentioned. Specifically, however, the pitfalls of such programs include the following points:

GOALS. Do these programs assist teachers toward the most desirable educational goals or do they, in reality, interfere with these goals? Once this question is answered, referral may be made on a more informed basis. When the programs are found to conflict with the school's goals, attempts should be made to reconcile the differences. When reconciliation is not possible, educators should strongly recommend nonparticipation by the parents of their students.

PERSONNEL. The effectiveness of all of these programs depends on the supervisory as well as the instructional personnel involved. Weakness in personnel means weakness in the program. No compromise can be made by educators in demanding that out-of-school programs meet certain quality standards.

INTENTION. Since each of these programs has aims beyond simply assisting students, it must be determined if assisting students is even included in their

A diagnostic teaching approach can help each student learn more successfully.

aims. Naturally, all programs claim to help readers having difficulties, but money or teacher education may become so important that the student does not seem to matter. When alternate aims prevail, the worth of the program is suspect.

Accountability

Teachers should be accountable for providing efficient instruction based on diagnostic techniques. If they lockstep students through one commercial program or are indifferent to students' individual learning styles they should be held accountable for student failure. The teacher who knows the strengths and needs of children and who provides the best possible instruction is truly teaching with accountability.

Accountability has nothing to do with obtaining the same results with all students. It has nothing to do with helping each student read on some mythical grade level. It refers to helping each student learn successfully—a task that can only be done with a diagnostic teaching approach.

Of necessity, accountability requires careful record keeping. Careful record keeping does not need to be a time-consuming activity. In some school districts and states, however, mandatory record keeping interferes with quality instructional programs. At times, different agencies request the same type of information but use different forms. Administrators at all levels should try to consolidate information needed and minimize record keeping while remaining able to account for student progress.

Legal Responsibilities

Teachers have always had to act within the law. Today, however, considerable attention has been directed to the rights of students under the law. Many school districts have developed student handbooks that identify particular student rights. Some entail using common sense, while others involve following special procedures under the law. All teachers should be well informed about the laws in their state, as well as local school district policies.

Some particular legal responsibilities need attention when working with test results. McClung discusses them at length.[8] Educators should be able to defend the validity and reliability of any tests used for making decisions about placing students. If the tests used in instructional planning cannot be defended, the decisions cannot very well be defended. Yet students continue to be labeled and grouped by the data obtained from tests of questionable reliability and validity. If such practices continue, educators are placing themselves in legal jeopardy.

Other matters also deserve attention. Students have the right to privacy, due process, and fair treatment. They should also be allowed to view their personal records. The technical discussion of these rights is beyond the scope of this text, but several suggested readings at the end of this chapter should be studied in order to obtain detailed information on student rights.

Be a Reader

Teachers must be readers. If they are to nurture students to value reading, they must set the example. How can one develop a love of reading in students when there is no love of reading within oneself?

Duffey found that 34 percent of the teachers surveyed in his study were not reading a book and that 50 percent had no plans to read a book.[9] Twenty percent reported that they were not reading any professional literature. Duffey states that the trend he reported is continuing as he collects data on teacher reading habits.

Teaching to strengths can make learning to read enjoyable and successful.

A determined effort can change the sorry picture painted by Duffey's data. Teachers should read to their students every day. They can go to a bookstore and pick a good book for their own reading enjoyment and provide time in school for student reading of personally enjoyable material. As the student reads, so should the teacher. Teachers should also subscribe to professional journals. They should talk with students about what they are reading, showing enjoyment and enthusiasm. A teacher's desire to be a reader can often make a difference to students' desire to be readers. They should not let this opportunity slip by them.

Summary

Once the professional roles of the classroom teacher and reading specialist are understood, programs can be developed to incorporate them appropriately. An awareness of the types of programs available within the realms of the school permits educators to strive to develop those that the needs of their community demand. All facilities—local school, county, state, college, and university—should be incorporated when it is felt that they can be helpful.

Out-of-school programs for children must be evaluated, and cooperation should be encouraged when possible. In areas where out-of-school programs proliferate, more concentrated efforts will be needed to assure educational programs of the greatest effectiveness for students.

Teachers should be aware of the legal ramifications of their actions in decision making. They should also model the reading habit for their students.

Notes

1. International Reading Association, "What's in a Name: Reading Specialist?" *Journal of Reading* 22, no. 7 (April 1979): 623–28.
2. Barbara Kapinus, "Miniclinics: Small Units of Reading Instruction Can Be a Big Help," *Journal of Reading* 24, no. 6 (March 1981): 516–18.
3. See *The Reading Teacher* and *Journal of Reading* published in Newark, Delaware by the International Reading Association.
4. See *Language Arts* and *The English Journal* published in Urbana, Illinois by the National Council of Teachers of English.
5. See *Reading Research and Instruction* published in Boone, North Carolina by the College Reading Association.
6. See the *Journal of Reading Behavior* published in Chicago, Illinois by the National Reading Conference.
7. Karla Hawkins Wendelin, R. Ann Zinck, and Sylvia M. Carter, "Teacher's Memories and Opinions of Children's Books: A Research Update," *Language Arts* 58, no. 4 (April 1981): 416–24.
8. Merle S. McClung, "Competency Testing: Potential for Discrimination," *Clearinghouse Review* 2, no. 3 (September 1977): 439–48.
9. Robert V. Duffey, "What to Do?" *The Reading Teacher* 27, no. 2 (November 1973): 132–33.

Suggested Readings

Bean, Rita M., and Robert M. Wilson. *Effecting Change in School Reading Programs.* Newark, Del.: International Reading Association, 1981. A thorough discussion of the reading resource role is presented in this book, with practical suggestions for making this role a successful one.

Clague, Monique W. "Competency Testing and Potential Constitutional Challenges of Every Student." *Catholic University Law Review* 28, no. 3 (Summer 1979): 469–509. Clague cites court cases relating to competency testing and discusses their implications.

Cohn, Stella M., and Jack Cohn. *Teaching the Retarded Reader.* New York: Odyssey Press, 1967. The authors discuss in detail the roles and responsibilities of reading personnel in establishing and administering reading programs. Based on experience in the New York city schools, this book offers many practical suggestions.

Combs, Arthur, Donald L. Avila, and William W. Purkey. *Helping Relationships.* Boston: Allyn & Bacon, 1971. This book provides an interesting discussion of the ways people relate to one another. It also provides specific suggestions for developing successful strategies when working as a resource to others.

Harper, Robert J., and Gary Kilarr, eds. *Reading and the Law.* Newark, Del.: International Reading Association, 1978. Seven articles regarding the law and the reader are presented. Written for laypersons, this book is essential reading for all educational decision makers.

Koskinen, Patricia S., and Robert M. Wilson. *Developing a Successful Tutoring Program.* New York: Teachers College Press, 1982. This book provides information for getting a tutoring program started and keeping it going, with general as well as specific teaching strategies. Two companion booklets, one for adults and one for student tutors, are also available.

McClung, Merle S. "Competency Testing: Potential for Discrimination." *Clearinghouse Review* 2, no. 3 (September 1977): 439–48. McClung discusses six potential areas of legal difficulty in the use and interpretation of competency testing as a criterion for high school graduation.

Roser, Nancy, and Margaret Frith, eds. *Teaching with Books Children Like.* Newark, Del.: International Reading Association, 1983. Practical suggestions for using trade books in the classroom to stimulate the desire to read. It also includes a very interesting chapter on writing by children for children.

EDITORIAL

Suzanne Clewell

is an educational specialist for the Montgomery County Public Schools in Maryland.

The resource role of the reading specialist in providing in-service education for teachers is an essential function that is often misunderstood by classroom teachers. Classroom teachers may view the reading specialist, their peer, as suspect in this role. However, in a leadership role, the reading specialist is often asked by the principal to provide in-service sessions for a variety of purposes.

Because time is precious in the instructional day, in-service sessions should be planned with a clear focus as efficiently as possible. Providing teachers with a written agenda stating objectives of the session helps to establish this purpose. One purpose may be to inform teachers of new curriculum materials adopted by the school district. In this case, modeling a specific lesson with teachers as learners is most effective. For example, if characterization is an instructional objective, the reading teacher could teach the lesson showing how to compare character traits from two folk tales. The teachers would be actively involved as the audience. In this way, teachers can take the demonstrated lesson and adapt it to their materials and student groups. It is important that interesting material be used and that the reading specialist does not "talk down" to the audience. Occasionally, adult reading material can be used as the source for a specific activity. A creative and enthusiastic idea which involves the audience as participants is more likely to be accepted than a lecture format with presentation of information.

Long-range planning of instructional units is a schoolwide purpose which the reading specialist can begin to address in an in-service session. Teachers welcome a format to use and appreciate a "sample plan" using their materials by grade level. From this sample, teachers can identify specific objectives and units to be taught and plot out their own plan. Individual follow-up sessions may be necessary to complete the task. If reading specialists are involved, they have a clear picture of how they might team with teachers in assisting students with remedial needs.

Another schoolwide in-service need may be to assist teachers with appropriate diagnostic strategies using their basal materials. The reading specialist can provide the guidelines for developing the informal assessment and establish the in-service time as a work session for teachers to prepare questions for passages. During the session, the reading specialist can assist individual teachers. Classroom teachers value productive time in making an assessment measure they understand and can use.

A final schoolwide purpose for in-service sessions is to share new instructional strategies or new ideas from conferences and journal articles that may have an impact on the schoolwide reading program. Both primary and intermediate levels of students should be addressed in this effort. For example, if the reading specialist shares a vocabulary strategy, it is useful to show its application with both easy and more difficult materials. A way to assess appropriateness for total staff is to survey teachers in their needs and provide the information that is most widely requested.

Suzanne F. Clewell

Diagnostic Instruments

Appendix A lists the tests cited throughout this textbook. Tests are cited under publisher name, listed alphabetically. No effort has been made to compile a comprehensive list of all known reading tests. The careful reader will note that most of the tests that follow are designed for individual administration, consistent with the authors' reservations about group testing instruments. The tests listed differ in their purposes, technical merits, comprehensiveness, time of administration, and value in assisting a reading diagnosis.

Teachers desiring to use any of the tests listed would be well advised to consult published evaluations and critiques of each test prior to using it. Test evaluations can be found in the *Mental Measurements Yearbooks* edited by James V. Mitchell (previously edited by Oscar K. Buros) and in *Test Critiques* edited by Daniel J. Keyser and Richard C. Sweetland. Critical reviews of recent tests also regularly appear in the *Journal of Reading* and *The Reading Teacher*.

Academic Therapy Press
20 Commercial Boulevard
Novato, California 94947
415-883-3314
    Receptive One-Word Picture Vocabulary Test

Allyn and Bacon
7 Wells Avenue
Newton, Massachusetts 02159
617-455-1200
    Ekwall Reading Inventory

American Guidance Service
Publisher's Building
Circle Pines, Minnesota 55014
800-328-2560
    Peabody Picture Vocabulary Test–Revised
    Woodcock Reading Mastery Tests–Revised
    Doren Diagnostic Test of Word Recognition
        Skills
    Goldman–Fristoe–Woodcock Test of
        Auditory Discrimination
    Kaufman Test of Educational Achievement
    Peabody Individual Achievement
        Test–Revised
    Kaufman Assessment Battery for Children

Merrill Publishing Company
1300 Alum Creek Drive
Box 508
Columbus, Ohio 43216
614-258-8441
    Analytical Reading Inventory
    Curriculum Referenced Tests of Mastery

CTB/McGraw-Hill
Del Monte Research Park
2500 Garden Road
Monterey, California 93940
800-538-9547
    Diagnostic Reading Scales Revised
    Sequential Tests of Educational Progress
    California Test of Personality
    California Achievement Tests: Reading
    Comprehensive Tests of Basic Skills
    Prescriptive Reading Performance Test

411

DLM Teaching Resources
P.O. Box 4000
One DLM Park
Allen, Texas 75002
800-527-4747
  Woodcock-Johnson Psycho-Educational
  Battery

Economy Company, The
P.O. Box 25308
1901 Walnut Street
Oklahoma City, Oklahoma 73125
405-528-8444
  New Sucher-Allred Reading Placement
  Inventory

Educational Development Corporation
P.O. Box 45663
Tulsa, Oklahoma 74145
800-331-4418
  Individualized Criterion Referenced
  Test–Reading

H & H Publishing Company
2165 Sunnydale Boulevard
Suite N
Clearwater, Florida 33575
813-442-7760
  Learning and Study Strategies Inventory

Heinemann Educational Books
70 Court Street
Portsmouth, New Hampshire 03801
603-431-7894
  Concepts About Print Test

Houghton Mifflin Company
One Beacon Street
Boston, Massachusetts 02108
617-725-5000
  Informal Reading Inventory (Burns and Roe)

Jastak Associates
1526 Gilpin
Wilmington, Delaware 19806
302-652-4990
  Wide Range Achievement Test–Revised

Macmillan Education
Houndmills, Basingstoke
Hampshire, RG 21 2XS
United Kingdom
  New Macmillian Reading Analysis

Modern Curriculum Press
13900 Prospect Road
Cleveland, Ohio 44136
216-238-2222
  Botel Reading Inventory

Prentice-Hall
Educational Books Division
Englewood Cliffs, New Jersey 07632
201-592-2000
  Individual Evaluation Procedures in Reading

PRO-ED
5341 Industrial Oaks Boulevard
Austin, Texas 78735
512-892-3142
  Detroit Tests of Learning Aptitudes–2
  Gray Oral Reading Tests–Revised
  Test of Reading Comprehension
  Test of Early Reading Ability
  Test of Written Language
  Diagnostic Achievement Battery
  Formal Reading Inventory
  Standardized Reading Inventory
  Diagnostic Achievement Test for Adolescents

Psychological Corporation, The
555 Academic Court
San Antonio, Texas 78204
512-299-1061
  Durrell Analysis of Reading Difficulty
  Gilmore Oral Reading Test
  Boehm Test of Basic Concepts–Revised
  Wechsler Intelligence Scale for
    Children–Revised
  Stanford Diagnostic Reading Test
  Metropolitan Achievement Tests: Reading

Riverside Publishing Company, The
8420 Bryn Mawr Avenue
Chicago, Illinois 60631
800-323-9540
  Gates–MacGinitie Reading Tests
  Revised Stanford–Binet Intelligence Scale
  Iowa Tests of Basic Skills

Science Research Associates
155 N. Wacker Drive
Chicago, Illinois 60606
312-984-7000
  Survey of Reading Study Efficiency

Slosson Educational Publications
P.O. Box 280
East Aurora, New York 14052
800-828-4800
  Slosson Intelligence Test, Revised
  Slosson Oral Reading Test

Teachers College Press
Teachers College
Columbia University
1234 Amsterdam Avenue
New York, New York 10027
212-678-3929
  Gates–McKillop–Horowitz Reading
    Diagnostic Tests

Western Psychological Services
12031 Wilshire Boulevard
Los Angeles, California 90025
213-478-2061
  Auditory Discrimination Test

William C. Brown Company
2460 Kerper Boulevard
Dubuque, Iowa 52001
319-588-1451
  Classroom Reading Inventory (Silvaroli)

Remedial Materials

Appendix B provides a reference list of commercial materials useful in remedial reading instruction. Specific information concerning these materials may be found in publishers' catalogs. A publisher key, which corresponds to a listing of publishers' addresses in appendix C, is provided.

Although the materials in this appendix have been grouped by areas of use, reading level, and interest level, many of the materials may be adapted for other uses or age levels. Several major journals carry periodic reviews of instructional materials. Teachers are encouraged to continually update their knowledge of available materials in the field.

Prepared by Anita Dempsey, Lorna Liswell, and Diane Strohecker, reading specialists in the Anne Arundel County Schools in Maryland.

Primarily Designed to Assist in Instruction of	Name of Material	Reading Level	Interest Level	Format	Publisher
All Skills	1. Action Reading System	E	S	Kit	SBS
	2. Addison-Wesley Reading Program	E	E	Basal	AD
	3. Audio Reading Kits	E	S	Kit	EPC
	4. Be a Better Reader	S	S	Workbook	PH
	5. Breaking the Code	E	E/S	Workbook	OH
	6. BRS Satellite	E	E	Kit	SRA
	7. Careers	E/S	E/S	Kit	HBJ
	8. Clues to Reading Progress	E	E/S	Kit	EPC
	9. Comics Reading Library	E	E/S	Kit	KIN
	10. Controlled Reader	E/S	E/S	Machine	EDL
	11. DISTAR Library	E	E	Kit	SRA
	12. F.A.C.T.	E/S	E	Kit	RAI
	13. The Game Drawer Series	E	E	Game	CP
	14. GO	E/S	E/S	Workbook	SBS
	15. Ginn Reading Program	E	E	Basals	Ginn
	16. HBJ Reading Program (Bookmark)	E	E	Book	HBJ
	17. Holt Reading Program	E	E	Basal	HRW
	18. Houghton Mifflin Reading	E	E	Basal	HMC
	19. Impressions	E	E	Kit	HRW
	20. IRP: Interactive Reading Program	E	E	Basal	BL
	21. Language Master	E/S	E/S	Machine	BHC
	22. Leavell Language Development Service	E	E	Machine	CLB
	23. Let's Read	E	E	Basal	CLB
	24. Listening Comprehension Skills Kit	E/S	E/S	Kit	CA
	25. Little Trolley Books	E	E	Kit	BL
	26. Lunch Box Library	E	E	Kit	SRA
	27. Macmillan Reading Program	E	E	Basal	MAC
	28. Merrill Linguistic Readers	E	E	Basal	MP
	29. Merrill Reading Skill Text	E	E	Books	MP
	30. Newslab	E/S	E/S	Kit	SRA
	31. Now Try This	E	E	Kit	HBJ
	32. Odyssey-HBJ Literature Program	E	E	Book	HBJ
	33. Open Highways	E/S	E/S	Basal	SF
	34. The Owl Books	E	E	Books	HRW
	35. Palo Alto Sequential Steps	E	E	Basals	HBJ
	36. Perceptual Activities (P)	E	E	Workbook	AAP
	37. Peabody Rebus Reading Program	E	E	Kit	AGS
	38. Pilot Library	E/S	E/S	Kit	SRA
	39. Phonetic Keys to Reading	E	E	Basal	WMcH

No.	Title				
40.	Plays for Reading Progress	E/S	E/S	Kit	EPC
41.	Point 31	E	E	Kit	RDS
42.	Practicing Reading	E/S	E/S	Workbook	RH
43.	PREP: Personalized Reading Enrichment Program	E/S	E/S	Kit	AR
44.	RD 2000	E	S	Kit	RDS
45.	Read Alongs	E	E	Books	SP
46.	Read Better—Learn More	E/S	E/S	Workbook	Ginn
47.	Readers' Workshop	E/S	E/S	Kit	RDS
48.	Reading Accelerator	E/S	E/S	Machine	SRA
49.	Reading Comprehension Basic Skills Centers	E	E	Kit	SCH
50.	Reading Connection	E	S	Kit	OP
51.	Reading for Concepts	E	E	Workbook	WMcH
52.	Reading for Understanding	E/S	E/S	Kit	SRA
53.	Reading Incentive Program	E/S	E/S	Kit	WMcH
54.	Reading Laboratory	E/S	E/S	Kit	SRA
55.	Reading Reinforcement Skill Text Series	E/S	E/S	Workbooks	MP
56.	Reading Skill Builders	S	S	Kit	RDS
57.	Reading Skills Practice Kit	E	E	Kit	CA
58.	Reading Skilltexts	E/S	E/S	Books	MP
59.	Reading Tactics	S	S	Workbooks	SF
60.	Resources for Teaching Young Children	E	E	Book	BJ
61.	Reading, Thinking and Reasoning	E/S	E/S	Workbook	SV
62.	Scholastic Literature Kits	S	S	Kit	SBS
63.	Scholastic Pleasure Reading Library	E/S	E/S	Kit	SBS
64.	Scope Skills Book	E	E	Workbook	SBS
65.	Scott Foresman, American Tradition	E	E	Basal	SF
66.	Signals	S	S	Basals	SF
67.	Six-Way Paragraphs	S	S	Workbook	JAM
68.	Spotlight on Reading	E/S	E/S	Workbook	RH
69.	Spotlight on Writing	E/S	E/S	Workbook	RH
70.	Sprint Libraries	E	E	Books	SBS
71.	SRS: Specific Reading Skills	E/S	E/S	Kit	AR
72.	Star Wars Attack on Reading	E	E	Workbook	RH
73.	The Superstars Series	E	E	Workbook	SV
74.	Supportive Reading Skills	E	E	Kit	BL
75.	The Super Kids Library	E	E	Kit	AD
76.	Triple Action Unit	S	S	Kit	SBS
77.	Triple Takes	E/S	E/S	Workbook	RDS
78.	Using the Context	E	E	Workbook	BL

Key: E = elementary, S = secondary, E/S = elementary/secondary.

Primarily Designed to Assist in Instruction of	Name of Material	Reading Level	Interest Level	Format	Publisher
Functional Reading	1. Following Directions	S	S	Visuals	SBS
	2. Getting Applications Right	S	S	Visuals	SBS
	3. How to Read for Everyday Living	S	S	Workbook Cassette	EA
	4. The Job Ahead	E	S	Workbook	SRA
	5. Modern Reading Skill Text Series	S	S	Basal	CEM
	6. On Your Own	S	S	Books	JAN
	7. Reading Contracts and Forms	S	S	Visuals	SBS
	8. Reading for the Real World	E/S	S	Workbook	MP
	9. Real Life Reading Skills	E	S	Kit	SBS
	10. Scoring High in Survival Reading	S	S	Workbook	RH
	11. Skill Builders	E/S	S	Workbook	GLN
	12. Spring Reading Skills Program	E	E	Kit	SBS
	13. SRA Basic Reading Series	E	E	Basal	SRA
	14. Super Kits	E	E/S	Basal	SF
	15. Survival Guides	E	S	Workbook	JAN
	16. Survival Signs	E	E	Posters	ID
	17. Survival Vocabulary	E	E	Kit	PPP
	18. Survival Words Program	E	E	Kit	DCM
	19. Tachistoscope	E/S	E/S	Machine	KEY
	20. Text Extenders	E	E	Kit	SBS
	21. The Thinking Box	E/S	E/S	Activity Cards	BP
	22. Top-Pick Readers	E/S	E/S	Books	RDS
	23. Troll Talking Dictionary	E	E	Books	TA
	24. Troll Read Alongs	E	E	Books	TA
	25. Troll I Can Read Series	E	E	Books	TA
	26. Websters Reading Centers	E/S	E/S	Kit	TA
	27. What's Cooking	E	E	Kit	WMcH

Primarily Designed to Assist in Instruction of	Name of Material	Reading Level	Interest Level	Format	Publisher
Comprehension	1. Adventures in Reading	E	E	Workbook	SCH
	2. Better Reading Books	E/S	E/S	Books	SRA
	3. Bill Martin Instant Readers	E	E	Books	HRW
	4. Bookshop	E	E	Kit	DCH
	5. Camera Patterns	E	E	Books	SAD
	6. Catching On	E	E	Workbook	OP
	7. CLUES for Better Reading Kit 1	E	E	Kit	CA
	8. CLUES for Better Reading Kit 2	E	E	Kit	CA
	9. CLUES for Better Reading Kit 3	E	E	Kit	CA
	10. Comprehension School Pack	E	E	Workbook	CP
	11. Comprehension Skills Laboratory	E/S	E/S	Kit	AR
	12. Comprehension Skills Station	E	E	Kit	MCP
	13. Comprehension We Use	E	E	Workbook	RM
	14. Critical Thinking Skills	E	E	Kit	SV
	15. Detecting the Sequence	E	E	Workbook	BL
	16. Developing Reading Comprehension Skills	E/S	E/S	Workbook	OC
	17. Drawing Conclusions	E	E	Workbook	BL
	18. Following Directions	E	E	Workbook	BL
	19. Getting the Facts	E	E	Workbook	BL
	20. Getting the Main Idea	E	E	Workbook	BL
	21. Guinness Book of World Records	E	E/S	Kit	SIN
	22. Incentive Language Program	E/S	E/S	Kit	BOW
	23. Invitations to Personal Reading	E	E	Kit	SF
	24. Listen and Think Series	E	E/S	Kit	EDL
	25. Locating the Answer	E	E	Workbook	BL
	26. The Monster Books	E	E	Books	WMcH
	27. Narrative Writing	E/S	E/S	Kit	PPP
	28. New Diagnostic Reading Workbook	E	E	Workbook	MP
	29. New Practice Readers	E	E/S	Workbook	WMcH
	30. Nichols Slides	E/S	E/S	Tachistoscope Materials	KEY
	31. Reading Drills	S	S	Workbook	JAM
	32. Single Skills	S	S	Kit	JAM
	33. SRA Skills Series	E	S	Kit	SRA
	34. Starting Comprehension (Visually, Phonetically)	E	E	Workbook	EPS
	35. Think Reader Books	E	E	Workbook	CP

Key: E = elementary, S = secondary, E/S = elementary/secondary.

419

Primarily Designed to Assist in Instruction of	Name of Material	Reading Level	Interest Level	Format	Publisher
Readiness	1. Adventures in Living	E	E	Books	WP
	2. Alpha Time	E	E	Kit	AR
	3. Auditory Discrimination Kit	E	E	Kit	DLM
	4. Beaded Alphabet Cards	E	E	Cards	ID
	5. Beginning to Read Series	E	E	Kit	MCP
	6. Building Pre-reading Skills Kit-a-Language	E	E	Kit	Ginn
	7. Concepts for Communication	E	E	Kit	DLM
	8. Developing Pre-reading Skills	E	E	Kit	HRW
	9. Explode the Code	E	E	Workbook	EPS
	10. Following the Path	E	E	Activity Cards	TE
	11. Happily Ever After	E	E	Kit	AD
	12. Invitations to Story Time	E	E	Books	SF
	13. Kindergarten Basic Skills Center	E	E	Kit	SCH
	14. Kindergarten Keys	E	E	Kit	WmCH
	15. Language Activity Cards	E	E	Kit	SAD
	16. Learning Basic Skills through Music	E	E	Record	EA
	17. Peabody Language Development Kit	E	E	Kit	AGS
	18. Peg Board with Designs	E	E	Activity Cards	DLM
	19. Phonics & Beginning Reading	E	E	Kit	DID
	20. Read and Tell (Level 3)	E	E	Pictures	MAC
	21. The Reading Bridge	E	E	Kit	BFA
	22. Ready Steps	E	E	Kit	HMC
	23. The Riverside Reading	E	E	Kit	RIV
	24. Sequential Cards	E	E	Game	ID
	25. Sound Order, Sense	E	E	Kit	FOL
	26. Sound Start	E	E	Kit	CA
	27. Sweet Pickles—Readiness Program	E	E	Kit	AR
	28. Target Read: Auditory-Visual Discrimination Kit	E	E	Kit	AD
	29. Teaching Reading through Creative Movements	E	E	Record	KIM
	30. Visual Discrimination	E	E	Ditto	CPP
	31. Visual Motor	E	E	Ditto	CPP
	32. Why/Because	E	E	Game	ID

420

Primarily Designed to Assist in Instruction of	Name of Material	Reading Level	Interest Level	Format	Publisher
Study Skills	1. Beginner's Dictionary	E	E	Book	MAC
	2. Dictionary Skills	E	E/S	Workbook	CA
	3. EDL Study Skills Library	E/S	E/S	Kit	EDL
	4. Graph and Picture Study Skills Kit	E	E/S	Kit	SRA
	5. Map and Globe Skills Kit	E/S	E/S	Kit	SRA
	6. News Lab	E	S	Kit	SRA
	7. Organizational Skills	E	E/S	Workbook	CA
	8. Organizing and Reporting Skills Kit	E	E	Kit	SRA
	9. Outline Building	E/S	E/S	Kit	CA
	10. Quick Word	E	E	Workbook	CA
	11. Reading Maps, Globes, Charts, Graphs	S	S	Workbook Cassette	EA
	12. Reading Skills for the Content Area	E	E	Kit	AR
	13. Reading without Words: How to Interpret Graphic	E/S	E/S	Workbook	SBS
	14. Research Lab	E	E/S	Kit	SRA
	15. Skimming & Scanning	S	S	Workbook	JAM
	16. Sports Superstars	E	S	Kit	AR
	17. Target Purple-Study Skills Kit	E/S	E/S	Kit	AD
	18. Try-a-Tile Words	E/S	E/S	Game	CP

Key: E = elementary, S = secondary, E/S = elementary/secondary.

Primarily Designed to Assist in Instruction of	Name of Material	Reading Level	Interest Level	Format	Publisher
Vocabulary	1. Basic Sight Cards	E	E	Cards	GP
	2. Comprehensive Signed English Dictionary	E	E	Book	GAL
	3. Developing Your Vocabulary	S	S	Workbook	SRA
	4. Dolch Group Word Teaching Game	E	E	Game	DLM
	5. Dolch Paper Words	E	E	Game	DLM
	6. Dolch Puzzle Books	E	E	Workbook	DLM
	7. Homonyms	E	E	Workbook	DW
	8. In Other Words	E	E	Book	SF
	9. Linguistic Block Series	E	E	Blocks	SF
	10. Pictocabulary Series	E	E	Workbook	BL
	11. Practical Vocabulary	E	S	Workbook	SBS
	12. Practicing Vocabulary in Context	E/S	E/S	Workbook	RH
	13. Sight Word Lab	E	E	Kit	DLM
	14. Signed English Starter	E	E	Book	GAL
	15. Spello Word Game	E	E	Game	ID
	16. Target Green—Vocabulary Development Kit 1	E/S	E/S	Kit	AD
	17. Target Orange—Vocabulary Development Kit 2	S	S	Kit	AD
	18. Vocabulary Fluency	E/S	E/S	Workbook	CA
	19. Vocabulary Improvement	E	S	Workbook	SBS
	20. Vocabulary Laboratories	E/S	E/S	Kit	AR
	21. Vocabulary Skills	S	S	Workbook	JAM
	22. Words to Use	E	E	Book	SAD

Primarily Designed to Assist in Instruction of	Name of Material	Reading Level	Interest Level	Format	Publisher
Word Attack	1. Alpha One	E	E	Kit	AR
	2. Can Do	E	E	Game	CP
	3. Context-Phonetic Clues	E	E	Kit	CA
	4. Lesson in Vowel and Consonant Sounds	E	E	Activities	CA
	5. Merrill Phonics Skill Text	E	E	Workbook	MP
	6. Phonics for Fun	E	E	Kit	AR
	7. Phonics Skilltext	E	E	Workbook	MP
	8. Phonics We Use	E	E	Game Kit	RM
	9. Reading Lab 1—Word Games	E	E	Game Kit	SRA
	10. Road Race	E	E	Game	CA
	11. Schoolhouse Kits	E	E	Kits	SRA
	12. Sea of Vowels	E	E	Game	ID
	13. Sound Hunt	E	E	Game	APA
	14. Speech to Print Phonics	E	E	Kit	HBJ
	15. Spelling Learning Games Kits	E	E	Game Kit	RM
	16. SRA Skill Series Phonics	E	E	Kit	SRA
	17. SRA Skill Series Structural Analysis	E	E	Kit	SRA
	18. Sweet Pickles Phonics Program	E	E	Kit	AR
	19. Target Blue: Structural Analysis Kit	E	E/S	Kit	AD
	20. Target Yellow: Phonetic Analysis Kit	E	E	Kit	AD
	21. Word Analysis Kit	E	E	Kit	CA
	22. Word with Sounds	E	E	Workbook	BL
	23. Working with Words	E	E	Workbook	Ginn

Key: E = elementary, S = secondary. E/S = elementary/secondary.

Key to Publishers Code

AAP   Ann Arbor Publishers
P.O. Box 7249
Naples, Florida 48104
813-775-3528

AD   Addison-Wesley Publishing Company
2725 Sand Hill Road
Menlo Park, California 94025
800-447-2226

AGS   American Guidance Service
P.O. Box 31552
Richmond, Virginia 23294
800-328-2560

APA   American Publishers Aids
Covina, California 91722

AR   Artista Corporation
Two Parr Avenue
New York, New York 10016
800-227-1606

BHC   Bell & Howell Company
7100 McCormick Road
Chicago, Illinois 60645

BL   Barnell Loft, Ltd.
111 S. Centre Avenue
New York, New York 11571

BP   Benefic Press
1250 Sixth Avenue
San Diego, California 92101

CA   Curriculum Associates
5 Esquire Road
N. Billerica, Massachusetts 01862-2589
800-225-0248

CAM   Cambridge Book Company
(Adult Education)
42 4th Avenue
Waltham, Massachusetts 02154
800-637-0047

CLB   Clarence L. Barnhart Reference Books
Box 359
Bronxville, New York 10708

CP   Creative Publications
5005 W. 110th Street
Oak Lawn, Illinois 60453

DCH   DC Heath & Company
Center Square
Hanover, Pennsylvania 17331
800-447-1210

DID   Didax, Inc. Educational Resources
Peabody, Massachusetts 01960
800-458-0024

DLM   Developmental Learning Materials
One DLM Park
P.O. Box 4000
Allen, Texas 75002
800-527-4747

EA   Educational Activities
     P.O. Box 392
     Freeport, New York 11520
     800-645-3739

EC   The Economy Company
     1200 Northwest 63d Street
     Oklahoma City, Oklahoma 73125

EDL Educational Development Laboratories
     Huntington, New York 11746

ENC Encyclopedia Britannica Educational
     Corporation
     425 N. Michigan Avenue
     Chicago, Illinois 60611
     800-554-9862

EPC Educational Progress Corporation
     P.O. Box 45663
     Tulsa, Oklahoma 74145

EPS Educators Publishing Service, Inc.
     75 Moulton Street
     Cambridge, Massachusetts 02238-9101
     800-225-5750

FOL Follett Publishing Company
     4506 Northwest Highway
     Crystal Lake, Illinois 60014-3397
     800-323-3397

GAL Gallaudet University Press
     800 Florida Avenue, NE
     Washington, D.C. 20002

Ginn Ginn & Company
     4343 Equity Drive
     P.O. Box 2649
     Columbus, Ohio 43216
     800-848-9500

GLN Glenco Pub
     15319 Chatsworth Street
     P.O. Box 9509
     Mission Hills, California 91345-9509
     800-423-9534

HBJ Harcourt Brace Jovanovich Inc.
     Orlando, Florida 32887
     305-345-3800

HMC Houghton Mifflin Company
     One Beacon Street
     Boston, Massachusetts 02108
     800-445-6575

HRW Holt, Rinehart and Winston
     16237 Woodland Avenue
     Austin, Texas 78741
     800-426-0462

ID   Ideal
     11000 S. Lavergne Avenue
     Oak Lawn, Illinois 60453

JAM Jamestown Publishers
     P.O. Box 9168
     Providence, Rhode Island 02940
     800-USA-READ

JAN Janus Book Publishers
     2501 Industrial Parkway West
     Hayward, California 94545
     800-227-2375

JBL J. B. Lippincott Company
     East Washington Square
     Philadelphia, Pennsylvania 19105

KEY Keystone View Company
     2212 East 12th Street
     Davenport, Iowa 52803

KIN King Features
     Department 1198
     235 East 45th Street
     New York, New York 10017

MAC The Macmillan Company
     Front & Brown Streets
     Riverside, New Jersey 08075-1197

MCP Modern Curriculum Press Inc.
13900 Prospect Road
Cleveland, Ohio 44136

MP Merrill Publishing Company
1300 Alum Creek Drive
Columbus, Ohio 43216

NY Nystrom
3333 Elston Avenue
Chicago, Illinois 60615
800-621-8086

OC Oceana Educational Communications
40 Cedar Street
Dobbs Ferry, New York 10522
914-693-8100

OP Open Court Publishing Company
P.O. Box 599
Peru, Illinois 61354-0599
800-435-6800

PE PRO-ED
5341 Industrial Oak Boulevard
Austin, Texas 78735

PH Prentice-Hall
Simon & Schuster
Englewood Cliffs, New Jersey 07632

PPP Pied Piper Productions
1645 Monrovica Avenue
Costa Mesa, California 92627
800-247-8308

PSY Psychological Corporation
555 Academic Court
San Antonio, Texas 78204-0952

RA Rodmar Associates
P.O. Box 354
Horsham, Pennsylvania 19044

RAI Raintree Publishers Group
310 W. Wisconsin Avenue
Milwaukee, Wisconsin 53203
800-558-7264

RDS Readers Digest Services
Pleasantville, New York 10570

RH Random House
201 E. 50th Street
New York, New York 10022
800-492-0782

RIV Riverside Publishing Company
Pennington-Hopewell Road
Hopewell, New Jersey 08525

RM Rand McNally & Company
P.O. Box 7600
Chicago, Illinois 60680
800-245-1647

SAD William H. Sadlier Inc.
11 Park Place
New York, New York 10007

SBS Scholastic Book Service
P.O. 7501
2931 E. McCarty Street
Jefferson City, Missouri 65102

SCH Frank Schaffer Publications
26616 Indian Park
Palos Verdes, California 90274

SEP Slosson Educational Publications Inc.
P.O. Box 280
East Aurora, New York 14052

SF Scott, Foresman & Company
1900 East Lake Avenue
Glenview, Illinois 60625

SP Sundance Paperbacks
Box 1326
Littleton, Massachusetts 01460

SRA Science Research Associates, Inc.
155 N. Wacker Drive
Chicago, Illinois 60606

SV Steck-Vaughn
P.O. Box 26015
Austin, Texas 78755

TA Troll Associates
100 Corporate Drive
Mahwah, New Jersey 07430
800-526-5289

TE Trend Enterprises
P.O. Box 8623
White Bear Lake, Minnesota 55110

WMcH Webster Division
McGraw-Hill Book Company
1154 Roco Avenue
St. Louis, Missouri 63126

WP Western Publishing Co. Inc.
P.O. Box 700
Racine, Wisconsin 53401

WWS Weston Woods Studios
Weston, Connecticut 06883-1199
800-243-5020

Selected Software Publishers

Addison-Wesley
School Products Division
2725 Sand Hill Road
Menlo Park, California 94025
415-854-0300

Advanced Ideas
2902 San Pablo Avenue
Berkeley, California 94702
415-526-9100

Broderbund Software
17 Paul Drive
San Rafael, California 94903-2101
800-527-6263
415-492-3200

Davidson and Associates
3135 Kashiwa Street
Torrance, California 90505
800-556-6141
213-534-4070

Developmental Learning Materials (DLM)
One DLM Park
P.O. Box 4000
Allen, Texas 75002
800-527-4747
214-248-6300

First Byte, Inc.
3333 E. Spring Street
Suite 302
Long Beach, California 90806
800-523-8070
213-595-7006

Hartley Courseware
133 Bridge Street
Dimondale, Minnesota 48821
800-247-1380
517-646-6458

Houghton Mifflin Company
Educational Software Division
P.O. Box 683
Hanover, New Hampshire 03755
603-448-3838

The Learning Company
6493 Kaiser Drive
Fremont, California 94555
800-852-2255
415-328-5410

Mindscape, Inc.
3444 Dundee Road
Northbrook, Illinois 60062
800-221-9884
312-480-8715

Prepared by Gordon B. Browning, Kent County Schools, Maryland.

Minnesota Educational Computing Corporation
  (MECC)
3490 Lexington Ave., N.
St. Paul, Minnesota 55126-8079
612-481-3500

Optimum Resources, Inc.
10 Station Place
Norfolk, Connecticut 06058
800-327-1473

Random House
201 E. 50th Street
New York, New York 10022
800-492-0782
212-572-2616

Scholastic, Inc.
2931 E. McCarty Street
P.O. Box 7502
Jefferson City, Missouri 65102
800-325-6149
212-505-3537

South-Western Publishing Co.
5101 Madison Road
Cincinnati, Ohio 45227
513-271-8811

Spinnaker Software
One Kendall Square
Cambridge, Massachusetts 02139
800-323-8088
617-494-1200

Springboard Software
7808 Creekridge Circle
Minneapolis, Minnesota 55435
612-944-3915

Sunburst Communications
39 Washington Avenue
Pleasantville, New York 10570
800-431-1934
914-769-5030

Troll Associates
100 Corporate Drive
Mahwah, New Jersey 07498-0025
800-526-5289
201-529-4000

Word Associates, Inc.
3096 Summit Avenue
Highland Park, Illinois 60035
312-291-1101

International Reading Association Code of Ethics

The members of the International Reading Association who are concerned with the teaching of reading form a group of professional persons obligated to society and devoted to the service and welfare of individuals through teaching, clinical services, research, and publication. The members of this group are committed to values which are the foundation of a democratic society—freedom to teach, write, and study in an atmosphere conducive to the best interests of the profession. The welfare of the public, the profession, and the individuals concerned should be of primary consideration in recommending candidates for degrees, positions, advancements, the recognition of professional activity, and for certification in those areas where certification exists.

See *Code of Ethics*, International Reading Association, Newark, Delaware. Reprinted by permission.

Ethical Standards in Professional Relationships

1. It is the obligation of all members of the International Reading Association to observe the Code of Ethics of the organization and to act accordingly so as to advance the status and prestige of the association and of the profession as a whole. Members should assist in establishing the highest professional standards for reading programs and services, and should enlist support for these through dissemination of pertinent information to the public.
2. It is the obligation of all members to maintain relationships with other professional persons, striving for harmony, avoiding personal controversy, encouraging cooperative effort, and making known the obligations and services rendered by the reading specialist.
3. It is the obligation of members to report results of research and other developments in reading.

431

4. Members should not claim nor advertise affiliation with the International Reading Association as evidence of their competence in reading.

Ethical Standards in Reading Services

1. Reading specialists must possess suitable qualifications . . . for engaging in consulting, clinical, or remedial work. Unqualified persons should not engage in such activities except under the direct supervision of one who is properly qualified. Professional intent and the welfare of the person seeking the services of the reading specialist should govern counseling, all consulting or clinical activities such as administering diagnostic tests, or providing remediation. It is the duty of the reading specialist to keep relationships with clients and interested persons on a professional level.

2. Information derived from consulting and/or clinical services should be regarded as confidential. Expressed consent of persons involved should be secured before releasing information to outside agencies.

3. Reading specialists should recognize the boundaries of their competence and should not offer services which fail to meet professional standards established by other disciplines. They should be free, however, to give assistance in other areas in which they are qualified.

4. Referral should be made to specialists in allied fields as needed. When such referral is made, pertinent information should be made available to consulting specialists.

5. Reading clinics and/or reading specialists offering professional services should refrain from guaranteeing easy solutions or favorable outcomes as a result of their work, and their advertising should be consistent with that of allied professions. They should not accept for remediation any persons who are unlikely to benefit from their instruction, and they should work to accomplish the greatest possible improvement in the shortest time. Fees, if charged, should be agreed on in advance and should be charged in accordance with an established set of rates commensurate with that of other professions.

Glossary

The number that appears in parenthesis following the definition denotes the chapter in which the term first appears.

acuity The sharpness of vision or hearing. (4)

aliteracy A lack of desire to read despite possessing average or above-average reading ability. (1)

amblyopia Visual difficulty resulting from suppression of the vision in one eye (sometimes called lazy eye). (4)

articulation The ability to speak clearly and distinctly. (8)

auding The ability to listen to and comprehend oral language. (4)

audiometer A screening device used to test ability to hear at various pitches and levels of loudness. (4)

baseline In single-subject research, the observed behavior of a student prior to an intervention. (13)

binocular fusion The ability of the brain to construct a single image from the sensory input of both eyes. (4)

closed-captioned television A technological aid to reading that produces written text on a television screen to accompany or replace the spoken message. (10)

cloze test A test constructed by deleting selected words from a passage. (5)

comprehension The ability to make sense of spoken or written language. (1)

comprehension monitoring The ability to continually assess one's understanding of what is being read and to take appropriate steps when understanding breaks down. (10)

computerized adaptive test A computer-presented ability test that individually tailors the difficulty of a test to the test taker. (12)

concurrent validity Establishing test validity by comparing a given test to another well-regarded test of similar abilities. (3)

content validity Establishing test validity by an expert examination of test items. (3)

context Skill in identifying unknown words through use of meaning cues in the text. (5)

criterion-referenced test (CRT) A test comprised of items matched to specific educational objectives (sometimes called a mastery test). (3)

database A large quantity of information that is stored and accessed through a computer. (12)

dialect A language variation that is common to a region or group that has certain identifiable characteristics. (1)

dialect transfer The ability of a language user to adapt the dialect used to the demands of a social situation. (8)

discrimination The ability to either see or hear likenesses and differences. (4)

dyslexic A label often used by medical professionals to describe a reader who is experiencing severe reading difficulties. (1)

free reading Reading sessions in materials of the reader's choice not followed by questioning. (8)

frustration level The level at which materials may be considered too difficult for a student to read successfully, even when given assistance. (5)

functional literacy   A term used to describe ability to perform minimal reading and writing skills necessary for everyday living. (1)

gain scores   Differences in student performance between pretest and posttest results. (13)

grade equivalent   A score on a norm-referenced test that compares a student's performance to the average performance of similar-age students from the standardization population. (3)

grapheme   A printed symbol. (5)

halo effect   The tendency of respondents on self-report instruments to attempt to cast themselves in a favorable light. (13)

independent level   The level at which a reader can successfully read without assistance. (5)

independent variable   The factor in an experimental research study that is manipulated by the researcher. (13)

Individualized Education Program (IEP)   A written plan required by law which details the current levels of performance, special services, and educational goals and objectives for each student who has been identified as requiring special education. (1)

informal reading inventory (IRI)   A test developed from materials used for reading instruction. (5)

instructional level   The level at which a reader can successfully read if given necessary assistance. (5)

intelligence quotient (IQ)   An estimate of a person's intellectual potential derived by dividing a person's mental age by that person's chronological age and multiplying by 100. (3)

intervention   In an educational research study, the action on the part of the researcher that is intended to produce learning. (13)

language disabled   A label used to identify a person who experiences difficulty in comprehending or using language. (1)

learning modalities   Those sensory systems through which a student evidences the greatest strengths. (6)

lockstepping   The tendency for students who are placed in groups or materials to remain in those groups or materials despite evidence that such placement may be inappropriate. (15)

mainstreaming   The educational practice of placing a handicapped student in a regular classroom for all or part of the school day. (11)

maze test   A variation on cloze testing in which three alternatives are presented in place of the deleted word. (5)

mean   The arithmetic average of a group of scores derived by dividing score totals by the number of students taking the test. (3)

median   The midpoint of a group of scores when the scores are arranged in ascending or descending order. (3)

mental age (MA)   An estimate of a person's intellectual potential derived by multiplying a person's intelligence quotient by that person's chronological age and dividing by 100. (4)

metalinguistic awareness   Knowledge of the jargon and conventions associated with language use. (8)

minimal brain dysfunction   A label used to identify students who experience learning difficulties which are attributed to presumed brain damage. (1)

mode   The most frequently reported score in a group of scores. (3)

neurological disorders   Difficulties associated with malfunctions of the central nervous system. (4)

normal curve   A mathematical model that represents the expected performance of large groups on a well-constructed ability test. (3)

norm-referenced test   A testing instrument that compares student performance to the average performance of students in the standardization population. (3)

ocular motility   Movements of the eye encompassing such abilities as fixations, pursuit, saccadic movement, accommodation, and convergence. (4)

orientation   The ability of the eyes to maintain proper spatial relationships on a page. (6)

out-of-level testing   Using a lower level test and appropriate norms to get a more reliable indication of a remedial student's abilities. (3)

paired scale   A forced-choice test which requires a student to express a preference between pairs of words, activities, and so forth. (13)

434

percentile   A statistical means of reporting test performance that designates the point on the normal curve at or below which a given percentage of students scored on the test. (3)

phonics   Use of sound-symbol relationships in identifying unknown words. (1)

predictive validity   The degree to which a score on a given test can be used to forecast future performance. (3)

Public Law 94-142   A federal law enacted to provide protective safeguards for handicapped students. (1)

range   An indication of the spread in a group of scores derived by subtracting the lowest reported score from the highest reported score. (3)

readability   The relative difficulty of a given piece of reading material for a student. (5)

reading expectancy level   An estimate of a student's reading potential that may be useful in helping to set realistic goals for that student. (4)

reading prosthesis   Initially developed for blind students, a computer-assisted "reading" machine that is capable of producing a voice-synthesized rendition of text. (12)

regression   Those portions of student scores that are obtained by chance will tend to move toward the mean on subsequent testing. (13)

reliability   A statistical term used to designate the ability of a test to measure consistently. (3)

reliability coefficient   A decimal measurement of test consistency. (3)

reluctant reader   A person who possesses reading skills but who is not inclined to read. (10)

semantic   The system of language that governs meaning. (5)

simulation program   A software program that presents some real-life situation or model usually involving the user in problem solving. (12)

Snellen Chart   A device for screening visual acuity at a distance of twenty feet. (4)

software   Computer programs, usually commercially produced, which make it possible for microcomputers to process information. (12)

specific reading disability   A term used to identify difficulty in reading which is attributable to poor perceptual processing. (1)

standard deviation   An indication of how widely scores vary around the average on a normal curve. (3)

standard error of measurement   An estimate of test reliability which represents the relationship between a student's obtained score and that student's hypothetical "true" score. (3)

standardized test   A test, often of achievement, in which standards of performance have been determined by the average performances of large groups of students. (3)

standard score   A score based on mean and standard deviation that permits comparisons between different tests. (3)

stanine   A statistical means of reporting test performance that divides the normal curve into nine parts. (3)

stereopsis   Visual ability to judge relative distances and depth. (4)

strabismus   Vision disorder resulting from poor eye muscle coordination. (4)

structural analysis   Skill in identifying unknown words through use of meaningful parts of words (such as prefixes, suffixes, etc.). (5)

summated rating scale   A test that requires responses to be made to statements on a continuum (usually a five-point scale). (12)

Sustained Silent Reading (SSR) or Sustained Quiet Reading Time (SQUIRT)   Time set aside in the school day for students and the teacher to read silently from materials of their choice. (8)

syntactic   The system of language which governs the arrangement of words into meaningful patterns. (5)

telebinocular   A screening device for a wide variety of vision abilities. (4)

teleconferencing   Communications that are made possible through computer links. (12)

tele-decoder   A device that enables a television set to produce text from closed-captioned programs. (12)

usability The practical considerations that influence test selection (time, expense, ease of administration, etc.). (3)

validity The ability of a test to measure what it purports to measure. (3)

validity coefficient A decimal measurement of a test's ability to measure what it claims to measure. (3)

word attack skills Those skills that a reader brings to bear in identifying an unknown word. (1)

word processor A computer-aided system for producing, storing, retrieving, and editing printed materials. (12)

Name Index

440

Subject Index

443

447

Robert Wilson is currently professor of education and director of the Reading Center at the University of Maryland, where he teaches courses in undergraduate and graduate reading education. His research interests are in the areas of captioned television, signing, and metacognition, and he has recently published books in each of those areas. His writing reflects his public school teaching experiences as well as his work with students in the University of Maryland Reading Clinic and in the public schools of Maryland. He has been honored by his undergraduate and graduate institutions for his accomplishments and is a past president of the College Reading Association.

Craig Cleland is currently an associate professor of education and director of the graduate reading program at Mansfield University in Pennsylvania. During the academic year, his teaching responsibilities include courses in reading education and children's literature. In summers he directs the Mansfield University Reading Clinic and codirects a European study tour for teachers. He has published in a variety of professional journals and has written elementary-level curriculum materials. A former public school teacher, he combines a dual background in elementary and special education with a practical approach to teacher education.

451

WE VALUE YOUR OPINION—PLEASE SHARE IT WITH US

Merrill Publishing and our authors are most interested in your reactions to this textbook. Did it serve you well in the course? If it did, what aspects of the text were most helpful? If not, what didn't you like about it? Your comments will help us to write and develop better textbooks. We value your opinions and thank you for your help.

Text Title _____ Edition _____

Author(s) _____

Your Name (optional) _____

Address _____

City _____ State _____ Zip _____

School _____

Course Title _____

Instructor's Name _____

Your Major _____

Your Class Rank _____ Freshman _____ Sophomore _____ Junior _____ Senior

_____ Graduate Student

Were you required to take this course? _____ Required _____ Elective

Length of Course? _____ Quarter _____ Semester

1. Overall, how does this text compare to other texts you've used?

_____ Superior _____ Better Than Most _____ Average _____ Poor

2. Please rate the text in the following areas:

	Superior	Better Than Most	Average	Poor
Author's Writing Style	_____	_____	_____	_____
Readability	_____	_____	_____	_____
Organization	_____	_____	_____	_____
Accuracy	_____	_____	_____	_____
Layout and Design	_____	_____	_____	_____
Illustrations/Photos/Tables	_____	_____	_____	_____
Examples	_____	_____	_____	_____
Problems/Exercises	_____	_____	_____	_____
Topic Selection	_____	_____	_____	_____
Currentness of Coverage	_____	_____	_____	_____
Explanation of Difficult Concepts	_____	_____	_____	_____
Match-up with Course Coverage	_____	_____	_____	_____
Applications to Real Life	_____	_____	_____	_____

3. Circle those chapters you especially liked:
   1   2   3   4   5   6   7   8   9   10   11   12   13   14   15   16   17   18   19   20
   What was your favorite chapter? _____
   Comments:

4. Circle those chapters you liked least:
   1   2   3   4   5   6   7   8   9   10   11   12   13   14   15   16   17   18   19   20
   What was your least favorite chapter? _____
   Comments:

5. List any chapters your instructor did not assign. _____

6. What topics did your instructor discuss that were not covered in the text?_____

   _____

7. Were you required to buy this book? _____ Yes _____ No

   Did you buy this book new or used? _____ New _____ Used

   If used, how much did you pay? _____

   Do you plan to keep or sell this book? _____ Keep _____ Sell

   If you plan to sell the book, how much do you expect to receive? _____

   Should the instructor continue to assign this book? _____ Yes _____ No

8. Please list any other learning materials you purchased to help you in this course (e.g., study guide, lab manual).

   _____

9. What did you like most about this text? _____

   _____

10. What did you like least about this text? _____

   _____

11. General comments:

   May we quote you in our advertising? _____ Yes _____ No

   Please mail to: Boyd Lane
                     College Division, Research Department
                     Box 508
                     1300 Alum Creek Drive
                     Columbus, Ohio 43216

   Thank you!

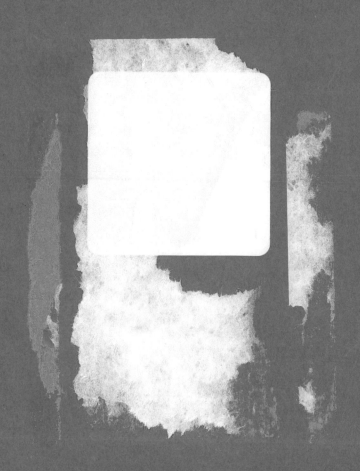